**The Sociology of Education**
A Sourcebook

372-7747

**The Dorsey Series in Sociology**

Editor
ROBIN M. WILLIAMS, JR.    *Cornell University*

# The Sociology of Education

## A Sourcebook

Edited by

**HOLGER R. STUB**
Temple University

 Third Edition   1975

THE DORSEY PRESS   Homewood, Illinois   60430

Irwin-Dorsey Limited, Georgetown, Ontario   L7G 4B3

Third Edition

5 6 7 8 9 0 ML 5 4 3 2 1 0 9

ISBN 0-256-01630-5

Library of Congress Catalog Card No. 74–29744

*Printed in the United States of America*

# Preface

The increased public interest and concern with education at all levels of modern society has stimulated a substantial amount of writing and research in the sociology of education. This has both necessitated and facilitated an extensive revision of the last edition of this book. Over three fourths of the material in this third edition was not published in the second edition. In addition, a new section on "Social Processes and Classroom Interaction" has been added. Although most of the articles included are from professional journals, some have come from more popular sources such as the *Atlantic Monthly* and *Transaction*. A number of excerpts from books are also included. Though not all are written by professionally trained sociologists, they are thought to contribute insight and understanding to the sociological analysis of education. The practice adopted in the earlier editions of reprinting complete articles rather than severely edited excerpts has with one exception been maintained. The assumption is that if an article merited inclusion it should generally be reprinted in its entirety. This not only allows the student to see fully the nature and logic of the work as provided by the author, but also allows him or her to experience the reading and study of unadulterated social scientific work as it is presented to the fraternity of social scientists. Though a small portion of the material may prove difficult to some students, the intent is to present the best rather than the easiest or the most readable.

The introductions to each of the seven sections were written with the intention of providing background material appropriate to the readings that follow. In contrast to some collections of this general type, we have chosen not to predigest the reprinted articles. The reprinted articles were selected to stand on their own without elaborate introduction or discussion.

The choice of topic subdivisions and accompanying articles is arbitrary. The aim was to reprint materials that are important *and,* though varied, fit together in a loosely coherent fashion. For some of the topics there were numerous articles to choose from; for others it was difficult to find appropriate ones for inclusion. The final choices were made in accordance with the editor's own predispositions regarding the theoretical importance of each article for presentation in a textbook in the *sociology* of education.

This sourcebook is aimed at meeting the needs of sociology of education courses in colleges and universities. It may also prove to be useful to a variety of other education courses that require a sociological perspective. Earlier editions have been used in courses such as: the social foundations of education (both graduate and undergraduate), educational administration, and comparative social structure. This volume was designed to serve as either a textbook along with supplementary articles or paperbacks, or in conjunction with a different type of textbook.

In a very fundamental sense whatever merit a book of this sort possesses must be credited to the authors of the articles presented. I am, therefore, deeply indebted to them and their publishers. Finally, I wish to express my appreciation to an understanding family—Elin H. Stub, Lisa, and Peter.

*Temple University*                                    HOLGER R. STUB
*Philadelphia, Pa.*
*April 1975*

# Contents

**part ONE**
Education and American Society . . . . . . . . . . . . . . . . . . . . . . . . . . . . . . . . . . . . 1

   1. Out of the Past: Sociological Perspectives on the History of Education, *Ronald G. Corwin,* 6
   2. Do Schools Make a Difference? *Godfrey Hodgson,* 32
   3. Value Orientations of High School Students, *Leo C. Rigsby and Edward L. McDill,* 53

**part TWO**
Socialization and Learning: Nonformal Aspects . . . . . . . . . . . . . . . . . . . 77

   4. Learning the Student Role: Kindergarten as Academic Boot Camp, *Harry L. Gracey,* 82
   5. Early Experience and the Socialization of Cognitive Modes in Children, *Robert D. Hess and Virginia C. Shipman,* 96
   6. Education and Socialization: A Complex Equation, *Edward Wynne,* 114
   7. Lower Class Negro Mothers' Aspirations for Their Children, *Robert R. Bell,* 125

**part THREE**
Social Status and Education . . . . . . . . . . . . . . . . . . . . . . . . . . . . . . . . . . . . . . 137

   8. Education and Class, *P.G. Squibb,* 142
   9. Changing Patterns of Education and Mobility, *Robert Perrucci,* 164

10.   Programmed for Social Class: Tracking in High School, *Walter E. Schafer, Carol Olexa, and Kenneth Polk*, 186

11.   Local Social Structure and Educational Selection, *Natalie Rogoff*, 200


**part FOUR**
The School As a Social Organization............................ 211

12.   The School Class as a Social System: Some of its Functions in American Society, *Talcott Parsons*, 216

13.   Open-Space Schools: The Opportunity to Become Ambitious, *Elizabeth G. Cohen*, 238

14.   The Character of Bureaucracy in Urban Schools, *Raymond C. Hummel and John M. Nagle*, 244


**part FIVE**
Social Processes and Classroom Interaction...................... 255

15.   Which Pupils Do Teachers Call On? *Thomas L. Good*, 261

16.   The Hidden Curriculum and the Nature of Conflict, *Michael Apple*, 269

17.   Language as Curriculum Content and Learning Environment, *Courtney B. Cazden*, 289


**part SIX**
The Teacher...................................................... 303

18.   The Teacher's Role—A Sociological Analysis, *Bryan R. Wilson*, 309

19.   Authority, Conflict, and Teacher Effectiveness, *William G. Spady*, 327

20.   Teaching the Teacher, *Estelle Fuchs*, 339

21.   The Professional Prestige of Classroom Teachers: A Consequence of Organizational and Community Status, *Holger R. Stub*, 349


**part SEVEN**
Higher Education................................................ 367

22.   The Triumph of Academic Man, *Christopher Jencks and David Riesman*, 372

23.  The "Cooling-Out" Function in Higher Education,
     *Burton R. Clark,* 391

24.  The Impact of College, *Kenneth A. Feldman and
     Theodore M. Newcomb,* 402

Name Index...................................................... 417

Subject Index .................................................. 423

# part ONE

# Education and American Society

Education in American society has emerged as one of the most preeminent social institutions. Since the building of the one-room school house run by a lone schoolmaster in the 17th century, the nation's schools have become one of the largest employers of manpower in the country, constitute the single most expensive social enterprise, and provide the daily habitat for millions of young citizens. The school and all its many offshoots—ranging from the pre-school, special schools for the retarded, blind, talented, trades and technology, and the two thousand-odd institutions of higher learning—have permeated every aspect of American life.

It is no small wonder that Americans have typically come to look to the educational establishment for answers to many of their most pressing problems. More and better education has become a knee-jerk like response to those concerned with social problems. The contemporary reliance on the school as a locus of problem-solving is a logical extension of the important functions that have been assigned to the schools.

The school has taken on the tasks of providing a literate population for a burgeoning industrialized country, the Americanization of millions of immigrants, the preparation of new professionals and technical experts in the emerging post-industrial age, and finally in the 1950s and 60s, the establishment of social equality.

It is not simply the development of mass education, which encompasses the vast majority of the population between five and 20, that has engendered the notion that the school is a key factor in the solution of social problems. Substantial changes in the function of the family, church, and local community have contributed to the burden placed on the school.

1

The important function of socializing the young to follow the accepted norms of the community and nation, as well as preparing them for a future place in the labor market have been passed on to the school. Parents, community leaders, and employers have tended to transfer responsibility for the socialization of the oncoming generation into the hands of the educators. This has occurred to such a degree that Christopher Jencks characterized the present as "an academic age."[1] Moreover, the observation has been made that "Graduate schools are the wave of the future."[2]

The speed of our technological development has been aided by education. In turn, a continuation of progress toward the improvement of life is assumed to be contingent on an increased level of education. The great development in professional specialization, giving rise to a whole new category of men, namely the experts, is a product of education and post-industrial society. Mass urban society, with a high degree of occupational specialization has come to rely upon and demand the use of credentials in the allocation of men to positions in the occupational structure. The certificate or diploma is often the key that unlocks the door to a decent job.

The reliance on credentials has increased the importance of schools, particularly from high school through higher education. The development of an ideology that assumed a high level of social mobility for all ranks in society has enhanced the position of schools and colleges as the prime providers of the standard credentials needed in achieving social mobility.

Many specific factors and events have given the educational organization an importance far exceeding that considered by the early colonials when they first instituted compulsory public education. The development of scientific and technological knowledge has been of great import. The focal point of the knowledge explosion has been the university. The practical success of fields such as engineering and medicine have provided ample testimony to the efficacy of education. Government subsidized higher education and research through G.I. Bill and government-funded fellowships have aided in making education a major element in all considerations related to problem-solving, expertise and the providing of reliable credentials.

The important role played in providing one of the most readily attained requirements (credentials) for social mobility has made the schools a key factor in the drive for social and economic equality among the nation's minority groups. To be directly charged with the task of implementing social equality has posed a serious problem for the educational establish-

---

[1] Christopher Jencks, "Who Shall Control Education?" *Dissent*, March–April 1966, p. 150.

[2] Ibid., p. 151.

ment. However, the expectation that education is capable of resolving the problem of inequality has been seriously challenged by the research work of Jencks. His findings state that differences in the quality of schools, when measured by money, curricula, and facilities, do not explain inequality. Overall academic differences between whites and minority group students are substantial even though the quality of the schools are not very different. Some educators have come to the conclusion that family background and social environment are much more important than the schools in giving the minority-group student the academic orientation and skills necessary for taking advantage of the opportunity to gain the educational credentials needed for social mobility. These findings have caused serious shock waves for the educational community as well as for liberal ideologues who have traditionally supported heavy fiscal investment in education.[3]

The challenge to the basic assumptions undergirding much of the recent moral and economic support for education has been compounded by an increase in research oriented toward a genetic explanation of inequality. The work of Professor Arthur Jensen in attempting to connect variations in I.Q. scores to genetic differences associated with race, as well as the studies of Herrnstein and Shockley, caused near riots in university lecture halls, and the charge of racism became a major element in the counterarguments.

The public controversies over education, which range from "how to pay for it" to "what's it good for," have stimulated great interest among social scientists as well as to biologically-oriented scientists who have contributed to the racist controversy. The profound importance of the major issues has done much to stimulate interest and research in the sociology of education, an interest that has only become full-blown during the last five to six years. The national prominence of the leading researchers and commentators such as Coleman, Jencks, Moynihan, Jensen, and Pettigrew is unique in the short history of the sociology of education.

Education has not only been one of the major focuses dealing with social and economic inequality, but also for public issues such as the space race, generation gap, youthful radicalism, alternative lifestyles, crime, delinquency, and the urban poor (who are also poorly educated). Moreover, the great expenditures of public funds for education at all three levels of government (local, state, and federal) has sensitized many groups to the issues confronting the schools. The ever-increasing demands for funds has generated considerable antagonism between those who view the schools as prime agents in facilitating social mobility and improving society and those who are primarily interested in the school as simply the

---

[3] These points are more fully discussed in Godfrey Hodgson, "Do Schools Make a Difference?" Reading No. 2 in this volume.

perpetuator of conventional norms and values. Of course, there are many persons who fall in between these two categories, but this dichotomy forms an important component in the present-day school funding controversy.

Another feature of the contemporary education scene is the small, but vocal minority, who view the nation's schools as total failures in preparing the coming generations for a fruitful and happy life. The new theme has spawned new labels: free schools, open schools, ungraded schools, alternative schools, and, finally, deschooling. The substance of most of these "reforms" basically concerns the degree to which educational activities are "child centered." To a substantial degree the new schools as well as the changes made in some existing schools is a result of a growing awareness that is based on a body of research findings that have emerged in the last quarter of a century.

Although at least 70,000 studies in education have been reported during the past 25 years, few have had significant consequences.[4] Bloom argues that only 70, or one per 1,000, reported studies are of substantial significance. Among the areas in which important work has been done are the processes of individual development and the effects of environment on individual development. An important sociological aspect of the latter is the educational effects of the classroom and school *as* social organizations. The multiple processes of individual growth and development have been brought out by the work of Eriksen, Piaget, Gesell, and Havighurst. The research conducted by these and others created a strong awareness regarding the importance of the close relationship between physical, psychological, and social development and the special learning (reading, writing, arithmetic) purported to be a major function of the school. The inferences drawn from the work of these scholars have greatly affected teacher training, attitudes and classroom organization. Much of the impetus for change in the direction of creating a child-centered context for learning has come from child development research.

Research has also established the effects of social environment on the development of the individual as he or she relates to school and learning. "Perhaps one of the most fundamental distinctions that is emerging is the veiw of the home as an educative environment with its own curriculum, in contrast to an earlier view of the home as a unit in a socio-economic or social class status system."[5] The influence of language learning in the home is illustrated in the article by Hess and Shipman.[6] This work, along with that done by Joseph Kahl, shows the influence of the class and status com-

---

[4] Benjamin S. Bloom, "Twenty-five Years of Educational Research," in Patricia C. Sexton, *Readings on the School and Society* (Englewood Cliffs, N.J.: Prentice-Hall, 1967), p. 233.

[5] Ibid., p. 232.

[6] Printed in Part Two of this volume.

munity environment on behavior in the school.[7] The work of James S. Coleman in studying the influence of adolescent sub-cultures on individual behavior has sharpened the awareness of the sociological consequences of organized education.[8]

An interesting aspect of most of the research in education is that the exact influence of the formal and official work of the school is constantly subject to debate. Findings continue to be equivocal; one study contradicts another when attempting to determine the effectiveness of one or the other ascertainable feature of a school, classroom, or teaching technique. This has now led to the asking of very serious questions by public figures and social commentators. The response of the educational institution to the question "Do schools make a difference?" will be felt for a long time to come. A significant part of any answer to this salient question is the fact that there are no fully adequate sociological and social psychological theories of human behavior that can explain the effects of social community, organization of the school, learning and socialization, teacher training and orientation, adult socialization and social change. Most of the needed theoretical development falls within the social science areas of sociology and social psychology.

To the practically oriented student a question frequently arises regarding the importance of theory. The philosopher A.N. Whitehead has stated that the "most practical thing in the world is a good theory." When one remembers that a theory provides one with a way of explaining a phenomenon in question, having a good theory allows one to change the behavior in question as well as predict certain behavior from knowable facts. For the pragmatists, nothing could be more useful than good theories. Sociologists of education are those social scientists who view their primary function as working toward the development of good theories for explaining some of the phenomena that occur in the social arena labelled education, be it in school, sports field, play group, home, or local community.

---

[7] Joseph A. Kahl, "Educational and Occupational Aspirations of 'Common Man' Boys," *Harvard Educational Review*, 23 (1953):186–203.

[8] James S. Coleman, *The Adolescent Society* (New York: Free Press, 1961).

# 1

# Out of the Past: Sociological Perspectives on the History of Education*

## RONALD G. CORWIN

The setting for education extends beyond the interpersonal context of the classroom; the most important setting is the institutional one. Indeed, schools cannot be understood apart from the social forces that have shaped them, their historical struggles and rivalries, and the past affiliations out of which their present character has emerged. Educational institutions are thus not autonomous structures but the historical product of a warfare of values among dominant institutional groups. Whether the family, the state, or business dominates has made a fundamental difference in the goals and procedures of schools.

This chapter reviews highlights of the transitions in these institutional values as they have influenced the character of public schools. The history of education in America is one of unmistakable domination by other institutions education traditionally has existed to serve; this fact has been the strength as well as the weakness of the public schools, because educators occasionally have been able to use their connections with dominant groups, in turn, to exert an influence of their own disproportionate to their position in society.[1]

Compared with the fragility of most social organizations (some of

* From Ronald G. Corwin, A Sociology of Education: Emerging Patterns of Class, Status, and Power in the Public Schools, © 1965. Reprinted by permission of Prentice-Hall, Inc., Englewood Cliffs, New Jersey.

[1] Burton R. Clark, Educating the Expert Society (San Francisco: Chandler Publishing Company, 1962), pp. 30–37.

which fail at the rate of 80 percent annually) the public schools have been relatively successful. It has been only within the past 30 years, with the success of the consolidation movement, that the rate of failure of public schools as organizations reached a magnitude that merits public attention; but the elimination of 50 percent of the school districts within the last 15 years does not signify the failure of individual organizations so much as the obsolescence of a *form* of organization. The otherwise exceptional capacity of public schools to survive can be partially attributed to what Carlson calls the domesticated environment in which they prevail; for example, they are publicly supported and are guaranteed both financial support and clientele.[2] In this nurtured culture, schools can exist despite inefficiencies and slow adaptations to change.

Another factor that accounts for the survival capacity of schools, besides public support, is the readiness with which schools have changed their goals and organizational structure to adapt to fluctuating circumstances. The history of education is, in fact, a history of successful adaptation to changing circumstances (although this statement will be qualified in the following chapter, which considers current lags). Therefore, as religion, the family, business, and the state successively have dominated society, their influences have been evident in the classroom.

## RELIGION AND EDUCATION

The initial settlement of America must be understood in the context of the Protestant revolt, which was essentially a middle-class struggle against the arbitrary power of the church and state in Europe. Protestant sects were attempting to establish a form of government that was less arbitrary and capricious than the ones in Europe, for the profits of middle-class businessmen depended on reducing risks and this required equalitarian legal procedures.

The significance of this religious movement for education has been elaborated by Newton Edwards in a remarkably sociological interpretation of educational history.[3] Although the Protestant revolt represented a middle-class struggle against traditional aristocracy, the intent of the struggle was not to establish a democratic form of government so much as to provide a government in which individualistic middle-class interests could

---

[2] Richard Carlson, *Executive Succession and Organizational Change: Place-Bound and Career-Bound Superintendents of Schools* (Midwest Administration Center, University of Chicago, 1962), p. 77.

[3] Newton Edwards and Herman Richey, *The School in the American Social Order* (Boston: Houghton Mifflin, 1947). Much of the following discussion is based on their analysis. See also Freeman Butts, *A Cultural History of Education* (New York: McGraw-Hill, 1947). Also Lawrence A. Cremlin, *The Transformation of the School: Progressivism in American Education, 1876–1957* (New York: Knopf, 1961).

flourish. This was not, then, a revolt against the established system of social classes; nor was it a revolt against religion per se. The revolt was
against the organized church, and it merely represented the efforts of a
group to ascend in the established social class system (which existed in
America as well as in Europe). The Puritans aimed at nothing less than
complete domination of the society and the strict imposition of their beliefs on others.[4] Consequently, both the privileged middle class and their
religion continued to dominate during the Colonial period. And not surprisingly, the school, which in Europe traditionally had been the hand-
maiden of the church, was completely dominated by religion in the Colonial period: the original primary function of schools was neither political
nor vocational but religious. The goals of teaching children to know "God's
word" and to read the Bible were primary. Because of their "holy" antecedents, classical languages and the traditional upper-middle-class curriculum also continued to dominate. Even servants were instructed in religion, and approval of the clergy was necessary before a teacher could be
employed. In short, early education in this country was totally dominated
by Protestant religious values.

Indeed, the whole society was under the control of the church; a secondary function of church schools was to develop attachments to the existing political order. In this sense, the first schools were neither secular
nor public. Members of the church hierarchy wrote the Massachusetts
Act of 1647 in which for the first time a state made public education mandatory. The purpose of the education prescribed in this act was to provide
the population with vocational training and information to help them to
"delude Satan." Universal education for members of society outside the
church was not to develop until later.

Due to internal conflicts among religious groups themselves and to the
ascending power of business over other institutions, these religious influences have declined considerably. Yet there remain traces of religion's
early influence over the public schools; it can be detected in the stress on
deportment and character training, the continued controversy over the
place of religion and spiritual training in the school, and the idealistic conception of teachers as dedicated people who should be disinterested in
high salaries while setting good moral examples. Narrowly behavior-cen-
tered moral criteria often have tended to take precedence over intellectual
ones in hiring and evaluating teachers; as a result, otherwise excellent
teachers may be excluded from the profession. Russell maintains that,
consequently, critical examination of religion and other sacred institutions
has been discouraged by teachers and that students have been encouraged
by their teachers to be timid and conventional, while otherwise intellectually superior nonconformists have been discouraged from exercising

---

[4] Edwards and Richey, ibid., p. 38.

their curiosity.[5] In short, religion has been not only a strong moral force, but also a conservative, anti-intellectual force in public education.

## BUSINESS AND EDUCATION

### The Transition from Religious to Business Control

Even after suffrage had been extended, Edwards notes, the clergy continued to exert a strong influence on education. In 1827 prayer and spiritual reading in public schools was nearly universal. Elementary spellers taught that "God governs the world" and is to be "worshipped by prayer." In fact, as one historian puts it, no great educational leader prior to the Civil War would have denied that the institution of education was subordinate to religion.[6] Yet the Colonial clergy had begun to align themselves with wealthy New England businessmen who were gaining influence independent of their religious connections. Because the clergy emulated these rising business leaders, they felt little sympathy for the lower-class movements that were beginning to threaten law and order, and which thus seemed to threaten Godliness itself; in 1847, Webster's spelling book suggested that pain and misfortune were to be endured and that the meanest trick was to steal a man's property.[7]

The transition from a religious- to a business-dominated society can be explained in terms of underlying similarities in the two value systems. Max Weber and R.R. Tawney both documented a thesis that the Protestant ethic was closely associated with the spirit of capitalism.[8] Calvin and Luther had maintained that salvation was part of a man's preordained destiny, that some men were predestined to be saved, others not. Such a depersonalized and orderly view of the universe, however, was hardly consoling to people who wanted clues as to how to achieve their own salvation. Successive misinterpretations of the doctrine eventually provided the means by which the saved could be identified: those predestined to salvation obviously would be privileged with a favorable position in this world too. From this interpretation it was but a short, logical step to the conclusion that a person could achieve salvation by achieving a favorable position in this world. This Protestant interpretation of salvation was expressed in a code of ethics that defined hard work and profit as moral virtues. Material success had become a means of salvation.[9]

---

[5] Bertrand Russell, *Education and the Social Order* (London: G. Allen, 1938).

[6] Merle Curti, *The Social Ideas of American Educators* (New York: Cooper Square Publishers, 1935).

[7] Ibid., pp. 33–34.

[8] Max Weber, *The Protestant Ethic and the Spirit of Capitalism*, Talcott Parsons, trans. (New York: Scribner, 1930).

[9] Ronald G. Corwin, *Social Mobility: A Dimension of Migration* (unpublished M.A. thesis, University of Minnesota, 1958).

From the beginning, then, profit motives had been at least as strong as religious motives among some New England colonists. Puritans were striving for ascendance in the society. As they achieved social position, the religious ideology became a less necessary and a less powerful influence. What prevailed was the commercial motive. The full success of the business ideology was symbolized by the Civil War in which Northern capitalists permanently subjugated the landed aristocracy in the South.

As the influence of religion declined, educational practices eventually became tailored to the needs of business. However, as Edwards observed, designed as it was primarily for religious purposes, the old educational system was not immediately useful to the expanding business economy; ambition and chance were more relevant factors to business success than character formation. Hence, as long as the economy could use child labor, education was neither necessary nor compulsory.[10]

It was only after labor unrest had developed in the middle of the 19th century that business leaders seriously turned their attention to the support of public education. It occurred to them that public schools could indoctrinate children with the business ideology as easily as they had formerly formed religious character. Hence, education for the masses promised the businessman security in face of the growing unrest among the working classes. Indoctrination with the business ideology and training for vocations became primary emphases of the curriculum. During the period, for example, the National Education Association consistently appealed to its members to help end strikes. While the nation was in the throes of labor disorder in 1877, said Curti, the president of the NEA said that schools should teach discipline and respect for property and for the rights of organized industry.[11] One educational leader asserted that teachers were employed to demonstrate the worthiness of the employers who hire their graduates and pay their salaries. The school was expected to teach children to respect the rights of organized industry; as one educator put it, "to the owner of property, no economy is more important than that which shall reform those who have it in their power to plunder and destroy" (i.e., the lower class).[12] The NEA was consistently opposed to strikes and other forms of resistance to big business. One educator observed that correct schooling for the masses must be supported by business in order to prevent the "foolish notion that there should be equality of condition"—the ideology that supported the strikes.[13]

Much of the renewed zeal for mass education prior to the turn of the century, then, was not simply an expression of a democratic desire to edu-

---

[10] Edwards, *School in the American Social Order*, pp. 97–109.

[11] William T. Harris, cited by Curti, *Social Ideas*, p. 330.

[12] B.P. Adydelott, cited by Curti, *Social Ideas*, pp. 80, 83; see also p. 218.

[13] Ibid., p. 83.

cate persons for their own good. Indeed, compulsory education itself came in the wake of mass unemployment and after labor leaders had begun to give active support to public education. The passage of state compulsory education laws requiring all children to remain in school until the age of 16 followed closely upon laws establishing the same minimum age requirement for child labor in industry; compulsory education was not instituted until children no longer were needed in the labor market.

Clearly, the new policies expressed by educational leaders were adapted to their need for the support of businessmen and property owners. Just as early education was designed to preserve the position of religion in the society, under early industrialism in this country the schools were expected to preserve the *status quo* of the commercial classes. Schoolmen had embraced the laissez-faire philosophy (that if individuals act selfishly the system will correct itself), which supported the industrial system. In a self-correcting system, there is little need for critical analysis either in the school or out of it. From Lincoln to Wilson, observed Curti, educators campaigned for the causes of capitalism and industry against farmers and organized labor; and just as Southern educators saw nothing ethically wrong with slavery, so Northern educators saw nothing ethically wrong in the exploitation of human and natural resources and of child labor for profit.[14] Education still was primarily a conservative and preservative force.

## THE IMPACT OF BUSINESS ON EDUCATION

The business principles that have been embraced by public school systems illustrate the profound forces that operate to keep the school program in line with current social values. One of the most perceptive analyses of the relation between business values and education is contained in an essay on higher education by Thorstein Veblen.[15] His observations are presented here not as final answers, but because they raise significant questions about the influence of business on public schools as well as on universities.

The core of his thesis is that higher education is based on the "price system"; i.e., the same values and procedures that dominate the business world. There are several reasons why the price system is a central part of educational organizations. First, the public, the board of governors, and the legislature, which determine a school's fate, are often made up of businessmen who are accustomed to evaluating business success rather than evaluating the success of scholarship and teaching. Second, big business

---

14 Curti, *Social Ideas*, p. 98.

15 Thorstein Veblen, *The Higher Learning in America* (New York: Sagamore Press, 1957). The discussion in this section follows Veblen's analysis.

and educational organizations share a common organizational structure; i.e., a large-scale, complex one. The difficulties that the layman and specialist alike have in evaluating intrinsically ambiguous educational activities, many of which are performed behind closed doors out of the sight of the public, would be problem enough; but they are compounded by the fact that there is no simple way of evaluating the teaching product. On the other hand, the criteria of business success ( e.g., profit or volume sales) are more observable and more easily applied; so schools and colleges are forced to justify their activities, their budget requests, and their reputations in terms of the business criteria to which the public is accustomed. Among these criteria are: financial solvency, advertising for clients, publicity and public relations, material symbols of success, and accountability.

_Financial Solvency._ Programs that can be justified as financially solvent are more appealing than those that cannot. It is easier to expand programs that bring a financial return, such as athletic programs, than those that do not guarantee financial solvency or profit, such as a program subsidizing advanced study for teachers. Similarly, the emphasis on attendance in public schools is supported not only by law, but also by the fact that state-supported schedules are based on average daily attendance.

_Advertising._ It is also easier to defend programs that act as a form of advertising and provide favorable publicity for the organization. Expanding the number of courses offered is justified in the same way that a department store justifies a new line of goods: it increases the potential market by attracting and holding a wider range of clientele. Raising the standards of performance has the opposite effect; it is therefore difficult to justify practices such as hard grading or heavy work loads. With semi-official approval, in many departments snap courses develop that attract and hold the students who have been discouraged by courses with higher standards.

Public schools advertise through handbills and letters sent home with the child. At levels of higher education as well, many colleges advertise for students. Speaking of the advertising functions of college catalogues, Clark observes, "the catalogue of a college so often portrays the campus as the nearest thing to an earthly paradise—ideally situated on a hill overlooking a beautiful valley, combining rural charm with urban convenience, peopled by scholars and dedicated youth of almost cinematic sex appeal."[16]

_Public Relations._ Most phases of school operation have effects on public relations. Administrators often try to keep their faculty in line with the sentiments of the community. Veblen charges that a good teacher, like a good administrator, is considered to be a safe one who has the proper religious and political affiliations.

Discrepancies sometimes develop between a school's internal status system and the status the public accords to various types of teachers. Col-

---

[16] Clark, _Educating_, p. 201.

leagues are probably more likely than the general public to judge one another on the basis of their day-to-day contributions to the intrinsic goals; the public is more likely than the faculty to be familiar with teachers who work in the public spotlight, such as coaches. The publicity accorded to a drama coach or athletic coach, for example, gives him an aura of public prestige not necessarily endorsed by other teachers in less publicized but important fields such as English, science, and mathematics.

It is often the very personnel least connected with the intrinsic functions of education who establish closest connections with the public; for example, the school nurse, the truant officer, or the guidance director has more opportunity than classroom teachers to work directly with parents. The outside contacts of the former groups increase their influence within the school, and quite possibly these persons—whose jobs involve contact with the public and whose reputations are therefore dependent on favorable public opinion—are most in favor of adapting to outside pressure. Vocational teachers are an example of persons who are in especially advantageous positions to develop good relations with important businessmen of the community. Their contacts can give them power within the school disproportionate to the respect accorded them by other teachers, and they can be expected to be sensitive to the wishes of businessmen.

For evidence that the prestige of teachers does not correspond to their autonomy Corwin asked teachers in seven schools to indicate the number of times they consulted with each administrator in the system about their problems.[17] The rate of consultation can be considered an index of the extent to which each department in a school is dependent on the administration to make its decisions. Generally, the language, mathematics, business, and athletic departments reported more autonomy from the administration than the other departments. Nonacademic departments, home economics, and English had the least autonomy. The prestige of these departments also was determined by asking teachers to assume that budget limitations have made it necessary to eliminate three courses from the present curriculum and to indicate the three courses that should be the first to be eliminated and the three that should be the last to be eliminated. The rank of each course was determined by the proportions of the faculty mentioning it as the last and as the first to be eliminated. Generally speaking, the academic subjects had more prestige, especially English, mathematics, and science. At the other extreme, the applied, vocational, and nonacademic (extracurricular) course areas ranked low. The correlation of this prestige ranking with autonomy was very low: for example,

---

[17] Preliminary findings reported in *The Development of an Instrument for Examining Staff Conflicts in the Public Schools*, U.S. Office of Education Report No. 1934, (Columbus: Department of Sociology and Anthropology, The Ohio State University, 1964).

English was accorded the highest prestige of all departments but it was among the lowest in autonomy.

The fact that the public receives much of its information and impressions of a school from persons in peripheral areas of the curriculum (such as student-activities departments in colleges) promotes public ignorance as to the school's intrinsic character. The same situation, however, also protects teachers by hiding the true character of the school.

*Success Symbols.*  Symbols of success must be visible and easily comprehended. Therefore, it is easier to justify budgets for modern buildings, late-model trucks, automobiles, and buses, and other visible symbols of material success than it is to justify budgets for salary increases for the faculty, financial support for advanced training for teachers, and other less visible forms of expense. While a community that builds new schools usually hires competent faculty as well, it is the school buildings rather than the scholarship that publicize the status of its educational program. The architecture of school buildings reflects the fashion of the era at least as much as it reflects the best use of space for educational purposes. This point recently was illustrated in a new school with large glass walls. Every classroom nevertheless was equipped with expensive velvet draperies that completely covered most of the windows. The explanation was one well known in education: when windows are exposed, sunlight makes the children sleepy and they are distracted by the events outdoors.

Because of the symbolic nature of success, failure to create the proper image can seriously impair the school's relationship with its public. The superintendent who must entertain the town's leading banker in a shabby office is therefore placed at an initial disadvantage. A similar situation exists at the level of state-local relationships, where personnel in the state departments of education often have less expensively decorated offices than the superintendents whom they are supposed to be advising.

*Accountability.*  The principle of accountability, which is a vital part of modern business practices, is widely used by public educators. It is generally easier to justify programs whose efficiency can be accounted for than those whose efficiency is not easily measured. The credit and grade-point systems, as Veblen notes, are parallels of the price system; credit hours are measures of the efficiency of students in the sense that "failure" is failure to achieve the proper point-hour within a specified period of time. Similarly, a course that cannot be taught in three semester credits is "inefficient."

Just as businesses maintain separate departments of accounting, so do schools. Special record-keeping offices constantly evaluate student and staff efficiency, attendance, promptness, grade-point ratios, and student–teacher loads. The standardized testing procedures teachers use also are essentially measures of teaching and learning efficiency. This stress on efficiency can distort the relative importance of measurement to the point that teachers are reluctant to teach that which cannot be easily measured. At the same time, there is pressure to administer tests even when it is not clear what is being tested.

### The Cult of Efficiency in Public Education

Veblen's observations on the influence that business has had on higher education have been documented also in the public schools by Callahan, who traced the diffusion of business principles from the factory into the classroom during the first part of this century.[18] In a nation whose educational leaders are more impressed by the accomplishments of the Andrew Mellons than of the John Deweys, Callahan observes that educational spokesmen such as William C. Bagley arose to proclaim that classroom management was primarily a business problem, a problem of economy.[19] The extent to which educators had embraced the desire of the age for practical education was perhaps expressed best by a superintendent of the Illinois Farmer's Institute, speaking before the National Education Association in 1909: "Ordinarily a love of learning is praiseworthy; but when this delight in the pleasures of learning becomes so intense and so absorbing that it diminishes the desire, and the power of earning, it is positively harmful."[20]

This was the era of scientific management in industry, and Callahan documents the influence that principles of scientific management had on the thinking of public school administrators. The principle of time-and-motion study was interpreted by schoolmen to mean that there was one best way of doing any job and that this method could be determined only through scientific job analysis. Teaching functions were reduced to a dollars and cents formula. Hence, Spaulding could demonstrate, "5.9 pupil-recitations in Greek are of the same value as 23.8 pupil-recitations in French," and "it takes 41.7 pupil-recitations in vocal music to equal the value of 13.9 pupil-recitations in art." He suggested that the price of Greek instruction at the rate of 5.9 pupil-recitations per dollar was too high; schools should invest in something else.[21] A contemporary of Spaulding observed with pride that, although some eighth-grade classes do addition only at the rate of 35 combinations per minute, the average rate of some classes is 105 combinations per minute.[22] In order to implement efficiency, it was felt that definite lessons should be prepared by the teacher for each day's work, just as the industrial supervisor laid out the day's work for the

---

[18] Raymond E. Callahan, *Education and the Cult of Efficiency* (Chicago: The University of Chicago Press, 1962).

[19] Cited by Callahan, ibid., p. 7.

[20] Cited by Callahan, ibid., p. 10.

[21] Cited by Callahan, ibid., p. 73.

[22] Ibid., p. 81.

men under him. Close supervision of teachers was considered necessary to assure adequate performance. Clearly, these policies were made not on educational, but on financial grounds.

The efficiency of education was measured in terms of the number of pupils, classes, and preparations per teacher and the proportion of the teacher's time devoted to school work each week. Remedies for inefficiency were as simple as the formula for computing them. If the objective is to reduce the cost of education, it is necessary to increase the number of classes per teacher and the class size, to cut teachers' salaries, to operate two shifts a day, to keep schools open in the summer and in the evening for the community, and to operate schools on a 12-month basis. Again, these decisions were made primarily as a matter of good business rather than educational policy.

Another innovation was to introduce an organizational scheme that would provide an economical basis for specialized study. It was the educators' answer to the industrial assembly line; i.e., the so-called platoon system. Under this plan, more of the rooms were in constant use for specialized purposes; the students shifted classes at the sound of a bell.

The productivity of the system was measured in terms of the proportion of the students in the system who enrolled and graduated in comparison with the proportion of withdrawals. The alarming number of dropouts, some educators thought, constituted a loss of "raw material during the process of production" such as would bankrupt a private manufacturing industry within a short period of time. One remedy for this problem was to change the curriculum from one which appealed to the bright child to one which would appeal to the average pupil.

Callahan notes a number of consequences of this development in education, especially the fact that the energies of a whole generation of educationalists had been diverted from the probem of assessing educational goals to problems such as the heating and ventilating of schools, school seating, decorating, operation of the school cafeteria, and school fire insurance. While practicing administrators were busy studying waste and efficiency and standardization of janitor service, still another entire generation of teachers and school administrators was being trained in this immensely practical way of thinking.[23] As Callahan points out, many educators still in positions of leadership were socialized at a time when this consciousness of efficiency dominated. It is this type of training in education which led Nicholas Murray Butler to remark in 1950 that there was "some measure of truth in the cynical suggestion that administration may best be defined as the doing extremely well of something that had better not be done at all."[24]

---

[23] Ibid., pp. 59, 187.
[24] Cited by Callahan, ibid., p. 195.

From business' stranglehold over the schools emerged the ideas that teachers are employees and that education is a marketable product. For example, a school board member wrote in 1911, "a board of education is only a board of directors; the taxpayers, the stockholders. The superintendent is a sales manager; the teachers salesmen."[25] As a school board president told the principals of Chicago schools in 1927, "You educators must understand that teaching is a business. You are salesmen. Your commodity is education. You must satisfy your customers, the taxpayers."[26] Thus had academic hucksterism matured in the schools; teachers had become one of the largest sales forces in the country.

There is little doubt that the biggest customer of educators was the business community. Teachers were counseled that the public controls education and the administration of it and that they would do well to resign themselves to the situation, or better still, to accept it with hardy approval. Many schoolteachers and administrators did. In their enthusiasm for the demands that the public was making on schools, educators of this era again demonstrated their remarkable capacity to adapt to changing social tides.

Traces of this business influence are still quite apparent. For example, when asked in 1960 which fields of study were most important, school administrators placed school finance at the top of the list, and public relations, human relations, and school business management within the first five.[27] Undoubtedly there are educators in positions of power and influence who still subscribe to the image of education expressed in the following statement:

> Our schools are, in a sense, factories in which the raw products (children) are to be shaped and fashioned into products to meet the various demands of life. The specifications for manufacturing come from the demands of twentieth-century civilization, and it is the business of the school to build its pupils according to the specifications laid down. This demands good tools, specialized machinery, continuous measurement of production to see if it is according to specifications, the elimination of waste in manufacture, and a large variety in the output.[28]

Callahan's analysis of the public schools, like Veblen's analysis of higher education, is one-sided and caustic. Neither analysis recognizes the bargaining role that administrators play in public organizations. . . . Administrators sometimes bargain away certain educational principles in order to accomplish others more effectively; thus the fact that educators sub-

---

[25] Cited by Callahan, ibid., p. 151.
[26] Ibid., p. 231.
[27] Ibid., p. 260.
[28] Ellwood P. Cubberley, *Public School Administration* (Boston, Houghton Mifflin, 1960), pp. 337–38, as quoted by Callahan, *Education*, p. 152.

scribed to principles of efficiency reduced the public's resistance to increasing costs of education. Nevertheless, there is merit in analyses such as these, for in relating educational practices to broader social movements, they demonstrate that organizational goals are not simply inherent in an organization but are imposed on it by broader social movements, and in the process these analyses illustrate how change in other institutions implement organizational change.

## THE FAMILY AND EDUCATION

Family control over education was established early in the Colonial period. Early compulsory education acts, among them the Massachusetts Act of 1647, did not provide for schools, but rather responsibility for educating children was delegated to parents. Families banded together to hire private teachers who were allowed to board with each of the families successively in exchange for their services. In this traditional setting, family influence was so far-reaching that it encompassed the entire community. Family control over education amounted to community control.

However, with the Industrial Revolution and the transfer of work outside the home to the factory, the family gradually diminished in importance, economically, educationally, and politically. As the family lost its economic importance, its cohesiveness and the ability of its members to control one another also were jeopardized. The attention of men was turned outside the family to their work. Women, who formerly had been partners in a common economic farm enterprise, no longer played a role in their husband's work and consequently experienced a prestige vacuum. Having lost the sense of importance that was hers on the frontier—where her canning, sewing, and bookkeeping functions had been essential for the survival of the family itself—the American woman was left with the menial tasks of cleaning, food preparation, and, particularly, child care.

Children followed their fathers' exodus from the home. At first they went into industry, but after a short but humanly degrading stint in the factories, children were barred from employment by depressions and subsequently by child labor laws. These events initially had the effect of transforming children, who had been economic assets on the farm, into liabilities; but they were soon to regain importance as a new "leisure class," one of the few groups in possession of the time and the facilities to play, read, create, and pursue other activities that formerly had been the exclusive prerogative of the upper socioeconomic strata. The new role of children as agents of family prestige and mobility, together with the disorganizing effects of the family's loss of economic function and the status vacuum of women, were to place the child in a strategic position within the family. Children were to become a central reason for the family's very existence, and perhaps its only essential purpose other than that of adult companionship. Hence, middle-class families became child centered. Children became especially relevant to the functions that remained for the woman within the family; the mother role appeared as the only essential remaining one in the family and the one which promised to compensate for some of the loss of importance women experienced during this period. Women were to elevate themselves primarily as mothers.

Given the role that the child has assumed in maintaining family integration, given the effects of children on the status of women, and given the traditional controls the family has exercised over education and over the legal apparatus for local control of the schools, it is natural that middle-class parents in this country exhibit anxieties about what teachers do to their children. Moreover, these anxieties were further provoked by the fact that teaching was professionalizing at the same time: teachers were assuming more control over the curriculum, and they were adopting a professional viewpoint that set them apart from parents.[29] In teaching the child to mature, the school is emancipating him from his mother's apron strings; for from their professional perspective, teachers naturally view children objectively in terms of their performance, while parents evaluate their children on subjective criteria. Whereas parents will love and reward the child regardless of what he accomplishes, teachers reward him primarily on the basis of performance. Under these conditions, the child's entrance into school can be a point of dethronement for the child and a point of origin for competition between teacher and family for the child's loyalty.

With the growing number of value conflicts in the society, the school's role in socializing children has become especially suspect to many whose values are different from those of teachers. The teacher who inspects fingernails is judging parents as well as children; the pupil who is asked by the teacher to describe his breakfast, only to be told that his mother is not providing him with nourishing meals, eventually is forced to consider the validity of his parents' way of life. Even the middle-class child may find that his parents and teachers disagree as to the merits of fluoridation, the way one can get ahead in the world, the validity of the theory of evolution, or the importance of cleanliness and hard work. As such incidents reoccur, they may lead to a generalized respect or disrespect for either parents or teachers, which may culminate in alienation from school or from family.

The teacher, then, has gained more influence over child rearing precisely at the time that children have become essential to family stability. At least some parents find that they have granted more authority to schools than they had bargained for and seek to retain control by exerting pressure through formal and informal channels. Generally speaking, pres-

---

[29] Willard Waller, *The Sociology of Teaching* (New York: Wiley, 1932), pp. 30, 40, 68 ff.

sure groups tend to form precisely at such times; i.e., when an activity that is crucial for the goals and survival of a group has been delegated to another agency.

The relationship that has developed between parents and teachers with respect to children is one of overlapping authority, or, in other words, two parties both seek to control a third. From the child's standpoint, this system of dual control creates a conflict of alternatives he is forced somehow to ignore, to compromise, or to reject. He is, for example, expected to learn to be modern and scientific while maintaining the traditions of his family. But while the overlapping authority of parents and teachers can be a source of confusion, it can also be a challenge and a source of stimulation to the child.

## THE STATE AND EDUCATION

It is certain that any group whose primary concern is to influence the younger generation will be carefully watched by political leaders. Indeed, the struggle to control education is largely political. At the local level, school boards control paid administrators, and education is becoming an increasingly prominent concern of legislative bodies at the state and federal levels.

Whenever men disagree, they turn to the state (i.e., a unit of regional government) for support: "There ought to be law." The greater the disagreement among groups in the society, the more frequently they turn to higher political authorities and the greater the power of the state becomes. During the past 30 years the Federal Government has gained enormous powers, and government officials themselves have become professionalized; whereas in preceding administrations officials were recruited from the ranks of business, in recent years they have come increasingly from a growing core of professional politicians, academicians, and technicians. Growing tensions and occasionally bitter conflicts between top business executives and the federal government signify the full maturation of big government as an independent institution.

As guardians of an institution whose function it is to conserve the social order, educators never have been radically disposed. Although it is true as Clark points out, that education often has a liberalizing effect on people, that among persons of similar occupational status, those with higher education tend to have more liberal attitudes; and that during their college years students become more liberal (the change in students in Ivy League colleges being greater than in those in publicly supported institutions).[30] Nevertheless, persons who expect the schools to eliminate the problems of racial prejudice or religious intolerance ignore the important

---

[30] Clark, *Educating*, pp. 20–37.

fact that schools traditionally have been places where such attitudes were reinforced. Schoolmen have always supported discrimination, segregation, and forms of religious bigotry. The schools are a part of society, not apart from it; and as a result, the beliefs of those in control of society find their way into the classroom.

As all levels of government have achieved more control, the goals of education have become more narrowly prescribed in terms of the interests of the state. In many circles, public education is believed to be equivalent to citizenship training; children traditionally have learned patriotism to the local region or to a specific country as opposed to more worldwide allegiances. As the nation has assumed growing importance in world affairs, however, the national government has become the primary object of patriotism, at the expense of community and regional loyalty. Accordingly, the public schools now offer courses in citizenship and American government, they sponsor the American Legion Boys State programs and patriotic essay contests, and they have other clearly nationalistic functions designed to increase loyalty to the nation. In the process, patriotic myths have sometimes been allowed to obscure objectivity and critical thinking, for state interests require the suppression of certain information, such as the proportion of time the state has spent in wars. Schools are expected to teach history in such a way that the country appears always to have been motivated by the highest and the noblest ideals, and, as M. Curti states it, to give the impression that there is no land where people are so prosperous, happy, or intelligent, nor so bent on doing just and right. The Spanish American War, which historians agree was initiated by militant and expansionist motives on the part of the United States, the NEA declared to have been "entered upon in the most unselfish spirit and from the loftiest of motives."[31] One educator was reportedly thrilled at seeing young Puerto Ricans singing "America" only five years after the United States had acquired the island.[32] At the peak of the corruption of Tammany Hall, Curti observes, educators did not attack such practices, preferring to wait for "character training" to eliminate the problem; and while Horace Mann deplored violence initiated by the common man in efforts to improve his lot, he considered war to be necessary for expansion.[33] Similarly, during wars educators have reinforced young children's hatred of the enemy. During World War II, for example, many children were taught that the "Japs" were a despicable people and that the Russians were our allies; the current generation learns the opposite.

Nationalism in public education has become even more pronounced during the current cold war crisis. The federal government's interest in

---

[31] Cited by Curti, *Social Ideas*, p. 225.
[32] Ibid., pp. 226–227.
[33] Ibid., p. 128.

education is clearly a patriotic one. Aids to math-science education are direct expressions of political concepts of education as a weapon in the cold war. Also, Conant's recommendation that all intellectually advanced children take four years of mathematics is directly predicated on the assumption that the public school's primary responsibility is to train citizens who are useful to their country, just as certainly as an earlier goal was to train religious zealots useful to the church.[34] Precisely as education has come to play a more important function in the economy, it has become more strategically involved in politics.

In a society where institutions are not entirely in harmony, the art of compromise, which is the basis of politics, begins to characterize the public school system as well, as for example released time represents a compromise between religious and secular interests. But as politics has infiltrated education, *educators, in turn, have engaged in politics. They have sometimes found political allies with power sufficient to grant education some independence and intellectual freedom of thought.* Ironically, as groups struggle among themselves for control over education, educators become involved in the political process and begin to exercise more control over their fate. . . .

## LEISURE AND EDUCATION

The growth of leisure is one of the most important institutional developments of this century. Americans now spend an estimated eight percent of the gross national product on leisure, which is nearly three times the amount spent on public education, and it is more than is spent each year on cars and houses. These figures reflect the expanding scope of leisure. The average workweek has declined from 66 hours in 1850 to less than 30 hours by 1975, as a result of population growth and the alarming effects of automation; while the average life span has increased from 48.2 years in 1900 to nearly 70 years in 1960; it will be near 73 years by the year 2000.[35] If the retirement age merely remains constant, the average time in retirement will triple to nine years by 2000; it has already doubled since 1900, there being now an average of five years of leisure at the end of the life span for the average person. Finally, during the work years, leisure in the form of annual vacations and lengthened lunch hours and coffee breaks also has increased.

But perhaps the greatest increases in leisure are those in the early part of the career cycle. In 1825 every Massachusetts town claimed at least 11

[34] James R. Conant, *Slums and Suburbs* (New York: McGraw-Hill, 1961), pp. 88–89.

[35] Joseph Zeisel, "The Work Week in American Industry, 1850–1956"; and Seymour L. Wolfbein, "The Changing Length of Working Life," in Eric Larrabee and Rolf Meyersohn (Eds.), *Mass Leisure* (New York: Free Press), pp. 145–161.

hours a day of labor of children ages 6 to 17 years; in many cases it was much higher. By 1900, 20 percent of the males aged 10 to 15 years were employed full time, and in 1950 this figure was less than one percent.

The last set of figures reflects a development that was closely associated with the growth of public education. Advanced education could not come into being until the society could afford to release children from gainful employment and until people had become sufficiently leisure oriented to consider education worthwhile. With the advent of universal education, school children became the new leisure class, and public schools were among the first institutions to face the problems of leisure. Free-moving, relaxed classrooms, employing progressive education, could not have been implemented if the society had not been leisure based; even business was relaxing its logic of efficiency to incorporate coffee breaks and extended lunch hours. Conversely, as someone has said, if Dewey had not invented progressive education someone would have invented Dewey, for progressive education represented a means of adapting schools to the changing times.

### The Conception of Leisure

The conception of leisure that schools have embraced must be understood within the framework of the Protestant ethic, which essentially is a work ethic. The Protestant ethic was this-worldly; although hard work, thrift, investment, and similar virtues necessary for economic success were believed essential for religious salvation as well. Based on a materialistic view of the universe, its major premise, that man is master over the universe, spurred growth of the nation's commerce and industry. That premise sustained a set of focal values which one anthropologist refers to as "effort-optimism," or the belief that through hard work and vigor man can harness the universe for his utilitarian purposes.[36] To lower-class immigrants who came into the country from the fields and the factories of Europe, work traditionally appeared as a virtue; and this impression did not suffer from the American frontier experience. Since hard work requires energy, vigorous and youthful adults were upheld as the American ideal; America learned to admire the young and to discard the aged who had retired from productive work. The sports complex symbolizes this appreciation of vigor and energy; sports are a means by which many mature adults desperately attempt to retain youthfulness. Cosmetics perform the same function for women in a more visible way. The American language, too, is an active one—compare the phrase "I've got it made" with the

---

[36] Cora Dubois, "The Dominant Value Profile of American Culture," *American Anthropologist* (December 1955):232–239; also Florence Kluckhohn, "Dominant and Variant Value Orientations," in Clyde Kluckhohn, et al. (Eds.), *Personality in Nature, Society and Culture* (New York: Knopf, 1953), pp. 342–360.

English equivalent, "It's jolly well done." The spectator is suspect in this atmosphere of effort-optimism, hard work, and vigor; so also the intellectual (who fits the image of the armchair observer) is a subject of scorn and suspicion, while the person with practical experience is admired.

There is little in this tradition to prepare middle-class Americans for the present onslaught of leisure. In a work-oriented, religious society, failure to work had connotations of sin.[37] Leisure itself, Mead notes, was defined primarily in its relation to work. Recreation literally meant to "re-create" oneself for the next day's work; Sunday was a day of rest to recuperate for the next workweek; meals were viewed as a means to sustain strength. Moreover, even leisure had to be earned with hard work, and as large amounts of unproductive leisure time have accrued in recent decades, the American has had difficulty justifying and utilizing it. But some writers suggest that one way people have attempted to justify it is by combining leisure with work.[38] On the one hand, the American people play at work, smuggling leisure into the work routine in the form of coffee breaks, extended lunch periods, business-over-lunch, office parties, and other ways in which it will go unnoticed. On the other hand, Americans work at play —the most acceptable hobbies involve manual labor or shop work; and athletic activities such as tennis, golf, and bowling have become increasingly popular pastimes.

One problem is that traditional areas of play have become professionalized at the very time that people have more time on their hands. For example, the lady bountiful, the upper-middle-class woman who handed out baskets of food on skid row, has been replaced by the professional social worker;[39] the amateur musician confronts a demanding audience that has become acquainted with superior musical performances through mass media; and amateur athletics suffers from competition with professional games. College and high school games are developing an increasingly professional character to hold their audiences. Indeed, the Little League ball clubs have become nearly as competitive as professional teams. With full-length, professional-like games, Little League managers are reluctant to interrupt the game to show a boy or girl how to bat or throw, or to pull out an ace pitcher before the arm is injured. In one metropolitan area coaches are given "points" to buy up players from around the city for their teams, which to say the least, represents a change from the traditional neighborhood basis of sandlot games. The pressure toward professionalization of leisure is also apparent in the craft hobbies. The amateur crafts-

---

[37] Margaret Mead, "The Pattern of Leisure in Contemporary American Culture," in *Mass Leisure* (New York: Free Press), pp. 10–15.

[38] David Riesman, et al., *The Lonely Crowd* (New York: Doubleday, 1956), Chap. 15.

[39] Ibid.

man with a basement full of power tools competes with professional manufacturers to build a coffee table identical to one that can be purchased in
the local department stores.[40]

As the traditional areas of play continue to increase in competitiveness,
the prospect is that more Americans will be forced to look for alternative
uses of leisure time. What then? One writer suggests that play increasingly will be used as "taste exchange." He visualizes the spread of intellectual discussion groups, which exchange judgments on jazz, literature,
TV programs, athletics, and other forms of armchair quarterbacking.[41]

### Institutionalization of Play

Frederick traces the status of leisure-time (extracurricular) activities
in public schools through at least four stages of development.[42] First, in
the Colonial period the initial attitude toward outside activities was one
of abstinence; children were expected to attend to their lessons. The second period, during the decline of religious influence and the emergence
of industry, may be characterized as a period of tolerance toward leisure
activity. School children organized dances, parties, and other activities
without faculty leadership or encouragement. During the third period,
from which schools have just recently begun to emerge, schools have been
developing extracurricular programs, with corresponding expansions of
plant and staff. Under the guidance of regular staff members, student activities have become a definite part of the school program. Frederick refers to this as the period of capitalization.

The phase into which schools now seem to be entering may be characterized as a period of formalization; it is the era of the "third curriculum,"
of cocurricular activities. The preliminary stages of formalization begin
with the later stages of capitalization when teachers begin to supervise
extracurricular activities on a part-time basis as an added part of their
normal duties. The next step is to assign academic credit to the activity,
which means that the teacher assumes full responsibility for it. Then, a
full-time staff member is hired to direct the activity, and finally, it may be
granted the status of a required course. Music, typing, homemaking, and
physical education have evolved through similar stages in many schools.

The prominent and formal role of the third curriculum in present-day
schools is illustrated in the following set of morning announcements which
appeared in one school:

---

[40] Reuel Denny, The Astonished Muse (Chicago: The University of Chicago Press,
1957). Denny points out that even amateur "hot rodders" have been crowded out by
Detroit professional models.

[41] Riesman, Lonely Crowd.

[42] Robert W. Frederick, The Third Curriculum: Student Activities in American
Education (New York: Appleton-Century-Crofts, 1959).

Band members whose last names begin with letters A–L will report to the gym for uniform fittings first period, letters M–Z report during second period.

The Track Team will leave at 2:10 for their afternoon meet.

The Prom Decorating Committee will be excused for the afternoon.

Invitation Committee will meet in the art room, fifth period.

Regular music classes will be cancelled third and fourth periods. The Girls' Chorus will practice for commencement at this time.

Otherwise classes will be regular.

Formalized as part of the curriculum, certain leisure activities have become standardized features of schooling; and significantly enough, others have been omitted or ignored. Struggles for favored status have developed between the teachers responsible for various activities; the band director who needs new uniforms and instruments complains that the athletic team is receiving too much money for its uniforms or that the drama coach's sets are too expensive. Under these circumstances, students also have become the object of many bitter struggles between the sponsors of activities, whose prestige depends on the number and caliber of students they attract. While logically these activities exist for students, in fact, once the activity is formalized, students sometimes are recruited for its benefit. In five of the seven schools in which the author interviewed, teachers volunteered descriptions of competitive incidents between extracurricular programs.[43] One teacher generalized as follows, "The music people might say, 'We want so and so in for music practice after school,' and the athletic team would say 'Well, we want him too; he's got to practice with us after school.'" An incident involving a music teacher and an athletic coach was summarized by a teacher like this, "There is a kind of bad feeling between the music department and the physical education department. Mr. L. kept a boy from going to a track meet, and now there is friction between the two because Mr. M. lost the track meet." Because these defeats are taken personally by activity sponsors, they develop tactics for holding favorite participants. A music director explains the consequences that competition for students had for his program:

I have had a boys' chorus before school took up in the morning. So, this year they instigated an early class to start at 7:30, which many of the boys who want to be in chorus had to be in; and it was for the benefit of the athletic program, so they could go to early class and get out early in the afternoon and practice. So, I can't have them before school or after school. In addition to that, they have been putting the pressure on for the last two years, on everybody who is going to take a composition literature course, also to take speech. Well, if you have to take speech, and the physical education requirement has been made so strong, people just can't get

---

[43] Unpublished material from the study by Corwin, *Social Mobility*.

into my course. Years ago when they tried to make a speech requirement, I stood up to *my* rights. [Author's italics]

Another tactic which is typically used is described by a teacher in another school: "Mr. A. would not allow anybody on his team to work in any of the other arts. It wasn't really a friction between personalities; he wanted a winning team, and we wanted a winning team." The pressure that this competition creates for students is noted by this teacher:

> Practices came at the same time; the coaches then saying that the individual is not considered a member of a team if he misses the practice; the dramatics coach saying that the individual can't be considered for a part in a play if he misses practice. So there is a conflict there that puts the student in the middle. . . . He gets bawled out by both individuals concerned. If he doesn't do too well, he drops out of one or the other.

When these conflicts come to the attention of the administration, policies are developed for regulating the student's decision; such a policy is described by a coach:

> The board actually made a policy that if a boy had a conflict with a (basketball) tournament and any other extracurricular activity, that the boy should go to the tournament. . . . I could have taken a definite stand and told the boy that he couldn't go to chorus practice, but I didn't because the boy is such a wonderful boy. He told the supervisor of music last year that everything was going to be basketball; he wasn't going to take part in the operetta this year. And then, when school started he (the music supervisor) talked him into it, taking a part against his wishes.

If a sponsor cannot persuade students to give their wholehearted allegiance to his activity, he must be willing to work out a compromise like one between a music director and a track coach, who allowed a boy to participate in a track meet on Friday and then fly to a music contest on Saturday.

Characteristically in this era of formalization, a prestige hierarchy of leisure-time activities develops from these interdepartmental struggles. The school officially encourages some activities, such as athletics and music, which gain dominance in the program, while other activities like the Latin club, the rifle team, or art are relatively ignored. The prestige ranking of 50 student organizations of one high school, which is probably typical of many high schools throughout the nation, is reproduced in Table 1.[44]

---

[44] C. Wayne Gordon, *The Social System of the High School* (New York: Free Press, 1957), p. 61. A team of investigators recently classified activities settings in a number of schools of various sizes. It was found that the most frequent type of behavior setting was "extracurricular," followed by educational, athletic, and operating. In the three largest schools, settings concerned with the operation of the school ranked second. Roger C. Barker, et al., *Big School–Small School: Studies of the Effects of High School Size upon the Behavior and Experiences of Students* (Midwest Psychological Field Station, University of Kansas, 1962), p. 59.

**TABLE ONE**
Prestige Rank of the 50 Student Organizations of Wabash High School (showing ranking by 50 12th grade girls, 50 12th grade boys, and combined ranking with assigned rank weights)

| Organization | Girls' Rank | Boys' Rank | Combined Rank | Weight Rank |
|---|---|---|---|---|
| Student Assembly (student government body) | 1 | 2 | 1 | 5 |
| Varsity Basketball | 3 | 1 | 2 | 5 |
| Varsity Football | 5 | 3 | 3 | 5 |
| National Honor Society | 4 | 8 | 4 | 5 |
| Cheerleaders | 2 | 9 | 5 | 5 |
| Crest Coronation (yearbook queen's court) | 6 | 7 | 6 | 5 |
| Varsity Baseball | 11 | 4 | 7 | 4 |
| Crest Staff (yearbook staff) | 9 | 5 | 8 | 4 |
| Varsity Track | 14 | 6 | 9 | 4 |
| Senior Play Cast | 7 | 13 | 10 | 4 |
| Junior Prom Committee | 8 | 12 | 11 | 4 |
| Scoop Staff (school newspaper) | 17 | 11 | 12 | 4 |
| Mixed Chorus | 10 | 14 | 13 | 4 |
| Varsity Wrestling | 20 | 10 | 14 | 4 |
| Girls' Athletic Association | 12 | 19 | 15 | 3 |
| Senior Dramatics Club | 16 | 15 | 16 | 3 |
| School Band | 15 | 18 | 17 | 3 |
| "B" Basketball | 18 | 16 | 18 | 3 |
| School Orchestra | 13 | 23 | 19 | 3 |
| Quill & Scroll (honorary publications) | 19 | 21 | 20 | 3 |
| Junior Ring Committee | 22 | 17 | 21 | 3 |
| "B" Football | 21 | 22 | 22 | 3 |
| Varsity Tennis | 28 | 20 | 23 | 3 |
| "T-13" (honorary girls' athletic) | 23 | 26 | 24 | 3 |
| Pep Club | 27 | 24 | 25 | 2 |
| Junior Dramatics | 25 | 28 | 26 | 2 |
| Junior Rotarians | 24 | 33 | 27 | 2 |
| Junior Town Meeting | 26 | 32 | 28 | 2 |
| Bowling Club | 30 | 27 | 29 | 2 |
| Rifle Club | 29 | 30 | 30 | 2 |
| Projection Staff | 31 | 29 | 31 | 2 |
| Varsity Golf | 37 | 25 | 32 | 2 |
| Intramural Basketball | 40 | 31 | 33 | 2 |
| Drum Majorettes | 34 | 35 | 34 | 2 |
| Stage Crew | 33 | 37 | 35 | 2 |
| Gym Assistants | 32 | 42 | 36 | 2 |
| Office Assistants | 35 | 41 | 37 | 2 |
| Chess Club | 49 | 48 | 38 | 2 |
| Art Club | 39 | 39 | 39 | 1 |
| Intramural Volleyball | 41 | 36 | 40 | 1 |
| Diversified Occupations (vocational club) | 43 | 38 | 41 | 1 |
| Student World Federalist | 36 | 45 | 42 | 1 |
| Intramural Tennis | 44 | 40 | 43 | 1 |
| Library Club | 42 | 44 | 44 | 1 |
| Junior Red Cross | 38 | 46 | 45 | 1 |
| Roller Skating Club | 45 | 43 | 46 | 1 |
| Outdoor Club | 50 | 34 | 47 | 1 |

TABLE ONE *(Continued)*

| Organization | Girls' Rank | Boys' Rank | Combined Rank | Weight Rank |
|---|---|---|---|---|
| Pencil Pushers (creative writing) ..... | 47 | 47 | 48 | 1 |
| Riding Club (horseback riding) ...... | 46 | 49 | 49 | 1 |
| Knitting Club ..................... | 48 | 50 | 50 | 1 |

Student ratings, May 1950.

Source: C.W. Gordon, "Formal Student Organizations," *The Social System of the Schools* (New York: Free Press, 1957), p. 61.

From this prestige structure, children vicariously learn which leisure activities are "good"; i.e., approved, and which are not. The prominence of these activities encourages some students to overextend themselves, to compete excessively in many activities in search for approval and popularity. An 11th-grade girl in one high school said this of "big wheels":

> Many of the students are chosen by teachers to be on the yearbook or *Bugle* and many of the Student Assembly committees were very mischosen. They are in so many different things that they don't have to work on any of them; they can just stand around and supervise. I don't imagine the teachers realize it.
>
> There are a lot of kids who really want to be on these things but the teachers just get in a rut and choose the same people year after year just because they don't want to be bothered with showing somebody new how things run. . . . I guess your school success is based on how many clubs and committees you have beside your picture in the yearbook.[45]

On the other hand, those students who do not wish to participate in activities feel pressures from their peers, teachers, and parents to join in, and the person who collects stamps or reads travel folders is defined as a wallflower. Activities that can be *dis*played are most admired.

Shaping of the child's leisure tastes in the schools begins very early. He learns these attitudes, for example, when the elementary teacher asks children to describe their activities over the summer and shows approval of some uses of time and not others; travel is good, but travel to a national shrine is better; tent camping is not as good as a Mediterranean cruise, but it is better than just staying at home; classical music or jazz is condoned, pop music is not; Shakespeare is, Tennessee Williams is not, etc.

The schools not only encourage uniform uses of leisure time, but often they convey the impression that leisure can be used appropriately only in organized activities that are set aside for *that purpose*. This impression is confirmed in an anthropologist's content analysis of home economics curriculum guides, which were found to reflect the traditional work-oriented ethic of efficiency as opposed to an orientation in which leisure

---

[45] C. Wayne Gordon, *Social System*, pp. 64–65.

values are permitted to dominate. Rather than daydreaming while doing the dishes, watching a sunset, or recalling their experiences of last summer, girls were encouraged to anticipate their next chore and organize their day.[46] Good housewives, like good businessmen, presumably are supposed to give priority to their work while relegating leisure to planned activities outside the work area where it will not interfere with efficiency. The guides showed less concern with what housewives were supposed to do with the time they saved, but they did suggest that nonproductive activity is inappropriate in a work setting.

In short, the formalization of leisure encourages children to participate in uniform, recognized activities rather than to explore the multitude of alternative available uses and conceptions of leisure. What is significant is not merely that the decisions being made in this area, as in others, are forming a pattern, but that this uniformity is being enforced by teachers, the very group that talks most of individuality and creativity. This fact further supports the thesis that educational practices are less a reflection of the personal philosophies of educators than they are direct responses to the oppressing realities of institutional change.

## Implications for Education

The formalization of leisure has far-reaching implications for the values of individualism and creativity. In the past it was argued that the detrimental effects of specialization and routine work would be counteracted by the increased opportunity that workers would have for creative, personally meaningful activities, opportunity made possible because of the time saved by automation. But this alternative seems not to have materialized except, ironically, in the lower classes. Social pressures and standards of propriety rather than personal inclination define leisure time uses. It is possible that the liberal arts curriculum will gain prestige if idleness becomes more acceptable, but it is also possible that liberal arts activities will become formalized and commercialized as well.

David Riesman anticipates the development of avocational counselors, who will advise students in the use of their leisure time.[47] In fact, it is quite possible that schools of the future will develop entire curriculums designed to increase the competence of people in a variety of nonvocational areas. Such curriculums already exist in adult education programs and in some types of extracurricular activities, but many of these seem to be based on the assumption that leisure is worthwhile only if it involves physical activity and companionship. More passive activities which re-

---

[46] H. Powdermaker's discussion in George P. Spindler (Ed.), *Education and Anthropology* (Stanford: Stanford University Press, 1955).

[47] Riesman, *Lonely Crowd*, Chap. 15.

quire solitude, such as reading, have not been particularly encouraged by schools as admirable extracurricular activities, although the popularity of paperback books and book clubs in the adult community suggests that the public's concept of leisure may be changing in advance of that of schools. Also, the government is still advertising the belief that leisure time activities should involve strenuous physical exercise. Consequently, the answers that schools have provided for the problem have been rather unimaginative—the development of a new game, or more of something else that already exists.

That there is a growing demand for types of nonvocational skills now being neglected by schools is perhaps suggested in the fan clubs that follow popular movie stars and popular singing personalities—which now are forced to procure their knowledge and cues for evaluating popular arts from lay teachers in the mass media; i.e., movie fan magazines and disc jockeys. Schools of the future can be expected to assume responsibility for more of these avocational types of counseling duties and to develop a broader curriculum dealing with the problems of leisure. As other types of activities do develop and press for recognition, however, struggles among the avocational counselors, such as those illustrated in this chapter, will increase. Athletic directors, liberal arts teachers, school librarians, home economists, and other as yet unknown types of teachers will struggle for dominance. Some interesting dramas concerning these developments will take place in the hallways of schools in the future.

In their preference for *organized* leisure activities—i.e., those that usually involve well-defined responsibilities and the companionship of other people—people seem to be using leisure to escape from solitude and from themselves. The fear of solitude on the part of the American people is an expression of a broader value system that appears to have become prominent, a value system Whyte has called the "social ethic." Attention is now turned to this development.

# 2

# Do Schools Make a Difference?*

GODFREY HODGSON

The day Daniel Patrick Moynihan arrived at Harvard in the spring of 1966, he met some of his new colleagues at the Faculty Club in Cambridge. One of those present that evening was Professor Seymour Martin Lipset of the Harvard government department. "Hello, Pat," said Lipset, "guess what Coleman's found?"

"Coleman" was James S. Coleman, professor of social relations at Johns Hopkins, who had been charged by the Johnson administration with conducting an extensive survey of "the lack of availability of equal educational opportunities" by reason of race, religion, or national origin. And what the Coleman survey had found, as Lipset paraphrased its voluminous findings, could hardly have come as more of a surprise. He had found, as Lipset told Moynihan excitedly, that "schools make no difference; families make the difference."

Some six years later, Moynihan arrived a few minutes late for lunch with a friend at the same club, in a mood of jubilant intellectual pugnacity unusual even for him. Both the delay and the mood, he explained, resulted from a demonstration he had run into on his way across Harvard Yard from a class. Some students were handing out leaflets. It was their content which had produced Moynihan's mood of sardonic amusement. "Christopher Jencks," they said, "is a tool of reactionary American imperialist capitalism."

*Christopher Jencks* a tool of capitalism? In the dozen years since he graduated from the Harvard Graduate School of Education, where he is now an associate professor, Sandy Jencks (as he is called) had moved perceptibly from the liberal toward the radical position. While an editor of *The New Republic* he began working with the distinctly New Left Institute for Policy Studies in Washington. He got into the neighborhood community control thing, and he helped to found the Cambridge Institute, which looks for "alternative visions of the American future": decidedly one of the rising intellectual reputations on the American left. Now he has written a book, *Inequality,* in association with other researchers, working in large part from the same Coleman report data which, in Lipset's words, showed that "schools make no difference."

Pat Moynihan had started on the left, too. Trained as an orthodox social scientist, he grew up among liberals, and then discovered a most unorthodox flair for polemical prose and persuasive speech. After a political apprenticeship working for Governor Averell Harriman of New York, he took office as a liberal intellectual in good standing as an Assistant Secretary of Labor in the Kennedy administration, and stayed on for a period under Johnson.

For some years now, however, he could hardly have been called a man of the left. His intellectual voyage can be dated from the publication of his report on the Negro family in 1965. Many liberals and blacks reacted with outrage to his dour assessment of the likelihood that orthodox liberal policies could eliminate the problems of the black under-class. He was outraged in turn by what he perceived as the liberals' dishonest and anti-intellectual refusal to follow where social science led. And by the time he returned to Washington in 1969 to serve Richard Nixon as a Cabinet-rank counselor, he could no longer be called a man of the left at all. In recent years he has in fact established himself as the shrewdest strategist and most flamboyant impresario of an intellectual movement that can perhaps be called neo-conservative—though Moynihan maintains that it is radical. Whatever the label, it is almost contemptuously skeptical of the New Left and of conventional liberal shibboleths alike.

Moynihan's amusement at seeing his colleague Jencks leafleted in Harvard Yard was not due to malice or *Schadenfreude.* On the contrary, it seemed to him to confirm that the argument between him and his friends and the left was over: that he had won. "Jencks ends up," he told me, "where Richard Nixon was in 1969."

Christopher Jencks does not see it that way. In fact, it is a strange kind of argument: one in which the participants largely agree about the Coleman survey, greatly as it surprised them when they first grasped it, but disagree, sometimes vehemently, on what it implies. The fight calls into question certain propositions which, until the Coleman report, few social scientists and few liberals dreamed of doubting: principally, that one of the main causes of inequality in American life has been inequality in education; and that education could be used as a tool to reduce inequality in society. The crucial role education has been assigned in the United States is under heavy challenge. Is there now to be a retreat from the traditional faith in education as a tool of social change in America?

Since the days of Horace Mann and John Dewey—indeed since the days of Thomas Jefferson, that child of the Enlightenment—education has occupied a special place in the optimistic vision of American progressives, and of many American conservatives, for that matter. As the historian David Potter pointed out in *People of Plenty*, the American left, encouraged by the opportunities of an unexhausted continent and by the experience of economic success, has always differed sharply from the European left in that it has generally assumed that social problems could be resolved out of incremental growth: that is, that the life of the have-nots could be made tolerable without taking anything from the haves. Education has always seemed one of the most acceptable ways of using the national wealth to provide opportunity for the poor without offending the comfortable. As a tool of reform, education had the advantage that it appealed to the ideology of conservatives, to that ethic of self-improvement that stretches back down the American tradition through Horatio Alger and McGuffey's *Readers* to Benjamin Franklin himself. This was particularly true in the age of the Great Migration. The public school systems of New York and other cities with large immigrant populations really did provide a measure of equality of opportunity to the immigrant poor. By the time the New Deal coalition was formed (and educators of one sort and another were to be a significant part of that coalition), these assumptions about education were deeply rooted. And they were powerfully reinforced, and virtually certified with the authority of social science, by the Supreme Court's 1954 desegregation decision in *Brown* v. *The School Board of Topeka*. *Plessy* v. *Ferguson*, the 1896 Supreme Court decision by which statutory and customary segregation in the South were reconciled with the Thirteenth, Fourteenth, and Fifteenth Amendments, was not a school case. (As it happens, it concerned segregation on a Lake Pontchartrain ferry steamer.) But when, in the late 1930s and the 1940s, the NAACP, its lawyers, and its allies began to go to court to lay siege to segregation, they deliberately, and wisely, chose education as the field of attack. This was not accidental; they well knew that education was so firmly associated with equality in the public mind that it would be an easier point of attack than, say, public accommodations or housing. Not coincidentally, they worked their way up to the main citadel of the 1954 *Brown* decision by way of a series of law school cases: lawyers would find it hard to deny that segregation in law school was irrelevant to success in professional life.

In *Brown*, the NAACP's lawyers deployed social science evidence in support of their contention that segregated education was inherently unequal, citing especially work done by psychologists Kenneth and Mamie Clark with black children and black and white dolls. The Clarks' conclusions were that segregation inflicts psychological harm.

The historical accident of the circumstances in which school segregation came to be overthrown by the Supreme Court contributed to the currency of what turned out to be a shaky assumption. The great majority of American liberals, and this included large numbers of judges, Democratic politicians, and educators, came to suppose that there was incontrovertible evidence in the findings of social science to prove not just that segregated education was unequal but that if you wanted to achieve equality, education could do it for you. Or, to put the same point in a slightly different way, the prominence given to footnote 11 in the *Brown* judgment, which listed social science research showing that education could not be both separate and equal, had the effect of partially obscuring the real grounds for overthrowing segregation, which were constitutional, political, and moral.

Then a contemporary development put education right at the center of the political stage. President Johnson's "Great Society" was to be achieved without alienating the power structure and, above all, the Congress. Education was an important part of the Great Society strategy from the start, but as other approaches to reducing poverty and racial inequality, notably "community action," ran into political opposition, they fell apart, and so the proportional emphasis on educational programs in the Great Society scheme grew. In the end, the Johnson administration, heavily committed to reducing inequality, was almost equally committed to education as one of the principal ways to do it.

Each of the events and historical developments sketched here increased the shock effect of the Coleman report—once its conclusions were understood. A handful of social scientists had indeed hinted, before Coleman, that the effect of schools on equality of opportunity might have been exaggerated. But such work had simply made no dent in the almost universal assumption to the contrary.

James Coleman himself has confessed he does not know exactly why Congress, in section 402 of the Civil Rights Act of 1964, ordered the Commissioner of Education to conduct a survey "concerning the lack of availability of equal educational opportunities for individuals by reason of race, color, religion or national origin." The most likely reason is that Congress thought it was setting out to document the obvious in order to arm the Administration with a public relations bludgeon to overcome opposition. Certainly James Coleman took it for granted that his survey would find gross differences in the quality of the schools that black and white children went to. "The study will show," he predicted in an interview more than halfway through the job, "the difference in the quality of schools that the average Negro child and the average white child are exposed to. You know yourself that the difference is going to be striking."

He was exactly wrong. Coleman was staggered—in the word of one of his associates—to find the *lack* of difference. When the results were in, from about 600,000 children and 60,000 teachers in roughly 4,000 schools, when they had been collected and collated and computed, and sifted with regression analysis and all the other refinements of statistical science, they were astonishing. A writer in *Science* called them "a spear pointed at the heart of the cherished American belief that equality of educational opportunity will increase the equality of educational achievement."

What did the figures say? Christopher Jencks later picked out four major points:

(1) Most black and white Americans attended different schools.

(2) Despite popular impressions to the contrary, the physical facilities, the formal curricula, and most of the measurable characteristics of teachers in black and white schools were quite similar.

(3) Despite popular impressions to the contrary, measured differences in schools' physical facilities, formal curricula, and teacher characteristics had very little effect on either black or white students' performance on standardized tests.

(4) The one school characteristic that showed a consistent relationship to test performance was the one characteristic to which poor black children were denied access: classmates from affluent homes.

Here is how James Coleman himself summed up the 737 pages of his report (not to mention the additional 548 pages of statistical explanation):

> Children were tested at the beginning of grades 1, 3, 6, 9 and 12. Achievement of the average American Indian, Mexican American, Puerto Rican, and Negro (in this descending order)[1] was much lower than the average white or Oriental American, at all grade levels . . . the differences are large to begin with, and they are even larger at higher grades. Two points, then, are clear: (1) these minority children have a serious educational deficiency at the start of school, which is obviously not a result of school, and (2) they have an even more serious deficiency at the end of school, which is obviously in part a result of school.

Coleman added that the survey showed that most of the variation in student achievement lay within the same school, and very little of it was between schools. Family background—whatever that might mean—must, he concluded, account for far more of the variation in achievement than differences between schools. Moreover, such differences as *could* be attributed to the schools seemed to result more from the social environment (Jencks's "affluent classmates," and also teachers) than from the quality of the school itself.

This was the most crucial point. For if quality were measured, as it had tended to be measured by administrators and educational reformers alike,

---

[1] Coleman oversimplified his own report slightly on this point: in the first grade blacks did better than Puerto Ricans, while in the 12th grade Mexican Americans did better than American Indians.

in material terms, then the quality of the school, on Coleman's data, counted for virtually nothing.

When other things were equal, the report said, factors such as the amount of money spent per pupil, or the number of books in the library, or physical facilities such as gymnasiums or cafeterias or laboratories, or even differences in the curriculum, seemed to make no appreciable difference to the children's level of achievement. Nothing could have more flatly contradicted the assumptions on which the administration in Washington, and urban school boards across the country, were pouring money into compensatory education programs.

As we shall see, the report exploded with immense force underground, sending seismic shocks through the academic and bureaucratic worlds of education. But on the surface the shock was not at first apparent. There were two main reasons for this. The first was that the report was, after all, long, tough, dry, and technical. It had been written in five months to comply with a congressional deadline, and it therefore made no attempt to point a moral or adorn a tale: it was essentially a mass of data. All of these characteristics militated against its being reported in detail by, for example, the Associated Press, the source from which most American newspapers get most of their out-of-town news.

The Office of Education, which realized all too clearly how explosive the report was, didn't exactly trumpet the news to the world. The report was released, by a hallowed bureaucratic stratagem, on the eve of July 4, 1966. Few reporters care to spend that holiday gutting 737 pages of regression analysis and standard deviations. And to head off those few who might have been tempted to make the effort if they guessed that there was a good story at the end of it, the Office of Education put out a summary report that can only be described as misleading. "Nationally," it said, to take one example. "Negroes have fewer of some of the facilities that seem most related to academic achievement." That was true. But it was not the significant truth.

The point was that the gap was far smaller than anyone expected it to be. To take one of the summary report's own examples, it was true that Negro children had "less access" to chemistry labs than whites. But the difference was that only 94 percent of them, as compared with 98 percent of whites, went to schools with chemistry labs. That was hardly the kind of difference that could explain any large part of the gap between white and black achievements in school, let alone that larger gap, lurking in the back of every educational policy maker's mind, between the average status and income of blacks and whites in life after they leave school.

A few attempts were made to discredit the survey. But the Coleman findings were in greater danger of being ignored than of being controverted, when, at the beginning of the academic year in the fall of 1966, Pat Moynihan began to apply his talents to make sure that the report should not be ignored. He and Professor Thomas Pettigrew of the Harvard School of Education organized a Seminar on the Equality of Educational Opportunity Report (SEEOR). The seminar met every week at the Harvard Faculty Club, and by the end more than 80 people had taken part.

Moynihan had taken the precaution of getting a grant for expenses from the Carnegie Corporation, some of which was laid out on refreshments stronger than coffee or cookies. "It was quite something, that seminar," says Jencks, reminiscing. "Pat always had the very best booze and the best cigars." But if Moynihan is a connoisseur of the good things in life, he also knows how to generate intellectual excitement, or to spot where it is welling up.

"When I was at the School of Education ten years ago," Jencks says, "almost nobody who was literate was interested in education. The educational sociologists and psychologists, the educational economists, they were all pretty near the bottom of the heap. Suddenly that's changed."

"That seminar taught me something about Harvard," Moynihan says. "People here are not interested in a problem when they think it's solved. There are no reputations to be made there. But when something which people think was locked up opens up, suddenly they all want to get involved." People started coming up to Moynihan in Harvard Yard and asking if they could take part—statisticians, economists, pediatricians, Professor Abram Chayes from the Law School (and the Kennedy State Department). Education had become fashionable. Jason Epstein of Random House and Charles E. Silberman from *Fortune* magazine started coming up from New York.

Harvard had seen nothing quite like it since the arms control seminars of the late 1950s, at which the future strategic policies of the Kennedy administration were forged and the nucleus of the elite that was to operate them in government was brought together. In the intervening decade, domestic social questions had reasserted their urgency. Education had emerged as the field where all the agonizing problems of race, poverty, and the cities seemed to intersect.

If schools, as Seymour Martin Lipset paraphrased Coleman, "make no difference," what could explain the inequalities of achievement in school and afterward? One school of thought was ready and waiting in the wings with an answer. In the winter of 1969, the following words appeared in an article in the *Harvard Educational Review:*

> There is an increasing realization among students of the psychology of the disadvantaged that the discrepancy in their average performance cannot be completely or directly attributed to discrimination or inequalities in education. It seems not unreasonable, in view of the fact that intelligence variation has a large genetic component, to hypothesize that genetic factors may play a part in this picture.

The author was Professor Arthur Jensen, not a Harvard man, but an educational psychologist from Berkeley with a national reputation. He had jabbed his finger at the rawest, most sensitive spot in the entire system of liberal thinking about education and equality in America. For after more than a generation of widespread I.Q. testing, it is an experimental finding, beloved of racists and profoundly disconcerting to liberals, that while the average white I.Q. is 100, the average black I.Q. is 85. Racists have seen in this statistical finding confirmation of a theory of innate biological inferiority. Conservatives have seen in it an argument against heavy expenditures on education, and against efforts to desegregate. And liberals have retorted that the lower average performance of blacks is due either to cultural bias in the tests used or to unfavorable environmental factors that require redoubled efforts on the part of social policy makers.

Jensen marched straight into the fiercest of this cross fire. He argued two propositions in particular in his article: that research findings suggest that heredity explains more of the differences in I.Q. between individuals than does environment, and that heredity accounts for the differences between the average I.Q.s of groups as well as between those of individuals.

The article was scholarly in tone. In form it was largely a recital of research data. And it was tentative in its conclusion that perhaps more of the differential between blacks' and whites' average I.Q.s was due to heredity than to environment. That did not stop it from causing a most formidable rumpus. It became a 90 days' wonder in the press and the news magazines. It was discussed at a Cabinet meeting. And Students for a Democratic Society rampaged around the Berkeley campus chanting "Fight racism! Fire Jensen!"

Two years later, a long article in *The Atlantic* by Professor Richard Herrnstein on the history and implications of I.Q. provoked a reaction that showed that the sensitivity of the issue had by no means subsided. Herrnstein touched only gingerly on the racial issue. "Although there are scraps of evidence for a genetic component in the black-white difference," he wrote, "the overwhelming case is for believing that American blacks have been at an environmental disadvantage . . . a neutral commentator (a rarity these days) would have to say that the case is simply not settled, given our present stage of knowledge."

Neutral commentators certainly proved rare among those who wrote in to the editor. Arthur Jensen wrote to say that Herrnstein's essay was "the most accurately informative psychological article I have ever read in the popular press"; while a professor from the University of Connecticut said: "This is not new. Hitler's propagandists used the same tactics in the thirties while his metal workers put the finishing touches on the gas ovens."

If Herrnstein—understandably enough—tiptoed cautiously around the outskirts of the black-white I.Q. argument, he charged boldly enough into another part of the field. The closer society came to its ideal of unimpeded upward social mobility, the closer he predicted it would come to "meritocracy," a visionary state of society described by the British sociologist Michael Young. A new upper class composed of the descendants of the most successful competitors with the highest I.Q.s would defend its own advantage far more skillfully and successfully than did the old aristocrats. Herrnstein did not welcome this trend; he merely argued that it might be inevitable. "Our society may be sorting itself willy-nilly into inherited castes," he concluded gloomily. Or, as his Harvard colleague David K. Cohen neatly epigrammatized Herrnstein's long article in a rejoinder in *Commentary,* "His essay questioned the traditional liberal idea that stupidity results from the inheritance of poverty, contending instead that poverty results from the inheritance of stupidity."

Cohen went on to disagree with Herrnstein's prediction. "America is not a meritocracy," he wrote, "if by that we mean a society in which income, status, or power are heavily determined by I.Q. . . . Being stupid is not what is responsible for being poor in America."

But that still left the original question open.

If differences in the quality of schools, as measured by money, facilities, and curricula, don't explain inequality, because the differences between the schools attended by children of different racial groups are simply not that great in those respects, then what does? Genetic differentials in I.Q., perhaps, says Jensen. Nonsense, says a majority of the educational community; the explanation is more likely to be integration—or rather the lack of it.

"I'm a Southern liberal," says Tom Pettigrew. "There are only about thirty of us, and my wife says we all know each other." Pettigrew comes from Richmond, Virginia, but his father immigrated from Scotland, and there is something about him that strikes one as more typically Scots than Southern. He is a shy man with a passion for methodological precision: "I really believe that data can free us," he says. He also has a deceptive, because quiet, commitment to the liberal faith.

The Coleman report gave only three pages to the effects of desegregation, and Pettigrew didn't think that was enough. At Jim Coleman's explicit insistence, the data bank of the survey was to be made generally available for the cost of the computer tapes. Pettigrew persuaded the Civil Rights Commission to take advantage of this and to reanalyze the data to see what light it cast on the effects of desegregation. David Cohen and Pettigrew were the main authors of the resulting survey, which came out in 1967 as *Racial Isolation in the Public Schools* and gave the impression that the Coleman data supported desegregation. This was true up to a point. Coleman had concluded that desegregation did have an effect. But his report also showed that social class had a greater effect. Pettigrew is not much troubled by this, because of the close connection between race and social class in America. "Two-thirds of the whites are middle-class," he says, "and two-thirds of the blacks are working-class."

Pettigrew also draws a sharp distinction between desegregation and integration. By integration he means an atmosphere of genuine acceptance and friendly respect across racial lines, and he believes that mere desegregation won't help blacks to do better in school until this kind of atmosphere is achieved. He is impressed by the work of Professor Irwin Katz, who has found that black children do best in truly integrated situations, moderately well in all-black situations, and worst of all in "interracial situations characterized by stress and threat."

Pettigrew believes, in other words, that integration, as opposed to mere desegregation, will be needed to bring black children's achievement up to equality with whites'. And he argues that no one can say that integration hasn't worked, for the simple reason that it hasn't been tried.

"The U.S. is going through a period of self-flagellation," he said to me. "I dispute the argument that Moynihan is forever putting out. He says liberalism was tried and didn't work." This, as we shall see, misstates Moynihan's views. The difficulty is partly semantic. Moynihan believes that past policies, which can be called "liberal," have "worked" in the sense that they have produced a surprising degree of equality in terms of all the resources that go into schools, without, however, achieving equality of outcome. "I say liberalism hasn't been tried," Pettigrew goes on. "Racial integration has yet to be tried in this country." Desegregation proceeded so slowly, Pettigrew says, that the courts "got mad and started ruling for busing in 1969 and 1970." Until desegregation is achieved, he argues, we won't know whether integration works.

The Civil Rights Commission's report on racial isolation did recommend that the federal government set a national standard that no black children should go to a school that was more than 50 percent black. In practical terms, that meant busing. And, in fact, Pettigrew argues that some busing will be needed to achieve desegregation—and thus to produce the physical circumstances in which integration as he understands it can take place. He has been actively involved as a witness in several desegregation suits in which he has advocated busing.

It is, therefore, as Pettigrew himself wryly remarks, an irony that he should have suggested to one of his junior colleagues at the Harvard School of Education that he do a study on busing. The colleague's name was David Armor, and Pettigrew's idea was that it would be interesting to take a look at Project Metco, a scheme for busing children out of Roxbury, the main Boston ghetto, into nearby white suburban schools.

That was in 1969. Three years later, a paper by David Armor called "The Evidence on Busing" was published in *The Public Interest*. Armor said he had concentrated on the question of whether "induced integration"—that is, busing—"enhances black achievement, self-esteem, race relations, and opportunities for higher education." In a word, Armor maintained that it did not.

The article used data not only from Project Metco but from reports of four other Northern programs for induced integration: in White Plains, New York; Ann Arbor, Michigan; Riverside, California; and New Haven and Hartford, Connecticut. And on the basis of this data,[2] Armor maintained that "the available evidence . . . indicates that busing is *not* an effective policy instrument for raising the achievement of blacks or for increasing interracial harmony."

"None of the studies," said Armor, "were able to demonstrate conclusively that integration has had an effect on academic achievement as measured by standardized tests." Aspirations, indeed, were high among the black children in Project Metco. But they might be too high, in view of the fact that, while 80 percent of them started college, half of them dropped out. As for race relations, Armor found the bused students not only more militant but actually more hostile to integration than the study's "control group," which was not bused. Militancy, as measured, for example, by sympathy with the Black Panthers, seemed to be particularly rife among those children who had high aspirations (such as going to college) but were getting C grades or below in competitive suburban high schools.

But Armor did not limit himself to reporting the results of his own Metco study and the other four studies. His article was a sweeping, slashing attack on the whole tradition of liberal social science. He described what he called the "integration policy model," based on social science research going back to the time of John Dollard and Gunnar Myrdal. Though the "real goals of social science and public policy are not in opposition," Armor said, he claimed that almost all of the "'major premises of the integration policy model are not supported by the data"—by which he meant the studies he quoted.

It was a frontal assault on the liberal tradition in the social sciences for a generation: on "forty years of studies," as one of his opponents put it. At one point Armor came close to accusing his opponents of deliberate dishonesty: "There is the danger that important research may be stopped when the desired results are not forthcoming. The current controversy over the busing of schoolchildren affords a prime example."

It was not likely that such an attack would go unanswered, and, in fact, the response was both swift and severe. Pettigrew and three colleagues fired back a critique which called Armor's article "a distorted and incomplete review." To back up their charge, they argued that the studies Armor had cited as "*the* evidence on busing" were highly selective. Armor had

---

[2] Armor mentioned three other studies: one from Berkeley, California, one from Evanston, Illinois, and one from Rochester, New York.

not discussed seven other studies which they said met his own methodological criteria—from New York, Buffalo, Rochester, Newark, Philadelphia, Sacramento, and North Carolina—surveys that had reported positive achievement results for bused blacks. The integrationists also found what they claimed were disastrous weaknesses in Armor's own Metco study. For one thing, they said, he compared the bused children with a control group that included children who were also attending desegregated schools, though not under Project Metco. "Incredible as it sounds," Pettigrew and his colleagues commented, "Dr. Armor compared children who were bused to desegregated schools with other children many of whom were also bused to desegregated schools. Not surprisingly he found few differences between them."

"We respect Dr. Armor's right to publish his views against mandatory busing," they said. "But we challenge his claim that those views are based on scientific evidence." (Armor is replying to the critique in *The Public Interest*, the journal that published his paper.)

If the tone of the public controversy sounds rough, it was positively courtly compared to the atmosphere inside William James Hall, the new Harvard high-rise where Pettigrew and Armor had their offices, two doors apart.

Armor, too, started out on the left. He was president of the student body at Berkeley in 1959–1960, and head of SLATE, a forerunner of the radical Free Speech Movement there. He was also a protégé of Pettigrew's at Harvard, and indeed a close friend. But by the spring of 1972, Pettigrew realized that Armor had become vehemently opposed to mandatory busing.

Both men became very bitter. Armor failed to get tenure at Harvard, and has now moved to a visiting professorship at UCLA. Armor accused one of Pettigrew's assistants of breaking into his office to steal his Metco data. Pettigrew wrote to the *New York Times:* "There is no evidence beyond the allegation itself for the charge, much less any link between the paper's critics and the alleged intrusion." Armor accused Pettigrew of suppressing his paper; Pettigrew does concede that he told Armor that he had done "incomparable harm" by publishing it.

Tempers, in short, were comprehensively lost over the Armor affair. Much of the bitterness, no doubt, must be put down to personal factors. But it would be wrong to dismiss the episode as a mere squabble between professors. For it shows just how traumatically a world where consensus reigned half a dozen years ago has been affected by the pressure to abandon certain cherished premises. And the issue, after all, is the interrelationship of education, race, and equality in America, which is not exactly a recondite academic quibble.

To an unbiased eye ("a rarity these days," as Richard Herrnstein might say), Armor's paper has been rather seriously impugned. It does not follow that his central thesis is entirely discredited. Even Pettigrew was quoted, at the height of the row, as saying that "nobody is claiming that integration has been a raving success." "That's not what they were saying before," says Moynihan. And Christopher Jencks, who can hardly be accused of conservative prejudice, has summed up the evidence in the most cautious and equivocal way. Blacks, he says, might do much better in "truly integrated schools, whatever they may be." Failing that consummation, devoutly to be wished, the benefits of desegregation appear to be spotty, and busing can be expected to yield contradictory results.

Jencks's position is easily misunderstood. In an interview, he drew some distinctions for me. He reminded me that he had himself written that the Coleman report "put the weight of social science behind integration." It was not until Armor's article was published, he said, that social scientists began to argue that desegregation itself might not work. Jencks personally feels that Armor's data were shaky, and that the effect of Armor's paper came from its review of other studies—a review which, as Pettigrew pointed out, does not refer to all the available studies, Jencks himself thinks that desegregation is probably necessary, simply in order to meet the constitutional requirements of the Fourteenth Amendment, in virtually every urban school district in the country. He does, however, have personal reservations about mandatory busing, on libertarian grounds. The furthest he would go was to say, "I think that a case can be made out that busing might be a useful part of an overall strategy of desegregation." That is not to say that he has any tenderness toward segregation. On the contrary, he rejects it as absolutely as any of the "integrationists." The difference is that Jencks does not think that segregation explains nearly as much of existing inequality as the integrationists think it does.

But with Armors' paper and its reception, we are getting ahead of the story. The Coleman report came out in 1966. It was not until 1972 that two major books appeared, each an attempt to reassess the whole question of the relationship between education and equality in America in the light of the Coleman data. Each was collaborative.

The first of these two books was the Random House collection of papers arising out of the SEEOR seminar, which was published as *On Equality of Educational Opportunity,* with Frederick Mosteller (professor of mathematical statistics at Harvard) and Daniel Patrick Moynihan as co-editors. Most of the leading participants in the debate contributed chapters: Pettigrew *and* Armor, Coleman, David Cohen, and Christopher Jencks among them. The introductory essay was signed jointly by Mosteller and Moynihan. If much of the technical analysis and of the drafting were Mosteller's, the essay's style and conclusions are vintage Moynihan.

Later in the year, Christopher Jencks and seven of his colleagues (two of whom, Marshall Smith and David Cohen, had also contributed to the Mosteller-Moynihan volume) published an only slightly less massive book: *Inequality: A Reassessment of the Effect of Family and Schooling in*

*America.* This work displays considerably more intellectual cohesion than the Mosteller-Moynihan book, presumably because Jencks actually wrote his group's text himself from start to finish and according to the preface, it "embodies his prejudices and obsessions, and these are not shared by all the authors." But again, though the book draws upon data from dozens of other large- and small-scale surveys, the data from the Coleman survey are the bedrock and foundation.

The enormous body of analysis and reinterpretation in these two books represents the completion of the first stage of the reaction to Coleman. I began by quoting Professor Lipset's hasty shorthand for Coleman's central discovery "schools make no difference." Professor Pettigrew draws an important distinction. "Never once was it said that schools make no difference. The belief that Coleman hit was the belief that you could make a difference with money." (He added: "Americans are crazy in the head about money: they think you can do everything with money.") However that may be, the nub of the discovery that has set off the whole prolonged, disturbing, confusing, sometimes bitter debate can be expressed as a simple syllogism:

(1) The "quality" of the schools attended by black and white children in America was more nearly equal than anyone supposed. (2) The gap between the achievement of black and white children got wider, not narrower, over twelve years at school. (3) Therefore there was no reason to suppose that increasing the flow of resources into the schools would affect the outcome in terms of achievement, let alone eliminate inequality.

Among the social scientists, the central ground of debate about the meaning of those findings now lies between Jencks and Moynihan. It is a strange debate, for the two protagonists have much in common, even if one does have New Left loyalties, and the other served in Nixon's White House and at one time as Nixon's Ambassador to India. Both use the same data. Indeed, the spectacle of social scientists reaching into the same data bank for ammunition to fire at each other is sometimes reminiscent of war between two legs of the same octopus. Both agree on many of the implications of the data, and on many of the conclusions to be drawn from them. Yet those who lump the two professors together, as many practical educators and civil rights lawyers do, as "Moynihan and Jencks and those people up at Harvard," could hardly be more wrong. The two men are divided by temperament and ideology in the preconceptions they bring to the data, and ultimately in the policy prescriptions they draw from that data.

Perhaps the very heart of their disagreement, after all, comes down to a matter of temperament. Is a glass half empty, or is it half full? A pessimist will say it is half empty when an optimist says it is half full. Pat Moynihan (and his co-author Mosteller—but I should be surprised if these particular thoughts were not Moynihan's contribution, since they coincide with so much that he has said and written elsewhere) looked at the Coleman data and made the very reasonable inference that if the differences in quality between the schools attended by different groups of children in the United States were so much smaller than everyone had expected to find them, then the United States had come much closer to realizing the goal of equality of educational opportunity than most people realized. He then chose to relate this to the general question of social optimism versus social pessimism. At the time of the Coleman report's publication, "a certain atmosphere of 'cultural despair' was gathering in the nation," they wrote, "and has since been more in evidence. Some would say more in order. We simply disagree with such despair."

One of the specific recommendations of the Mosteller-Moynihan essay is optimism. The electorate should maintain the pressure on government and school boards, the essay urges, "with an attitude that optimistically expects gains, but, knowing their rarity, appreciates them when they occur." Yet on examination this is a strange use of the word optimism. For optimism normally connotes an attitude toward the future. But the emotion that is being evoked here has more to do with the past: it is not optimism so much as pride. "The nation entered the middle third of the 20th century bound to the mores of caste and class. The white race was dominant. . . . Education beyond a fairly rudimentary point was largely determined by social status. In a bare third of a century these circumstances have been extensively changed. *Changed!* Not merely a sequence of events drifting in one direction or another. To the contrary, events have been bent to the national will." True, the essay concedes, the period ended with racial tensions higher than ever before, and with dissatisfaction with the educational system approaching crisis. Nevertheless, say Moynihan and Mosteller, we should accentuate the positive. "It is simply extraordinary that so much has been done. . . . No small achievement! In truth, a splendid one. . . . It truly is not sinful to take modest satisfaction in our progress."

Swept along by the dithyrambic rhythm of these tributes to past policies, it would be easy to conclude that Moynihan thinks they should be pressed to the utmost. But he does not. When I asked him why not, he replied promptly, if cryptically: "Production functions." In an article in the fall 1972 issue of *The Public Interest*, he spells out what he means. The argument is characteristically simple, forceful, and provocative.

Proposition 1: "The most striking aspect of educational expenditure is how large it has become." It has now reached $1,000 per pupil per annum, and it has been rising at 9.7 percent annually for the last ten years, while the GNP has risen 6.8 percent.

Proposition 2 (the Coleman point): Maybe not much learning takes place in a school without teachers or a roof. But "after a point school expenditure does not seem to have any notable influence on school achievement."

There are, Moynihan concedes, considerable regional, class, racial, and ethnic variations in achievement, and he would like to see them disappear. "But it is simply not clear that school expenditure is the heart of the matter."

This is where the production function, or what is more familiar to laymen as the law of diminishing returns, comes in, according to Moynihan. The liberal faith held that expenditure of resources on education would produce not merely a greater equality in scholastic achievement, but greater equality in society. On the contrary, says Moynihan, additional expenditure on education (and indeed on certain other social policies) is likely to produce greater *inequality*, at least of income.

The day the students leafleted Christopher Jencks in Harvard Yard, Moynihan said to me: "They're defending a class interest." What he meant was that as future teachers, or social workers, or administrators of education or social policies, left-wing students had a vested economic interest in the high-investment "liberal" policies they defended.

"Any increase in school expenditure," Moynihan wrote in *The Public Interest*, "will in the first instance accrue to teachers, who receive about 68% of the operating expenditure of elementary and secondary schools. That these are estimable and deserving persons none should doubt"— Brutus is an honorable man—"but neither should there be any illusion that they are deprived." With teachers earning some $10,000 a year on the average, he argues, and with many of them married women with well-paid husbands, "increasing educational expenditures will have the short-run effect of income inequality."

As a matter of statistical fact, that may be literally true. But it is a peculiar argument nonetheless, for several reasons. For, leaving aside the matter of their spouses' incomes, teachers are not, relatively, a highly paid group. Marginal increases in their salaries have an imperceptible effect on inequality in the national income distribution.

Whatever its merits, however, Moynihan's position is plain. But it is worth noting that this position fits oddly with an exhortation to optimism. There is indeed nothing sinful about taking satisfaction in past progress; but when this attitude is combined with skepticism about the benefits to be expected from future public expenditure, it is usually called not optimistic but conservative.

Like Moynihan, Christopher Jencks is concerned with equality, not only in the schools but also in the world after school. The essence, and the originality, of his thinking lie in the use he makes of two crucial, though in themselves unoriginal, distinctions.

The first distinction is between equality of opportunity and equality of condition. Most Americans say they are in favor of equality. But what most of them mean by this is equality of opportunity. What we have learned from the Coleman report, says Jencks, and from the fate of the reforms of the 1960s, is that contrary to the conventional wisdom, you cannot have equality of opportunity without a good deal of equality of condition—now and not in the hereafter.

This is where the second of Jencks's distinctions comes in. Where the Coleman survey, and most of the work published in the Mosteller-Moynihan volume, looked at the degree of equality between *groups*, Jencks is more interested in inequality between individuals. Coleman's conception of equality looked at the distribution of opportunity between two groups. For Coleman, as Marshall Smith puts it, if you laid the distribution curve of one group over the distribution curve of the other, and they coincided exactly, then you could say that the two groups were equal. And Coleman found that between white and black Americans, this was closer to being true than most people had suspected. "Sandy Jencks is saying that though this may apply as between groups, this approximate equality disappears when you look at individuals."

It is cause for shock, he says in the preface to his book, "that white workers earn 50 percent more than black workers." But it is a good deal more shocking "that the best-paid fifth of all white workers earns 600 percent more than the worst-paid fifth. From this point of view, racial inequality looks almost insignificant"—by comparison with economic inequality.

Is the glass half empty, or half full? If Moynihan's instinct is to emphasize the real progress that has been made toward reducing inequality in America, Jencks stresses how much inequality remains, not only in educational opportunity, in learning skills, and in educational credentials but also in job status, in job satisfaction, and in income.

The trouble is, he points out—and here I am summarizing an argument which is based, step by step, on mountains of statistical data—that whatever measure you take—income, socioeconomic status, or education—there is plenty of inequality among Americans. But the same people by no means always come out at the same point on each measure. In the social scientists' terms, these different kinds of inequality don't "correlate" very closely. It follows that school reform is not likely to effect much greater equality outside the school. The "factory model," which assumes that the school's outcome is the direct product of its inputs, must be abandoned, says Jencks. For him, a school is in reality more like a family than a factory.

This idea underlies a surprising strand in Jencks's thought. If there is no direct correlation between expenditure on schools and effects on society—for example, in producing greater equality between racial groups—some would draw the lesson that it is not worth spending more than a (possibly quite high) minimum on schools. (That is something like Moynihan's theoretical position, as we have seen.) No, says Jencks, spend more money; not because of the benefits it will bring in some sociological hereafter but simply because people spend something close to a fifth of their life in school, and it is better that they spend that time in a pleasant and comfortable environment.

"There is no evidence," Jencks writes, "that building a school playground will affect the students' chances of learning to read, getting into college, or earning $50,000 a year when they are 50. Building a playground may, however, have a considerable effect on the students' chances of having a good time during recess when they are eight." And in a recent statement protesting the use of the conclusions which *Inequality* reaches "to justify limiting educational expenditures and abandoning efforts at desegregation," Jencks writes that "educators will have to keep struggling," and that "they need more help than they are currently getting." But he concludes that the egalitarian trend in American education over the last 30 years has not made the distribution of either income or status outside the schools much more equal. He writes: "As long as egalitarians assume that public policy cannot contribute to economic equality directly, but must proceed by ingenious manipulation of marginal institutions like the schools, progress will remain glacial."

"Marginal institutions like the schools"! The phrase sets Jencks every bit as far outside the old liberal orthodoxy as Moynihan's suggestion that spending money on schools may actually increase inequality. Fourteen words from the end of his book Jencks unfurls a word which startles many of his readers. "If we want to move beyond this tradition, we will have to establish political control over the economic institutions that shape our society. That is what other countries usually call socialism. Anything less will end in the same disappointment as the reforms of the 1960s."[3]

Norman Drachler was superintendent of the huge, tormented Detroit public school system from 1966 to 1971. When I talked to him recently, he was going through the anguish of liberal educators who had the intellectual honesty to try to reconcile the new teachings of the social scientists with the working assumptions of a lifetime of effort.

He showed me a headline from the *New York Times* of December 4, 1966, which perfectly summed up the pre-Coleman orthodoxy. WHEN

---

[3] In one sense, Moynihan is closer to Jencks than is generally supposed. When he went to work for President Nixon, both he and the President were fully aware of the Coleman conclusions. At that point, in February 1969, two documents arrived on Moynihan's desk within 72 hours. The first was Arthur Jensen's article, which started from the proposition that compensatory education wasn't working. The second document, the Ohio Westinghouse report, was a gloomy appraisal of one major experiment with compensatory education, Project Headstart. Moynihan says that the conception of his Family Assistance Plan was directly influenced by the social science findings about education and equality. "The argument was put to the President," he says, "that enormous expectations had built up that you could achieve racial equality through compensatory education, and it was not working. Point two: a proposition had been put forward by Dr. Jensen which the democracy could not live with. Therefore, point three: you had to move directly to income redistribution." There is an ironic parallel here—if a distant one—to the way in which Christopher Jencks concludes his book *Inequality*.

SPENDING FOR EDUCATION IS LOW, it said, ARMY INTELLIGENCE TEST FAILURES ARE HIGH. And he showed me figures to prove that when federal money under Title I of the Elementary and Secondary Education Act of 1965 was concentrated on the schools with the greatest need in Detroit, reading scores improved by two months from 1965 to 1971, while the city-wide average declined by two months. "In the worst schools, Title I helped to arrest a disastrous fall," says Drachler. "Where we spent more money, we did do better."

How did he square this with the Coleman report?

"I think Coleman is basically correct. With better schools we can only make a small difference. But it is worth that investment."

The post-Coleman challenge to the case for spending money on education is beginning to echo through the halls of Congress, ominously for the supporters of federal aid to education, who include both Representative John Brademas, Democrat of Indiana, the chairman of the House Select Subcommittee on Education, and one of his Republican colleagues, Representative Albert Quie of Minnesota. In a recent speech Quie has made it plain that he remains to be convinced that compensatory education makes no difference. John Brademas is afraid that the social science findings, misunderstood or deliberately misrepresented, will be used to justify savage cuts in federal aid to elementary and secondary education and to make opposition to such programs respectable. He is deeply skeptical of the case against the efficacy of educational spending, pointing out not only that federal aid still amounts to only seven percent of the cost of elementary and secondary schooling but also that in many cases funds intended under Title I for compensatory education for underprivileged children have been indiscriminately spent for political reasons on middle-class children, so that few valid conclusions can be drawn from the experience of Title I. He feels adrift without adequate information, while the opponents of educational spending are able to use the social scientists' evidence, often disingenuously. In his own reelection campaign in Indiana last fall he was amused, but not happy, to find his Republican opponent quoting what he called the "Colombo report" (meaning the Coleman report) at him.

Education lobbyists claim that the "Jencks report" was freely cited by the Nixon Administration's Office of Management and Budget on Capitol Hill in justification of the cuts in the fiscal 1974 budget. And even in some of the more conservative governors' offices, one lobbyist for elementary and secondary education told me there is a widespread feeling that "Coleman and Jencks" have the effect of giving education a low priority.

Money is one issue; integration is another. Although, as Christopher Jencks put it to me, "the impact both of Coleman and of the Moynihan-Mosteller book is to put the support of social science behind integration," and even though a majority of the social scientists who have spoken up remains integrationist, there is no mistaking the chill the Armor paper, supported as it has been to some extent by various influential figures in the intellectual community, has sent down the spines of the integrationists. Last November, for example, Harold Howe, U.S. Commissioner for Education in the Johnson Administration (he is now with the Ford Foundation), conceded that "the lively researches of statistically oriented social scientists have cast some shadows on conventional assumptions about the benefits of integration, particularly in the schools."

The first place where those shadows would fall is in the courts, which are now jammed with cases arising from the tough desegregation orders made by federal judges in all parts of the country since 1969. Integrationists insist that the law requires school desegregation under the Fourteenth Amendment, wholly independent of social science data regarding its effect. As former Chief Justice Earl Warren put it in a recent interview with Dr. Abram Sachar of Brandeis, *Brown* was a race case, not an education case. And so far the judges have upheld the principle that the requirement of desegregation in the law is independent of evidence about its effect.

But already the courts have begun to hear social science evidence about the equality of achievement in schools. In *Keyes* (the Denver school desegregation case which the Supreme Court has already heard, but on which it has not yet handed down its opinion), Judge William Doyle, in the district court, asked for evidence about the achievement of 17 schools which he found to be segregated, though not as a result of public policy. James Coleman himself was one of the witnesses, and he testified that while compensatory education had proved disappointing, desegregation might be helpful.

David Armor was a witness on the other side in one of the Detroit desegregation hearings. But in the Memphis case, where his paper was produced in evidence, the court of appeals gave it short shrift. Judge Anthony Celebrezze (a former Democratic Secretary of HEW) dismissed it as "a single piece of much criticized sociological research," and said "it would be presumptuous in the extreme for us to refuse to follow a Supreme Court decision on the basis of such meager evidence."

Judicial reaction generally, says Louis Lucas, a Memphis lawyer who appeared for plaintiffs in both the Detroit and Memphis cases, "has been to say 'a plague on both your houses' to the social scientists. They have noticed how much criticism of the new findings there has been, and they say in effect, 'We are not going to re-try *Brown*.'"

But that is exactly what less sanguine integrationists are afraid the Supreme Court will do, with respect to the most difficult Northern desegregation cases: not frontally, but by erosion. Norman Drachler, for example, told me he thought it very probable that the Burger Court would find some way to re-try *Brown* without seeming to do so. Nick Flannery, of the Harvard Center for Law and Education, told me that "the Burger Court will almost certainly be looking for distinctions to draw that will narrow the scope of *Brown*."

Flannery suggested some possibilities. The Court could adopt Judge Doyle's argument (in the Denver case) that not all segregation results from public policy. Or it could adopt the Justice Department's contention that the wrong to be remedied is not segregation itself, but discrimination, so that the plaintiff can get relief only when he can show not merely generalized segregation but particular instances of discrimination. In the *Swann* case, in 1971, having to do with Charlotte, North Carolina, Chief Justice Warren Burger laid down the principle that the scope of the remedy need not exceed the scope of the violation. That might seem to lay the groundwork for limiting *Brown* in this way. Alternatively, the Court might reverse the integrationist doctrine that has been developing in the lower courts, by imposing burdens of proof on the plaintiffs which would make the process of bringing a school desegregation case even lengthier and more expensive than it is already.

Some years ago, the great historian of the South, C. Vann Woodward of Yale, compared the civil rights movement of the 1960s to the Reconstruction period after the Civil War and said that he thought this second Reconstruction was ending. There is a parallel in the intellectual world that Woodward did not draw. The 1870s—the years of "reunion and reaction," when the nation wearied of the political impasse created by white resistance to the Radicals' drive for Negro equality—were also the years when American intellectual life was swept by the ideas of Herbert Spencer and his followers, the Social Darwinists. Their enthusiasm for ruthless competition that would drive the weakest to the wall, for "anarchy with a policeman" as the type of society most likely to produce the highest evolution of man, did much to rationalize and to justify public indifference as white supremacy reasserted itself after Reconstruction. The skepticism about the efficacy of social reform which seems to be emerging from the social science of the Nixon era in itself, of course, bears no resemblance to the harsh Social Darwinism of the age of the Robber Barons. The only parallel would lie in the danger that this new skepticism that is eroding the confident liberal assumptions could be distorted and used to rationalize a second period of indifference in a nation once again weary of the stress of reform.

What can be said, at the end of the first stage of the reception of the Coleman doctrine, is that—whether you believe with Daniel Patrick Moynihan that liberal education policies of the last few generations have succeeded so well that they have run into diminishing returns, or with Christopher Jencks that they have proved disappointing—those policies, and the intellectual assumptions on which they were built, are in bad trouble. They have lost support in the ranks of the social scientists who provided America, from Roosevelt to Johnson, with a major part of its operating ideology.

# 3

# Value Orientations of High School Students*

## LEO C. RIGSBY and EDWARD L. McDILL

This paper will examine some of the literature on adolescence in an effort to clarify some issues relating to the phrase "adolescent subculture" and more generally to the value orientations of adolescents. First we will briefly review several themes from the literature on the sociology of adolescence. The first theme, and one on which there is consensus, is that adolescents share some values, norms, experiences, and world views that set them off from other stage-of-life groups. A second theme is that the dominant shared concerns of adolescents subvert the formal goals of school and are, on the whole, counterproductive to the educational and occupational preparation of young people. The third theme, one on which there is less consensus, is that the above two generalizations characterize most adolescents—that it is meaningful to speak of *an* adolescent society. Further, some treatments of the theme seem to suggest that to the extent that subcultural variation exists among adolescents, it can be summarized in a single dimension (Coleman, 1961). One pole of this dimension is seen as being "school oriented" (or "responsible" or "adult oriented") and the other pole is "peer oriented" (or "hedonistic" or "social life and activity oriented"). A major purpose of this paper is to call into question whether

* An earlier version of this paper was presented at the Annual Meetings of the Southern Sociological Society, April 1970. McDill's contributions to this paper were supported in part by a Ford Foundation Fellowship which is gratefully acknowledged. We wish to thank John Boston, Robert A. Gordon, and John D. McCarthy for helpful comments on an earlier version of this paper. Responsibility for the interpretations and analysis remain solely ours, of course. Finally, we wish to thank the Center for the Study of Social Organization of Schools at Johns Hopkins University for technical, intellectual, and financial support.

the value and behavioral commitments of adolescents are adequately summarized by this dimension. Further, we will suggest some special considerations of these themes as they relate to important sex role socialization. We will discuss each of these themes briefly and propose a modification of the third theme.

Regarding the first theme, theory and evidence are plentiful. General assessments of the separation of youth from their parents and other adults have been made by Davis (1940), Eisenstadt (1962), and Matza (1964), among others. Coleman's *The Adolescent Society* (1961) typifies recent empirical studies which have codified the peculiar concerns of adolescents. He paints a picture of the "subculture" of the typical high school as being a peer-oriented society whose main concerns are athletics, clothes, cars, popular music, dates, and extracurricular activities. His data reveal that popularity was bestowed on members of the leading crowd and leaders of activities in each school more often than on those who devoted their time to school work. That is, peer status rewards went to those who ostensibly devoted themselves to nonintellectual rather than scholastic endeavors.

While the whole of Coleman's argument may be something of an overstatement, other research supports the basic contention that ". . . American high-school students throughout much of the twentieth century have been strongly influenced if not dominated by values and practices that range from nonintellectual to anti-intellectual and subvert the formal purposes of the school" (Clark, 1962:246). The work of Turner (1964) and of Gordon (1957) give additional supporting evidence.

Regarding the second theme, it seems intuitive that effort spent on nonscholastic activities would by necessity restrict effort spent on scholastic activities. This is at least an implicit assumption of most criticisms of what is seen as the overdevelopment of extracurricular activities in the modern high school. Without elaborating at this point, we would raise the question of whether the situation is necessarily zero-sum—that is, whether effort spent on extracurricular matters is necessarily counterproductive to scholastic enterprise. It would seem that school officials, who support many of these activities with released time, facilities, and adult sponsorship, do not view them as completely unsupportive of scholastic concerns.

On the other hand, one must differentiate between nonintellectual interests that are centered in the school and may promote commitment to the (broadly defined) school community and those that do, in fact, pull students' attention away from the school community. Interests of the former kind—athletics, school clubs, pageants, dances, and so forth—may and seemingly do, in some cases, promote identification with and commitment to the school. Waller (1932) initially recognized the integrative functions (both for students and the larger community) of nonintellectual school activities. Further, Gordon (1957) pointed out that some activities in high schools that are nonintellectual in focus have minimum grade requirements as a criterion of participation. Coleman's (1961:82) data reveal that the average grades of male and female "leading crowd" members in each school he studied are from slightly to substantially higher than the same sex average grades in that school (with one exception out of 17 comparisons). Other studies have shown that participation in high school athletics or service organizations or both is positively related to educational aspirations (Rehberg and Schafer, 1968; Spady, 1970) even with "relevant personal attributes" controlled.

One would suppose that activities such as movie going, drag racing, dating, and so forth would have no positive consequences whatever for the school, since they fail even to contribute to the development of school or community identification.

Finally, regarding the third theme mentioned above, the notion of an adolescent subculture has widespread, if not unanimous, acceptance. Clark (1962) suggested that the visibility and clamor of a national adolescent culture centered around pop music, styles of dress, and pop culture, and a supporting mass media gives credence to the notion of an adolescent subculture. That the image of this national "culture" as reflected in the mass media is somewhat alien to most adults reinforces the popular impressions regarding the irresponsibility and hedonistic nature of adolescents in general.

Some controversy, however, has been generated over the question of whether the values, norms, and experiences of adolescents are sufficiently autonomous and differentiated from those of their parents to justify the use of the term "subculture." Berger (1963) argued, in a review of Coleman's book, that adolescents share a majority of their values with their parents. His point is that most adult Americans are not terribly intellectual either. He argued, as others have, that much of adults' involvement in the schooling of their children is predicated on nonintellectual or antiintellectual interests similar to those which motivate the children themselves. Epperson (1964) questioned Coleman's conclusion regarding the degree of estrangement of adolescents from their parents. Even granting some divergence of values and interests (in both the political and social senses) between adolescents and their parents, it is important to be cognizant of Katz's (1964:424) caveat that ". . . the 'adolescent subculture' theme may exaggerate the existence of conflict between youths and adults by assuming that divergence necessarily implies conflict." Turner (1964) suggested that the influence of the peer group is segmental; that is, youth culture influences only selected aspects of the lives of adolescents. He further holds that participation in youth subculture often is characterized by ritualistic adherence rather than deep, inner conviction (see Turner, 1964:138–147).[1]

---

[1] In an article that appeared well before most of the literature being discussed here, Elkins and Westley (1955) were led to reject the popular notion of an "adolescent

Jahoda and Warren (1965) suggested that the controversy over whether there is *an* adolescent subculture results from a definitional problem.[2] They argue that the fact that youth is assigned a special status in society is not sufficient reason to conclude that there is a separate youth culture. Contending that the major part of the culture of young people is shared with adults, they suggest that youth can as well be studied from the point of view of the culture they have in common with adults as from the point of view of the culture that is uniquely theirs. We would add to this that, in addition, adolescents may fruitfully be studied from the point of view of what they hold in common (regardless of whether it is parallel with or in opposition to adults) or from the point of view of the diversity of values and behavior among themselves. Toward the end of making explicit certain aspects of this diversity we will mention briefly some of the research literature on adolescents. In order to emphasize one aspect of the diversity of adolescents' values, we will organize our comments on this literature around the levels of aggregation on which different writers have focused their attention.[3]

Coleman (1961) focused his attention primarily on differences between schools in the degree to which the student status system supported the general scholastic enterprise by giving status for scholastic performance. Since differences between schools were small, and since the students in each school were more likely to indicate a preference for "nonintellectual" than "intellectual" images, he was led to concentrate more on the communalities among adolescents than on differences among them. The thrust of Coleman's book, then, is in describing and examining the implications for school-related behavior of the adolescent subculture.

Clark (1962), in looking at the value orientations of high school students, suggested the existence of several subcultures, He described the value configuration, the originating and sustaining processes, and the im-

---

culture." See also the view presented by Lipset and Bendix (1963:227): ". . . the subculture of the school is almost everywhere defined largely in intellectual terms. High status within a school's social system is given to those who are best in their school work (although nonintellectual factors such as athletic prowess and social-class background also effect status within schools)."

[2] Berger (1963) makes a different point relative to the definitional problem. Accepting the premise that adolescents' values and interests are inimical to the formal academic aims of the schools, Berger points out that ". . . whether the anti-intellectual character of adolescent life is attributed primarily to autonomous social processes *within* the adolescent groups, or primarily to the larger culture which adolescents simply 'reflect'" is a crucial question. He adds that in the latter case, one is led to a critical examination of adult institutions, while in the former case one is led to devise strategies for redirecting adolescent energies toward scholastic pursuits.

[3] For the sake of brevity we will confine our remarks regarding literature to essentially three works we believe are fairly representative of the literature in this area. The reader who wishes to consult a wider range of literature should see in addition, Stinchcombe (1964), Turner (1964), Campbell (1969), Berger (1963), Cohen (1955), Gordon (1957), and Douvan and Adelson (1966).

plications of a "fun subculture" (drawing on Coleman's work for the description), an "academic subculture," and a "delinquent subculture." Clark suggested that in most high schools there are a number of distinguishable subcultures that have somewhat autonomous and self-sustaining life styles, values, norms, and so forth. His conceptualization explicitly posits a lower-than-school-level set of cultural systems that shapes the behavior of adolescents.

Matza (1964) described variations in adolescents' value orientations and behavior that parallel the variations discussed by Clark. However, Matza focuses on variations that are conceived at the level of individuals; that is, personality variations. He described youthful styles as being the outcomes of identity-seeking by adolescents and as being transitory in nature. The particular styles he emphasizes are "studious youth," "athletic-sports oriented youth," and "rebellious youth."

No conflict is to be implied among these three broad views of adolescent value orientations. Matza does not preclude the possibility that adolescents of similar orientation will coalesce into subcultures. Neither does Clark's formulation preclude that, in some cases, a single subculture may dominate a high school. Coleman acknowledges some value differentiation within schools, both at the subgroup and individual levels. It is conceivable that meaningful contextual variations in values and behavior can occur simultaneously at several levels of social aggregation—for example, at the immediate peer group level, at the level of grade in school, and at the level of the school.[4]

Although these authors conceptualize their ideas at different levels of abstraction, the specific variations they discuss are parallel. Thus, for example, Coleman describes schools whose value climates are "academically-oriented" (relative to other schools), Clark describes "academic subcultures" in high schools, and Matza describes a youthful style he calls "studious youth." Each of these conceptions provides useful insights and meaningful organizing principles for different research problems. We suspect that there may be more variation in the value orientations of students within schools than between schools, though this does not nullify the theoretical and empirical importance of between-school differences.

We will focus our attention in the remainder of this paper on value differences among high school students that can be characterized as being social psychological in nature. We will refer hereafter to "student styles" by which we wish to connote different patterns of values, norms, and behaviors that are embedded in loosely defined structures of interpersonal influence (i.e., that of peers, family, teachers, etc.). Our view is that different styles define alternative orientations toward school and the intellectual and social activities centered in the school. This view of style does

---

[4] A similar suggestion was made by Boocock (1966:27).

not exclude the possibility that any style is "subcultural" in the strictest sense of that term. Whether a style is subcultural presumably depends on the composition of the interpersonal influence structure and the nature and origin of the norms and values characterizing the style and is a matter for empirical determination rather than definition.

A useful way to orient further discussion of the styles is to consider whether there are common dimensions implicit in the descriptions of different constellations of adolescents' values that we reviewed above that will allow us to construct an analytic typology. We wish to avoid what we view as the distorting oversimplification brought about by the use of a single dimension such as the "school oriented" versus "peer oriented" dimension mentioned earlier. This dimension seems particularly inadequate when one considers what we regard as the high value American culture places on being "well-rounded"—being outstanding in scholastic as well as athletic and social endeavors.[5] The extensive documentation of the importance of peer group norms and peer-oriented activities makes clear that these normative influences and activities cannot be ignored. Further, the importance to some students of academic achievement and its lack of importance to other students suggests that this is another broad sphere that is centrally relevant to students' orientations toward school.

It is these considerations that lead us to suggest the importance of two dimensions of students' orientations, conceptually separating scholastic and peer orientations. These dimensions are (1) orientation toward the formal or scholastic status (reward) system of the school and (2) orientation toward and involvement in the informal status (reward) system. In dealing with these abstract dimensions we would suggest that one's orientation may vary from strong commitment to strong rejection (or alienation) on each one. A brief description of our view of the content of these status systems may help the reader to appreciate their meaning.

The formal reward system of the school dispenses grades, scholastic honors, and prestige in a sponsored status system designed to give support to the implementation of the formal educational goals of the school. To array students according to their degree of commitment to this status system is to order them, in general, by their desire to succeed in school. The dimension is defined broadly enough to encompass commitment due to intrinsic intellectual values, instrumental motivation, reaction to external (e.g., parents') pressures, and so forth.

The informal status system of the school is the guardian of the core values, the social activities, and the well-being (comfort, solidarity, collective pride, and spirit) of student life. It should be clear that we do not conceive this dimension to be an "adult authority" versus "peer orienta-

---

[5] This image is implicit in Coleman's (1961, Chapter 5, *passim*) discussion of student elites who are "athlete-scholars."

tion" construct. Our conception of it is based on the assumption that a good part of the content of even the nonscholastic sector of student life is nurtured by the school and/or derives from the values and priorities held in common between students and their parents. To array students according to their degree of commitment to and involvement in the informal status system is to order them by their visibility, fame, and likely "success" in the social life of the school and its informal group extensions.

It should be clear to the reader that we are orienting our inquiry to adolescents *in school*. Our orientation clearly omits, for the present, consideration of an important and interesting segment of young people, namely the "dropouts" of several meanings for this term—the social and intellectual dropout (hippie), those who have left school to work or seek work, and so forth. Our inability to differentiate among these young people or to clearly fit them into our typology points to the need for additional, or for some uses, different dimensions with which to characterize adolescents. Nevertheless, we feel that the dimensions we have employed here are, for many purposes, quite useful. We would argue that any study of young people that is concerned with the dominant orientations of youth would have to incorporate these or similar dimensions. Given the importance of education generally in our society, and the importance of education in structuring the day-to-day lives of most adolescents in particular, we believe these dimensions are paramount for the study of school-related behavior of adolescents. This is not to say that other dimensions would not be useful for other purposes.

## DATA AND METHOD

Rather than pursuing further these abstract dimensions of students' orientations, we will at this point introduce empirical measures of them, propose a typology of student styles based on them, and illustrate the efficacy of the typology in sorting students with respect to selected school-related attitudes and behaviors.

The data we will use in operationalizing the typology and in relating it to the attitudes and behaviors of high school students come from three schools taken for arbitrary reasons from a larger, 1964 study of 20 public high schools.[6] Two of the schools are middle-class suburban schools—one

---

[6] These schools were used rather than all the schools from the larger study because the three had been included in a second study, being directed by Drs. Denise Kandel and Gerald Lesser of Harvard University. Data they had collected on parents of the students in the three schools were exchanged for the data McDill, et al. had collected on students. The two sets of data for these three schools are the subject of extensive analysis in Rigsby (1970). In that study the typology proposed herein is treated as a dependent variable and its relations with individual ability, family background, peer group supports, and parental values and expectations are analyzed.

located in the midwest and the second in the northeast—and the other is the only school serving a small (1960 population about 26,000) southern city.[7] Questionnaires were administered to 3,588 students in these three schools, as well as to teachers and principals. Questionnaires were mailed to the parents of all students enrolled in these schools, 65 percent of which were returned. In addition, students were given a mathematics achievement test and a test of abstract reasoning ability.[8] Data for this paper come from the student questionnaires for the 2,528 cases where data were available from both student and parents.[9]

For our measure of students' commitment to the formal status system of the school we have taken a six-item summated binary scale developed by McDill, Meyers, and Rigsby (1966). The scale,[10] which they called Personal Orientation Toward Intellectualism (POTI), is composed of indicators of (1) desire to use extra time in school for studying or coursework, (2) importance placed on learning, (3) personal acceptability of the brilliant student image, (4) importance placed on getting good grades, (5) satisfaction received from working hard on studies, and (6) admiration of brightness in other students.

The measure of students' commitment to the informal status system of the school,[11] referred to hereafter as Student Involvement in the Informal Status System (SIISS), is composed of items relating to (1) the number of leading crowd choices received from other students, (2) whether the respondent placed himself in the leading crowd, (3) whether the respondent indicated he was near the center of social activities in the school, (4) the number of school activities in which the respondent was a participant, (5) the number of school leadership roles occupied by the respondent, and (6) the respondent's choice of a "social" or "activity" leader, as opposed to a "scholastic" leader, as a preferred date.

---

[7] For detailed information about the schools, see McDill, et al. (1966; 1967). The three schools from which the present data are drawn are referred to in the above references as schools 05, 14, and 17. Each is a three-year public high school with comprehensive curricula.

[8] The two tests were taken from the Project TALENT battery (see Dailey and Shaycoft, 1961). For a description of the tests and the standardization procedure used to produce the C-scale scores, see McDill, et al., 1966:III-47.

[9] See Rigsby (1970) for an exposition of the details of the sample and for evidence that the reduction in cases due to parental nonresponse does not affect the relationships reported here or any of the arguments or conclusions presented herein.

[10] Internal consistency reliability for this index (KR-20) is .52. Inter-item correlations vary from .11 to .41 (phi/phi max) and item-total correlations vary from .45 to 73. These are well within the ranges suggested by Guilford (1954:471–472). For more details regarding the scales, see Rigsby, 1970:446–470.

[11] Internal consistency reliability for this index is .63. Inter-item correlations vary from .11 to .67 and item-total correlations vary from .47 to .86.

RESULTS

To give the reader an intuitive feel for the meaning of the indexes, we will summarize some data relating them to their leading correlates. First, in Table 1 students' reports of their feelings about their over-all social and intellectual experiences in school are given by their score on the academic values index (POTI). For both boys and girls there is a fairly strong, direct relationship between POTI score and the proportion of respondents saying their time in school has been "interesting and filled with hard work" as opposed to one of the other responses (the higher the POTI score, the more likely they are to say their time in school has been "interesting and filled with hard work.") There is an inverse relationship between scores on the index and the proportion of students choosing the social life-oriented response ("filled with fun and excitement") or one of the neutral or negative responses ("fairly pleasant, somewhat dull, or unhappy"). In Table 2 students' responses to this question are given by their index score on involvement in the informal status system (SIISS). The data in Table 2 show that the higher the students' scores on SIISS, the greater the proportion whose response to the time-in-school question was "filled with fun and excitement" and the lower the proportion who gave a neutral or negative response to the question. Data from these two tables, then, give some support to the idea that those who are more strongly committed to the formal status system of the school more frequently respond to school experience in scholastic terms, while those who are more committed to the informal status system more frequently respond to school experience in "fun and excitement" terms.

As one would expect, scores on index of commitment to the formal status system (POTI) are positively correlated with measures of scholastic effort and scholastic achievement. Strength of academic values is positively associated with reporting two or more hours of studying per day, with doing "serious" reading other than that required in school, with planning to go to college, with math achievement, and with score on the ability test. (Data not shown.)

Interestingly, scores on the index of Student Involvement in the Informal Status System are likewise positively correlated with most of these indicators of scholastic effort and achievement. The single exception to this pattern is that involvement in the informal status system is uncorrelated with doing "serious" reading outside school assignments. These associations give some support to our earlier raising doubt that involvement in the informal status system is necessarily inimical to scholastic endeavor. We shall return to this issue later. Further validation of this index is made by noting that it, but not the academic values index, is strongly correlated with the number of choices students received as persons other students

## TABLE ONE
Students' Scores on the Index of Personal Orientation Toward Intellectualism (POTI) Related to Their Assessment of Their Over-all High School Experience, Separately for Boys and Girls[1]

| | Number of Cases[2] | | Percentage Saying Their Time in School Has Been | | | | | |
| | | | Filled with Fun and Excitement | | Interesting and Filled with Hard Work | | Fairly Pleasant, Somewhat Dull, Unhappy | |
| POTI Score | Boys | Girls | Boys | Girls | Boys | Girls | Boys | Girls |
|---|---|---|---|---|---|---|---|---|
| 0 | 134 | 64 | 28% | 33% | 7% | 9% | 65% | 58% |
| 1 | 260 | 219 | 26 | 42 | 23 | 21 | 51 | 38 |
| 2 | 291 | 291 | 25 | 29 | 30 | 33 | 46 | 38 |
| 3 | 261 | 267 | 22 | 24 | 36 | 45 | 42 | 31 |
| 4 | 219 | 208 | 22 | 18 | 46 | 50 | 33 | 32 |
| 5 | 116 | 114 | 10 | 16 | 64 | 56 | 26 | 28 |
| 6 | 29 | 48 | 10 | 13 | 72 | 73 | 17 | 15 |

[1] The exact question was: My time in this school has been . . . . (1) filled with fun and excitement, (2) interesting and filled with hard work, (3) fairly pleasant, (4) somewhat dull, and (5) unhappy.

[2] Respondents with "no answer" on the index or the question are excluded from the bases. Nine boys are "no answer" on the index and eight boys plus five girls are "no answer" on the question.

## TABLE TWO

Students' Scores on the Index of Student Involvement in the Informal Status System (SIISS) Related to Their Assessment of Their Over-all High School Experience, Separately for Boys and Girls[1]

| SIISS Score | Number of Cases[2] | | Percentage Saying Their Time in School Has Been | | | | | |
| | | | Filled with Fun and Excitement | | Interesting and Filled with Hard Work | | Fairly Pleasant, Somewhat Dull, Unhappy | |
| | Boys | Girls | Boys | Girls | Boys | Girls | Boys | Girls |
| --- | --- | --- | --- | --- | --- | --- | --- | --- |
| 0........ | 358 | 193 | 14% | 18% | 25% | 30% | 61% | 52% |
| 1........ | 362 | 254 | 16 | 22 | 35 | 33 | 49 | 45 |
| 2........ | 232 | 266 | 29 | 26 | 35 | 42 | 36 | 33 |
| 3........ | 171 | 215 | 33 | 25 | 38 | 47 | 29 | 29 |
| 4........ | 112 | 154 | 29 | 31 | 26 | 43 | 26 | 26 |
| 5........ | 63 | 89 | 33 | 43 | 46 | 40 | 21 | 17 |
| 6........ | 16 | 36 | 63 | 56 | 25 | 42 | 13 | 3 |

[1] See footnote 1 of Table 1 for the exact wording of the question.

[2] Respondents with "no answer" on the index or the question are excluded from the bases. Three boys and four girls are "no answer" on SIISS and ten boys plus five girls are "no answer" on the question.

would "like to be friends with" and "would like to be like." (Data not shown.)

Having described the content of these measures of students' orientations and having mentioned some of the leading correlates of each, we refer the reader to Figure 1. Shown there is a typology of student styles

FIGURE ONE
A Typology of Student Styles Deriving from Their Orientations
Toward the Formal and Informal Status Systems

|  | | Commitment to the Formal Reward System of the School | |
|  | | High | Low |
|---|---|---|---|
| Involvement in the Informal Social System of the School | High | Well Rounded | Fun Culture |
|  | Low | Studious | Uninvolved |

that we derive from these two dimensions. Briefly, students who have a high degree of commitment to both dimensions of students' orientations are termed "well-rounded."[12] Students highly committed to and involved in the informal status system, but with low commitment to the formal reward system, are termed "fun culture." Students having a high degree of commitment to the formal reward system and a low degree of commitment to the informal status system are called "studious." Finally, those who are characterized by low commitment to both status systems are the "uninvolved."[13]

What do we mean by student styles? One of the most salient features of adolescence as an age status is its characterization as a period of change or transition. In light of the emphasis on adolescence as a period of change, it may seem a fruitless endeavor to talk of adolescent styles as though style were a fixed attribute to be "explained" in the same manner we might explain educational achievement. While it is clear that an adolescent's style changes and adjusts to new circumstances over time, it also seems

---

[12] No value judgment is implied in applying this label. We suspect that the label as a stimulus would elicit the response "both socially and scholastically active" on the part of most people. This is why we use it here.

[13] More variety could be added to this typology by considering an extension of each dimension to include an "alienation" segment. That is, one could imagine that students may be strongly committed to, neutral toward, or strongly alienated from the formal or informal status systems. Unfortunately, the items from which these measures were derived were not expressly designed for the purpose to which they have been put here. No items were included in the questionnaire that would allow us to construct measures tapping the alienation spectrum of these dimensions.

to be true that, on the whole, such changes are gradual and evolutionary.

We would suggest that adolescent styles are functions of a complex set of background characteristics and social forces including basic abilities, personal goals, expectations of others, social experience and values. Styles are conceived at a higher level of abstraction than the personal identity concept from social psychology, though we would suggest that personal identity forms the foundation for an adolescent's style in the sense that one's identity must in most respects be consistent with his style. Styles, as we have operationalized them, are predominant orientations that students adopt toward the social and intellectual activity centers that dominate students' lives. This notion of style specifically includes the relevance of interpersonal supports, but it does not carry the necessary implication of subculture.

While we will argue that these style characterizations create meaningful categories with respect to certain kinds of behavior, it should be evident that in many other respects they are of necessity heterogeneous categories. For example, in the "uninvolved" style would be included not only apathetic students but also delinquent, bohemian, radical, and other nonconforming styles as well. These are grouped together simply because, with respect to the dimensions of student orientations used here, they cannot be distinguished. One would have to take into account additional dimensions of students' values to further differentiate within any of these four styles. From our perspective they are all excluded from, or exclude themselves from, the dominant scholastic and social-activity sectors of school life. The burden of proof that these style categories are useful in understanding the quality of adaptation to school and its social life, in spite of some obvious heterogeneity within categories, lies with the authors. We turn to this task next.

That these dimensions are, at least for the populations used in this study, not highly correlated can be seen by examining Table 3. Shown there are the distributions of scores on the index of involvement in the informal status system (SIISS) by scores on the academic values index (POTI) for boys and girls separately. One can see by examining the marginals for each segment of the table that the distribution of scores on both indexes is skewed toward the low end for boys and toward the high end for girls. The skewness is particularly marked for girls on the index of involvement in the informal status system. This is primarily a function of the greater participation of girls in activities in the school.

In Tables 4 (for girls) and 5 (for boys) are presented data relating student styles to various indicators of scholastic effort and orientation and to indicators of one aspect of social life (dating).[14] First we will discuss the data for girls. In general, well-rounded girls are more likely than girls

---

[14] It should be made clear that these indicators are arbitrarily chosen from a much

TABLE THREE
The Relationship between Index of Personal Orientation Toward
Intellectualism (POTI) and Index of Student Involvement in the
Informal Status System (SIISS), for Boys and Girls Separately[1]

| POTI Score | SIISS Score | | | |
|---|---|---|---|---|
| | Low | High | Total | Number |
| Boys:[2] | | | | |
| Low .......... | 56% | 44% | 100% | 698 |
| High ......... | 53 | 47 | 100 | 627 |
| Total ......... | 55 | 45 | 100 | 1,316 |
| Girls:[3] | | | | |
| Low .......... | 34 | 66 | 100 | 572 |
| High ......... | 39 | 61 | 100 | 640 |
| Total ......... | 37 | 63 | 100 | 1,212 |

[1] For both sexes SIISS is dichotomized 0, 1 versus 2, 3, 4, 5, 6. POTI is dichotomized 0, 1, 2 versus 3, 4, 5, 6.

[2] The association (phi expressed as a proportion of its maximum value) for boys is .032. The unadjusted correlation is not significant ($.20 < p < .30$, chi square, 1 d.f.).

[3] The association (phi expressed as a proportion of its maximum value) for girls is −.061. The unadjusted correlation is not significant ($.05 < p < .10$, chi square, 1 d.f.).

of other styles to be high achievers, to apply themselves to school work and to have a high level of confidence in their scholastic images and performance. They, relative to other girls, are less likely to report never dating but are also less likely to report dating more than once a week. In summary, relative to girls of the other styles, they are most likely to have the attitudes and behavior of the "model" student. At the other extreme in terms of modal values and behavior for a category of students is the style we have called uninvolved. These girls, relative to those of other styles, are least often high achievers, hard workers, or confident regarding their scholastic images and performance. With respect to dating behavior, few of these girls report that they never date at all. Further, these girls are among the most likely to date outside their own school.

The studious and fun culture styles present the most interesting contrasts among the possible comparisons of styles. These two groups are the "pure" types in our typology—each being defined by high commitment to only one of the dimensions. In terms of scholastic behavior they tend to fall between well-rounded girls and uninvolved girls. In terms of social behavior, they often are the extreme styles. Contrary to what one might have expected given the usual ideas regarding consonance between values and behavior, studious girls are less often high performers than are fun culture girls. Further, although as a group studious girls more often report being hard workers and perceiving that they have a "hard working" image,

---

larger set of potential items to illustrate certain kinds of differences among the styles. Other similar items show similar patterns, though to a greater or lesser extent depending on the item.

TABLE FOUR
Percentage of Girls of Each Student Style Making the Indicated Response to
Designated Attitudinal and Behavioral Items

| Item | Student Style[1] | | | |
| | Well Rounded | Studious | Fun Culture | Uninvolved |
| --- | --- | --- | --- | --- |
| Planning to go to college ...... | 89% | 62% | 82% | 52% |
| Above median score on MATH Test ............ | 63 | 41 | 47 | 33 |
| Average 2+ hours per day studying .............. | 70 | 62 | 51 | 33 |
| Do "much" or "a great deal" of serious reading .......... | 32 | 26 | 21 | 15 |
| Believe most teachers would rate as "bright" ............ | 48 | 27 | 27 | 17 |
| Believe most teachers would rate as "hard working" ...... | 74 | 72 | 60 | 45 |
| Agree "I am often not able to keep up with the rest" ...... | 23 | 38 | 26 | 38 |
| Agree "I am not doing so well at school" ................ | 18 | 34 | 26 | 51 |
| Average frequency of dating: | | | | |
| Not at all ................. | 14 | 36 | 12 | 19 |
| More than once per week ..... | 28 | 25 | 32 | 39 |
| Of those who date, the percentage who most often date a boy from the same school .............. | 59 | 35 | 54 | 38 |

[1] Approximate bases for the percentages are: well-rounded, 389; studious, 251; fun culture, 375; and uninvolved, 197. Nonresponse to a question caused elimination of the case for only that question.

they less often believe that they are "doing well in school." In addition, more than one-third of the studious girls and only one-eighth of the fun culture girls report that they never date. Finally, while more than half of the fun culture girls who date do so with boys in their own high school, only one-third of the studious girls who date do so with boys from their own high school. These results raise some doubts about the meaning of the styles and the dimensions on which they are based. Before we present arguments to resolve the doubts, we will briefly discuss similar data for boys, which are presented in Table 5.

As was true for girls, well-rounded boys and uninvolved boys occupy the extreme positions regarding scholastic performance, effort, and attitudes. Well-rounded boys, of all styles for boys are most frequently models of scholastic behavior. They most frequently are high performers and hard workers and most frequently express confidence in their school work. With respect to social life, most well-rounded boys date, but they, like most other boys, tend not to date more than once a week. Further, more than other boys except for fun culture boys, well-rounded boys date girls in their own high schools.

At the opposite extreme from well-rounded boys in terms of scholastic behavior are the uninvolved boys. Relative to all other styles, their school performance is more often low, fewer of them report that they devote much time to studying or reading, and more frequently their confidence in their school work is low. The dating behavior of uninvolved boys is about average for these schools, though they are somewhat less likely than other boys to date girls who attend their own high schools.

**TABLE FIVE**
Percentage of Boys of Each Student Style Making the Indicated Response to Designated Attitudinal and Behavioral Items

| | Student Style[1] | | | |
|---|---|---|---|---|
| Item | Well Rounded | Studious | Fun Culture | Uninvolved |
| Planning to go to college ...... | 91% | 74% | 78% | 52% |
| Above median score on MATH test ............. | 76 | 60 | 54 | 40 |
| Average 2+ hours per day studying .............. | 54 | 43 | 28 | 21 |
| Do "much" or "a great deal" of serious reading .......... | 31 | 29 | 14 | 18 |
| Believe most teachers would rate as "bright" ............ | 59 | 35 | 36 | 24 |
| Believe most teachers would rate as "hard working" ...... | 57 | 53 | 38 | 29 |
| Agree "I am often not able to keep up with the rest" ...... | 21 | 30 | 32 | 44 |
| Agree "I am not doing so well at school" ................. | 23 | 37 | 42 | 55 |
| Average frequency of dating: | | | | |
| Not at all ................ | 19 | 40 | 8 | 24 |
| More than once per week ..... | 20 | 10 | 27 | 20 |
| Of those who date, the percentage who most often date a girl from the same school .............. | 72 | 64 | 72 | 52 |

[1] Approximate bases for the percentages are: well-rounded, 293; studious, 334; fun culture, 301; and uninvolved, 388. Nonresponse to a question caused elimination of the case for only that question.

Next we turn to a comparison of studious and fun culture boys. With the single exception of the percentage of boys of each style saying they intend to go to college, studious boys equal or exceed fun culture boys in the proportion who are more "scholastic" on each measure shown in Table 5. That is, studious boys more frequently had high scores on the mathematics test, more frequently report working hard, and more often express confidence in their school work. In terms of dating behavior, the fun culture and studious styles are the extremes for boys. Fun culture boys more often date, more often date more than once a week, and, among those who do date, are more likely to date girls from their own schools.

Thus the data for boys fairly well fit the popular notions of student styles. Relative to other boys, those who are withdrawn from the formal and informal status systems of the school—the uninvolved—do poorly, do not work hard, and are less frequently integrated even into the dating activities of the school. At the other extreme, boys who are committed to the formal status system and are involved in the informal status system— the well-rounded—are most often good students, most often work hard, most often have positive attitudes toward school, and are further integrated through dating girls from their own schools. Studious boys and fun culture boys fall between these extremes, with studious boys more often excelling in scholastic matters and fun culture boys being more active socially. Stated differently, among boys, a high degree of commitment to the formal reward system of the school goes with relatively high scholastic output. This is complemented to some degree by concomitant orientation toward the informal status system.[15]

TABLE SIX
Correlations of Personal Orientation Toward Intellectualism (POTI) and Student Involvement in the Informal Status System (SIISS)[1] With Students' Mathematics Achievement, Ability, and College Plans, Separately for Boys and Girls[2]

|  | Mathematics Achievement[3] | | Ability | | College Plans[4] | |
|---|---|---|---|---|---|---|
|  | SIISS | POTI | SIISS | POTI | SIISS | POTI |
| Boys ..... | .15 | .23 | .07 | .15 | .35 | .33 |
| Girls ..... | .22 | .13 | .18 | .10 | .41 | .12 |

[1] POTI and SIISS are dichotomized as they were for purposes of the typology construction, as near as possible to the median score for the total sample.

[2] The measure of association is phi expressed as a proportion of its maximum value.

[3] C-scale scores for the MATH and ability tests were dichotomized at their medians.

[4] College plan responses are dichotomized "yes as a full-time student right after high school" ( = high) versus all other responses ( = low). Nonresponses were eliminated.

Why, then, are the results for girls different? Why are studious girls disadvantaged relative to fun culture girls? Some suggestions can be gleaned from the pattern of correlations given in Table 6. In this table are given, for boys and girls separately, the correlations between the two dimensions of the style typology and three performance-ability measures. Two patterns are evident in these correlations. First, scholastic commit-

---

[15] We note that those of both sexes who are relatively uninvolved in the informal status system of the school—the studious and the uninvolved—also, relative to the other styles, are less likely to regularly date people from their own school. This may be indicative of their involvement in other social circles (e.g., a sizable proportion of the girls indicated that they dated boys who were already in college). It is not clear whether involvement elsewhere is the cause of or the result of lack of involvement in their own school. Probably to some extent it is both.

ment (POTI) has higher correlations with the performance measures for boys than is true for girls. The opposite is true for involvement in the informal status system. This index (SIISS) has higher correlations with the performance measures for girls than is true for boys. The second pattern evident is that for boys, with the exception of its correlation with college plans, scholastic orientation (POTI) has higher correlations with the performance measures than does involvement in the informal status system (SIISS). For girls the opposite is true; namely, involvement in the informal status system (SIISS) has higher correlations with the performance measures than does scholastic orientation (POTI).

Part of the explanation that we would offer in trying to account for these differences between boys and girls builds upon conventional notions about sex role differences. With respect to scholastic endeavors, girls are more conforming than boys. They study harder and make better grades (Lavin, 1965:128–129; Coleman, 1961:18; McDill, et al., 1966:IV–14). Yet, the school performance of girls is less concretely relevant to the determination of their future status since most will not have work careers other than that of housewife. The lack of relevance of educational performance for an expected business world career may partially explain why girls are less frequently over- or under-achievers than boys. (See Lavin, 1965, for evidence that the latter is true.)

Boys, on the other hand, are not as conforming to the general performance norms and typically are high performers only if they are motivated to be for more concrete reasons—e.g., performance is instrumental for the attainment of future goals or they are intrinsically interested in particular subject matter. This would lead one to expect that a measure of scholastic orientation would predict performance better for boys than for girls.

The importance of involvement in the informal status system for girls, is, of course, related to this explanation. A girl can act to enhance her visibility and attractiveness to boys by being socially adept and popular. Social competence and popularity are attributes that can be enhanced through experience in and involvement in the informal status system. Angrist (1969:226) made a similar point in her discussion of sex role socialization:

> While man's strait jacket during socialization is occupational choice, woman's strait jacket is marriage. . . . one contingency takes priority during late adolescence and early adulthood rendering others subordinate. It is preparation for, even overstress on, marriage and the marital role. . . . As the key contingency, preparation to fit the unknown spouse leads girls to tailor their behavior for maximum eligibility. This means acting feminine (passive, cooperative, non-intellectual) in dating situations . . . and high school girls' acceptance of traditional but disliked domestic responsibilities for their married lives. . . . It means perception of limited options in the occupational world. The inability of occupational choice theories to han-

dle women's patterns reflects women's contingency orientations. . . . Women's expectations for adult roles have been dubbed unrealistic . . . ; on the contrary, one could argue that they are concretely realistic. While a boy enters college considering types and conditions of work, the girl's primary focus is on marriage. Work is peripheral. College then becomes important —as broadening social experience, for self-development for mate-finding. Whereas during the preteen years boys and girls tentatively consider occupations, only boys consistently pass into the reality stages of exploring, crystallizing and specifying an occupation.

Some credence can be added to this explanation by the following test. If the explanation is even partially true, then it should be the case that for girls for whom the occupational arena *is* relevant—those who want to have careers other than, or in addition to, homemaker roles—the pattern of relationships between scholastic values (POTI) and the performance measures should be more like the pattern of relationships among these variables for boys. We can divide the girls in our sample into two groups: (1) those who named a definite occupation in answer to a question on what they would like to be doing 15 years hence and (2) those who said they would like to be housewives or who named nothing specific that they wished to be doing. The relationships between measures of the two dimensions of the styles typology and the ability-performance measures are given in Table 7 separately for girls who named an occupation and those who did not name an out-of-the-home occupation. These results lend substantial support to our argument.

What can be seen in Table 7 is a partial duplication of the pattern of correlations that was shown in the previous table. Scholastic commitment (POTI) has higher correlations with the performance-ability measures for

TABLE SEVEN
Correlations of Girls' Scores on Personal Orientation Toward Intellectualism (POTI) and on Student Involvement in the Informal Status System (SIISS) With Their Mathematics Achievement, Ability, and College Plans, by Whether They Desire to Work Outside the Home 15 Years Hence[1]

| Desires Regarding Work[2] | Mathematics Achievement[3] | | Ability | | College Plans | |
|---|---|---|---|---|---|---|
| | SIISS | POTI | SIISS | POTI | SIISS | POTI |
| Desires to be working 15 years hence . . . . . . . . . . . . | .18 | .15 | .14 | .11 | .36 | .25 |
| Does not desire to be working 15 years hence . . . . . | .29 | .09 | .25 | .07 | .49 | −.07 |

[1] Correlations are phi expressed as a proportion of its maximum value given the marginals.

[2] Labor force participation desires were tapped by the following questions: If your desires could be realized, what one job would you *like* to have 15 years from now? (*Be specific;* for example, saleslady, nurse, secretary, housewife, school teacher, etc.) If a girl named any occupation (other than housewife), she is considered for these purposes to desire to be in the labor force (N = 707). Any other response ("I don't know," no answer, or "housewife") is considered to indicate no desire to be in the labor force (N = 447).

[3] Ability-achievement items are dichotomized as in Table 6.

girls desiring to work outside the home than it (POTI) does for girls not desiring to work outside the home. In addition, involvement in the informal status system (SIISS) has higher correlations with the performance measures for girls not desiring to work than it does for those who do name an occupational choice other than housewife. The other pattern shown in Table 6—that for boys the correlations of POTI with the performance measures are higher than the correlations of SIISS with these variables and that for girls the correlations of SIISS with the performance measures are higher than the correlations of POTI with these variables—is not fully duplicated in the results of Table 7.

These data support our general *post hoc* argument then. Those girls for whom the traditional occupational choice and educational attainment theories should be relevant—those desiring out-of-the-home occupations—are most like boys in the pattern of correlations between ability-performance measures and scholastic commitment. While the relationships are not strong, and the differences among the correlations are not large, the pattern of correlations is too consistent to be dismissed. It would seem that girls opt for the success model that is most relevant to their personal desires. When the desires lead them to select the "traditional" feminine role, their relative "success" in filling the high school-level counterpart of the role—active, demure, visible, etc.—is correlated with (a function of) their general capacity to function in the scholastic sector of school life. When their desires lead them to the "non-traditional" feminine role, the strength of their commitment to this role is related to their ability to function in the scholastic sector of school life. That is, girls invest their abilities to capitalize on preparation to fit the role model they deem most appropriate for themselves. Their general abilities (social as well as intellectual) should be related to the degree of "success" they have in their role preparation. Obviously many things impinge both on the role choice (traditional vs. nontraditional) and on the degree of success in pursuit of either role. Our (limited) purpose has been to suggest how general orientation to the formal and informal status systems relate to these processes.

## DISCUSSION AND CONCLUSIONS

We have shown that, even though adolescents may have experiences and normative elements in common that separate them from adults (we have not addressed the validity of this common assumption), they also have many differences with regard to experiences and normative elements among themselves. Further, we have shown that some of these differences —i.e., on orientations that are the defining elements of the style typology —are related to important aspects of the scholastic and social behavior of high school students. These latter behaviors are some of the behaviors that writers who argue that an adolescent subculture does exist claim to be substantially dominated by the adolescent subculture. We have not by any means shown that the notion of an adolescent subculture is an empty or fallacious notion. That is not the question we have addressed here. We have shown that involvement in the informal status system of the high school is not necessarily inimical to the scholastic effort of high school students. The currency of the idea that involvement in the informal status system of the school is contradictory to involvement in or commitment to the formal, scholastic status system probably derives in part from the fact that at any given instant involvement in one or the other approaches total involvement. Instantaneous total commitment may lead to an impression of mutual exclusiveness between scholastic activity and peer-centered social activity, when in reality there is probably some phasing between the two in the lives of most people.[16]

We think we have added some clarity to the concept of "adolescent subculture" through our examination of what we have called student styles. Though the conception of "adolescent subcultures" is at a different level of abstraction than that of "student styles," we would suggest that our results on the latter can inform the perception of the former. We would suggest that an implicit dimension of adolescents' commitments that varies from "peer group oriented" to "scholastic oriented" is too simplistic. Researchers may be able to derive typologies of subcultures that parallel what we have done here with student styles. Other dimensions may be relevant for other purposes. But we suggest that to the extent that a notion of adolescent subculture is useful for given research problems, then it probably is most fruitfully conceived as being multi-dimensional.

In a different vein, we have suggested that the typology (and its constituent dimensions) has a different pattern of relationships with aspects of scholastic and social behavior for girls than the pattern which exists for boys. Our explanation for the differences draws on the sex role socialization literature, which argues that females, being socialized to expect and desire marriage and family commitments for the future, lack (or have less fully developed) outside-the-home career plans. For this reason, we argue, the model of success for high school girls typically has emphasized interpersonal and "social" skills rather than scholastic excellence and career preparation (the success model for boys).

## REFERENCES

Angrist, Shirley S. "The Study of Sex Roles." *Journal of Social Issues* 25 (1969):215–32.

---

[16] We are grateful to Professor Robert A. Gordon for suggesting this point to us in reacting to a different version of this manuscript.

Berger, Bennet.   "Adolescents and Beyond." *Social Problems* 10 (Spring 1969):
394–408.

Boocock, Sarane S.   "Toward a Sociology of Learning: A Selective Review of
Existing Research." *Sociology of Education* 39 (1966):1–45.

Campbell, Ernest Q.   "Adolescent Socialization." *Handbook of Socialization
Theory and Research*. ed. David A. Goslin. New York: Rand McNally &
Company, 1969.

Clark, Burton R.   *Educating the Expert Society*. San Francisco: Chandler Publishing Co., 1962.

Cohen, Albert K.   *Delinquent Boys*. Glencoe, Ill.: The Free Press, 1955.

Coleman, James S.   *The Adolescent Society*. New York: The Free Press of
Glencoe, 1961.

Dailey, John T., and Shaycoft, Marion F.   *Types of Tests in Project TALENT*.
U.S. Department of Health, Education and Welfare, Office of Education,
Cooperative Research Branch Monograph No. 9. Washington: U.S. Gov-
ernment Printing Office, 1961.

Davis, Kingsley.   "Sociology of Parent-Youth Conflict." *American Journal of
Sociology* 5 (August 1940):523–35.

Douvan, Elizabeth, and Adelson, Joseph.   *The Adolescent Experience*. New
York: John Wiley & Sons, Inc., 1966.

Eisenstadt, S.N.   "Archetypal Patterns of Youth." *Daedalus* (Winter 1962):
28–46.

Elkin, Frederick, and Westley, William A.   "The Myth of Adolescent Culture."
*American Sociological Review* 20 (1955):680–84.

Epperson, D.C.   "A Reassessment of Indices of Parental Influence in 'The Adolescent Society.'" *American Sociological Review* 29 (1964):93–96.

Gordon, C. Wayne.   *The Social System of the High School*. Glencoe: The Free
Press, 1957.

Guilford, J.P.   *Psychometric Methods*. 2nd ed. New York: McGraw-Hill Book
Company, Inc., 1954.

Jahoda, Marie, and Warren, Neil.   "The Myths of Youth." *Sociology of Education* 39 (1965):138–49.

Katz, Fred E.   "The School as a Complex Social Organization." *Harvard Educational Review* 34 (Summer 1964):428–55.

Lavin, David E.   *The Prediction of Academic Performance*. New York: Russell Sage Foundation, 1965.

Lipset, Seymour Martin, and Bendix, Reinhard.   *Social Mobility in Industrial
Society*. Berkeley and Los Angeles: University of California Press, 1963.

Matza, David.   "Position and Behavior Patterns of Youth." *Handbook of Modern Sociology*. Edited by Robert E.L. Faris. Chicago: Rand McNally & Co.,
1964.

McDill, Edward L., Meyers, Edmund D., Jr., and Rigsby, Leo C.   *Sources of
Educational Climates in High Schools*. Final Report to the Office of Edu-
cation, U.S. Department of Health, Education and Welfare under Contract
OE–3–10–080. December 1966.

————.   "Institutional Effects on the Academic Behavior of High School Students." *Sociology of Education* 40 (Summer 1967):181–99.

Rehberg, Richard A. and Schafer, Walter E.   "Participation in Interscholastic

Athletics and College Expectations." *American Journal of Sociology* 73 (May 1968):732–40.

Rigsby, Leo C.  *Life Styles of High School Students: Sources and Consequences.* Unpublished dissertation. Johns Hopkins University, 1970.

Spady, William G.  "Lament for the Letterman: Effects of Peer Status and Extracurricular Activities on Goals and Achievement." *American Journal of Sociology.* 75 (January 1970):680–702.

Stinchcombe, Arthur L.  *Rebellion in the High School.* Chicago: Quadrangle Books, 1964.

Turner, Ralph H.  *The Social Context of Ambition.* San Francisco: Chandler Publishing Co., 1964.

Waller, Willard.  *The Sociology of Teaching.* New York: John Wiley & Sons, 1932.

# part TWO

# Socialization and Learning:
# Nonformal Aspects

Socialization and learning are frequently defined as being almost synonymous. But, when viewed in the context of education, socialization is more apt to pertain to the nonformal aspects of the educational process—a process that takes place inside as well as outside of school. All of the various components of the social environment contribute to the socialization of the young and involve learning of one kind or another. The formal learning that takes place in school is greatly influenced by the processes of socialization and informal learning that go on constantly during a person's waking hours, both in the early years and throughout the entire life course.

The locus of early socialization and learning is the family. A vast amount of learning takes place during the preschool years. Much of the learning that occurs in this early period of socialization is neither self-consciously or systematically carried out. Parents, brothers and sisters, grandparents, and other adults all contribute to the process. The basic requirements involved in walking, talking, playing with other children, eating, toilet training, sleeping, and generally dealing with adults are learned in an informal way. Actually, more learning takes place informally during the course of a person's life than could conceivably take place in the formal classroom and related activities of the school.

A large part of the learning that takes place within the family, as well as later on among friends and age peers, occurs under circumstances in which feelings of love, hate, fear, anxiety, pride, guilt, and affection abound; that is, learning frequently takes place within an emotionally charged social context. Though this is often also true in the formal setting

77

of the school, attempts are made to minimize the degree of emotional interference. However, when psychic or emotional circumstances can be used to motivate students in school, efforts are frequently made to encourage it. The same holds for that proportion of *conscious* teaching and training carried on by parents. Parents vary in their ability to mix discipline leading to the learning of social norms with continuous acceptance and love. Each succeeding generation of parents goes through a process of socialization based partly on past modes of teaching and discipline, on the rejection of past modes, and on the adoption of new ways of teaching the young to respond to the adult world they will soon enter. Parents and grownups both consciously and unconsciously teach by example and precept how to avoid the dangers as well as how to take advantage of the opportunities of life.

Sometimes middle-class parents will make a conscious effort to use the latest theories of child-rearing in preparing their children for the adult world. Magazines and books devoting thousands of pages to the latest theories and practices are printed every year. Child-rearing is also a favorite topic for inclusion in the Sunday newspaper supplements. Television gives considerable time to documentaries and commentary on child-rearing practices. In most cases much of the effort is aimed at giving the child those preschool experiences, knowledge, and skills needed for success in the more formal world of school.

When education and its related activities such as reading, writing, study, and discussion are considered important in the home, the young members of the family generally come to place high value on formal education. When the socialization process includes, not only education as an important value, but also the activities that are an important element of formal education, the likelihood of success in school is vastly increased. In most cases it is the mother who is in the best position to both emphasize the value of reading, writing, and study as well as specifically teach many skills important to the education process.

The all-important mother, as seen also in Hess and Shipman's discussion of the influence of her mode of communicating with her child, has an important place in the development of the basic medium for learning language.[1] Since modes of communicating are generally neither consciously learned or deliberately transmitted to the next generation, this critical feature of the learning process is nonformal and frequently unintentional. Although a great many important aspects of learning and socialization take place in the family setting, the attribution of cause for behavior is much more complicated than is frequently implied when the importance of the family is being extolled. The interplay of family relationships, kin-

---

[1] See Robert D. Hess and Virginia C. Shipman, "Early Experience and the Socialization of Cognitive Modes in Children," chapter 5 of this volume.

groups, teachers, age peers, status community, mass media, besides such characteristics as health and temperament, is extremely complicated. At this stage of social science the interplay is only partially understood and no comprehensive theory adequately explains the consequences of many of the specific behaviors involved.

It can be observed that the mass media, as well as the vast bulk of pronouncements coming from officials and others in the news, periodically attest to the importance of education. Officially, Americans place a very high value on formal education, and continuously verbalize this fact. Nevertheless, a great many Americans grow up with a rather low estimation of formal education. This is based partly on distinct family, peer group, and community attitudes relative to the function of the school, who should be educated and how it ought to be carried out. Status and class differences also have a powerful influence on who goes on to school after the initial ten to 12 years. Not all families view upward mobility for their children as an unmixed blessing. Families with strong kingroup, ethnic and religious attachments see economic and social mobility as a major cause in family disintegration. When such is the case education is generally not viewed as the key to insuring success in adult life, but rather as the time for growing up and learning the "basics." In such families the value placed on education is of a different order than that exhibited by the professional, or upper middle class family. In the former, high school is viewed as terminal, whereas for the latter the high school diploma and corresponding academic record is critical for moving on to college or university. The foregoing variation in the value placed on education as well as how much and what type is a crucial factor in the informal learning that influences behavior in school.

In addition to expressing "official" values, the mass media (comic books, radio, movies, and television) has had a powerful effect on learning. Little solid information is available on how much the average child learns from television, for example, but its impact is considered important. Bringing the whole world in "living color" into the home for several hours every day has created a childhood environment of sight and sounds never before experienced in the history of man. The differences between the world of today's children and that of their parents is profound, even when only considering the exposure to the influences of the mass media. The impact of the newer mass media has been dramatized by Marshall McLuhan. McLuhan characterized the recent development as creating a "classroom without walls," and states that "these mass media threaten, instead of merely reinforce, the procedures of the traditional classroom."[2]

---

[2] Marshall McLuhan, "Classroom Without Walls," in Edmund Carpenter and Marshall McLuhan, *Explorations in Communication* (Boston: Beacon Press, 1960), pp. 1–3.

The vast bulk of the socialization and learning that provides the basis for the major roles played by youth and adults takes place informally. Family roles are primarily learned within family and kingroup, but the remainder are learned in the groups we are members of or with which we come into contact. Among the most powerful are the various groups made up of our age and status peers. For the small child the play group provides the social setting for learning how to adjust needs and desires to the behavior of peers. The child begins to develop an identity of his own and to model behavior in ways that are defined as appropriate. In a very real sense the child begins to develop a sense of self as distinct from the family.

As the child develops a social self he also learns to participate in the cultural norms and practices of childhood. Much of what is learned is gained directly from slightly older members of the child peer group. For example, social scientists have shown that the rather specific rules of many childhood street games are learned, not from adults who might still remember them, but from older children. It has been estimated that such rules and practices have been passed from generation to generation since the days of ancient Rome without reliance on adult memory or example. The same can be said for many rhymes, myths, and examples of childhood logic. In childhood we briefly belong to a unique world and are taught a great deal, albeit informally. Peer influences begin before school intrudes and continues with varying degrees of importance for the rest of life.

The norms, values, and expectations of the peer groups of late childhood and adolescence tend to compete or even conflict with those of the immediate family. Behaviors that are deemed proper and right within the family are at times incompatible with those expected by the adolescent gang or peer group. Initiation requirements like shoplifting, "borrowing" someone's car for a joy ride, or experimenting with drugs are not unknown in some adolescent peer groups.

Most directly related to education is the powerful influence of the teenage sub-culture of the junior and senior high school. The norms and values of this sub-culture, as reported by Coleman, indicate that for boys academic attainment ranks far below such other values as being an athlete or being a member of a leading crowd. Similarly, for girls, membership in a leading crowd, leadership in activities, or having nice clothes far outranks high grades.[3] It is quite apparent from Coleman's study that powerful forces operate in the informal structure of schools to generate and foster norms and values that may go counter to the generally accepted function of the school itself.

The power of peer group interaction and pressure is probably at its extreme in cases similar to that provided by the living conditions at the

---

[3] James S. Coleman, "The Adolescent Society," in *Studies in American Society* by Derek L. Phillips (Ed.) (New York: Thomas Y. Crowell Co., 1965), pp. 136 ff.

famous English "public" schools such as Eton, Harrow, Winchester, or Marlborough. For example, by curtailing privacy, group loyalty and cooperation is fostered while individuality is inhibited. One writer on the English public school noted that:

> The more boys live in their own rooms, the more intimate, . . . , will be their talk. . . . On the other hand, the more they live in common rooms, the more they will be likely to restrict themselves to general topics, such as the obvious one of the doings of the house team, and by so doing incline to a more passionate local patriotism.[4]

An observation by a headmaster of one of these prestigious boarding schools indicated that the sharing of one large study hall tended to influence the rapid abandonment of individual hobbies by newcomers.[5] The claim was also made that the close collective type of living found in the public schools tended to inhibit the expression of individual emotions that might threaten or challenge the prevailing esprit de corps or school spirit.[6] "Lack of privacy meant that the minority who might have resisted irrational appeals to tradition and good taste were confronted abruptly and constantly by the majority, those who are always content to follow convention."[7] Beyond the issues of individuality and group loyalty, the informal aspects of learning carried on in the English public school is probably many times more pervasive and important in the lives of the participants than the formal features of these schools. Since they are largely boarding schools, the force of the peer group, backed by intricate traditions and living conditions involving lack of privacy and rather severe austerity is extremely powerful and effective.

Although the vast majority of men are not subjected to the kind of social environment epitomized by the English public school, the power of peer group influences of late childhood and youth are very important. The peer group is generally the most effective force, along with the family, in shaping norms, values, and expectations during the school years. Sometimes peer group influences run counter to family and teachers. At other times they are primarily competitive for the time and energy of the young. In contrast, at other times they may support the norms and values of parents and teachers. No categorical blame or praise for inhibiting or promoting formal learning can characterize the social groups of the young. It is, nevertheless, clear that the peer group is a potent informal learning environment.

---

4 Bernard Darwin, *The English Public School* (Longmans, 1929), p. 88 quoted from Rupert Wilkinson, *Gentlemanly Power: British Leadership and the Public School Tradition* (London: Oxford University Press), p. 45.

5 Wilkinson, Ibid., p. 45.

6 Ibid., p. 45.

7 Ibid., p. 45.

# 4

# Learning the Student Role: Kindergarten as Academic Boot Camp*

## HARRY L. GRACEY

### INTRODUCTION

Education must be considered one of the major institutions of social
life today. Along with the family and organized religion, however, it is a
"secondary institution," one in which people are prepared for life in society as it is presently organized. The main dimensions of modern life, that
is, the nature of society as a whole, is determined principally by the "primary institutions," which today are the economy, the political system, and
the military establishment. Education has been defined by sociologists,
classical and contemporary, as an institution that serves society by socializing people into it through a formalized, standardized procedure. At the
beginning of this century Emile Durkheim told student teachers at the
University of Paris that education "consists of a methodical socialization
of the younger generation." He went on to add:

> It is the influence exercised by adult generations on those that are not
> ready for social life. Its object is to arouse and to develop in the child a
> certain number of physical, intellectual, and moral states that are de-

From: *Readings in Introductory Sociology* by Dennis Wrong and Harry L. Gracey.
Copyright © 1967 by Macmillan Publishing Co., Inc.

* This article is an abridgment of a chapter from a work tentatively titled *The
American Elementary School, a Case Study in Bureaucracy and Ideology;* a report of
research supported by Grant No. MH 9135 from the National Institute of Mental
Health. The author wishes to thank Arthur Vidich for his helpful criticisms and
suggestions.

manded of him by the political society as a whole and by the special milieu for which he is specifically destined. . . . To the egoistic and asocial being that has just been born, [society] must, as rapidly as possible, add another, capable of leading a moral and social life. Such is the work of education.[1]

The educational process, Durkheim said, "is above all the means by which society perpetually recreates the conditions of its very existence."[2] The contemporary educational sociologist, Wilbur Brookover, offered a similar formulation in his textbook definition of education:

Actually, therefore, in the broadest sense education is synonymous with socialization. It includes any social behavior that assists in the induction of the child into membership in the society or any behavior by which the society perpetuates itself through the next generation.[3]

The educational institution is, then, one of the ways in which society is perpetuated through the systematic socialization of the young, while the nature of the society that is being perpetuated—its organization and operation, its values, beliefs and ways of living—are determined by the primary institutions. The educational system, like other secondary institutions, *serves* the society that is *created* by the operation of the economy, the political system, and the military establishment.

Schools, the social organizations of the educational institution, are today for the most part large bureaucracies run by specially trained and certified people. There are few places left in modern societies where formal teaching and learning is carried on in small, isolated groups, like the rural, one-room schoolhouses of the last century. Schools are large, formal organizations that tend to be parts of larger organizations, local community school districts. These school districts are bureaucratically organized and their operations are supervised by state and local governments. In this context, as Brookover says:

the term education is used . . . to refer to a system of schools, in which specifically designated persons are expected to teach children and youth certain types of acceptable behavior. The school system becomes a . . . unit in the total social structure and is recognized by the members of the society as a separate social institution. Within this structure a portion of the total socialization process occurs.[4]

Education is the part of the socialization process that takes place in the

---

[1] Emile Durkheim, *Sociology and Education* (New York: The Free Press, 1956), pp. 71–72.

[2] Ibid., p. 123.

[3] Wilbur Brookover, *The Sociology of Education* (New York: American Book Company, 1957), p. 4.

[4] Ibid., p. 6.

schools; and these are, more and more often today, bureaucracies within bureaucracies.

Kindergarten is generally conceived by educators as a year of preparation for school. It is thought of as a year in which small children, five or six years old, are prepared socially and emotionally for the academic learning that will take place over the next 12 years. It is expected that a foundation of behavior and attitudes will be laid in kindergarten on which the children can acquire the skills and knowledge they will be taught in the grades. A booklet prepared for parents by the staff of a suburban New York school system says that the kindergarten experience will stimulate the child's desire to learn and cultivate the skills he will need for learning in the rest of his school career. It claims that the child will find opportunities for physical growth, for satisfying his "need for self-expression," acquire some knowledge, and provide opportunities for creative activity. It concludes, "The most important benefit that your five-year-old will receive from kindergarten is the opportunity to live and grow happily and purposefully with others in a small society." The kindergarten teachers in one of the elementary schools in this community, one we shall call the Wilbur Wright School, said their goals were to see that the children "grew" in all ways: physically, of course, emotionally, socially, and academically. They said they wanted children to like school as a result of their kindergarten experiences and that they wanted them to learn to get along with others.

None of these goals, however, is unique to kindergarten; each of them is held to some extent by teachers in the other six grades at the Wright School. And growth would occur, but differently, even if the child did not attend school. The children already know how to get along with others, in their families and their play groups. The unique job of the kindergarten in the educational division of labor seems rather to be teaching children the student role. The student role is the repertoire of behavior and attitudes regarded by educators as appropriate to children in school. Observation in the kindergartens of the Wilbur Wright School revealed a great variety of activities through which children are shown and then drilled in the behavior and attitudes defined as appropriate for school and thereby induced to learn the role of student. Observations of the kindergartens and interviews with the teachers both pointed to the teaching and learning of classroom routines as the main element of the student role. The teachers expended most of their efforts, for the first half of the year at least, in training the children to follow the routines which teachers created. The children were, in a very real sense, *drilled* in tasks and activities created by the teachers for their own purposes and beginning and ending quite arbitrarily (from the child's point of view) at the command of the teacher. One teacher remarked that she hated September, because during the first month "everything has to be done rigidly, and repeatedly, until they know exactly what they're supposed to do." However, "by January," she said, "they know exactly what to do [during the day] and I don't have to be after them all the time." Classroom routines were introduced gradually from the beginning of the year in all the kindergartens, and the children were drilled in them as long as was necessary to achieve regular compliance. By the end of the school year, the successful kindergarten teacher has a well-organized group of children. They follow classroom routines automatically, having learned all the command signals and the expected responses to them. They have, in our terms, learned the student role. The following observation shows one such classroom operating at optimum organization on an afternoon late in May. It is the class of an experienced and respected kindergarten teacher.

## AN AFTERNOON IN KINDERGARTEN

At about 12:20 in the afternoon on a day in the last week of May, Edith Kerr leaves the teachers' room where she has been having lunch and walks to her classroom at the far end of the primary wing of Wright School. A group of five- and six-year-olds peers at her through the glass doors leading from the hall cloakroom to the play area outside. Entering her room, she straightens some material in the "book corner" of the room, arranges music on the piano, takes colored paper from her closet and places it on one of the shelves under the window. Her room is divided into a number of activity areas through the arrangement of furniture and play equipment. Two easels and a paint table near the door create a kind of passageway inside the room. A wedge-shaped area just inside the front door is made into a teacher's area by the placing of "her" things there: her desk, file, and piano. To the left is the book corner, marked off from the rest of the room by a puppet stage and a movable chalkboard. In it are a display rack of picture books, a record player, and a stack of children's records. To the right of the entrance are the sink and clean-up area. Four large round tables with six chairs at each for the children are placed near the walls about halfway down the length of the room, two on each side, leaving a large open area in the center for group games, block building, and toy truck driving. Windows stretch down the length of both walls, starting about three feet from the floor and extending almost to the high ceilings. Under the windows are long shelves on which are kept all the toys, games, blocks, paper, paints and other equipment of the kindergarten. The left rear corner of the room is a play store with shelves, merchandise, and cash register; the right rear corner is a play kitchen with stove, sink, ironing board, and bassinette with baby dolls in it. This area is partly shielded from the rest of the room by a large standing display rack for posters and children's art work. A sandbox is found against the back wall between these two areas. The room is light, brightly colored and filled with things adults feel five- and six-year-olds will find interesting and pleasing.

At 12:25 Edith opens the outside door and admits the waiting children. They hang their sweaters on hooks outside the door and then go to the center of the room and arrange themselves in a semi-circle on the floor, facing the teacher's chair which she has placed in the center of the floor. Edith follows them in and sits in her chair checking attendance while waiting for the bell to ring. When she has finished attendance, which she takes by sight, she asks the children what the date is, what day and month it is, how many children are enrolled in the class, how many are present, and how many are absent.

The bell rings at 12:30 and the teacher puts away her attendance book. She introduces a visitor, who is sitting against the right wall taking notes, as someone who wants to learn about schools and children. She then goes to the back of the room and takes down a large chart labeled "Helping Hands." Bringing it to the center of the room, she tells the children it is time to change jobs. Each child is assigned some task on the chart by placing his name, lettered on a paper "hand," next to a picture signifying the task—e.g., a broom, a blackboard, a milk bottle, a flag, and a Bible. She asks the children who wants each of the jobs and rearranges their "hands" accordingly. Returning to her chair, Edith announces, "One person should tell us what happened to Mark." A girl raises her hand, and when called on says, "Mark fell and hit his head and had to go to the hospital." The teacher adds that Mark's mother had written saying he was in the hospital.

During this time the children have been interacting among themselves, as well as with Edith. Children have whispered to their neighbors, poked one another, made general comments to the group, waved to friends on the other side of the circle. None of this has been disruptive, and the teacher has ignored it for the most part. The children seem to know just how much of each kind of interaction is permitted—they may greet in a soft voice someone who sits next to them, for example, but may not shout greetings to a friend who sits across the circle, so they confine themselves to waving and remain well within understood limits.

At 12:35 two children arrive. Edith asks them why they are late and then sends them to join the circle on the floor. The other children vie with each other to tell the newcomers what happened to Mark. When this leads to a general disorder Edith asks, "Who has serious time?" The children become quiet and a girl raises her hand. Edith nods and the child gets a Bible and hands it to Edith. She reads the Twenty-third Psalm while the children sit quietly. Edith helps the child in charge begin reciting the Lord's Prayer, the other children follow along for the first unit of sounds, and then trail off as Edith finishes for them. Everyone stands and faces the American flag hung to the right of the door. Edith leads the pledge to the flag, with the children again following the familiar sounds as far as they remember them. Edith then asks the girl in charge what song she wants and the child replies, "My Country." Edith goes to the piano and plays "America," singing as the children follow her words.

Edith returns to her chair in the center of the room and the children sit again in the semi-circle on the floor. It is 12:40 when she tells the children, "Let's have boys' sharing time first." She calls the name of the first boy sitting on the end of the circle, and he comes up to her with a toy helicopter. He turns and holds it up for the other children to see. He says, "It's a helicopter." Edith asks, "What is it used for?" and he replies, "For the army. Carry men. For the war." Other children join in, "For shooting submarines." "To bring back men from space when they are in the ocean." Edith sends the boy back to the circle and asks the next boy if he has something. He replies "No" and she passes on to the next. He says "Yes" and brings a bird's nest to her. He holds it for the class to see, and the teacher asks, "What kind of bird made the nest?" The boy replies, "My friend says a rain bird made it." Edith asks what the nest is made of and different children reply, "mud," "leaves," and "sticks." There is also a bit of moss woven into the nest and Edith tries to describe it to the children. They, however, are more interested in seeing if anything is inside it, and Edith lets the boy carry it around the semi-circle showing the children its insides. Edith tells the children of some baby robins in a nest in her yard, and some of the children tell about baby birds they have seen. Some children are asking about a small object in the nest which they say looks like an egg, but all have seen the nest now and Edith calls on the next boy. A number of children say, "I know what Michael has, but I'm not telling." Michael brings a book to the teacher and then goes back to his place in the circle of children. Edith reads the last page of the book to the class. Some children tell of books they have at home. Edith calls the next boy, and three children call out, "I know what David has." "He always has the same thing." "It's a bang-bang." David goes to his table and gets a box which he brings to Edith. He opens it and shows the teacher a scale-model of an old-fashioned dueling pistol. When David does not turn around to the class, Edith tells him, "Show it to the children," and he does. One child says, "Mr. Johnson [the principal] said no guns." Edith replies, "Yes, how many of you know that?" Most of the children in the circle raise their hands. She continues, "That you aren't supposed to bring guns to school?" She calls the next boy on the circle and he brings two large toy soldiers to her which the children enthusiastically identify as being from "Babes in Toyland." The next boy brings an American flag to Edith and shows it to the class. She asks him what the stars and stripes stand for and admonishes him to treat it carefully. "Why should you treat it carefully?" she asks the boy. "Because it's our flag," he replies. She congratulates him, saying, "That's right."

"Show and Tell" lasted 20 minutes and during the last ten one girl in particular announced that she knew what each child called upon had to show. Edith asked her to be quiet each time she spoke out, but she was not content, continuing to offer her comment at each "show." Four children from other classes had come into the room to bring something from another teacher or to ask for something from Edith. Those with requests were asked to return later if the item wasn't readily available.

Edith now asks if any of the children told their mothers about their trip to the local zoo the previous day. Many children raise their hands. As Edith calls on them, they tell what they liked in the zoo. Some children cannot wait to be called on, and they call out things to the teacher, who asks them to be quiet. After a few of the animals are mentioned, one child says, "I liked the spooky house," and the others chime in to agree with him, some pantomiming fear and horror. Edith is puzzled, and asks what this was. When half the children try to tell her at once, she raises her hand for quiet, then calls on individual children. One says, "The house with nobody in it"; another, "The dark little house." Edith asks where it was in the zoo, but the children cannot describe its location in any way which she can understand. Edith makes some jokes but they involve adult abstractions the children cannot grasp. The children have become quite noisy now, speaking out to make both relevant and irrelevant comments, and three little girls have become particularly assertive.

Edith gets up from her seat at 1:10 and goes to the book corner, where she puts a record on the player. As it begins a story about the trip to the zoo, she returns to the circle and asks the children to go sit at the tables. She divides them among the tables in such a way as to indicate that they don't have regular seats. When the children are all seated at the four tables, five or six to a table, the teacher asks, "Who wants to be the first one?" One of the noisy girls comes to the center of the room. The voice on the record is giving directions for imitating an ostrich and the girl follows them, walking around the center of the room holding her ankles with her hands. Edith replays the record, and all the children, table by table, imitate ostriches down the center of the room and back. Edith removes her shoes and shows that she can be an ostrich too. This is apparently a familiar game, for a number of children are calling out, "Can we have the crab?" Edith asks one of the children to do a crab "so we can all remember how," and then plays the part of the record with music for imitating crabs by. The children from the first table line up across the room, hands and feet on the floor and faces pointing toward the ceiling. After they have "walked" down the room and back in this posture they sit at their table and the children of the next table play "crab." The children love this; they run from their tables, dance about on the floor waiting for their turns and are generally exuberant. Children ask for the "inch worm" and the game is played again with the children squirming down the floor. As a conclusion Edith shows them a new animal imitation, the "lame dog." The children all hobble down the floor, table by table, to the accompaniment of the record.

At 1:30 Edith has the children line up in the center of the room; she says, "Table one, line up in front of me," and children ask, "What are we going to do?" Then she moves a few steps to the side and says, "Table two over here, line up next to table one," and more children ask, "What for?" She does this for table three and table four and each time the children ask, "Why, what are we going to do?" When the children are lined up in four lines of five each, spaced so that they are not touching one another, Edith puts on a new record and leads the class in calisthenics, to the accompaniment of the record. The children just jump around every which way in their places instead of doing the exercises, and by the time the record is finished, Edith, the only one following it, seems exhausted. She is apparently adopting the President's new "Physical Fitness" program in her classroom.

At 1:35 Edith pulls her chair to the easels and calls the children to sit on the floor in front of her, table by table. When they are all seated she asks, "What are you going to do for worktime today?" Different children raise their hands and tell Edith what they are going to draw. Most are going to make pictures of animals they saw in the zoo. Edith asks if they want to make pictures to send to Mark in the hospital, and the children agree to this. Edith gives drawing paper to the children, calling them to her one by one. After getting a piece of paper, the children go to the crayon box on the right-hand shelves, select a number of colors, and go to the tables, where they begin drawing. Edith is again trying to quiet the perpetually talking girls. She keeps two of them standing by her so they won't disrupt the others. She asks them, "Why do you feel you have to talk all the time," and then scolds them for not listening to her. Then she sends them to their tables to draw.

Most of the children are drawing at their tables, sitting or kneeling in their chairs. They are all working very industriously and, engrossed in their work, very quietly. Three girls have chosen to paint at the easels, and having donned their smocks, they are busily mixing colors and intently applying them to their pictures. If the children at the tables are primitives and neo-realists in their animal depictions, these girls at the easels are the class abstract-expressionists, with their broad-stroked, colorful paintings.

Edith asks of the children generally, "What color should I make the cover of Mark's book?" Brown and green are suggested by some children "because Mark likes them." The other children are puzzled as to just what is going on and ask, "What book?" or "What does she mean?" Edith explains what she thought was clear to them already, that they are all going to put their pictures together in a "book" to be sent to Mark. She goes to a small table in the play-kitchen corner and tells the children to bring her their pictures when they are finished and she will write their message for Mark on them.

By 1:50 most children have finished their pictures and given them to Edith. She talks with some of them as she ties the bundle of pictures together—answering questions, listening, carrying on conversations. The children are playing in various parts of the room with toys, games, and blocks they have taken off the shelves. They also move from table to table examining each other's pictures, offering compliments and suggestions. Three girls at a table are cutting up colored paper for a collage. Another girl is walking about the room in a pair of high heels with a woman's purse over her arm. Three boys are playing in the center of the room with the large block set, with which they are building walk-ways and walking on them. Edith is very much concerned about their safety and comes over a number of times to fuss over them. Two or three other boys are driving trucks around the center of the room, and mild altercations occur when they drive through the block constructions. Some boys and girls are playing at the toy store, two girls are serving "tea" in the play kitchen and one is washing a doll baby. Two boys have elected to clean the room, and with large sponges they wash the movable blackboard, the puppet stage, and then begin on the tables. They run into resistance from the children who are working with construction toys on the tables and do not want to dismantle their structures. The class is like a room full of bees, each intent on pursuing some activity, occasionally bumping into one another, but just veering off in another direction without serious altercation. At 2:05 the custodian arrives pushing a cart loaded with half-pint milk containers. He places a tray of cartons on the counter next to the sink, then leaves. His coming and going is unnoticed in the room (as, incidentally, is the presence of the observer, who is completely ignored by the children for the entire afternoon).

At 2:15 Edith walks to the entrance of the room, switches off the lights, and sits at the piano and plays. The children begin spontaneously singing the song, which is "Clean up, clean up. Everybody clean up." Edith walks around the room supervising the clean-up. Some children put their toys, the blocks, puzzles, games, and so on back on their shelves under the windows. The children making a collage keep right on working. A child from another class comes in to borrow the 45-rpm adaptor for the record player. At more urging from Edith the rest of the children shelve their toys and work. The children are sitting around their tables now and Edith asks, "What record would you like to hear while you have your milk?" There is some confusion and no general consensus, so Edith drops the subject and begins to call the children, table by table, to come get their milk.

"Table one," she says, and the five children come to the sink, wash their hands and dry them, pick up a carton of milk and a straw, and take it back to their table. Two talking girls wander about the room interfering with the children getting their milk and Edith calls out to them to "settle down." As the children sit many of them call out to Edith the name of the record they want to hear. When all the children are seated at tables with milk, Edith plays one of these records called "Bozo and the Birds" and shows the children pictures in a book which go with the record. The record recites, and the book shows the adventures of a clown, Bozo, as he walks through a woods meeting many different kinds of birds who, of course, display the characteristics of many kinds of people or, more accurately, different stereotypes. As children finish their milk they take blankets or pads from the shelves under the windows and lie on them in the center of the room, where Edith sits on her chair showing the pictures. By 2:30 half the class is lying on the floor on their blankets, the record is still playing and the teacher is turning the pages of the book. The child who came in previously returns the 45-rpm adaptor, and one of the kindergarteners tells Edith what the boy's name is and where he lives.

The record ends at 2:40. Edith says, "Children, down on your blankets." All the class is lying on blankets now, Edith refuses to answer the various questions individual children put to her because, she tells them, "it's rest time now." Instead she talks very softly about what they will do tomorrow. They are going to work with clay, she says. The children lie quietly and listen. One of the boys raises his hand and when called on tells Edith, "The animals in the zoo looked so hungry yesterday." Edith asks the children what they think about this and a number try to volunteer opinions, but Edith accepts only those offered in a "rest-time tone," that is, softly and quietly. After a brief discussion of animal feeding, Edith calls the names of the two children on milk detail and has them collect empty milk cartons from the tables and return them to the tray. She asks the two children on clean-up detail to clean up the room. Then she gets up from her chair and goes to the door to turn on the lights. At this signal the children all get up from the floor and return their blankets and pads to the shelf. It is raining (the reason for no outside play this afternoon) and cars driven by mothers clog the school drive and line up along the street. One of the talkative little girls comes over to Edith and pointing out the window says, "Mrs. Kerr, see my mother in the new Cadillac?"

At 2:50 Edith sits at the piano and plays. The children sit on the floor in the center of the room and sing. They have a repertoire of songs about animals, including one in which each child sings a refrain alone. They know these by heart and sing along through the ringing of the 2:55 bell. When the song is finished, Edith gets up and coming to the group says, "Okay, rhyming words to get your coats today." The children raise their hands and as Edith calls on them, they tell her two rhyming words, after which they are allowed to go into the hall to get their coats and sweaters. They return to the room with these and sit at their tables. At 2:59 Edith says, "When you have your coats on, you may line up at the door." Half of the children go to the door and stand in a long line. When the three o'clock bell rings, Edith returns to the piano and plays. The children sing a song called "Goodbye," after which Edith sends them out.

## TRAINING FOR LEARNING AND FOR LIFE

The day in kindergarten at Wright School illustrates both the content of the student role as it has been learned by these children and the processes by which the teacher has brought about this learning, or, "taught" them the student role. The children have learned to go through routines and to follow orders with unquestioning obedience, even when these make no sense to them. They have been disciplined to do as they are told by an authoritative person without significant protest. Edith has developed this discipline in the children by creating and enforcing a rigid social structure in the classroom through which she effectively controls the behavior of most of the children for most of the school day. The "living with others in a small society" the school pamphlet tells parents is the most important thing the children will learn in kindergarten can be seen now in its operational meaning, which is learning to live by the routines imposed by the school. This learning appears to be the principal content of the student role.

Children who submit to school-imposed discipline and come to identify with it, so that being a "good student" comes to be an important part of their developing identities, become the good students by the school's definitions. Those who submit to the routines of the school but do not come to identify with them will be adequate students who find the more important part of their identities elsewhere, such as in the play group outside school. Children who refuse to submit to the school routines are rebels, who become known as "bad students" and often "problem children" in the school, for they do not learn the academic curriculum and their behavior is often disruptive in the classroom. Today schools engage clinical psychologists in part to help teachers deal with such children.

In looking at Edith's kindergarten at Wright School, it is interesting to ask how the children learn this role of student—come to accept school-imposed routines—and what, exactly, it involves in terms of behavior and attitudes. The most prominent features of the classroom are its physical and social structures. The room is carefully furnished and arranged in ways adults feel will interest children. The play store and play kitchen in the back of the room, for example, imply that children are interested in mimicking these activities of the adult world. The only space left for the children to create something of their own is the empty center of the room, and the materials at their disposal are the blocks, whose use causes anxiety on the part of the teacher. The room, being carefully organized physically by the adults, leaves little room for the creation of physical organization on the part of the children.

The social structure created by Edith is a far more powerful and subtle force for fitting the children to the student role. This structure is established by the very rigid and tightly controlled set of rituals and routines through which the children are put during the day. There is first the rigid "locating procedure" in which the children are asked to find themselves in terms of the month, date, day of the week, and the number of the class who are present and absent. This puts them solidly in the real world as defined by adults. The day is then divided into six periods whose activities are for the most part determined by the teacher. In Edith's kindergarten the children went through Serious Time, which opens the school day, Sharing Time, Play Time (which in clear weather would be spent outside), Work Time, Clean-up Time, after which they have their milk, and Rest Time, after which they go home. The teacher has programmed activities for each of these Times.

Occasionally the class is allowed limited discretion to choose between proffered activities, such as stories or records, but original ideas for activities are never solicited from them. Opportunity for free individual action is open only once in the day, during the part of Work Time left after the general class assignment has been completed (on the day reported the class assignment was drawing animal pictures for the absent Mark). Spontaneous interests or observations from the children are never developed by the teacher. It seems that her schedule just does not allow room for developing such unplanned events. During Sharing Time, for example, the child who brought a bird's nest told Edith, in reply to her question of what kind of bird made it, "My friend says it's a rain bird." Edith does not think to ask about this bird, probably because the answer is "childish"; that is, not given in accepted adult categories of birds. The children then express great interest in an object in the nest, but the teacher ignores this interest, probably because the object is uninteresting to her. The soldiers from "Babes in Toyland" strike a responsive note in the children, but this is not used for a discussion of any kind. The soldiers are treated in the same way as objects which bring little interest from the children. Finally, at the end of Sharing Time the child-world of perception literally erupts in the class with the recollection of "the spooky house" at the zoo. Apparently this made more of an impression on the children than did any of the animals, but Edith is unable to make any sense of it for herself. The tightly imposed order of the class begins to break down as the children discover a universe of discourse of their own and begin talking excitedly with one another. The teacher is effectively excluded from this child's world of perception and for a moment she fails to dominate the classroom situation. She reasserts control, however, by taking the children to the next activity she has planned for the day. It seems never to have occurred to Edith that there might be a meaningful learning experience for the children in re-creating the "spooky house" in the classroom. It seems fair to say that this would have offered an exercise in spontaneous self-expression and an opportunity for real creativity on the part of the children. Instead, they are taken through a canned animal imitation procedure, an activity they apparently enjoy but which is also imposed upon them rather than created by them.

While children's perceptions of the world and opportunities for genuine spontaneity and creativity are being systematically eliminated from the kindergarten, unquestioned obedience to authority and rote learning of meaningless material are being encouraged. When the children are called to line up in the center of the room they ask "Why?" and "What for?" as they are in the very process of complying. They have learned to go smoothly through a programmed day, regardless of whether parts of the program make any sense to them or not. Here the student role involves what might be called "doing what you're told and never mind why." Activities that might "make sense" to the children are effectively ruled out and they are forced or induced to participate in activities that may be "senseless," such as the calisthenics.

At the same time the children are being taught by rote meaningless sounds in the ritual oaths and songs, such as the Lord's Prayer, the Pledge to the Flag, and "America." As they go through the grades children learn more and more of the sounds of these ritual oaths, but the fact that they have often learned meaningless sounds rather than meaningful statements is shown when they are asked to write these out in the sixth grade; they write them as groups of sounds rather than as a series of words, according to the sixth grade teachers at Wright School. Probably much learning in the elementary grades is of this character; that is, having no intrinsic meaning to the children but rather being tasks inexplicably required of them by authoritative adults. Listening to sixth grade children read social studies reports, for example, in which they have copied material from encyclopedias about a particular country, an observer often gets the feeling that he is watching an activity which has no intrinsic meaning for the child. The child who reads, "Switzerland grows wheat and cows and grass and makes a lot of cheese" knows the dictionary meaning of each of these words but may very well have no conception at all of this "thing" called Switzerland. He is simply carrying out a task assigned by the teacher *because* it is assigned, and this may be its only "meaning" for him.

Another type of learning that takes place in kindergarten is seen in children who take advantage of the "holes" in the adult social structure to create activities of their own, during Work Time or out-of-doors during Play Time. Here the children are learning to carve out a small world of their own within the world created by adults. They very quickly learn that if they keep within permissible limits of noise and action they can play much as they please. Small groups of children formed during the year in Edith's kindergarten who played together at these times, developing semi-independent little groups in which they created their own worlds in the interstices of the adult-imposed physical and social world. These groups remind the sociological observer very much of the so-called "informal groups" adults develop in factories and offices of large bureaucracies.[5] Here too, within authoritatively imposed social organizations people find "holes" to create little sub-worlds that support informal, friendly, nonofficial behavior. Forming and participating in such groups seems to be as much part of the student role as it is of the role of bureaucrat.

The kindergarten has been conceived of here as the year in which children are prepared for their schooling by learning the role of student. In the classrooms of the rest of the school grades, the children will be asked to submit to systems and routines imposed by the teachers and the curriculum. The days will be much like those of kindergarten, except that academic subjects will be substituted for the activities of the kindergarten. Once out of the school system, young adults will more than likely find themselves working in large-scale bureaucratic organizations, perhaps on the assembly line in the factory, perhaps in the paper routines of the white collar occupations, where they will be required to submit to rigid routines imposed by "the company" which may make little sense to them. Those who can operate well in this situation will be successful bureaucratic functionaries. Kindergarten, therefore, can be seen as preparing children not only for participation in the bureaucratic organization of large modern school systems, but also for the large-scale occupational bureaucracies of modern society.

---

[5] See, for example, Peter M. Blau, *Bureaucracy in Modern Society* (New York: Random House, 1956), Chapter 3.

# 5

# Early Experience and the Socialization of Cognitive Modes in Children*

## ROBERT D. HESS and VIRGINIA C. SHIPMAN

### THE PROBLEM

One of the questions arising from the contemporary concern with the education of culturally disadvantaged children is how we should conceptualize the effects of such deprivation upon the cognitive faculties of the child. The outcome is well known: children from deprived backgrounds score well below middle-class children on standard individual and group measures of intelligence (a gap that increases with age); they come to school without the skills necessary for coping with first grade curricula; their language development, both written and spoken, is relatively poor; auditory and visual discrimination skills are not well developed; in scholastic achievement they are retarded an average of two years by grade six and almost three years by grade eight; they are more likely to drop out of school before completing a secondary education; and even when they have adequate ability are less likely to go to college (Deutsch, 1963;

* From: *Child Development*, Vol. 36, No. 4, December 1965, pp. 869–85. © Society for Research in Child Development, Inc. Reprinted by permission.

This research is supported by the Research Division of the Children's Bureau, Social Security Administration; Department of Health, Education, and Welfare; Ford Foundation for the Advancement of Learning; and grants-in-aid from the Social Science Research Committee of the Division of Social Sciences, University of Chicago. Project staff members who made specific contributions to the analysis of data are Jere Brophy, Dina Feitelson, Roberta Meyer, and Ellis Olim. Hess's address: Committee on Human Development, University of Chicago, Chicago, Ill. 60637.

Deutsch & Brown, 1964; Eells et al., 1951; John, 1963; Kennedy, Van de Riet, & White, 1963; Lesser, 1964).

For many years the central theoretical issues in this field dealt with the origin of these effects, argued in terms of the relative contribution of genetic as compared with environmental factors. Current interest in the effects of cultural deprivation ignores this classic debate; the more basic problem is to understand how cultural experience is translated into cognitive behavior and academic achievement (Bernstein, 1961; Hess, 1964).

The focus of concern is no longer upon the question of whether social and cultural disadvantage depress academic ability, but has shifted to a study of the mechanisms of exchange that mediate between the individual and his environment. The thrust of research and theory is toward conceptualizing social class as a discrete array of experiences and patterns of experience that can be examined in relation to the effects they have upon the emerging cognitive equipment of the young child. In short, the question this paper presents is this: what *is* cultural deprivation, and how does it act to shape and depress the resources of the human mind?

The arguments we wish to present here are these: first, that the behavior that leads to social, educational, and economic poverty is socialized in early childhood—that is, it is learned; second, that the central quality involved in the effects of cultural deprivation is a lack of cognitive meaning in the mother-child communication system; and, third, that the growth of cognitive processes is fostered in family control systems, which offer and permit a wide range of alternatives of action and thought, and that such growth is constricted by systems of control that offer predetermined solutions and few alternatives for consideration and choice.

In this paper we will argue that the structure of the social system and the structure of the family shape communication and language and that language shapes thought and cognitive styles of problem-solving. In the deprived-family context this means that the nature of the control system that relates parent to child restricts the number and kind of alternatives for action and thought that are opened to the child; such constriction precludes a tendency for the child to reflect, to consider and choose among alternatives for speech and action. It develops modes for dealing with stimuli and with problems that are impulsive rather than reflective, which deal with the immediate rather than the future, and which are disconnected rather than sequential.

This position draws from the work of Basil Bernstein (1961) of the University of London. In his view, language structures and conditions what the child learns and how he learns, setting limits within which future learning may take place. He identifies two forms of communication codes or styles of verbal behavior: *restricted* and *elaborated*. Restricted codes are stereotyped, limited, and condensed, lacking in specificity and the exactness needed for precise conceptualization and differentiation.

Sentences are short, simple, often unfinished; there is little use of subordinate clauses for elaborating the content of the sentence; it is a language of implicit meaning, easily understood and commonly shared. It is the language form often used in impersonal situations when the intent is to promote solidarity or reduce tension. Restricted codes are nonspecific clichés, statements, or observations about events made in general terms that will be readily understood. The basic quality of this mode is to limit the range and detail of concept and information involved.

Elaborated codes, however, are those in which communication is individualized and the message is specific to a particular situation, topic, and person. It is more particular, more differentiated, and more precise. It permits expression of a wider and more complex range of thought, tending toward discrimination among cognitive and affective content.

The effects of early experience with these codes are not only upon the communication modes and cognitive structure—they also establish potential patterns of relation with the external world. It is one of the dynamic features of Bernstein's work that he views language as social behavior. As such, language is used by participants of a social network to elaborate and express social and other interpersonal relations and, in turn, is shaped and determined by these relations.

The interlacing of social interaction and language is illustrated by the distinction between two types of family control. One is oriented toward control by *status* appeal or ascribed role norms. The second is oriented toward *persons*. Families differ in the degree to which they utilize each of these types of regulatory appeal. In status- (position-) oriented families, behavior tends to be regulated in terms of role expectations. There is little opportunity for the unique characteristics of the child to influence the decision-making process or the interaction between parent and child. In these families, the internal or personal states of the children are not influential as a basis for decision. Norms of behavior are stressed with such imperatives as, "You must do this because I say so," or "Girls don't act like that," or other statements which rely on the status of the participants or a behavior norm for justification (Bernstein, 1964).

In the family, as in other social structures, control is exercised in part through status appeals. The feature that distinguishes among families is the extent to which the status-based control maneuvers are modified by orientation toward persons. In a person-oriented appeal system, the unique characteristics of the child modify status demands and are taken into account in interaction. The decisions of this type of family are individualized and less frequently related to status or role ascriptions. Behavior is justified in terms of feelings, preference, personal and unique reactions, and subjective states. This philosophy not only permits but demands an elaborated linguistic code and a wide range of linguistic and behavioral alternatives in interpersonal interaction. Status-oriented families may be regulated by less individuated commands, messages, and responses. Indeed, by its nature, the status-oriented family will rely more heavily on a restricted code. The verbal exchange is inherent in the structure—regulates it and is regulated by it.

These distinctions may be clarified by two examples of mother-child communication using these two types of codes. Assume that the emotional climate of two homes is approximately the same; the significant difference between them is in style of communication employed. A child is playing noisily in the kitchen with an assortment of pots and pans when the telephone rings. In one home the mother says, "Be quiet," or "Shut up," or issues any one of several other short, preemptory commands. In the other home the mother says, "Would you keep quiet a minute? I want to talk on the phone." The question our study poses is this: what inner response is elicited in the child, what is the effect upon his developing cognitive network of concepts and meaning in each of these two situations? In one instance the child is asked for a simple mental response. He is asked to attend to an uncomplicated message and to make a conditioned response (to comply); he is not called upon to reflect or to make mental discriminations. In the other example the child is required to follow two or three ideas. He is asked to relate his behavior to a time dimension; he must think of his behavior in relation to its effect upon another person. He must perform a more complicated task to follow the communication of his mother in that his relationship to her is mediated in part through concepts and shared ideas; his mind is stimulated or exercised (in an elementary fashion) by a more elaborate and complex verbal communication initiated by the mother. As objects of these two divergent communication styles, repeated in various ways, in similar situations and circumstances during the preschool years, these two imaginary children would be expected to develop significantly different verbal facility and cognitive equipment by the time they enter the public-school system.

A person-oriented family allows the child to achieve the behavior rules (role requirements) by presenting them in a specific context for the child and by emphasizing the consequences of alternative actions. Status-oriented families present the rules in an assigned manner, where compliance is the *only* rule-following possibility. In these situations the role of power in the interaction is more obvious, and, indeed, coercion and defiance are likely interactional possibilities. From another perspective, status-oriented families use a more rigid learning and teaching model in which compliance, rather than rationale, is stressed.

A central dimension through which we look at maternal behavior is to inquire what responses are elicited and permitted by styles of communication and interaction. There are two axes of the child's behavior in which we have a particular interest. One of these is represented by an *assertive, initiatory* approach to learning, as contrasted with a *passive, compliant* mode of engagement; the other deals with the tendency to reach solutions impulsively or hastily as distinguished from a tendency to *reflect,* to compare alternatives, and to choose among available options.

These styles of cognitive behavior are related, in our hypotheses, to the dimensions of maternal linguistic codes and types of family control systems. A status-oriented statement, for example, tends to offer a set of regulations and rules for conduct and interaction that is based on arbitrary decisions rather than upon logical consequences that result from selection of one or another alternatives. Elaborated and person-oriented statements lend themselves more easily to styles of cognitive approach that involve reflection and reflective comparison. Status-oriented statements tend to be restrictive of thought. Take our simple example of the two children and the telephone. The verbal categoric command to "Be quiet" cuts off thought and offers little opportunity to relate the information conveyed in the command to the context in which it occurred. The more elaborated message, "Would you be quiet a minute? I want to talk on the phone" gives the child a rationale for relating his behavior to a wider set of considerations. In effect, he has been given a *why* for his mother's request and, by this example, possibly becomes more likely to *ask* why in another situation. It may be through this type of verbal interaction that the child learns to look for action sequences in his own and others' behavior. Perhaps through these more intent-oriented statements the child comes to see the world as others see it and learns to take the role of others in viewing himself and his actions. The child comes to see the world as a set of possibilities from which he can make a personal selection. He learns to role play with an element of personal flexibility, not by role-conforming rigidity.

## RESEARCH PLAN

For our project a research group of 163 Negro mothers and their four-year-old children was selected from four different social status levels: Group A came from college-educated professional, executive, and managerial occupational levels; Group B came from skilled blue-collar occupational levels, with not more than high-school education; Group C came from unskilled or semiskilled occupational levels, with predominantly elementary-school education; Group D from unskilled or semiskilled occupational levels, with fathers absent and families supported by public assistance.

These mothers were interviewed twice in their homes and brought to the university for testing and for an interaction session between mother and child in which the mother was taught three simple tasks by the staff member and then asked to teach these tasks to the child.

One of these tasks was to sort or group a number of plastic toys by color and by function; a second task was to sort eight blocks by two characteristics simultaneously; the third task required the mother and child to work together to copy five designs on a toy called an Etch-a-Sketch. A description of various aspects of the project and some preliminary results have been presented in several papers (Brophy, Hess, & Shipman, 1965; Jackson, Hess, & Shipman, 1965; Meyer, Shipman, & Hess, 1964; Olim, Hess, & Shipman, 1965; Shipman & Hess, 1965).

## RESULTS

The data in this paper are organized to show social-status differences among the four groups in the dimensions of behavior described above to indicate something of the maternal teaching styles that are emerging and to offer examples of relations between maternal and child behavior that are congruent with the general lines of argument we have laid out.

### Social-Status Differences

**Verbal Codes: Restricted versus Elaborated.**    One of the most striking and obvious differences between the environments provided by the mothers of the research group was in their patterns of language use. In our testing sessions, the most obvious social-class variations were in the total amount of verbal output in response to questions and tasks asking for verbal response. For example, as Table 1 shows, mothers from the middle-class gave protocols that were consistently longer in language productivity than did mothers from the other three groups.

TABLE ONE
Mean Number of Typed Lines in Three Data-Gathering Situations

|  | Upper Middle N = 40 | Upper Lower N = 40 | Lower Lower N = 36 | ADC N = 36 |
|---|---|---|---|---|
| School situations ......... | 34.68 | 22.80 | 18.86 | 18.64 |
| Mastery situations ........ | 28.45 | 18.70 | 15.94 | 17.75 |
| CAT card .............. | 18.72 | 9.62 | 12.39 | 12.24 |
| Total ................ | 81.85 | 51.12 | 47.19 | 48.63 |

Taking three different types of questions that called for free response on the part of the mothers and counting the number of lines of typescript of the protocols, the tally for middle-class mothers was approximately 82 contrasted with an average of roughly 49 for mothers from the three other groups.

These differences in verbal products indicate the extent to which the maternal environments of children in different social-class groups tend to be mediated by verbal cue and thus offer (or fail to offer) opportunities for labeling, for identifying objects and feelings and adult models who can demonstrate the usefulness of language as a tool for dealing with interpersonal interaction and for ordering stimuli in the environment.

In addition to this gross disparity in verbal output there were differences in the quality of language used by mothers in the various status groups. One approach to the analysis of language used by these mothers was an examination of their responses to the following task: They were shown the Lion Card of the Children's Apperception Test and asked to tell their child a story relating to the card. This card is a picture of a lion sitting on a chair holding a pipe in his hand. Beside him is a cane. In the corner is a mouse peering out of a hole. The lion appears to be deep in thought. These protocols were the source of language samples that were summarized in nine scales (Table 2), two of which we wish to describe here.

**TABLE TWO**
Social Status Differences in Language Usage (scores are the means for each group)

| | Social Status | | | |
|---|---|---|---|---|
| Scale | Upper Middle $N = 40$ | Upper Lower $N = 42$ | Lower Lower $N = 40$ | ADC $N = 41$ |
| Mean sentence length[a] ..... | 11.39 | 8.74 | 9.66 | 8.23 |
| Adjective range[b] .......... | 31.99 | 28.32 | 28.37 | 30.49 |
| Adverb range[c] ............ | 11.14 | 9.40 | 8.70 | 8.20 |
| Verb elaboration[d] ........ | .59 | .52 | .47 | .44 |
| Complex verb preference[e] ............ | 63.25 | 59.12 | 50.85 | 51.73 |
| Syntactic structure elaboration[f] ............ | 8.89 | 6.90 | 8.07 | 6.46 |
| Stimulus utilization ........ | 5.82 | 4.81 | 4.87 | 5.36 |
| Introduced content ........ | 3.75 | 2.62 | 2.45 | 2.34 |
| Abstraction[g] .............. | 5.60 | 4.89 | 3.71 | 1.75 |

[a] Average number of words per sentence.

[b] Proportion of uncommon adjective types to total nouns, expressed as a percentage.

[c] Proportion of uncommon adverb types to total verbs, adjectives, and adverbs, expressed as a percentage.

[d] Average number of complex verb types per sentence.

[e] Proportion of complex verb types to all verb types, simple and complex.

[f] Average number of weighted complex syntactic structures per 100 words.

[g] Proportion of abstract nouns and verbs (excluding repetitions) to total nouns and verbs (excluding repetitions), expressed as a percentage.

The first scale dealt with the mother's tendency to use abstract words. The index derived was a proportion of abstract noun and verb types to total number of noun and verb types. Words were defined as abstract when the name of the object is thought of apart from the cases in which it is actually realized. For example, in the sentence, "The lion is an *animal*," "animal" is an abstract word. However, in the sentence, "This animal in the picture is sitting on his throne," "animal" is not an abstract noun. In our research group, middle-class mothers achieved an abstraction score of 5.6; the score for skilled work levels was 4.9; the score for the unskilled group was 3.7; for recipients of Aid to Dependent Children (ADC), 1.8.

The second scale dealt with the mother's tendency to use complex syntactic structures such as coordinate and subordinate clauses, unusual infinitive phrases (e.g., "To drive well, you must be alert"), infinitive clauses (e.g., "What to do next was the lion's problem"), and participial phrases (e.g., "Continuing the story, the lion . . ."). The index of structural elaboration derived was a proportion of these complex syntactic structures, weighted in accordance with their complexity and with the degree to which they are strung together to form still more complicated structures (e.g., clauses within clauses), to the total number of sentences.

In the research group, mothers from the middle class had a structure elaboration index of 8.89; the score for ADC mothers was 6.46. The use of complex grammatical forms and elaboration of these forms into complex clauses and sentences provides a highly elaborated code with which to manipulate the environment symbolically. This type of code encourages the child to recognize the possibilities and subtleties inherent in language not only for communication but also for carrying on high-level cognitive procedures.

*Control Systems: Person versus Status Orientation.* Our data on the mothers' use of status- as contrasted with person-oriented statements comes from maternal responses to questions inquiring what the mother would do in order to deal with several different hypothetical situations at school in which the child had broken the rules of the school, had failed to achieve, or had been wronged by a teacher or classmate. The results of this tally are shown in Table 3.

As is clear from these means, the greatest differences between status groups is in the tendency to utilize person-oriented statements. These dif-

TABLE THREE
Person-Oriented and Status-Oriented Units on School Situation Protocols (mothers)

| Social Class | Person-Oriented | | Status-Oriented | | P/S Ratio | N |
|---|---|---|---|---|---|---|
| A. *Mean number:* | | | | | | |
| Upper middle ...... | 9.52 | (1–19) | 7.50 | (0–19) | 1.27 | 40 |
| Upper lower ....... | 6.20 | (0–20) | 7.32 | (2–17) | 0.85 | 40 |
| Lower lower ....... | 4.66 | (0–15) | 7.34 | (2–17) | 0.63 | 35 |
| ADC ............ | 3.59 | (0–16) | 8.15 | (3–29) | 0.44 | 34 |
| B. *Mean percent:* | | | | | | |
| Upper middle ...... | 36.92 | | 27.78 | | | 40 |
| Upper lower ....... | 31.65 | | 36.92 | | | 40 |
| Lower lower ....... | 26.43 | | 40.69 | | | 35 |
| ADC ............ | 20.85 | | 51.09 | | | 34 |

ferences are even greater if seen as a ratio of person-to-status type responses.

The orientation of the mothers to these different types of control is seen not only in prohibitive or reparative situations but in their instructions to their children in preparing them for new experiences. The data on this point come from answers to the question: "Suppose your child were starting to school tomorrow for the first time. What would you tell him? How would you prepare him for school?"

One mother, who was person-oriented and used elaborated verbal codes, replied as follows:

"First of all, I would remind her that she was going to school to learn, that her teacher would take my place, and that she would be expected to follow instructions. Also that her time was to be spent mostly in the classroom with other children, and that any questions or any problems that she might have she could consult with her teacher for assistance."

"Anything else?"

"No, anything else would probably be confusing for her at her particular age."

In terms of promoting educability, what did this mother do in her response? First, she was informative; she presented the school situation as comparable to one already familiar to the child; second, she offered reassurance and support to help the child deal with anxiety; third, she described the school situation as one that involves a personal relationship between the child and the teacher; and, fourth, she presented the classroom situation as one in which the child was to learn.

A second mother responded as follows to this question:

"Well, John, it's time to go to school now. You must know how to behave. The first day at school you should be a good boy and should do just what the teacher tells you to do."

In contrast to the first mother, what did this mother do? First, she defined the role of the child as passive and compliant; second, the central issues she presented were those dealing with authority and the institution, rather than with learning; third, the relationship and roles she portrayed were sketched in terms of status and role expectations rather than in personal terms; and, fourth, her message was general, restricted, and vague, lacking information about how to deal with the problems of school except by passive compliance.

A more detailed analysis of the mothers' responses to this question grouped their statements as *imperative* or *instructive* (Table 4). An imperative statement was defined as an unqualified injunction or command, such as, "Mind the teacher and do what she tells you to do," or "The first thing you have to do is be on time," or "Be nice and do not fight." An instructive statement offers information or commands which carry a rationale or justification for the rule to be observed. Examples: "If you are tardy or

TABLE FOUR
Information Mothers Would Give to Child on the First Day at School

| Social Status | Impera-tive | Instruc-tive | Support | Prepara-tion | Other | N |
|---|---|---|---|---|---|---|
| % of Total Statements: | | | | | | |
| Upper middle ...... | 14.9 | 8.7 | 30.2 | 8.6 | 37.6 | 39 |
| Upper lower ....... | 48.2 | 4.6 | 13.8 | 3.8 | 29.6 | 41 |
| Lower lower ....... | 44.4 | 1.7 | 13.1 | 1.2 | 39.6 | 36 |
| ADC ............ | 46.6 | 3.2 | 17.1 | 1.3 | 31.8 | 37 |
| % of Mothers Using Category: | | | | | | |
| Upper middle ...... | 48.7 | 38.5 | 76.9 | 33.3 | 87.2 | ... |
| Upper lower ....... | 85.4 | 17.1 | 39.0 | 19.5 | 70.7 | ... |
| Lower lower ....... | 75.0 | 5.6 | 36.1 | 8.3 | 77.8 | ... |
| ADC ............ | 86.5 | 16.2 | 43.2 | 8.1 | 86.5 | ... |

if you stay away from school, your marks will go down"; or "I would tell him about the importance of minding the teacher. The teacher needs his full cooperation. She will have so many children that she won't be able to pamper any youngster."

*Status Differences in Concept Utilization.* One of the measures of cognitive style used with both mothers and children in the research group was the S's mode of classificatory behavior. For the adult version, ( Kagan, Moss & Sigel, 1963) S is required to make 12 consecutive sorts of MAPS figures placed in a prearranged random order on a large cardboard. After each sort she was asked to give her reason for putting certain figures together. This task was intended to reveal her typical or preferred manner of grouping stimuli and the level of abstraction that she uses in perceiving and ordering objects in the environment. Responses fell into four categories: descriptive part-whole, descriptive global, relational-contextual, and categorical-inferential. A descriptive response is a direct reference to physical attributes present in the stimuli, such as size, shape, or posture. Examples: "They're all children," or "They are all lying down," or "They are all men." The subject may also choose to use only a part of the figure—"They both have hats on." In a relational-contextual response, any one stimulus gets its meaning from a relation with other stimuli. Examples: "Doctor and nurse," or "Wife is cooking dinner for her husband," or "This guy looks like he shot this other guy." In categorical-inferential responses, sorts are based on nonobservable characteristics of the stimulus for which each stimulus is an independent representative of the total class. Examples: "All of these people work for a living" or "These are all handicapped people."

As may be seen in Table 5, relational responses were most frequently offered; categorical-inferential were next most common, and descriptive

**TABLE FIVE**
Mean Responses to Adult Sigel Sorting Task (maps)

| | Social Status | | | |
|---|---|---|---|---|
| Category | Upper Middle $N = 40$ | Upper Lower $N = 42$ | Lower Lower $N = 39$ | ADC $N = 41$ |
| Total descriptive .......... | 3.18 | 2.19 | 2.18 | 2.59 |
| Descriptive part-whole ..... | 1.65 | 1.33 | 1.31 | 1.49 |
| Descriptive global ......... | 1.52 | 0.86 | 0.87 | 1.10 |
| Relational-contextual ....... | 5.52 | 6.79 | 7.38 | 6.73 |
| Categorical-inferential ...... | 3.30 | 3.00 | 2.23 | 2.66 |

most infrequent. The distribution of responses of our status groups showed that the middle-class group was higher on descriptive and categorical; low-status groups were higher on relational. The greater use of relational categories by the working-class mothers is especially significant. Response times for relational sorts are usually shorter, indicating less reflection and evaluating of alternative hypotheses. Such responses also indicate relatively low attention to external stimuli details (Kagan, 1964). Relational responses are often subjective, reflecting a tendency to relate objects to personal concerns in contrast with the descriptive and categorical responses which tend to be objective and detached, more general, and more abstract. Categorical responses, in particular, represent thought processes that are more orderly and complex in organizing stimuli, suggesting more efficient strategies of information processing.

The most striking finding from the data obtained from the children's Sigel Sorting Task was the decreasing use of the cognitive style dimensions and increasing nonverbal responses with decrease in social-status level. As may be seen in the tables showing children's performance on the Sigel Sorting Task (Tables 6 and 7), although most upper middle-class children

**TABLE SIX**
Children's Responses to Sigel Sorting Task (means)

| | Social Status | | | |
|---|---|---|---|---|
| Category | Upper Middle $N = 40$ | Upper Lower $N = 42$ | Lower Lower $N = 39$ | ADC $N = 41$ |
| Descriptive part-whole ..... | 2.25 | 0.71 | 0.20 | 0.34 |
| Descriptive global ......... | 2.80 | 2.29 | 1.51 | 0.98 |
| Relational-contextual ....... | 3.18 | 2.31 | 1.18 | 1.02 |
| Categorical-inferential ...... | 2.02 | 1.36 | 1.18 | 0.61 |
| Nonscorable verbal responses ......... | 5.75 | 6.31 | 6.64 | 7.24 |
| Nonverbal ................ | 3.00 | 6.41 | 7.08 | 8.76 |
| No sort ................. | 1.00 | 0.62 | 2.21 | 1.05 |

TABLE SEVEN
Percentage of Four-Year-Old Children Responding in Each of the Categories

|  | Social Status | | | |
|---|---|---|---|---|
| Category | Upper Middle N = 40 | Upper Lower N = 42 | Lower Lower N = 39 | ADC N = 41 |
| Descriptive part-whole . . . . . | 40.0 | 28.6 | 18.0 | 14.6 |
| Descriptive global . . . . . . . . . | 70.0 | 54.8 | 53.8 | 31.7 |
| Total descriptive . . . . . . . . . . | 80.0 | 66.7 | 59.0 | 39.0 |
| Relational-contextual . . . . . . . | 77.5 | 66.7 | 41.0 | 43.9 |
| Categorical-inferential . . . . . . | 52.5 | 45.2 | 30.8 | 24.4 |
| Nonscorable verbal . . . . . . . . | 85.0 | 88.1 | 92.3 | 85.4 |
| Nonverbal . . . . . . . . . . . . . . . . | 52.5 | 66.7 | 82.0 | 87.8 |
| No sort . . . . . . . . . . . . . . . . . . | 12.5 | 7.1 | 25.6 | 19.5 |

and a majority of the upper lower-class children use relational and descriptive global responses, there is no extensive use of any of the other cognitive style dimensions by the two lower lower-class groups. In looking at particular categories one may note the relative absence of descriptive part-whole responses for other than the middle-class group and the large rise in nonverbal responses below the middle-class level. These results would seem to reflect the relatively undeveloped verbal and conceptual ability of children from homes with restricted range of verbal and conceptual content.

Relational and descriptive global responses have been considered the most immature and would be hypothesized to occur most frequently in preschool children. Relational responses are often subjective, using idiosyncratic and irrelevant cues; descriptive global responses, often referring to sex and occupational roles, are somewhat more dependent upon experience. On the other hand, descriptive part-whole responses have been shown to increase with age and would be expected to be used less frequently. However, these descriptive part-whole responses, which are correlated with favorable prognostic signs for educability (such as attentiveness, control, and learning ability), were almost totally absent from all but the upper middle-class group. Kagan (1964) described two fundamental cognitive dispositions involved in producing such analytic concepts: the tendency to reflect over alternative solutions that are simultaneously available and the tendency to analyze a visual stimulus into component parts. Both behaviors require a delayed discrimination response. One may describe the impairment noted for culturally disadvantaged children as arising from differences in opportunities for developing these reflective attitudes.

The mothers' use of relational responses was significantly correlated with their children's use of nonscorable and nonverbal responses on the

Sigel task and with poor performance on the 8-Block and Etch-a-Sketch tasks. The mothers' inability or disinclination to take an abstract attitude on the Sigel task was correlated with ineffectual teaching on the 8-Block task and inability to plan and control the Etch-a-Sketch situation. Since relational responses have been found (Kagan, Moss, & Sigel, 1963) to be correlated with impulsivity, tendencies for nonverbal rather than verbal teaching, mother-domination, and limited sequencing and discrimination might be expected and would be predicted to result in limited categorizing ability and impaired verbal skills in the child.

### Analysis of Maternal Teaching Styles

These differences among the status groups and among mothers within the groups appear in slightly different form in the teaching sessions in which the mothers and children engaged. There were large differences among the status groups in the ability of the mothers to teach and the children to learn. This is illustrated by the performance scores on the sorting tasks.

Let us describe the interaction between the mother and child in one of the structured teaching situations. The wide range of individual differences in linguistic and interactional styles of these mothers may be illustrated by excerpts from recordings. The task of the mother is to teach the child how to group or sort a small number of toys.

The first mother outlines the task for the child, gives sufficient help and explanation to permit the child to proceed on her own. She says:

"All right, Susan, this board is the place where we put the little toys; first of all you're supposed to learn how to place them according to color. Can you do that? The things that are all the same color you put in one section; in the second section you put another group of colors, and in the third section you put the last group of colors. Can you do that? Or would you like to see me do it first?"

Child: "I want to do it."

This mother has given explicit information about the task and what is expected of the child; she has offered support and help of various kinds; and she has made it clear that she impelled the child to perform.

A second mother's style offers less clarity and precision. She says in introducing the same task:

"Now, I'll take them all off the board; now you put them all back on the board. What are these?"

Child: "A truck."

"All right, just put them right here; put the other one right here; all right put the other one there."

This mother must rely more on nonverbal communication in her commands; she does not define the task for the child; the child is not provided with ideas or information that she can grasp in attempting to solve the problem; neither is she told what to expect or what the task is, even in general terms.

A third mother is even less explicit. She introduces the task as follows: "I've got some chairs and cars, do you want to play the game?" Child does not respond. Mother continues: "O.K. What's this?"

Child: "A wagon?"

Mother: "Hm?"

Child: "A wagon?"

Mother: "This is not a wagon. What's this?"

The conversation continues with this sort of exchange for several pages. Here again, the child is not provided with the essential information he needs to solve or to understand the problem. There is clearly some impelling on the part of the mother for the child to perform, but the child has not been told what he is to do. There were marked social-class differences in the ability of the children to learn from their mothers in the teaching sessions.

Each teaching session was concluded with an assessment by a staff member of the extent to which the child had learned the concepts taught by the mother. His achievement was scored in two ways: first, the ability to place or sort the objects correctly and, second, the ability to verbalize the principle on which the sorting or grouping was made.

Children from middle-class homes were well above children from working-class homes in performance on these sorting tasks, particularly in offering verbal explanations as to the basis for making the sort (Tables 8 and 9). Over 60 percent of middle-class children placed the objects cor-

TABLE EIGHT
Differences Among Status Groups in Children's Performance
in Teaching Situations (toy sort task)

| Social Status | Placed Correctly (%) | Verbalized Correctly (%) | | N |
|---|---|---|---|---|
| A. Identity sort (cars, spoons, chairs): | | | | |
| Upper middle ..... | 61.5 | 28.2 | 45.8[a] | 39 |
| Upper lower ...... | 65.0 | 20.0 | 30.8 | 40 |
| Lower lower ...... | 68.4 | 29.0 | 42.3 | 38 |
| ADC ........... | 66.7 | 30.8 | 46.2 | 39 |
| B. Color sort (red, green, yellow): | | | | |
| Upper middle ..... | 69.2 | 28.2 | 40.7[a] | 39 |
| Upper lower ...... | 67.5 | 15.0 | 22.2 | 40 |
| Lower lower ...... | 57.9 | 13.2 | 22.7 | 38 |
| ADC ........... | 33.3 | 5.1 | 15.4 | 39 |

[a] Percentage of those who placed object correctly.

TABLE NINE
Differences Among Status Groups in Children's Performance
in Teaching Situations (8-block task)

| Social Status | Placed Correctly (%) | One-Dimension Verbalized (%) | | Both Verbalized (%) | | N |
|---|---|---|---|---|---|---|
| A. Short O: | | | | | | |
| Upper middle ....... | 75.0 | 57.5 | 57.5[a] | 25.0 | 33.3[a] | 40 |
| Upper lower ........ | 51.2 | 39.0 | 43.2 | 2.4 | 4.8 | 41 |
| Lower lower ........ | 50.0 | 29.0 | 33.3 | 15.8 | 31.6 | 38 |
| ADC ............. | 43.6 | 20.5 | 22.2 | 2.6 | 5.9 | 39 |
| B. Tall X: | | | | | | |
| Upper middle ....... | 60.0 | 62.5 | 64.1[a] | 27.5 | 45.8[a] | 40 |
| Upper lower ........ | 48.8 | 39.0 | 42.1 | 17.1 | 35.0 | 41 |
| Lower lower ........ | 34.2 | 23.7 | 26.5 | 7.9 | 23.1 | 38 |
| ADC ............. | 28.2 | 18.0 | 20.0 | 0.0 | 0.0 | 39 |

[a] Percentage of those who placed object correctly.

rectly on all tasks; the performance of working-class children ranged as low as 29 percent correct. Approximately 40 percent of these middle-class children who were successful were able to verbalize the sorting principle; working-class children were less able to explain the sorting principle, ranging downward from the middle-class level to one task on which no child was able to verbalize correctly the basis of his sorting behavior. These differences clearly paralleled the relative abilities and teaching skills of the mothers from differing social-status groups.

The difference among the four status levels was apparent not only on these sorting and verbal skills but also in the mother's ability to regulate her own behavior and her child's in performing tasks which require planning or care rather than verbal or conceptual skill. These differences were revealed by the mother-child performance on the Etch-a-Sketch task. An Etch-a-Sketch toy is a small, flat box with a screen on which lines can be drawn by a device within the box. The marker is controlled by two knobs: one for horizontal movement, one for vertical. The mother is assigned one knob, the child the other. The mother is shown several designs which are to be reproduced. Together they attempt to copy the design models. The mother decides when their product is a satisfactory copy of the original. The products are scored by measuring deviations from the original designs.

These sessions were recorded, and the nonverbal interaction was described by an observer. Some of the most relevant results were these: middle-class mothers and children performed better on the task (14.6 points) than mother and children from the other groups (9.2; 8.3; 9.5; [Table 10]). Mothers of the three lower-status groups were relatively persistent, rejecting more complete figures than the middle-class mothers; mothers from the middle class praised the child's efforts more than did other mothers but gave just as much criticism; the child's cooperation as

TABLE TEN
Performance on Etch-a-Sketch Task (means)

| | Social Status | | | |
|---|---|---|---|---|
| | Upper Middle N = 40 | Upper Lower N = 42 | Lower Lower N = 40 | ADC N = 41 |
| Total score (range 0–40) ....... | 14.6 | 9.2 | 8.3 | 9.5 |
| Average number of attempts ......... | 12.7 | 17.2 | 12.2 | 15.1 |
| Complete figures rejected ........... | 2.3 | 3.6 | 3.5 | 3.4 |
| Child's total score ..... | 5.9 | 4.0 | 3.4 | 4.0 |
| Child's contribution to total score (percentage) ....... | 40.4 | 43.5 | 41.0 | 42.1 |

rated by the observer was as good or better in low-status groups as in
middle-class pairs (Table 11), there was little difference between the
groups in affection expressed to the child by the mother (Brophy et al.,
1965).

TABLE ELEVEN[a]
Mother-Child Interaction on Etch-a-Sketch Task (means)

| | Social Status | | | |
|---|---|---|---|---|
| | Upper Middle N = 40 | Upper Lower N = 41 | Lower Lower N = 39 | ADC N = 39 |
| Praises child .......... | 4.6 | 6.9 | 7.2 | 7.5 |
| Criticizes child ........ | 6.4 | 5.5 | 6.4 | 5.9 |
| Overall acceptance of child ........... | 2.2 | 3.2 | 3.4 | 3.6 |
| Child's cooperation ..... | 5.6 | 5.3 | 4.5 | 5.1 |
| Level of affection shown to child ...... | 4.8 | 5.4 | 5.2 | 5.8 |

[a] Ratings made by observer; low number indicates more of the quality rated.

In these data, as in others not presented here, the mothers of the four
status groups differed relatively little, on the average, in the affective elements of their interaction with their children. The gross differences appeared in the verbal and cognitive environments that they presented.

Against this background I would like to return for a moment to the
problem of the meaning, or, perhaps more correctly, the lack of meaning
in cultural deprivation. One of the features of the behavior of the working-
class mothers and children is a tendency to act without taking sufficient
time for reflection and planning. In a sense one might call this impulsive

behavior—not by acting out unconscious or forbidden impulses, but in a type of activity in which a particular act seems not to be related to the act that preceded it or to its consequences. In this sense it lacks meaning; it is not sufficiently related to the context in which it occurs, to the motivations of the participants, or to the goals of the task. This behavior may be verbal or motor; it shows itself in several ways. On the Etch-a-Sketch task, for example, the mother may silently watch a child make an error and then punish him. Another mother will anticipate the error, will warn the child that he is about to reach a decision point; she will prepare him by verbal and nonverbal cues to be careful, to look ahead, and to avoid the mistake. He is encouraged to reflect, to anticipate the consequences of his action, and in this way to avoid error. A problem-solving approach requires reflection and the ability to weigh decisions, to choose among alternatives. The effect of restricted speech and of status orientation is to foreclose the need for reflective weighing of alternatives and consequences; the use of an elaborated code, with its orientation to persons and to consequences (including future), tends to produce cognitive styles more easily adapted to problem-solving and reflection.

The objective of our study is to discover how teaching styles of the mothers induce and shape learning styles and information-processing strategies in the children. The picture that is beginning to emerge is that the meaning of deprivation is a deprivation of meaning—a cognitive environment in which behavior is controlled by status rules rather than by attention to the individual characteristics of a specific situation and one in which behavior is not mediated by verbal cues or by teaching that relates events to one another and the present to the future. This environment produces a child who relates to authority rather than to rationale, who, although often compliant, is not reflective in his behavior, and for whom the consequences of an act are largely considered in terms of immediate punishment or reward rather than future effects and long-range goals.

When the data are more complete, a more detailed analysis of the findings will enable us to examine the effect of maternal cognitive environments in terms of individual mother-child transactions, rather than in the gross categories of social class. This analysis will not only help us to understand how social-class environment is mediated through the interaction between mother and child but will give more precise information about the effects of individual maternal environments on the cognitive growth of the young child.

## REFERENCES

Bernstein, B.  "Social Class and Linguistic Development: A Theory of Social Learning." In A.H. Halsey, Jean Floud, and C.A. Anderson (Eds.), Education, Economy, and Society. Glencoe, Ill.: Free Press, 1961.

Bernstein, B.  *Family Role Systems, Communication, and Socialization.* Paper presented at Conf. on Develpm. of Cross-National Res. on the Education of Children and Adolescents, Univer. of Chicago, February 1964.

Brophy, J., Hess, R.D., and Shipman, Virginia.  *Effects of Social Class and Level of Aspiration on Performance in a Structured Mother-Child Interaction.* Paper presented at Biennial Meeting of Soc. Res. Child Develpm., Minneapolis, Minn., March 1965.

Deutsch, M.  "The Disadvantaged Child and the Learning Process." In A.H. Passow (Ed.), *Education in Depressed Areas,* pp. 163–80. New York: Columbia Univer. T.C., 1963.

Deutsch, M., and Brown, B.  "Social Influences in Negro-White Intelligence Differences." *J. Soc. Issues* 20 (2; 1964):24–35.

Eells, K., et al.  *Intelligence and Cultural Differences.* Chicago: Univer. of Chicago Press, 1951.

Hess, R.D.  "Educability and Rehabilitation: The Future of the Welfare Class." *Marr. Fam. Lvg.* 26 (1964):422–29.

Jackson, J.D., Hess, R.D., and Shipman, Virginia.  *Communication Styles in Teachers: An Experiment.* Paper presented at Amer. Educ. and Res. Ass., Chicago, February 1965.

John, Vera.  "The Intellectual Development of Slum Children: Some Preliminary Findings." *Amer. J. Orthopsychiat.* 33 (1963):813–22.

Kagan, J., Moss, H.A., and Sigel, I.E.  "Psychological Significance of Styles of Conceptualization." *Monogr. Soc. Res. Child Develpm.* 28 (1963):No. 2.

Kagan, J.  "Information Processing in the Child: Significance of Analytic and Reflective Attitudes." *Psychol. Monogr.* 78 (1964):No. 1 (Whole No. 578).

Kennedy, W.A., Van de Riet, V., and White, J.C., Jr.  "A Normative Sample of Intelligence and Achievement of Negro Elementary School Children in the Southeastern United States." *Monogr. Soc. Res. Child Develpm.* 28 (1963):No. 6.

Lesser, G.  *Mental Abilities of Children in Different Social and Cultural Groups.* New York: Cooperative Research Project No. 1635, 1964.

Meyer, Roberta, Shipman, Virginia, and Hess, R.D.  *Family Structure and Social Class in the Socialization of Curiosity in Urban Preschool Children.* Paper presented at APA meeting in Los Angeles, Calif., September 1964.

Olim, E.G., Hess, R.D., and Shipman, Virginia.  *Relationship Between Mothers' Language Styles and Cognitive Styles of Urban Preschool Children.* Paper presented at Biennial Meeting of Soc. Res. Child Develpm., Minneapolis, Minn., March 1965.

Shipman, Virginia, and Hess, R.D.  *Social Class and Sex Differences in the Utilization of Language and the Consequences for Cognitive Development.* Paper presented at Midwest. Psychol. Ass., Chicago, April 1965.

# 6

# Education and Socialization:
# A Complex Equation*

EDWARD WYNNE

A group of provocative and romantic critics (e.g. Illich, 1971; Goodman, 1969; and Reimer, 1971) have proposed the radical reform, or even
total abolition of our school systems. These proposals have excited interest
in the press, in journals such as the *New York Review*, and in some academic quarters. But the proposals have not had noticeable impact on the
educational R&D community.

Despite the petulence underlying these writings, their authors are ad-
dressing a basic problem of all education: the articulation between childhood and adulthood; that is, the child is largely ignorant and undeveloped:
how can educators and the education system help him move into productive adulthood? If the educational system is inadequate for the task, we
will have, by definition, unhappy adults and an unhappy, unstable society. But the romantic critics are not the only writers who sense that modern learning and socialization systems provide poor articulation between
childhood and adulthood. A growing number of historians and sociologists
have been concerned with these issues, and have reached conclusions that
tend in the same direction as those of the popular critics. This paper surveys these writings, suggests their interrelationships, and presents implications for research.

## THE PAST

Philipe Ariès, a French demographer-historian (1961) analyzed the
continuing redefinition of the concept of childhood throughout Western

---

* From: *Educational Researcher*, 1, #12 (December 1972), pp. 5–9. Copyright,
1972, American Educational Research Association, Washington, D.C.

history from the 12th to the 18th century. Centering his analysis on developments in France, he demonstrated that what Western society has viewed as the "natural and proper" attitude toward children has undergone continuous redefinition. Thus, at one stage, it was seen as natural that children under ten should be grouped together in one classroom with adults in their 20s, and all be simultaneously taught an unsequenced curriculum that might include algebra, Latin, handwriting, and theology. Or that 15 year olds might be given serious responsibilities, for example, as officers in a military expedition. In contrast, today, the prevailing paradigm includes a homogeneous classroom, a sequenced curriculum, and the isolation of the young from important public responsibilities until their mid-20s.

Ariès suggests that many of the more "primitive" definitions of childhood held because they were supported by public expectations. (See also Van den Berg, 1961.) When, in the past, children were troubled by age diversity in a classroom, or by a disorganized curriculum, they were implicitly told that they were expected to overcome the problem. Neither has society always placed so high a value on cognitive scholastic success as it now does. Thus, some children learned the proffered academic skills, and all of them learned how to get along with adults. Similarly, in the military situation, the competent 15 year old acquired important responsibilities at a vigorous age; if he proved incompetent, he would be dismissed or tolerated, like any other incompetent officer.

Modern concepts of childhood "work" for largely the same reasons the more primitive ones did: they are supported by powerful social expectations, and where difficulties arise in applying the concept to concrete situations, the society is prepared to pay a price to maintain the concept. Thus, modern schools are far more orderly than the equivalent medieval institutions. It is possible that they are compelled to this characteristic by the absence of adults attending schools as co-students with the children (see also Elder, 1967). This modern emphasis on relatively impersonal order may in turn effect anomie and boredom among students. But since we are prepared to accept a certain proportion of bored and withdrawn students, modern society views the situation as tolerable. Again, we assume that teenagers should spend most of their time in school—as opposed to working. When young people are made restless by school or call it irrelevant, we strive to improve school—and usually do not consider that current arrangements for the prolonged schooling of the young have inherent dysfunctional consequences.

The proposition is this. If you believe in some concept, problems that arise consequently are simply difficulties to be overcome. And if you persist or believe enough, many difficulties may be solved or, at least, buried. Each of the diverse concepts of the nature of childhood accepted in Western history "worked" for awhile because of the combination of persistence, widespread supportive beliefs, and social *ignorance*. However, most of the concepts eventually changed because of gaps between the concept and social environment.

Ariès contends that we have been witnessing a long-range shift in youth socialization and learning: from activities that integrate youths and adults and that emphasize affect-oriented activities, toward activities that isolate the young from adult life and emphasize cognitive learning. Further background on this development in American history is offered by Cremin (1970) and Bailyn (1960) in treatments of evolution of educational patterns in America from the first settlements up to the Revolution. Despite incidental differences, both authors largely agree with the evaluation uttered by Jonathan Mitchell in Massachusetts in 1663: "We in this country, being far removed from the more cultivated parts of the world, had need to use utmost care and diligence to keep up learning and all helps to education among us, lest degeneracy, barbarism, ignorance and irreligion do by degrees break in upon us" (Cremin, p. 177).

Many forces in the colonial environment lessened the usefulness of the Old World structures that helped the articulation between childhood and responsible adulthood. These included the weakening of extended family ties due to the geographic mobility demanded of New World settlers, the lessening of apprenticeship bonds as a result of the perennial labor shortages in the society, etc. Such forces diminished the opportunities of the young to learn how to become adults and compelled the society to devise new tools for articulation. One major tool was formal education: schooling would become more widespread and so help to transform children into adults. This view of formal education was an important American social invention. Colonial developments established a formative framework for the appearance of the modern American pattern.

## THE PRESENT

Most youths in contemporary America spend most of their away-from-home time in formal education systems. Thus, the articulation between childhood and adulthood in modern society has become largely the responsibility of the school and the nuclear family. This is an historically unique development, and even within America the development is comparatively new. In 1915 the average youth was exposed to half as much school attendance as his modern contemporary (Dennison, 1962, p. 73); even as late as 1940, 23% of American families lived on farms where a diversity of intergenerational contacts might arise. The current figure is 5% (U.S. Department of Agriculture, 1969, p. 441).

In America, the degree of reliance on school and the nuclear family as socializers varies between different socio-economic classes. While precise studies are unavailable, it is likely that we can construct a continuum ranging from emphasis at one end on school, nuclear family, and suburban contacts limited to a narrow SES class, to an emphasis at the other end on work experience (for the young) and a diversity of contacts with relatives and members of other classes and generations. The one end of this continuum probably coincides with higher SES families and their children, the other with lower SES families. In other words, better-off families tend to give greater emphasis to formal education for their children, their children are less likely to work, and their children will be shielded from contacts with other economic classes. Families with lower SES have a converse pattern of child rearing; for example, there is no stigma attached to a lower SES child coming into contact with an upper SES world. There is such a stigma applied to higher SES children who are in close contact with the poor. (That is one reason why busing is opposed.)

Several researchers have raised serious questions about the efficiency of modern socialization arrangements. Coleman's important work *The Adolescent Society* (1961) noted the appearance of a highly peer-focused adolescent culture in Illinois high schools. This culture may be largely accounted for by the forces outlined above. Since the young have been cut off from most adult life and responsibilities while isolated in school they developed youth-oriented values divergent from those sustained by the adult society. These values varied from community to community, but they tended to center about sports, popularity with the crowd, cars, and dating. Generally, learning achievements were given a low priority. Coleman asked: is such a situation good for these youths or for society?

A number of later studies partly disagreed with Coleman's contentions (Kandel and Lesser, 1972; Flacks, 1967; Kenniston, 1967). While they found that American youths, particularly those from higher SES groups, are highly peer-oriented, they also found that the values promoted by the youths and their peer groups are not necessarily divergent from those of their nuclear families. In a sense, these studies suggest that there may not be a generation "gap" between peer-centered children and their parents.

However, the findings of both Coleman and his critics may be seen in another light: modern adolescents from high SES families are, in some senses, well socialized. They are carrying out the implicit wishes of their schools and parents: but these patterns do not teach the young how to be adults, and how to live in an adult society away from their schools and nuclear families. Thus, the alleged generation gap is not between parents and their children; it is between certain classes of youths and the bulk of society. The youths are being socialized with values that are inappropriate to adult life in the larger society.

Upper middle class families and schools often stimulate certain patterns of youth and adolescent conduct that are appropriate to these limited environments. However, these patterns make for poor articulation between childhood in upper middle class enclaves and adulthood in the larger society. The families and schools do not intend to prevent these children from maturing, but they naturally structure and focus the development of the young. The process they apply heavily emphasizes in-school and book learning, and systemically shields the young from diversified life experiences. This handicaps their transition from youth to adulthood. The children do essentially what their parents and their schools want—and end up inadequately matured.

Erikson (1950) recognized that this pattern of upbringing results in extended adolescence, a period of freedom from many life demands, which he termed a "moratorium." Erikson suggested that the outcome of such freedom might be a fuller and more informed commitment to adult life, but there are other implications. When people are isolated from others, their views may well spring from projected fear and ignorance; thus, lack of relatedness can promote disequilibrium as well as clear thought. Even Erikson, in recent writings (1970), suggested that moratoriums must have a time of ending. As we will discuss below, there are indications that contemporary youths participating in such moratoriums seem to be adapting poorly to adulthood.

Parenthetically we may note that research and analysis on upper middle class socialization is influenced by the tendency of successful American academics to identify with students who graduate from well-established institutions. For instance, one researcher remarked that, "the personal antecedents of the student activist—for example, economic security; committee parents; humanitarian, liberal, and permissive home environments; good education—are those which would promote unusually high levels of psychological functioning" (Kenniston, 1970, p. 172). Whether these antecedents promote "high levels of psychological functioning" is problematic. However, it is certain that the antecedents reflect the modal social values of American academics. Thus, any charge that these youths are poorly socialized is an attack on the values of their socializers.

A reader may agree that upper middle class youths are raised in an environment that significantly differs from that of most other youths, but disagree that such an environment is related to poor socialization. There is, however, increasing evidence that youths from upper SES backgrounds are not adapting well to the transition between youth and adulthood.

(1) A nationwide survey disclosed that 19% of all youths between 12 and 17 from families earning $15,000 a year and over had used marijuana; 14% of youths from families earning between $10,000 and $14,999 had used that drug, while only 6% of youths from families earning under $10,000 had been users (Josephson, 1971). Furthermore, marijuana use was highly associated with the use of other drugs, and with drinking liquor away from home. Regardless of whether the drug should be legalized, it seems likely that youths interested in drugs are evincing symptoms of withdrawal from social concerns. Such withdrawal is inconsistent with the acquisition of adult skills and perspectives.

(2) There is a trend among college graduates to seek employment in

manual labor after college graduation (Office of Graduate and Career Plans, 1970; *Chicago Maroon*, 1971). The numbers of students involved are small, but the signs suggest that the students are motivated by a desire to "find themselves." Should not 21 and 22 year old persons have some idea of "who they are" after a prolonged and costly education at a prestigious college? In addition, the alleged "finding" process is greatly complicated by the post-graduate nature of the work experience. It is one thing to work between high school and college, or to work one's way through college; but when one becomes a moving man after graduating from a quality institution, that manual job assumes a certain degree of artificiality. The Harvard graduate can probably quit the moving business and find work more relevant to his training—the job is sort of a game.

(3) The demonstrations and college unrest of the 1960s were initially concentrated among students from upper middle class backgrounds (Flacks, 1967; Kenniston, 1967). Although student unrest is not a new phenomenon in America, the recent outbursts were the most intense in our history (Feuer, 1969). Regardless of the pros and cons about the Vietnam War, or the students' tactics, it is clear that the protests evinced one major sign of immaturity: despite the energy displayed, the protestors were unable to form any continuing institution(s) for persistently pressing for their goals. This failure argues that the protestors were largely engaged in the cathartic release of stored frustration—and that the War served as a convenient and socially acceptable target of that frustration. However, when youths from our better families and schools evince such intense frustration and desire for catharsis, it suggests that their frustrations may be related to the socialization system that surrounds them, and to the poor articulation between their youth and the adult challenges they sense lying before them.

(4) Interest in communes and rock festivals is concentrated among students and ex-students from upper middle class environments (Houriet, 1971). These activities are highly peer-centered and unrelated to the adult responsibilities that the youths are of an age to face. Press reports and other writings suggest that participants in both these activities are seeking a form of emotional release that is antithetical to the demands of adulthood. The youths involved appear desirous of avoiding the challenges of adult life and of being solaced by a pool of homogeneous allies. Incidentally, in other cultures and in earlier Western society (according to Ariès) communal occasions, as compared to rock festivals, were usually occasions to bind young and old together in intergenerational festivities.

(5) Longitudinal studies show that successive cohorts of college students are displaying less and less pro-social attitudes; Heath found that cooperative attitudes among students (with equivalent backgrounds) at Haverford College diminished about 20% between 1948 and 1968 (1968, p. 67).

## THE PRESCRIPTIONS

The socialization dysfunctions outlined above have attracted the attention of a number of commentators. Kenniston (1960, 1967, 1969, 1970) described the tensions and alienations affecting many upper middle class youths and sensitively portrayed the emotions underlying their rhetoric. Despite his perceptiveness, Kenniston's writings lack concrete, focused prescriptions that directly relate to the environments surrounding these youths and which can be translated into social policy.

But other writers have come up with more specific suggestions. Bronfenbrenner (1970), for instance, compared many aspects of elementary and high school programs in America and the Soviet Union. In the Soviet schools great stress is placed on developing cooperative and work-oriented attitudes in all students. Tutorial arrangements, group assignments, and student responsibilities for school upkeep all play a heavy part in school programs (see also Melaragno, 1971). The Soviets use these techniques to develop skills and attitudes among students that equip them for participation in cooperative work in later life. Bronfenbrenner contrasts these Soviet patterns with (a) the emphasis on individual student assignments and responsibilities in American schools; (b) the assumption that only teachers are responsible for instruction (and the success or failure of pupils); and (c) the relegation of school maintenance to custodial staff—so that student time may be available for cognitive learning. He urges efforts to correct the excessive adult-youth isolation and individualism fostered by American schooling.

The Carnegie Commission (1971), Drucker (1969), Pfifer (1972), and Newman (1971) all conclude that the modern American college is poorly adapted to assisting youths to learn the essential skills related to effective adulthood. They attribute this inadequacy to diverse shortcomings. Many of these shortcomings are most heavily concentrated in more prestigious colleges populated with upper middle class students. The shortcomings include the overprofessionalization of the staff, the relatively homogeneous character of the student body (i.e., referring to age and SES), and the limited work experience of many of the students attending college.

These critics suggest a number of related remedies. In general, the remedies aim at increasing the average age of college students; increasing the diversity of types going into college teaching; and increasing the interrelationship between college and student work opportunities and experience. This last recommendation warrants elaboration, inasmuch as the matter is receiving increasing governmental attention.

Two themes underlie proposals for such work experience. One class of proposals aims to improve many of the recognized shortcomings within current vocational and technical education (e.g., Marland, 1972). Such proposals are attempting to increase the on-the-job training for sub-professional and technical jobs. Presumably, the youths enrolled in such programs might ordinarily go no higher than high school or a two-year college. However, other change advocates contend that upper middle class youths need work experience as much, or more than lower or middle class youths (Coleman, 1972 a and b; Wynne, 1971 a and b). The precise character of such experience is not easily defined; for all their cognitive sophistication, these youths lack many necessary job skills; e.g., tact, negotiation experience. So it is not easy to see where they should fit in. And there is the additional problem of persuading such youths and their parents that the experience is worth the time (and cost; one program providing one year of such experience to high school graduates charges a "tuition" of $4,000 a year [Life, 1972, p. 73]).

On the whole, the prescriptions for better articulation we have thus far discussed have focused on reorganizing a limited triad: the relation between schools, work, and the young. This is an understandable first stage. But the writings of Ariès, Bailyn, and Cremin suggest that this triad is only part of the socialization structure found in all societies. Socialization structures have also included (a) devices to bring together youths and more remote relatives and/or adults from outside the family to provide varied experiences and role models for the young; (b) community structures that integrate youths into many adult-type activities; (c) incentives that stimulate youths to seek and accept the challenges of adult responsibilities; and (d) rites of passage that demarcate the transition between youth and adulthood (Bettleheim, 1962; Eisenstadt, 1956).

The patterns of American upper middle class life are hostile to many of these elements. For example, the focus on the nuclear family isolates youths from adults outside of the immediate family. Specialization, bureaucracy, and credentialism in work—and the remoteness of work from most suburban communities—leaves little room for joint adult-youth responsibilities. Parental affluence has removed a major stimulus that provoked many youths toward adulthood, namely, the desire to earn money. The rationalistic environment surrounding upper middle class life is inherently hostile to ritualized, periodic ceremonies and rites of passage.

In sum, even if the proposed changes in the school and work environments surrounding upper middle class youths were carried out, we would still have poor articulation between youth and adulthood. We may need to borrow a leaf from early American history and try to devise new socialization systems that can correct the shortcomings. One cannot specify the appropriate remedies with particularity. However, the listing of suburban and family socialization deficiencies suggests it should be possible to develop social or legal policies that would stimulate parents to increase communication between their children and other relatives. For instance, if suburbs were reorganized to make large numbers of jobs available for older adults, more grandparents might live near their grandchildren. Local tax benefits might be offered to upper middle class families with other relatives living in their homes. To bring adults and youths together in adult activities and community chores (e.g., garbage collection, care of the sick or indigent) might be allocated to families or neighborhoods, with the provision that the work must be performed by residents, not by hired specialists or outsiders. Suburban zoning codes might be revised to bring more diversity into such communities by encouraging the entry of industry, corner stores, or middle income housing.

Obviously changes of this type would require revision of many popularly accepted values. They would encounter intensive resistance from numerous interest groups, as well as from parents and youths who have assumed that affluence could buy isolation, and that isolation was desirable. Since current social and educational arrangements are the product of many decades and centuries of evolution, immediate change is unlikely. And given the scope of these issues, an incremental approach is desirable.

## RESEARCH IMPLICATIONS

It is evident that more data are needed to further clarify the relationship between youth dysfunctions and their cultural determinants. As such data are collected, we will concurrently need research and development on means of improving youth articulation to adulthood; e.g., the economics of restructuring youth employment, the sociology of youth employment, the effect of community environments on youth socialization, the interrelationship between the varied proposals and existing institutions such as schools and colleges. These questions will require consideration from many fields, ranging from anthropology to social history.

The correction of systemic socializing deficiencies is only partly the responsibility of the schools. But educational researchers can have an important effect on these issues since their concerns are already heavily focused on the young. The following statement by Dewey (1916, p. 10) suggests an appropriate perspective:

> As formal training and teaching grow in extent, there is a great danger of creating an undesirable split between the experience gained in more direct associations and what is acquired in school. This danger was never greater than at the present time, on account of the rapid growth in the last few centuries of knowledge and technical modes . . . To avoid the split between what men have consciously known because they have learned it in the specific job of learning, and what they unconsciously know because they have absorbed it in the formation of their characters by their intercourse with others becomes an increasingly delicate task with every development in schooling.

## REFERENCES

Ariès, P.  *Centuries of Childhood.* New York: Alfred A. Knopf, 1962.

Bailyn, B.  *Education in the Forming of American Society.* Chapel Hill: University of North Carolina Press, 1960.

Bettleheim, B.  *Symbolic Wounds.* New York: Collier Books, 1962.

Bronfenbrenner, U.  *Two Worlds of Childhood.* New York: Russell Sage Foundation, 1970.

Carnegie Commission on Higher Education.  *Less Time, More Options.* New York: McGraw-Hill, 1971.

*Chicago Maroon.*  June 9, 1971, p. 1.

Coleman, J.S.  "How the Young Become Adults." *National Conference of the American Educational Research Association,* April 5, 1972. (a)

————.  "The Children Have Outgrown the Schools." *Psychology Today,* 1972, 5, 72 ff. (b)

————.  *The Adolescent Society.* New York: The Free Press, 1961.

Cremin, L.A.  *American Education, the Colonial Experience.* New York: Harper & Row, 1970.

Dennison, E. F.  *The Sources of Economic Growth in the United States.* New York: Committee for Economic Development, 1962.

Dewey, J.  *Democracy and Education.* New York: Macmillan Company, 1916.

Drucker, P.  *The Age of Discontinuity.* New York: Harper & Row, 1969.

Eisenstadt, S.N.  *From Generation to Generation.* New York: The Free Press, 1956.

Elder, G.H., Jr.  "Age Integration and Socialization in an Educational Setting." *Harvard Educational Review* 37 (1967):594–619.

Erikson, E.H.  *Childhood and Society.* New York: W.W. Norton, 1950.

————.  "Reflections on Dissent in Contemporary Youth." *Daedalus* 99 (1970): 154–76.

Feuer, L.F.  *The Conflict of Generations: The Character and Significance of the Student Movement.* New York: Basic Books, 1969.

Flacks, R.  "The Liberated Generation: An Exploration of the Roots of Student Protest." *Journal of Social Issues* 23 (1967):52–75.

Goodman, P.  *New Reformation.* New York: Vintage Books, 1969.

Heath, Douglas H.  *Growing Up in College.* San Francisco: Jossey-Bass, 1968.

Hollingshead, A.B.  *Elmstown's Youth.* New York: John Wiley and Sons, 1961.

Houriet, R.  *Getting Back Together.* New York: Coward, McCann & Geoghean, 1971.

Illich, I.  *Deschooling Society.* New York: Harper and Row, 1971.

Josephson, E. et al.  "Adolescent Marijuana Use: A Report of a National Survey." Paper presented September 14, 1971, in Newark, N.J., *First International Conference on Student Drug Use.*

Kandel, D.B. and Lesser, G.S.  *Youth in Two Worlds.* San Francisco: Jossey-Bass, 1972.

Kenniston, K.  *The Uncommitted.* New York: Harcourt, Brace and World, 1960.

————. "The Sources of Student Unrest." *Journal of Social Issues* 23 (1967): 108–37.

————. "You Have to Grow Up in Scarsdale to Know How Bad Things Are." *New York Times Magazine,* April 1969, p. 27–29.

Kenniston, K., E.E. Simpson, H.A. Korn, and associates (Eds.). *Student Activism and Protest,* pp. 87–106. San Francisco, 1970.

*Life.* The Big Year Off, 1972, 72 (June 16, 1972), 72–78.

Marland, S.P. "Career Education, a New Priority." *Science* 176 (1972):585.

Melaragno, R.J., and Newmark, G. "The Tutorial Community Concept" in J.W. Guthrie and E. Wynne (Eds.), *New Models for American Education,* pp. 98–113. Englewood-Cliffs, New Jersey: Prentice-Hall, 1971.

Newman, F. et al. *Report on Higher Education.* Washington: U.S. Department of Health, Education and Welfare, 1971.

Office of Graduate and Career Plans. *The Harvard Class of 1970.* Cambridge: Harvard University, 1970.

Pifer, A. *The Responsibility for Reform in Higher Education.* New York: The Carnegie Corporation, 1972.

Reich, C.A. *The Greening of America.* New York: Random House, 1970.

Reimer, E. *School Is Dead.* Garden City, N.Y.: Doubleday, 1971.

U.S. Census. *Statistical History of the United States.* Washington: Government Printing Office, 1960.

U.S. Department of Agriculture. *Agricultural Statistics,* 1969. Washington: Government Printing Office, 1969.

Van den Berg, J.H. *The Changing Nature of Man.* New York: W.W. Norton, 1961.

Wynne, E. "On Mentorship," in Guthrie and Wynne, *supra.,* pp. 230–49. (a)

————. "Student Unrest Reconsidered." *Phi Delta Kappan* 53 (1971):102–04.

# 7

# Lower Class Negro Mothers'
# Aspirations for Their Children*

ROBERT R. BELL

Social values are primarily transmitted to the growing child through the major social agencies of the family, the school, and the peer group. When those three agencies are in basic agreement as to values they tend to reinforce one another and thereby minimize personal or social conflict for the individual in the socialization process. However, there are two general ways in which the transmission of social values may lead to conflict: first, if the agencies of society transmit values that are in conflict with one another; second, even when the values of the various agencies are in essential agreement the realities of the social milieu may make the achievement of internalized values difficult or impossible for the individual.

There has been in the past some disagreement among social scientists as to the relationship between general American values and social class. One view has been that major American values are a part of the total American society, regardless of social class level, and therefore shared by almost all Americans. The opposite view has been that many American values are unshared and often vary by social class.[1] Because the focus of this paper centers on some lower class values the above disagreements are

* Revision of a paper read at the annual meeting of the Eastern Sociological Society, April, 1964. We wish to acknowledge partial support for this study by a Ford Foundation grant administered through the Philadelphia Council for Community Advancement. We also extend our thanks to those teachers and administrators in the four elementary schools who cooperated in helping make this study possible.

Reprinted from *Social Forces*, 43, No. 4, (May 1965):493–500; by permission of the University of North Carolina Press.

[1] For a comprehensive discussion of these points of view, see Hyman Rodman, "The Lower Class Value Stretch," *Social Forces* (December 1963):205–15.

conceptually important. A useful approach for resolving this disagreement has been suggested by Hyman Rodman through his concept of "the lower class value stretch." Rodman writes, "by the value stretch I mean that the lower class person, without abandoning the general values of the society, develops an alternative set of values. The result is that the members of the lower class, in many areas, have a wider range of values than others within the society. They share the general values of the society with members of other classes, but in addition they have stretched these values, or developed alternative values, which help them to adjust to their deprived circumstances."[2] Rodman goes on further to suggest that the result is "a stretched value system with a low degree of commitment to all the values within the range, including the dominant, middle class values."[3]

A related area of disagreement among sociologists has been whether or not values that tend to be peculiar to a social class level are essentially the same within both the dominant white and Negro social class systems. The general consensus of research findings offers support for the position that the class structures of the dominant white and Negro systems are basically the same, at least in reference to general values.[4] For example, in a recent study of Negroes in Philadelphia, Parker and Kleiner came to the conclusion that "Negroes in the higher status positions tend to have values more similar to those of the white middle class, stronger desires to associate with whites, more internalization of negative attitudes toward other Negroes, and relatively weaker ethnic identification, than individuals in lower status positions."[5]

Therefore, on the basis of the research findings and interpretations discussed above two assumptions are made about the Negro mothers to be discussed in this paper: first, that the Negro lower class, of which the mothers are a part, has a greater spread of values than does the Negro middle class; second, that the Negro lower class is similar to the white lower class in its acceptance of general social values. In this paper the interest centers around one category of values—the aspirations (i.e., ideal expectations) given by Negro mothers for their children's futures. In the lower class Negro family the mother has long been recognized as the most important adult figure—especially in reference to her children.[6] In our population

---

[2] Ibid., p. 209.

[3] Ibid., p. 209.

[4] See E.F. Frazier, *Black Bourgeoisie* (New York: Collier Books, 1962), p. 195, and August B. Hollingshead, and Fredrick C. Redlich, *Social Class and Mental Illness* (New York: John Wiley & Sons, 1958), p. 65.

[5] Seymour Parker and Robert J. Kleiner, "Status Position, Mobility, and Ethnic Identification of the Negro," manuscript copy, pp. 18–19.

[6] See Arnold Rose, *The Negro in America* (Boston: Beacon Press, 1956), p. 228 and

the mother was the only common parent figure because no husband/father was present in 27 percent of the Negro families.


## POPULATION STUDIED

On October 1, 1963, experimental nursery school classes started in four elementary school districts in Philadelphia. An attempt was made to acquire as random a group of nursery school pupils as possible from each of the four school districts. The four elementary schools had been asked to provide a list of children who would qualify by age for the nursery classes. During the spring of 1963 the schools had sent home with pupils requests to their mothers to send back information on any children of pre-school age. It was decided to use the lists of mothers' replies from the four schools to draw nursery school pupils who qualified by age and who had at least one older sibling in kindergarten, first or second grade. However, the lists from the four schools were incomplete and often factually inaccurate. As a result it was only possible to contact and interview between 25 and 35 mothers in three of the four elementary school districts. Within each of those three elementary school areas the 15 children picked to enter the nursery classes were selected on a random basis. The mothers of nursery school children in the fourth school district were not included in this study because they were a racially and ethnically mixed group. Therefore, 90 of the mothers interviewed were those in three elementary school districts who had a child who qualified by age for the nursery school classes.

The range of mother interviews was expanded because the major focus of the study was on the lower class Negro woman's self-role image. This was done by acquiring a list of mothers and their home addresses who had a child in kindergarten and at least one other child in the same elementary school districts where the nursery class mothers were interviewed. From the kindergarten lists 65 percent of the mothers were interviewed. Five percent of the kindergarten mothers refused to be interviewed and another 30 percent could not be contacted after three attempts by the interviewers. The failure to contact and interview the 30 percent group was because many of them were working mothers, and this biased the population interviewed because of underrepresentation of working mothers.

The population to be discussed consists of 202 Negro mothers with a minimum of two children, one of whom was in nursery school or kindergarten, and who lived in three elementary school districts in Philadelphia. The three school districts are essentially alike and may be described as

---

George E. Simpson and J. Milton Yinger, *Racial and Cultural Minorities* (New York: Harper & Bros., 1958), pp. 518–23.

almost totally Negro and on the basis of demographic data classified as lower class.

The interviewing was done by three Negro female graduate students using a schedule consisting of 102 items. An initial interview schedule was pretested with 15 interviews and as a result of the pretest about 20 percent of the items used in the final questionnaire were added or modified. The final items included in the interview schedule were designed to get at various aspects of the Negro woman's self-role image; i.e., background data, her views of her marriage and her wife role, patterns and techniques of child rearing, her feelings about the schools and her expectations for her children when they reach their adult years.

### ANALYSIS OF DATA

Hyman Rodman's concept of the lower class "value stretch" suggests that certain subgroups may fall at different points along a lower class continuum. Therefore, through the use of selected social variables an attempt was made to distinguish different lower class subgroups within the Negro mother population. It was hypothesized that *if* the selected Negro mother subgroups were in fact different from each other, they would show significant differences in, first, descriptive social class variables and, second, the aspirations they held for their children's futures. Therefore, the primary interest was to examine the Negro mother subgroups for any significant differences, with a secondary interest in whether or not the mother population can be established as falling into the Negro lower class.

In the analysis of the population four Negro mother subgroups were defined on the basis of their education and the number of their children. The use of education is supported by the conclusions of a number of researchers who have found education to be the best single index of Negro social class differences.[7] The size of family (number of children) has also been correlated with social class differences by researchers.[8] Therefore, amount of education and number of children provide a two-variable index for attempting to distinguish Negro social class differences. These two

---

[7] See Frazier, *Black Bourgeoisie*, p. 23; Joseph A. Kahl, *The American Class Structure* (New York: Rinehart & Co., 1957), pp. 236–37, 276–79; Rose, *The Negro in America*, p. 281; and Simpson and Yinger, *Racial and Cultural Minorities*, p. 686.

[8] See Ronald Freedman, Pascal K. Whelpton, and Arthur A. Campbell, *Family Planning, Sterility and Population Growth* (New York: McGraw-Hill Book Co., 1959), pp. 288–95; Paul H. Gebhard et al., *Pregnancy, Birth and Abortion* (New York: Harper & Bros., 1958), p. 154; Frank W. Notestein, "Class Differences in Fertility," in Reinhard Bendix and Seymour M. Lipset (Eds.), *Class, Status and Power* (New York: Free Press of Glencoe, 1953), p. 276; and Leonard Reissman, *Class in American Society* (New York: Free Press of Glencoe, 1959), pp. 450–59; and Rose, *The Negro in America*, p. 56.

variables were used to divide the Negro mother population into the following four subgroups:

Group A:   Low education (0 to 8 years) and a large number of children (7 or more), *low status*[9] mothers (N = 37).

Group B:   Low education (0 to 8 years) and a small number of children (6 or fewer), *middle status* mothers (N = 43).

Group C:   High education (9 or more years) and a large number of children (7 or more), *middle status* mothers (N = 29).

Group D:   High education (9 or more years) and a small number of children (6 or fewer), *high status* mothers (N = 93).

Using the four subgroups as defined above it was possible to make a comparison of six different paired subgroups. Using 11 items related to the mother's aspirations for her children five of the six possible paired subgroup comparisons showed three or fewer significant differences.[10] In the sixth paired subgroup comparison, Group A: *low status* mothers and Group D: *high status* mothers, eight of the 11 aspiration items showed statistically significant differences.

In the discussion of data that follows, the major focus is on the differences between the *low status* and *high status* mothers. If those two subgroups represent real social class differences then the data will show differences in several ways. First, the two mother subgroups will be different in reference to social variables found to be meaningful in other studies as helping to distinguish social class differences. Second, the aspirations for their children will not only be different for the two Negro mother subgroups but the direction of difference will be logically and conceptually consistent. Third, if the *low status* and *high status* mother groups *do* represent social class extremes in the population studied the other two mother groups (Group B and Group C, *middle status* mothers) will fall between them in aspirations they give for their children.

**Background Factors.**  Do the *low status* and *high status* mothers differ in social class variables other than education and number of children? Negroes born and reared in the south and migrating to the north have been found in studies to be overrepresented in the Negro lower class of northern cities.[11] In our population 65 percent of the *low status* mothers had been born and reared, until at least ten years of age, in the south as compared with 41 percent of the *high status* mothers.

---

[9] *Status* is used to describe different social class levels within the Negro lower class.

[10] Significant differences refer to chi-square tests with differences at least at the .05 level of confidence.

[11] See Rose, *The Negro in America*, pp. 64–67, 228; and Simpson and Yinger, *Racial and Cultural Minorities*, p. 520.

Younger age at marriage and age when the first child is born have also been related to the lower class.[12] In our population 35 percent of the *low status* mothers had been married at 16 years of age or younger as compared with 12 percent of the *high status* mothers. In the *low status* mother group 56 percent had given birth to their first child at 18 years of age or younger as contrasted with 33 percent of the *high status* mothers.

Finally, crowded living conditions have been determined as a characteristic of the lower class.[13] A ratio of the number of rooms divided by the number of persons living in the housing unit was used in this study as a measurement of housing conditions; i.e., over-crowded defined as a room-to-person ratio of .9 or below. Eighty-two percent of the *low status* mothers and 50 percent of the *high status* mothers lived in housing units with a ratio of .9 or below.

The background variables of place of birth, age at marriage, age when first child born, and living conditions were all statistically significant and in the predicted direction when comparing the two mother groups. When those differences are added to the differences of education and number of children the evidence contributes support to the contention that the *low status* and *high status* mothers represent different social class levels.

## ASPIRATIONS FOR CHILDREN

Rodman has pointed out that in most aspiration studies the respondent "is asked to give a simple, single response and it is then impossible to tell exactly what the response means."[14] This suggests that not only should a number of different aspirational questions be used but they also should be examined for overall logical consistency. In the discussion that follows the aspirations given by the Negro mothers for their children's futures are examined for internal consistency within the three response categories as well as to logical relationships between the three categories.

*Education and Occupation.* In the first category the mothers were asked how many years of education they would like to see their son(s) get and also how many years for their daughter(s). For the sons there was a statistically significant difference between the educational aspirations given by the *low status* and *high status* mothers. In the *low status* mother group 44 percent wanted a college education for their sons as compared with 65 percent of the *high status* mother group. For daughters there was also a significant difference in the mothers' responses. Thirty-nine percent

---

[12] See Hollingshead and Redlich, *Social Class and Mental Illness,* p. 126; and Kahl, *The American Class Structure,* p. 212.

[13] See Rose, *The Negro in America,* pp. 209–12, 313; and Simpson and Yinger, *Racial and Cultural Minorities,* p. 490.

[14] Rodman, *The Lower Class Value Stretch,* pp. 210–11.

of the *low status* mothers and 61 percent of the *high status* mothers wanted a college education for their daughters. There were no differences by the sex of the child in either of the two mother groups in desired educational achievement for their children.

The mothers were also asked what kind of occupation they would like to see their son(s) and daughter(s) fill when they reached their adult years. The occupational responses given by the mothers were classified as "office and clerical," "skilled," "professional," and "don't know." In occupational aspirations for their sons the responses given by the *low status* and *high status* mothers showed no significant differences. They were equally apt to respond "professional" (47 percent), but the *low status* mothers were slightly higher in giving "skilled" occupations for their sons than were the *high status* mothers (21 percent vs. 12 percent). For the daughters there was a significant difference in one type of job aspiration given by the two mother groups. Thirty-eight percent of the *low status* mothers said "office or clerical" as the level of occupational aspiration they held for their daughters as contrasted to 21 percent of the *high status* mothers' responses for the same occupational grouping.

When the occupational choices are compared for sons and daughters the *low status* mother group shows no difference in the "professional" group, but there were significant differences in the combined groupings of "office, clerical and skilled" with occupations in that grouping suggested for 48 percent of their daughters and 25 percent of their sons. The *low status* mothers were less sure about their aspirations for their sons' occupations as illustrated by 29 percent responding "don't know" as compared to only 10 percent saying "don't know" for their daughters. In the *high status* mother group there were no significant differences in their occupational aspirations for sons and daughters. Our data suggest a lower level of educational and occupational aspirations by the *low status* mothers for both sons and daughters than was true for the *high status* mothers.

*Marriage and Parenthood.* Educational and occupational items are the measures most commonly used to determine aspirational levels. Yet, other adult role expectations may also be important not only as independent measures but also because they may influence the achievement of educational and occupational goals. For example, if a mother holds high educational and occupational aspirations for her children and at the same time thinks they should marry young and have a large family, there is often, by implication, a contradiction in her aspirations. Therefore, one might expect that those mothers who have high educational and occupational aspirations for their children would also hold aspirations for them of older age at marriage and to have fewer children.

The mothers were asked what they thought would be the best ages for their children to marry. Best age given for son(s) showed significant differences between the two mother groups. Fifty percent of the *low status* mother group responded 21 years of age or under as compared to only 17 percent of the *high status* mothers; and in the older age range 37 percent of the *low status* mothers and 63 percent of the *high status* mothers answered that 24 years of age and older was the best age for a son to marry.

There were also significant differences between the two mother groups regarding the best age for daughters to marry. Thirty-five percent of the *low status* mothers and 7 percent of the *high status* mothers responded with 19 years of age or younger, and in the older age range 10 percent of the *low status* mothers and 27 percent of the *high status* mothers gave 24 years of age or older as the best age for a daughter to marry. As would be expected both the *low status* and *high status* mothers gave younger ages for the marriage of daughters than they did for sons.

The mothers were also asked what would be the best number of children for a son and daughter to have. There were significant differences in the number given by *low status* and *high status* mothers for their son(s). Sixty-one percent of the *low status* mothers and 41 percent of the *high status* mothers felt that two or fewer children were the best number for a son. At the other extreme 21 percent of the *low status* and 36 percent of the *high status* mothers suggested four or more children for their sons. The difference in ideal number of children for daughters given by the mothers was not statistically significant but the direction of difference was the same as that given for sons. Sixty percent of the *low status* and 50 percent of the *high status* mothers said two or fewer children and 19 percent of the *low status* and 33 percent of the *high status* mothers said four or more children. There were no differences as to ideal number of children for sons and daughters within either the *low status* or *high status* mother groups.

A question may be raised that if the *high status* mothers suggest a higher ideal number of children for both their sons and daughters than the *low status* mothers, doesn't that contradict their higher aspirational levels for their children? It is suggested that there may be no contradiction for several reasons. First, the range of ideal children suggested by the *high status* mothers is not greater than commonly found in studies of fertility ideals. Second, with the older age at marriage suggested by the mothers, the having of children generally would not occur until after the achievement of educational aspirations. Third, the smaller number of children suggested by the *low status* mothers was probably a reflection of their personal problems with their own large families, leading to the belief that if their children have smaller families they might escape some of the same problems.

**The American Dream.** The mothers' aspirations for their children in such areas as education, occupation, age at marriage and number of children were generally influenced by the realities of personal experience and interpretation. Yet, a part of the value system of aspirations for children also includes more abstract or less experimental values; i.e., what may be called "American dream" values. The already discussed aspirational values may be defined as essentially concrete and as Rodman points out, "the more concrete a value, the more differentiated a society may be with respect to it"; and further suggests that, "the more abstract a value, the more integrated a society may appear."[15] We would therefore expect the two mother groups to be less differentiated in their acceptance of more general or abstract American values than they were with the more concrete aspirational items.

While the mothers were asked specific questions in reference to educational aspirations for their children they were also asked a more general question about education. The mothers were asked what kind of education they thought a young man needed these days to be successful. On this item there were significant differences between the responses of *low status* and *high status* mother groups. Fifty percent of the *low status* mothers and 32 percent of the *high status* mothers said "high school" or "technical education" with the rest of the mothers in each group saying "college." This item as a general value is closely related to the more concrete item on educational aspirations for their sons. The number of years of schooling they would like to have their son(s) receive and the kind of education they think a young man needs to be successful are essentially the same. This would suggest that the general ideal held for educational success by each of the two mother groups was influenced by what each sees as the reality of the situation; i.e., what each mother group defines as the educational level they would like to see their sons achieve.

A second item focused on a more abstract value by asking the mother if she believed any young man with ability and hard work could hope to earn $10,000 a year. There were no differences between the *low status* and *high status* mothers in their responses to this question, with 72 percent of the *low status* mothers and 74 percent of the *high status* mothers answering "yes." For the *low status* mother group their high acceptance of that aspect of the "American dream" would suggest that on an abstract level they verbalize high aspirations although in the more concrete aspirational areas they do not.

A third item focused on one other aspect of the "American dream." The mothers were asked what they believed to be most important for a man to get ahead in his job: (1) hard work and ambition; (2) playing up to the boss; or, (3) to socialize with the boss. There were significant differences in the responses of the two mother groups with 69 percent of the *low status* and 95 percent of the *high status* mothers giving the traditional "American dream" response of "hard work and ambition." Even with the differences in responses between the two mother groups it is of interest that two-thirds of the *low status* mothers gave the traditional response.

---

[15] Ibid., p. 210.

The data on two of the items suggests there are differences between the *low status* and *high status* mothers in their acceptance of general "American dream" values. While there is a common acceptance of those values by the *low status* mother group it seems probable that for them the abstract values have minimal influence and are replaced by more concrete values to a greater degree than among *high status* mothers.

## DISCUSSION

The data presented in this paper offers support for the hypothesis that it is possible to distinguish significantly different subgroups at relative points along the Negro lower class continuum. Support for the hypothesis was given by differences in variables that help distinguish social class levels as well as in the differences between the two mother subgroups in aspirations for their children.

It was suggested earlier in the paper that *if* the *low status* and *high status* Negro mother groups were representative of the social class extremes in our population, then the other two mother groups (*middle status:* Group B, low education and small family and Group C, high education and large family) should fall between in the aspirational responses for their children. When a comparison was made between the responses of the Group B and Group C mothers on the 11 aspirational items only one showed a significant difference. Because of the lack of difference between the Group B and Group C mothers the two groups were combined.

It was found that on all 11 aspirational items the combined BC (*middle status*) mother group fell between the *low status* and *high status* mothers. Furthermore, on only two of the 11 items were there significant differences between the combined BC mother group and *either* the *low status* or *high status* mothers.

While the two extreme groups used for comparison were designated as *low status* and *high status* groups it was assumed that the overall mother population studied would fall within the Negro lower class. While there are probably some exceptions within the *high status* mother group it is suggested that even for that group the greatest number are at least within the upper range of the Negro lower class. This suggestion is based on a comparison of the mother population to other studies of Negro social class. For example, the descriptions provided by other researchers of the Negro middle class are generally different from what was found in reference to even our *high status* mother group.[16]

More specifically it is possible to make a general comparison of our *high status* mothers with a population of Negroes in Philadelphia recently stud-

---

[16] See Frazier, *Black Bourgeoisie,* Chapter 9; and Simpson and Yinger, *Racial and Cultural Minorities,* pp. 523–24.

ied by Parker and Kleiner.[17] In their study they interviewed a random sample of Philadelphia Negroes between the ages of 20 and 60, and while they did not divide their sample into traditional social class levels (i.e., upper, middle and lower) they did rank them by status (social class) on a four-point scale, ranging from 1 (lowest) to 4 (highest). Their Group I and part of Group II corresponds to what is usually described as the Negro lower class. Parker and Kleiner asked their respondents two questions similar to two of the aspirational questions asked of the Negro mother population. They asked the respondent for educational *and* occupational aspirations in regard to a hypothetical son.

A comparison of the responses given only by the Group I (lowest) respondents in the Parker and Kleiner sample is made with the responses given by our *high status* mother group. In reference to educational aspirations 74 percent of the Group I respondents in the Parker and Kleiner sample said "college" as did 64 percent of the *high status* mother group. As to occupational aspirations 32 percent of the Parker and Kleiner Group I responded "unskilled, semi-skilled, skilled and clerical" as did 31 percent of the *high status* mother group.[18] Therefore, if the criteria used by Parker and Kleiner reliably place their Group I in the Negro lower class then by comparison our *high status* mothers can also be described as being in the Negro lower class.

## CONCLUSIONS

It must be recognized that the aspirational values discussed in this paper were verbalized only by mothers. It is certainly possible that the mother's aspirations for her children may be altered through the influence of other family members, the school, peer groups or a variety of other social or personal forces. However, given the importance of the family, and especially the mother in the Negro lower class family, her values and aspirations in reference to her children are meaningful and influential for the children's future. It seems reasonable to assume that the closer the mother's aspirations for her children are to the lower end of the lower class value range the less likely are her children to be greatly influenced by other agencies and persons reflecting more middle class values. Therefore, the relative positions of Negro mothers in the lower class may be related to different aspirational values transmitted to their children, and may also contribute to a way of life which makes any alternative aspirational levels difficult for their children to internalize and possibly achieve.

The data in this paper provide some empirical support for Rodman's concept of the "lower class value stretch." The differences found between

---

[17] Parker and Kleiner, "Status Position," Table 1.

[18] For this comparison the "don't know" responses of Negro mothers were eliminated.

the Negro mother subgroups, at least in reference to aspirations, suggest a range of beliefs and values in the Negro lower class. Furthermore, the findings offer support for Rodman's suggestion that general social values have less exclusive force in the lower class and also indicate that the closer the mother is to the bottom of the lower class range the greater the deviation of her stated aspirations from those values.

# part THREE

# Social Status and Education

No one doubts that there is a close relationship between education, social stratification, and mobility. In studying social life sociologists rely heavily on factors related to the stratification of society; and education ranks high on the list of important stratification variables. The amount and type of education possessed by a person is closely related to the socioeconomic status of his family of origin, his peer groups, as well as his location in geographical space. Whether he lives on a farm, in a village, or a city makes a difference. Moreover, the status or prestige assigned to the *particular* farm, house in the village, or area of the city is also important in looking at the totality of influences that emanate from the relationship between education and socioeconomic status. Like status and prestige, income is also important in determining education. Although we may pride ourselves on tuition-free public education, going to school still costs money. Clothing, books, travel to school must all be paid for. Above all, after the age of adolescence school attendance means that the labor of youth must be given up in favor of education. For poor families the loss of income from a young family member may negate any idealistic notions of the importance of school.

To Americans high value is placed upon education because it is considered as the major avenue of upward social mobility. As noted in Part One, the schools have also come to be viewed as the chief agents in providing for equality of opportunity. It has been assumed that access to good schools would ultimately solve the problem of inequity in the distribution of wealth and privilege. The school not only is considered a key to mobility but also helps to support the traditional mythology seen in phrases like "rags to riches" and "there's plenty of room at the top." The implication being that America is possessed of an open opportunity structure, at times

137

also labeled as an open class system. The ideology of opportunity and success has long been faced with the paradox of long-term or permanent unrelenting poverty for several million citizens.

In those individual cases when it became apparent that the school had little influence on the lives of children from poverty-ridden slums, the blame for the failure was attributed to the parents and, in turn, the nature of life in the home. As Rogoff states in this section, the two major causal agents chosen to account for social mobility are either education, family background, or both.

When Michael Harrington helped us rediscover poverty and when Christopher Jencks concluded that schools were unable to influence greatly the inequities in the distribution of those material goods and privileges associated with the pursuit of the "good life," our faith in education began to falter. Strong support for an ever more comprehensive educational system had been given in the belief that it could solve one of our toughest social problems, large scale inequality. Such support may have been a convenient and easy way of avoiding a full confrontation with the problem of inequality. This serious problem can only be solved by making changes in *all* of the institutions of modern society, and education should not be blamed for failing when there was never much chance that it would succeed alone.

Despite the decline in the presumed power of education in affecting social changes desired by liberal middle level status groups, education is still high on the list of priorities in expenditure of tax money. There remains little doubt that continued technological growth and development is dependent on people with specialized education. Although voices are now heard that question our traditional ideology of "growth and development," they have not yet reached a level that seriously threatens the immediate position of our large comprehensive educational system. Higher education is, however, currently under serious attack.

The apparent truism that upward mobility was dependent on increased education has also been questioned in the light of contemporary statistics on employment. Minority groups and other disadvantaged elements in the population, such as the very poor, have long found that completion of high school, for example, is of dubious value in affecting upward mobility. The greatly increased number of college graduates has not only lowered the value of the bachelor's degree, but the overproduction of highly visible categories such as teachers and aerospace engineers has weakened the reliance on college education as the surest route to high income and status. All of these developments, and their extensive discussion in the mass media are contributing to a redefinition of the efficacy of more and more education.

The cracks in the shining armor of education is felt differentially in the evaluation and attitudes held toward education manifested by the various classes and status groupings in American society. As mentioned, the lower class levels made up of the poor and unskilled working people, frequently view the pursuit of education as a difficult and hopeless endeavor. Family, peer group, and the expectations of failure seemingly fostered in lower class schools frequently act to inhibit those attitudes and behaviors necessary for success in school. Among groups for whom ethnic and religious ties are strong, going to college and moving up the status ladder may be seen as negative in that it tends to break up the family and ethnic community. In contrast with the lower class, the middle level status groupings respond differently to education.

The middle level status communities are comprised of people who have recently climbed from the working class, and of those who are the descendants of several generations of middle status families. For all of these types a prime concern is the maintenance of their accustomed life style, whether it be recent or of an earlier vintage.

In modern industrial society the middle strata has been the most expansive and dynamic part of the stratification structure. It has been the spawning ground of the majority of new occupations, which, in turn, comprises the bulk of the technical expertise upon which modern industrialization is dependent. Technology implies training, though originally informal and acquired "on the job," it is ultimately taken over by the educational institution. In addition, the ever-increasing educational requirements of the professions, plus the positive status implications of the traditional liberal arts education, have made the college and university a key element in thinking of the middle strata. The norms of businessmen have changed. No longer is the young man urged to start in business at the bottom by climbing the ladder from "office boy to chairman of the board." This approach has been relinquished in favor of college first and work later, preferably with a Master of Business Administration degree in hand. In general, credentials have become of increasing importance in the modern society.

In the middle strata the importance of credentials is intensified. Most of the breadwinners in middle level families are employed in large bureaucratic organizations, be they business, governmental, religious or educational; and the ability of a father to pass on his position in a large organization is virtually impossible. Middle class parents are usually concerned that their children end up living at roughly the same status level as themselves. To insure this they perceive that the best legacy they can leave their children is to provide them with the opportunity for a "good" education. Good often means the kind of education that is most likely to facilitate the maintenance of the status of the family.

In former times middle class families hoped to leave a legacy consisting of a business and/or other assets that would insure their offspring a reasonable level of living. Present-day levels of consumption in the middle strata make the accumulation of such wealth almost impossible. High consumption, the threats of status loss for the next generation, and the assumption that some kind of advanced education will "pay off" in prestige and income, has caused many parents to go to unusual lengths to insure that their children will have the full opportunity of going to a college or university.

The perceived necessity of a college education for the maintenance of middle level life styles reaches such intensity that parents frequently put undue psychological pressure on their offspring to "succeed" in grade school and high school in order to go to college. Youth subjected to parental pressures of this sort frequently rebel with the result that colleges and universities contain substantial numbers who are disorganized and unmotivated, when it comes to academic work. This phenomenon helps to account for the large numbers of youth who enter college but leave before earning a degree.

The norms that lead such large proportions of youth from the middle strata to spend 14 to 16 years in school creates a dependency relationship between parents and youth that is vastly different from that considered appropriate by lower working class families. In effect, middle level parents exhibit a much greater willingness to maintain or subsidize their children all through youth and even into early adulthood, provided the reason is educational.

The basis for such an investment on the part of parents is to maintain the status continuity of the family. Part of the reason, however, for urging their children to pursue a college education is the belief that the college experience provides the individual with some of the informal prerequisites for upward mobility. The American liberal arts college remains the best place, next to the family and kingroup, for acquiring "taste and breeding," both of which are considered important for upward mobility as well as maintaining status in the middle strata.

The upper class and top elite status groups have a somewhat different conception of education from that exhibited in the ranks below them. Upper class children are usually sent to private schools, which tend to be somewhat exclusive in that children of the same high status and affluent life style spend most if not all of their school years with their status peers. The norms governing upper class education tend to stress individual growth and development rather than competition for place and vocational objectives. Although most male members of the upper strata in the United States have a vocation and work at some kind of appropriate job, the emphasis on vocational training is highly selective. It is primarily only in cases involving offspring who desire to go into the traditional professions such as law or medicine, who are oriented toward vocational education. In general, a liberal arts degree from a prestigious college or university is the common educational objective for upper class members. Attendance at an appropriate college should involve participation and the establishment of friendship relationships with one's upper status peers. Thus, membership in a prestigious student club at an Ivy League school is considered more important than grades or recommendations from professors.

For the upper status family, education is considered as part of a carefully orchestrated environment for the socialization of the next generation. The socialization is oriented toward learning the values and norms of a substantial number of socially interrelated families, as well as kingroups, who have a distinctive life style governed to a considerable extent by early access to wealth, power, and prestige.

For a member of the upper class the educational process can be carefully controlled, a characteristic that is in sharp contrast to the lack of choice and control available to the lower class and generally to the middle strata, as well.

Sociological research clearly points to some of the phenomena that affirm the importance of the critical relationship between education and stratification and mobility.

# 8

# Education and Class*

## P.G. SQUIBB

"The social system is, to be sure, made up of the relationships of individuals, but it is a system which is organized around the problems inherent in or arising from social interaction of a plurality of individual actors rather than around the problems which arise in connection with the integration of the actions of an individual actor. . . ."

Parsons, T. and Shils, E. (1962)

"To be aware of the idea of social structure and to use it with sensibility is to . . . possess the sociological imagination."

Mills, C. Wright (1970)

"We can speak sensibly of social stratification in relatively stable societies only, where the same class has dominated . . . for many generations, . . . shaping for many decades the uniform cultural framework for the processes of socialising individuals . . . their values, which are functional to the existing social system and therefore supported by all means the dominating class can utilize, become an integral part of the common culture; they are internalized during and through the process of societally organized education; general consensus concerning the inequality of social positions . . . is an outcome of this process. . . . Thus the final result is the emergence of large self-accepting and self-perpetuating groups, having an attitude of superiority towards some, and of inferiority towards others."

Bauman, Z. (1967)

* From: *Educational Research,* Vol. 15, #3 (June 1973), pp. 194–209. Reprinted by permission.

I must express gratitude for comments and suggestions to Douglas Barnes of Leeds University and Simon Frith of Warwick University.

142

## A THEORETICAL FRAMEWORK

That there is some connection between the value systems of socioeconomic groups and their educational attainment has been adequately demonstrated by much empirical research. Research has also shown some connection between values, attainment, and social mobility (Banks, 1968). It is, I think, obvious that some values must, over time, come to be shared by all groups, or at least by most groups, within an on-going social system and that these values must include differential evaluation of self and other. In social research in education, however, there has generally been a failure to see these values as part of a universal, self-sustaining pattern. Consequently, variations in values, differences between sub-cultural attributes, as for example differences in aspiration and motivation and differences in language usage between the classes, have tended to be seen as dysfunctional to the social system as a whole (Musgrave. 1965; Clegg and Megson, 1968). Owing to this failure to see the various parts of the overarching value system as complementary there has been the far more important failure to see the connections among the sub-value system, the stratification system, and the social system. As a result, social and educational reformers have gone on to propose measures designed to bring about changes in particular parts of the value system without reference to the effect this may, theoretically, have on other sets of values; nor have they tried to anticipate the ways in which other social groups, who may feel threatened by the proposed reforms, may seek to protect themselves and restore the previous balance of evaluations. Most important, however, due to the failure to see values as related to the social system as a whole, they have proposed remedies largely condemned to failure from the start or that will produce results different from those intended. One example of this is the general interpretation by the teaching profession of Bernstein's theories as meaning that all we have to do is to increase the vocabulary of the working-class child. Another is the inability of the teacher training institutions to give their students a professional ideology that can resist for long the retraining or detraining that goes on in the staffrooms of schools (Perry, 1969).

Of course, in a perfectly rigid stratified society the distributed values will be such that no one will seek to change the social structure; mobility will not exist and the members of each stratum will accept as immutable not only the rightness of their own position but also that of all other groups superior or inferior to themselves. In such a society there will be no socio-psychological motivation to move; self-perception and perception of others will be such that ambition will be confined to the ends attainable within the groups and not beyond its boundaries. In a society subject to some change, internal or external, where there are, as a consequence, discernible redistributions of wealth, power, or status, there will develop areas in which values will overlap and come to be shared by members of adjoining strata. Also values will begin to be questioned by those who see others, hitherto superior or inferior, change their position. In a perfectly mobile society, a model probably even theoretically impossible, one would expect one common value system to be held by all that did not differentiate between groups.

British society, of course, lies somewhere between the two ideal extremes. There is some mobility, the extent of which is in dispute; there is some acceptance of common values relating to the differential evaluation of the various strata; and there is some movement along the lines differentiating the different groups. Research into, for example, educational attainment and its associated values has tended to assume, in accordance with the dominant socio-political ideology, a higher degree of mobility than possibly actually exists (this, of course, hinges on the definition of "mobility"), and more important, it has seen the distribution of values not only, as argued above, as divorced from the social structure, but also as static and not related to changes in the social distribution of power and status. Consequently, the formation of values has not been seen as the outcome of historic forces; research has described the present "what" but has not gone on to undertake the sociologically necessary task of attempting to explain the "why" and the educationally necessary task of explaining the "how."

Therefore, firstly, we must spell out what is known about the different clusters of values and attitudes of the social groups and what is known about changes that have taken place or are currently occurring.

Having done this we must then attempt to relate these clusters to the social experience of these groups. This can only be done by deductive, historical, and comparative methods, using both concepts drawn from the "functional" and the "conflict" schools in an attempt to suggest causal connections. Thus, we may ask what "eufunctions" (supportive of the status quo) are obtained by a given system and distribution of values and whose or what interests are protected. Then we must try to discover what "dysfunctions" are created and for whom, whether part or all of the social system suffers. And we must also be aware of the possibility of "non-functions" existing, attributes that seem to serve no discoverable purpose of interest (Merton, 1968).

Thirdly, having discovered the "what" and attempted to suggest the "why" we must then, if this whole exercise is to have educational relevance, seek to understand the process by which individuals come to accept a given cluster of values and psychological attributes that constrain their educational attainment and how these may possibly, if at all, be changed by conscious policy without causing disproportionate damage to the individual psyche or to the social structure. It is possibly necessary, to disarm readers who may think I am implicitly arguing a crude socially determinist, infinite malleability theory of personality, to say, without going in detail into the sociology of personality, that I am assuming that personality is an open rather than a closed system; that is, its characteristics are determined by social experiences rather than merely modified by them: that social experience structures the biologically given characteristics into the abstracted concept we call personality (Spitzer, 1969).

At this point it is probably necessary to attempt to state a general thesis relating to the various value systems held within stratified societies. This I will attempt; then I will try to do the same for the values of the working class as a special case of the general theory.

The general theory is something like this:

1. A society will create, over time and through the different social experiences of the groups within it, an interrelated pattern of value systems that will tend to give cohesion and stability to the social structure.

2. These value systems will be such that each will give moral/ethical/cognitive/religious/psychological/etc., support to the social structure and its differential distribution of access to wealth, power, and status.

3. Each group or class will have a different perception of itself and the self-perceptions of each group will complement each other. These self-perceptions will protect the position within the social structure of each class and will also preclude attempts by individuals, or segments of classes, to change their self-perceptions and their social positions. The values held by self and other will have the effect of making change both socially and psycho-socially difficult.

4. Difficulty will arise because the value system held by members of a class will contain specific values about their abilities, aptitudes, and potential that will constrain the aspirations, motivations, expectations, etc., of that class.

5. Members of a class who do develop values that implicitly or explicitly challenge the value system balance will be "cooled out" of their "deviance" by pressures from within their class and from outside by other social processes that will redirect them back into their value system of origin. Education plays an important part in this "cooling out" process.

6. In a society with some social mobility the process described in 5 will not operate perfectly and there may well be some signs of strain exhibited by those who do change class and value system but this strain will not be intolerable because of the large area of symmetrical and common assumptions and values contained in the operant systems within reasonable reach of any individual.

7. Education, in modern industrial society, is a critical component of the "cooling out" process although the mode of operation may be different in different national cultures.

Our particular thesis, or the special case of the lower classes in Britain and applicable, with modifications, to the lower classes of all nations with similar social histories runs like this:

1. The value system of the lower class is such that it constrains their behavior, their self-perception, and their aspirations and defines their aptitudes and abilities in such a way that to engage successfully in middle class behaviour is very difficult. The corollary of this is that the value system of the middle class is such that it not only prevents itself from recognizing unexpected behaviour from the lower classes but it also acts in such a way as to reinforce and even create that behaviour it expects from the working class.

2. The genesis of this system of values must be looked for structurally and historically. In other words it is the result of previous social experience; of the way in which the lower class has been treated and of the way it has perceived that treatment and reacted to it. Its values are both the consequence of social facts, the rationalizations of those social facts and accommodations to them. They are the product of their experience and the cause of their experience. They have been forged and are still being forged by socially external and objective forces and by the internal adjustments needed to fit them into a pattern acceptable and explicable in terms of the values and expectations held.

3. In a society with compulsory education for all and where some social mobility is possible through education, the function of education and the role of the teacher in this sphere of value dissemination becomes critical (Smith, 1973). The sting in the tail of Durkheim's famous definition of education has usually been missed: "Education is the influence exercised by the older generations upon those who are not yet ready for social life. Its object is to awaken and develop in the child those physical, intellectual and moral states which are required of him both by his society and *by the milieu for which he is specifically destined*" (my italics). For, although the function of education and the role of the teacher is important in selecting those who will be given the opportunity of attainment and in providing the symbols by which mobility may occur and be legitimated through attainment this is only for an undetermined but small minority; the major function of education is in reinforcing those value systems that will prevent attainment by lower class members, thereby restricting mobility and so stabilizing the pattern of stratification. It is the failure, or unwillingness to recognize this major function of education that makes non-

sense of and prevents the success of attempts to improve the education of the underprivileged, the poor, and powerless.

## RESEARCH

This section is devoted to brief accounts of research and descriptions of the apparent characteristics of lower class children, largely British and American, which will illustrate their value system and the behaviour deriving from it. It will also, of course, include illustrations of the values of other classes and of teachers and schools, which, it is hoped, will show not only the differences but also the results of the interactions between them. The selection does not claim to be complete. It is given in alphabetical order. It is necessary to give it in this way to avoid giving the impression that scientific research proceeds in an ordered and theoretically structured manner and, equally important, this manner of presentation reduces the danger of not seeing social structure, value systems, and the relationship between them as essentially dynamic and dialectic.

One or two words of warning are perhaps in order, however, before we go on to describe the research. Firstly, as will be evident, the level of scientific neutrality is not as high in every piece of research as might be desirable. In some cases "middle-class" values are taken as being "better" implicitly than corresponding working-class values without the author having stated explicitly his criteria. Secondly, most of the writers have taken a psychological definition of personality as unquestioned (the sociologists do this as much as the psychologists!), which means that, not only is their account of the interaction between the two static but they give a priorness and independence to personality that should not be acceptable to sociologists unless, of course, they are prepared to deny Durkheim's (1927) assertion that social facts must be explained by social facts.

*Ausubel (1963).* Ausubel defines intelligence tests as measuring "function or operating capacity at a given point." The culturally deprived have few test-making skills; they are less responsive to pressure of time; they are less highly motivated to do well; they are less familiar with the language of tests. He examined the "critical period," or "stage of readiness" hypothesis and argues that this is difficult to apply to the cognitive development of children. Older children seem to have a distinct advantage in learning new skills. But the result of missing early learning is to build up a "cumulative deficit," which limits later learning. It is from this that the possibility of the irreversibility of cultural deprivation may arise and from the fact that learning becomes increasingly differentiated and specialized with age and the child who has missed the early undifferentiated learning may not have the basis on which to specialize.

*Bernstein.* The following is a summary of Bernstein's early major article, "Social class and linguistic development: a theory of social learning" (Bernstein, 1958).

He discusses the centrality of language in the process of socialization and the ways in which it depends on social structure and relationships. He suggests that observable linguistic differences are associated with social class membership. Middle-class children learn both formal (elaborated) and public (restricted) codes. Most lower working class children are restricted to the use of a public code. The formal code is grammatically more complex, permits greater elaboration of meaning and the articulation of subjective feelings and "points to the prohibition inherent in a complex conceptual hierarchy for the organization of experience." Public language is simple grammatically and does not allow precise explicit statement of ideas or emotions. It is a language in which much of the meaning is assumed or implicit.

Bernstein has several times emphasized that the restricted code is not *per se* inferior to the elaborated code and he says that the educational failure of lower class children is a "culturally induced backwardness transmitted and sustained through the effects of linguistic processing" and is not due, therefore, to psychological factors. He also argues that educational means taken to assist the lower class child should not destroy his restricted code and the cultural values from which it is derived; the "powerful forthrightness and vitality" of the restricted code must be preserved. The characteristics of the restricted code include the following: short, simple often incomplete sentences; frequent use of personal pronouns, but not "I"; repetition of conjunctions; few subordinate clauses; few qualifiers; much "sympathetic circularity" repetition of idiomatic phrases; dislocated, discontinuous argument; much extra-verbal communication.

In other articles Bernstein attacked the concept of compensatory education on the grounds that the working class child has not yet been offered even fair access to educational facilities; that the concept is a value-laden one, which implies the superiority of middle-class culture, and, that anyhow "education cannot compensate for society" (Bernstein, 1971).

*Bronfenbrenner (1961).* Bronfenbrenner sees the lower classes adopting middle class patterns of child rearing, but important differences between the classes remain. Psychological disciplinary techniques are increasingly being used; parents are more permissive, affection is more openly expressed; reason is taking over from personalized authority as a means of exacting compliance; feelings of guilt are encouraged by these techniques. There is a risk that boys in lower class families are not "adequately" disciplined and that girls will be overprotected. Mothers tend to use love-based techniques in all classes but fathers use direct methods with boys in the lower classes. He sees these trends as increasing achievement motivation but fears they will also lead to increases in aggression, cruelty, and tenseness.

*Bronfenbrenner (1957).* Bronfenbrenner emphasizes the importance of the mother in the formation of attitudes and values, particularly achievement motivation. High achievement motivation seems to flourish within families with an atmosphere of "cold democracy" and families with early maternal involvement and then strong pressures for independence and achievement. These are the characteristics more of the middle than lower classes. The middle class family is accepting and egalitarian, the lower class family is oriented toward obedience and order. Lower class fathers are more authoritarian. Lower class boys who do succeed at school often have mothers who have married "downward" socially.

*Caro (1966).* Caro's research shows working class boys to be less confident of their ability to achieve goals. He sees the acceptance by the working class of lower degrees of success as a necessary adjustment on their part to their circumstances. They are, in fact, "realistic" and anticipate greater difficulties in their efforts to achieve success by scaling their goals down.

*Coleman (1969).* Coleman looks here at the problem presented by working class children who do succeed at school. He compares the attitudes of the parents of such children with those of upper middle class parents. He finds that both use similar control techniques; both use similar reinforcement behavior; both have similar family characteristics and both share many attitudes of behavior in common.

*Deutsch (1963).* The argument here is that the skills the lower class child brings to school with him are such as to make early failure almost inevitable. Therefore, "school experience is negatively, not positively, reinforced." The confusion and noise of the home means that skills of inattention are learned. The lack of expectation of reward means that the tasks undertaken are "motoric," have a short time span, and are likely to be related to concrete objects or services for people.

*Drews and Teahan (1957).* Drews and Teahan conclude that "the achieving child is conforming, docile, and conventional."

*Floud and Halsey (1957).* Floud and Halsey reported that in South West Hertfordshire material environment was less important in differentiating between unsuccessful children than family size, education, and attitudes of parents. But, in Middlesbrough successful children were distinguishable by the relative prosperity of their homes.

*Fuchs (1968).* The value system of the slum school contains the tacit belief that social conditions outside the school are such that failure by the children is inevitable. This *belief* makes such failure inevitable. The school socializes new teachers into its values and attitudes whereby they are perpetuated. Therefore, failure is perpetuated because teachers learn how to help children fail.

*Golden and Birns (1968).* This reports research that indicates that social class differences in test scores do not become evident until the age of two. The authors conclude that either (1) class does not affect pre-verbal cognitive development, or (2) the tests used do not show it!

*Harrison (1968).* This is a study of "inconsistent" children; those from "good" homes who do badly and those from "bad" homes who do well. He finds that the advantaged children who are unsuccessful in school have similar attitudes to those of disadvantaged non-successful children. The disadvantaged but successful children have similar attitudes to the advantaged and successful.

*Henry (1971).* In a passage in which he is talking about the "randomness" of the behavior of lower class people he says that wherever, in our culture, achievement and security cease to be components of perception, behavior will appear to the middle class observer to be random. "An important modality of achievement is hope and a central modality of hope is time . . . the person who has no hope of achievement or security will have no conception whatever of the organization of behaviour (relative to middle class behaviour) at all." He characterizes lower class behavior as subject to entropy—which is the measure of randomness—and hence of loss of organization.

*Himmelweit (1955).* Here research shows prejudice by teachers against working class boys. The teachers chose more middle class boys as being popular than the boys themselves chose. Moreover, teachers from working class background tended to have opinions that asserted that the "wrong sort" of boy was being allowed into grammar schools today—this in spite (or because?) of the fact that they were themselves the "wrong sort" of boy.

*Hoggart (1962).* "Grammar schools can exert a great—if well meant or even unconscious—pressure to remove their working class pupils from attachment to their homes and neighbourhoods; they (teachers) seek to attach them to middle class values. . . . A substantial proportion (of teachers) not only reject their working class background but reject it with scorn and adhere to their new middle class attitudes; they are rigidly orthodox and wish to preserve a hierarchical society."

*Hyman (1967).* The lower classes have a system of beliefs and values that inhibit or prevent them from undertaking those actions that would improve their low status. This value system places less emphasis upon the traditional high success goals, increases their awareness of the lack of opportunity to achieve success, and puts less emphasis upon the achievement of goals, which in turn would be necessary for success. The lower class child does not want as much success, does not expect to get it if he wants it, and does not want that which might help him to get it.

*Kahl (1965).* Kahl summarizes the research on the social class distribution of value orientations: ". . . their results are comparable and parallel. Simple attitude items were devised to measure abstract values about certain social relationships and behaviors connected with achievement orientation and they produced scales that 'worked' in two senses; the same items clung together to define given scales despite distances of time, geography and language that divided the field studies; and the co-relations of the scales with an outside variable, socio-economic status, were stable."

**Kahl (1957).** In this work Kahl shows that only the boys who had internalized what he calls "getting ahead" values were sufficiently motivated to overcome the obstacles, which, as lower middle class or working class boys, they had to face in schools. He shows the great importance of parental value orientation.

**Kahl (1953).** Kahl argues that the evidence shows that while native ability is an important factor in determining success in the first few years of school social class and related values soon take over and strongly influence the school work of the student. Studies also show, he says, that those students who do succeed in school despite negative values in their social environment usually have strong motivations or important encouragement.

**Katz (1964).** Katz argues, on evidence, that the middle classes emphasize status achievement and utilize a procedure emphasizing personal effort and personal worthiness. The working classes (particularly the lower working class) define success in terms of possessions.

**King (1969).** King claims that the "social value component of the culture transmitted by the School had a high middle class loading." The sons of parents who had been to grammar school themselves held grammar school values. There was a high level of involvement in the school by boys who viewed it as an avenue to vocational success. There was some difference, however, between the declared aims of the teachers and the perceived aims of the boys; the former talked more of educational values, the latter saw the school more instrumentally.

**Kluckhohn (1961 and 1970).** Value orientations are "complex but definitely patterned . . . principles which give order and direction to the ever flowing stream of acts and thoughts as these relate to the solution of common human problems." Kluckhohn sees these problems as relating to the nature of man; relationships between man and nature; the evaluation of time; the meaning of activity and the nature of significant relationships. These works suggest that there are several different solutions which may be given to these problems and that there is a definite patterning of the answers given by the different social classes. For example, the middle classes see human nature as a mixture of good and evil, see man as exercising mastery over nature, place high value on time future and on doing, and emphasizes individuality. Whereas the working class possibly see man's nature as good, see him as subordinate to nature, emphasize time present and being rather than doing, and emphasize collectivity.

**Knupfer (1947).** Knupfer argues that the psychological characteristics of the underdog constrain and restrict his behavior in ways that reflect and reinforce the restrictions imposed upon him by external economic and social forces.

*Kohn and Schooler (1969).* Kohn and Schooler relate social class to orientation and values. They refer to other research by Kohn (1959 and 1966). These researchers found a significant difference between middle class and working class parents' values for their children. The middle class favoured self-direction and the working class favoured conformity to externally imposed rules. They argue that social class is consistently related to the values held for self, for one's children and to orientation to self, society and work. They suggest that these values and their class distribution can be explained as the cumulative effects of education and occupational position. Occupational position is important because it determines the conditions that give or deny the opportunity for self direction. Education is also important because it can give the necessary flexibility and perspective for self direction.

*Kohn (1959).* On evidence from his own research Kohn says that the working class parent reacts to his child's behavior in terms of its immediate results; the middle class parent reacts in terms of the intentions. The working class parent emphasizes acceptance of one's environment and one's lot in life; the middle classes emphasize acting in accordance with one's own principles and assume that one's environment and lot can be changed. The working classes value for their children qualities that assure respectability, "desirable" behavior is not violating proscriptions; the middle classes value the child's internalization of standards of conduct, "desirable" behavior is acting on principle.

*Le Shan (1952).* Temporal goal orientations vary by class. Lower class orientation is seen by Le Shan as quick sequences of tension and relief and there is very little planning for the future. In the middle class the tension–relief sequences are longer and planning into the future develops as the individual grows older. Le Shan says that the child rearing practices of the classes encourage this difference. The lower class train by immediate punishment and reward whereas the middle classes often defer punishment and reward. In a piece of research in which eight- to ten-year olds were asked to tell stories, the working class children's stories spanned a shorter period of time than those of the middle classes.

*Mays (1962).* Mays sees slum neighbourhoods acting as a collectivity or cluster of factors acting together to produce poor schools and poor school attainment and educational deprivation. He sees social, economic, and attitudinal factors reinforcing and supporting each other.

*Musgrove (1965).* Musgrove found that working class parents wanted teachers to encourage such basic behavior as cleanliness and obedience and the acceptance of authority. They also wished to restrict their children's friendship groups and were less educationally and occupationally ambitious for their children. They tended also to undervalue their children's educational ability and potential. If they criticized the schools it was because they thought the schools neglected practical and applied subjects. In each of these attitudes the working classes were different from the middle classes.

*Parsons and White (1961).* Parsons has summarized much of the research relating to value differences between the working and middle classes. The working classes exhibit more co-operativeness, dependence, mutuality, and less awareness of self, less competitiveness, less concern with privacy, less concern with ritual and courtesy; they are also more subject to externally imposed controls and so are more "other directed"; they show less anxiety, they are more egalitarian and prefer informality.

The middle classes on the other hand are more competitive, they exercise more personal autonomy, they establish ego early, they value privacy and courtesy, they are inward looking and "self directed" with internalized controls.

*Reisman (1962).* Reisman's account of the culturally deprived child is somewhat loaded but is an attempt to synthesize much of the relevant work. He sees the "weaknesses" as being traditional and narrow in outlook, pragmatic, anti-intellectual; individualism and creativity are only slightly developed. They show signs of alienation, political apathy, suggestibility and naiveté; they have boring occupational tasks and crowded homes. Their "strengths" lie in the co-operativeness and mutual aid of the extended family, they exhibit less tension and strain, they are more egalitarian and value informality and humour, they are relatively free from self-blame and parental over-protection, they show less sibling rivalry and enjoy a degree of security in the extended family and in their traditional outlook. Reisman describes the "style" of the deprived child in the following way. They are content rather than form centered, they are externally orientated rather than introspective, they are physical and visual rather than aural, problem centered rather than abstract centered, inductive rather than deductive, spatial rather than temporal, slow, careful, persevering rather than quick, facile, and flexible. They have a lack of formal language skills but a highly developed system of informal language and gestures.

*Rist (1970).* Rist's work is a study of the teacher and the organization of the classroom on the basis of his perceptions of children. Initially the teacher perceives the child on social class rather than academic criteria and the children are grouped within the classroom on social scale criteria. Then, over time, academic criteria are used to differentiate within the social class groups. Hence there develops what Rist calls a caste system within the classroom.

*Roberts (1968).* Roberts advances here the theory that the ambitions and aspirations of young workers are determined by their careers and not vice versa. He argues that young workers and dropouts believe that they have a career choice but that the career and employment opportunity structure, the school and the home determine their choice. The process operates upon the individual through the necessity of a "job identity" before personal identity can fully develop.

*Rosen (1956).* Rosen found that achievement value correlated with both educational aspirations and with social class. He also found that those with higher aspirations than the norm for their class also had higher achievement value and under-aspirers had lower achievement scores.

*Schneider and Lysgaard (1953).* Schneider and Lysgaard advance the theory that the working classes seek immediate gratification and the middle classes are prepared to plan ahead and thereby postpone gratification.

*Schwebel and Bernstein (1970).* Schwebel and Bernstein show that working class children exhibit more impulsiveness than middle class children in test situations and that this can be seen as a defensive reaction to the tension generated in such a situation. They also showed that this impulsiveness can significantly affect performance on tests.

*Stephenson (1958).* In a comparison of English and American youths Stephenson found that it was the working class pupils "who must lower their aspirations when it comes to considering plans or expectations."

*Swift (1965).* Swift suggests that there are two "ideal" family types for educational success. The first is the usual "ideal-type" of "cultured" upper middle class family in which the child is stimulated in a general tolerant fashion to develop his capacities in many directions. The second is characterized by its lower middle class status and by a high degree of mobility pessimism, it views education instrumentally as a means of improving career prospects—the father blames his own relative failure on the inadequacy of his own educational qualifications. Discipline in the family is of the traditional type, it is not permissive or tolerant. Because of the lower middle class nature of the father's occupation he has wider career horizons for his children than the working class parent.

*Yee (1969).* Yee found that "the most significant factor" in determining teacher–pupil interaction was the social class of the pupil. Middle class pupils saw their teachers as warm, trusting, and sympathetic, and working class pupils saw their teachers as cold, blaming, and punitive. Attitude patterns of the middle class pupils matched the attitude patterns of teachers better than did the attitude patterns of working class pupils. Working class pupils' attitudes toward male teachers were significantly more favourable than their attitudes toward female teachers.

## DISCUSSION AND CONCLUSION

I suggest that there is enough evidence, accepting qualifications and hesitations arising from the limitations of the methodology of some of the work, to indicate that the lower or working classes exhibit in the context of educational processes a cluster of attitudes, perceptions, and aspirations that are cohesive enough to be called a system tending to be self-supporting internally and self-differentiating externally.

I further suggest that this system is sufficiently coherent and has the necessary width and depth to justify being described as what Clyde Kluckhohn (1961) has called a "philosophy." "There is a 'philosophy' behind the way of life of every individual and of every relatively homogeneous group at any given point in their histories. This gives, with varying degrees of explicitness, some sense of coherence or unity both in cognitive and affective dimensions. Each personality gives to this 'philosophy' an idiosyncratic colouring, and creative individuals will markedly reshape it. However, the main outlines of the fundamental values, existential assumptions and basic abstractions have only exceptionally been created out of the stuff of unique biological heredity and peculiar life experience. The underlying principles arise out of, or are limited by, the givens of biological human nature and the universalities of social interaction. The specific formulation is ordinarily a cultural product. In the immediate sense it is from the life-ways which constitute the designs for living of their community or tribe or region or socio-economic class or nation or civilization that most individuals derive their 'mental-feeling outlook.'"

What this passage does not do—and neither does most of the research into the "philosophies" of the working class—is to attempt to locate the system of the lower classes into the overall pattern of value systems of the other groups in their society. Kluckhohn suggests that a "philosophy" is created from the folk-ways of their community but the folk-ways of a community can only be properly seen as the product of reciprocal interaction between the various communities within a social system. And, I argue, this is a dialectical process which must be seen through time, historically, to be understood. When, therefore, Olive Banks (1968a) says in talking of the influence of material conditions on the attitudes and attainments of working class children: "moreover, even when these adverse conditions are no longer present, the fact that they have existed in the recent past, or were a feature of the parents' own childhood, may exert an influence on attitudes, values, and aspirations for a generation or even more," she is grossly underestimating the capacity for survival of such characteristics, which may make it necessary to go back many generations to understand their origins. Similarly, when she (1968b) is discussing Turner's critique of some of the work on the class distribution of value orientations and suggests that "the expectations and perceptions both of themselves and of others, held by working class parents and their children, have perhaps been neglected as a subject of study," she neglects to make the further suggestion that such perceptions are structured socially and can only be understood as part of a social matrix.

The argument then runs something like this: given an adequate sociology of education it should be possible to predict with some accuracy, allowing for ethnic, religious, and sub-cultural variations deriving from the varieties of past experience, the core cognitive and perceptual characteristics of the members of a definable strata within a stratified society. In other words, given the understanding that the lower classes in Great Britain have been subject to relative poverty, to inadequate housing, to unemployment, to personal and group insecurity, to limited vocational choice, to noncreative repetitive, concrete, physical work, to subjection and subordination, to a relatively higher birth rate and death rate, to a political system that seemed ineffective in improving their lot and an educational system that was imposed upon them and a knowledge industry that seemed irrelevant to their perceptions—given this understanding it should have been possible to predict those characteristics that have been discovered only after much research. The necessary analytical concepts have existed, in Marx, in G.H. Mead, in Durkheim; and the factual knowledge has also existed in, for example, Engels and Booth. The descriptive insights have been there in novelists like Robert Tressel (1965), Jack London, and to some extent Orwell; they have also been seen by people like Lawrence and Hoggart. But all these strands have not been brought together and so the sociologist of education, professionally preoccupied by the needs for scientific respectability through empirical quantification procedures has failed to develop either his imagination or his perspective and consequently his theory has atrophied. As a result, in the sociology of education, we are only just beginning to see the characteristics of the working class child as something other than manifestations of his peculiar psychology.

The American sociologist, Bernard Barber, wrote the following in 1957: "Family solidarity will cause the members of different classes to have different interests in social mobility . . . different political interests . . . different attitudes toward income . . . different economic interests . . . different educational interests. . . . And so it will be with every kind of social interest: recreational, cultural, and even religious." One is tempted to ask whether research like the Douglas work on "Home and School" (1964) and "All Our Future" (1968) is really necessary and particularly to question the value of such writers as Clegg and Megson (1968); for emotion unbridled by understanding is even more dangerous than statistics uninformed by theory.

At this point I tentatively want to carry my argument one stage further. I have suggested that the cultural-historical approach, deriving its direction from the body of sociological theory I have mentioned, would have enabled us to have predicted with some accuracy the "characteristics" and responses of the working classes in the educational context they have been offered. It is necessary to simplify this. The way in which one, as a member of a group, is treated indicates the perceptions other groups have of one's own. The treatment of the lower class derives from its subordination and the structural necessity to maintain that subordination. All known societies have had a differential distribution of status, of power, of wealth. All societies have a division of labour, a division of roles and a concomitant differential distribution of knowledge and a consequential differential distribution of self perceptions. These various distributions will inevitably tend to cluster and certain groups will, over time, exhibit consistent characteristics. Where formal educational institutions are introduced the perceptions and understandings of those who structure the form and determine the content of education will tend to ensure that the educational processes will work to this end. There will be a tendency for education to emphasize the subordination of the subordinate and there will be the development of curricula, methods, and techniques and uses of language that will have this function in both latent and manifest forms.

Jules Henry (1971) refers widely to the work of anthropologists to show that in racially divided societies, in colonial societies or in societies split by class divisions the dominant or exploiting group "tends to organize the educational system so as to strengthen and maintain its own position. The anthropologists stress the repressive and destructive effects on the subordinate group of education by the dominating group."

Henry emphasizes the political use of education to perpetuate dominance and subordination. But the subjection of the lower classes is not only to other men, or to other groups. It is also to the material environment that surrounds them and on which they are dependent not only for sustenance but against which they perceive their own being. This material environment includes not only the urban industrialized world of today but all other manifestations of the work of nature and of man-upon-nature. Thorsten Veblen (1918) argued persuasively that the nature of the dominant occupational pattern created a "philosophy on life" and particular perceptions and attitudes to the world. The environment includes not only cotton mills, council flats, and supermarkets in Lancashire but also tractors and milking machines and the land-use of rural Wiltshire. Subordination is to man, machines, and "natural" environment (Bennet and Bennet, 1970). Each of these environments will co-operate with any political subordination to produce similar socio-psychological characteristics in the subordinated. The major social contexts of man are his family, his place of work, his topographical environment, and his school; the family alone of these will retain, while it remains nuclear or extended and not collectivized, a degree of autonomy, scope for individuality, and a potentiality for deviance. But work, environment, and school will emphasize and support, for most, a state of subordination, a condition of dependence and an acceptance of powerlessness to effect change. Where there is a religious context this, again, for the lower strata, will emphasize subordination; where there is an intimate and immediate community context this may support the family influence but this combined influence will tend to divert or protect from or compensate for and not direct against or conflict with the other subordination-making pressures for, in part at least, they will merely provide the framework for local or personal reforms. Factors making for subordination will dominate the major social process and institutions, the work situation and the environment.

Joan Simon (1970) drew upon the work of Homans (1960), which suggests that the "philosophy" of the medieval peasant was similar to that of our contemporary lower urban classes. Agricultural work reinforced certain ways of thought. There was a tendency to see the future in terms of the past, to think in terms of cycles equivalent to the agricultural year, and of human life following a similar cycle from birth through the different ages of man to death. Related to this were the ways of preparing the young to fit into social life, as it was and would continue to be. This form of upbringing had few specific features. In a restricted community it was subject to few intellectual influences. The oral culture emphasizes memory and logic-empirical thought was not absent but it was only directed at specific aspects of work; "most teaching and preaching was directed to persuading them that unremitting toil was the lot God had appointed for those at the base of society." Too great an awareness of oppression was avoided by clinging to the pattern of life and to the vernacular oral tradition. This largely protected the peasant from teaching and preaching directed from outside—as may even be the case today, despite all the modern technology of education—and ensured the maintenance of a distinctive popular culture and outlook. As a result, Simon suggests, "the worker saw himself as a part of nature, as co-operating with the elements; accordingly his tendency is to placate, since he lacks the means to coerce, to value security above adventure, to surrender to providence rather than tempting it. . . ."

Even more strikingly reminiscent is Joan Simon's description of the attitudes of the Florentine merchants of the early 15th century. This time the similarity is with our contemporary middle classes. Their domestic life was well regulated both as a background to efficient business and as a base for bringing up healthy children with a sound moral outlook; their education was directed toward communication and, more specifically, to encouraging the individual skills and attitudes needed in business affairs; the aim was to avoid making enemies and to acquire friends; to be of good appearance, courteous, equable and not eccentric. On the other hand, the potential merchant had also to avoid timidity and conformism, he needed judgment and strength of character, energy, versatility, a readiness to take control of events. Literacy was a practical necessity, also an apprenticeship in the art of communication "beginning with active participation in the community of the household . . . the need for love and understanding rather than force and fear enter into this. . . . Parents should try to ensure that a child develops his own particular characteristics, for individual character is an asset in social life and active qualities such as willpower are needed in business."

So we can see parallels between the attitudes of the modern middle classes and their emerging if still marginal predecessors in the middle ages and the characteristics of their social subordinates. In each case the value system exhibited can be hypothesized as a function both of the relative position of each within the total social system and as a function of the relationship of each to the surrounding material environment. Subordination, inferiority, and dependence will encourage the development of one system of values; superordination, superiority, and independence will encourage the development of different but complementary values. It is worth pointing out in particular one aspect of the values of the peasants and the merchants described by Simon—that is the function assigned to language in each system. This would seem to give interesting implicit support for the thesis about language advanced in recent years by B. Bernstein.

Similarly Kluckhohn and Leighton (1946) in contrasting the Navaho, a people without the technology for challenging nature and therefore subordinated to it, with Europeans suggest that the former accepted nature and adapted themselves to her demands as best they could, but they were not utterly passive. They tried many things designed to control nature physically and to repair damage caused by the elements. But they did not expect to conquer nature. The Navaho tried to influence her with songs and rituals but they knew that the forces of nature, rather than anything that man did determines success or failure.

It is, then, the relevance of all this to teaching that must concern us now. Those who deplore, for whatever reasons—be they economic, cultural, political, or aesthetic—the "failure" of the lower classes to benefit from the educational process, in this country or America, assume that there would be net gain, individual or social, if this wastage could be reduced. Some have challenged this, in part or in whole. Jackson and Marsden (1966) have spoken of the destruction of valuable components of working class culture by the grammar schools; Bernstein has argued that working class language and culture have an intrinsic and aesthetic value; Nye Bevan once deplored the fact that the grammar school castrated the potential political leaders of the labour movement. In this country the Welsh and Scottish nationalists and certain ethnic minority groups in the United States are demanding an education that will preserve and not destroy their cultures. On similar arguments some are suggesting deschooling on the theory that this will both relieve working class children from the oppressive effects of an alien and exploitive culture and enable them to develop the educational means of developing their own. Unfortunately an intensification of stratification or cultural differentiation probably will be subject to a sort of multiplier effect and create even wider gaps in communication and understanding leading on the one hand to even greater inequality in the distribution of power, wealth, and influence; and on the other hand it will lead to greater social tensions and strains which will bring in train further repression and coercion.

So we are, at the moment, left with the reformers and apparently an unreconcilable contradiction. The argument of this essay has been that the educational "inadequacy" of the lower classes is the corollary of the cluster of attitudes and characteristics one would expect to find in subordinated groups with a similar social and cultural history. Therefore, reform measures that see the attitudes it wishes to change as mere superficial and idiosyncratic psychological peculiarities are almost certainly doomed to failure, and, if they were to have any effect, we certainly could not be sure what these effects would be. Reform that does derive from a diagnosis of causes may theoretically have a greater chance of success and may also enable some speculative prediction to be made. But, our argument has been that it is the interaction of social groups through time and in the social structure that create the conditions necessary for the emergence of a system of values or "philosophy"; therefore, logically, structural changes are required to create the conditions necessary for attitudes to change. Also, logically, it would seem most probable that a new subordinated group would be produced within the new social structure. Therefore the contradiction: change is considered desirable, only structural change will make this possible, structural change, even if it were to happen, would bring about, in its turn, problems similar to those with which we began. So, it would seem nothing can, in fact, be done.

This conclusion, however, is not inescapable. Firstly, it is ethically unacceptable and secondly it does not necessarily follow from the sociological analysis which precedes it.

I have argued that it is a group's position in the social structure that is one essential precondition for the development of a "philosophy." The "social structure" is an abstraction, however, that constrains and impinges upon the individual through other micro social structures that are more "real" like the family, the place of work, and the school.

This is not the place to discuss the role of the first two of these institutions, beyond pointing out that both are subject to continuous change and that, currently, trends toward greater democratic participation seem to be gathering speed, but it is appropriate to look at the school. It is equally appropriate to suggest that changes in the internal structure and relations within the school might well be the one educational change that might create the conditions necessary for the desired attitudinal changes. What is certain is that reforms that take place in the context of the traditional hierarchically structured school and thereby replicate and support the external social subordination of the lower class child are probably thereby condemned from the start. Whereas changes in the school that gave the subordinate parents and even their children the opportunity to exercise some of the power usually reserved for the Head, the Governors and the Education Officer might well have that cumulative effect upon attitudes and self images and perceptions of parents, children, and teachers that might tip the balance in favour of some of the other reforms that could then be tried in the changed structure of the school. At least the results could not be more, educationally, disastrous than those which obtain at the moment.

## REFERENCES

Ausubel, D.P. "How Reversible Are the Cognitive and Motivational Effects of Cultural Deprivation?" (1963) in Bloom, B. and Hesa, R. *Compensatory Education for Cultural Deprivation*, pp. 76–77. New York: Holt, Rinehart & Winston, 1965.

Banks, O. *The Sociology of Education*. a. p. 74; b. p. 81. London: Batsford, 1968.

Barber, B. *Social Stratification*. New York: Harcourt Brace, 1957.

Bauman, Z. "Economic Growth, Social Structure, Elite Formation," in Bendix, R. and Lipset, S.M. (Eds.) *Class, Status, and Power*, p. 538. London: Routledge & Kegan Paul, 1967.

Bennet, M. and Bennet, P. "Social Psychology through Symbolic Interaction," in Dale, R. et al. (Eds.) *School and Society*. London: Routledge & Kegan Paul and Open University Press, 1971.

Bernstein, B. "Some Sociological Determinants of Perception." *Br. J. Sociol.*, 1X (June 1958):159–74.

———. *Class, Codes and Control*. London: Routledge & Kegan Paul, 1 (1971).

Bronfenbrenner, U. "Socialization and Social Class through Time and Space," in Maccoby, E., Newcombe, T., and Hartley, E. *Readings in Social Psychology*. New York: Holt, 1957.

———. ."The Changing American Child." *Merrill-Palmer Quarterly*, 7 (1961): 2, 73–84.

Caro, F.G. "Social Class and Attitudes of Youth Relevant for the Realization of Adult Goals." *Social Forces* 44 (1966):492–98.

Clegg, A. and Megson, B. *Children in Distress*. Harmondsworth: Penguin Press, 1968.

Coleman, A. "Parents Help Their Children Succeed." *The High School Journal*, 15 (1969):3, 48–59.

Deutsch, M. "The Disadvantaged Child and the Learning Process," in Passow, A.H. (Ed.) *Education in Depressed Areas*, pp. 163–80. New York: Teachers College Press Columbia University, 1963.

Douglas, J.W.B. *The Home and the School*. London: Macgibbon & Kee, 1964.

Douglas, J.W., Ross, J.M., and Simpson, H.R. *All Our Future*. London: Peter Davies, 1968.

Drews, E.M. and Teahan, J.E. "Parental Attitudes and Academic Achievement." *J. Clin. Psychol.*, 21 (1957):2.

Durkheim, E.  *Les Règles de la Méthode Sociologique.* Paris: Libraire Felix Alcan, 1927.

Floud, J. and Halsey, A.H.  "Intelligence Tests, Social Class and Selection for Secondary Schools." *Brit. J. Sociol.,* 8 (1957):33–39.

Fuchs, E.  "How Teachers Learn to Help Children Fail." *Transaction,* 5 (1968):9.

Golden, H. and Birns, P.  "Social Class and Cognitive Development in Infancy." *Merrill-Palmer Quarterly,* 3 (1968):121–37.

Harrison, F.I.  "Relationship Between Home Background, School Success and Adolescent." *Merrill-Palmer Quarterly,* 4 (1968):331–44.

Henry, J.  *Essays in Education.* Harmondsworth: Penguin, 1971.

Himmelweit, H.  "Socio-economic Background and Personality." *Internat. Soc. Sc. Bull.,* 7 (1955):29–35.

Hoggart, R.  Review article, *Observer,* 2/11/62.

Homans, G.  *English Villagers of the Thirteenth Century.* New York: Russell, 1960.

Hyman, H.H.  "The Value System of Different Classes," in Bendix, R. and Lipset, S.M. (Eds.) *Class, Status, and Power,* pp. 488–99. London: Routledge & Kegan Paul, 1967.

Jackson, B. and Marsden, D.  *Education and the Working Class.* Harmondsworth: Penguin, 1966.

Kahl, J.A.  "Educational and Occupational Aspirations of 'Common Man' Boys." *Harvard Educ. Rev.,* 22 (1953):186–204.

———.  "The American Class Structure." *Harvard Educ. Rev.,* 26 (1957):261–83.

———.  "Some Measurements of Achievement Orientation." *Amer. J. Sociol.,* 70 (1965):669–81.

Katz, F.M.  "The Meaning of Success." *J. Soc. Psychol.,* 62 (1964):182–96.

King, R.  *Values and Involvement in a Grammar School.* London: Routledge & Kegan Paul, 1964.

Kluckhohn, C.  (1961). In Kluckhohn, F. R. (1970) see below.

Kluckhohn, C. and Leighton, R.  "The Navaho," in Hymes, D. *Language in Culture and Society,* pp. 211–12. New York: Harper & Row, 1946.

Kluckhohn, F. R.  "Variations in the Basic Values of Family Systems," in Swift, D.R. (Ed.) *Basic Readings in the Sociology of Education.* London: Routledge & Kegan Paul, 1970.

Knupfer, P.  "Portrait of the Underdog." *Public Opinion Quarterly,* 3 (1947):121–23.

Kohn, M.L.  "Social Class and the Exercise of Parental Authority." *Amer. Sociol. Rev.,* 24 (1959):352–66.

Kohn, M.L. and Schooler, T.  "Class, Occupation and Orientation," *Amer. Sociol. Rev.,* 34 (2; 1969):659.

Le Shan, J.  "Time Orientation and Social Class." *J. Abnorm. Psychol.,* 47 (1952):589–92.

London, J.  *The People of the Abyss.* Harmondsworth: Penguin, 1951.

Mays, J.B.  *Education and the Urban Child.* Liverpool University Press, 1962.

Merton, R.K.  *Social Structure and Social Theory,* pp. 73–136. New York: The Free Press, Collier-Macmillan, 1968.

Mills, C. Wright.  *The Sociological Imagination,* p. 17. Harmondsworth: Penguin, 1970.

Musgrave, P.  *The Sociology of Education.* London: Methuen, 1965.

Musgrove, F.  "Parents' Expectations of the Junior School." *Brit. J. Educ. Psychol.,* 35 (1965):2.

Parsons, T. and White, W.  "The Link Between Character and Society," in Lipset, S.M. and Lowenthal, L. (Eds.) *Culture and Social Character.* Illinois: Free Press of Glencoe, 1961.

Parsons, T. and Shils, E.  *Towards a General Theory of Action,* p. 7. New York: Harper Torchbooks, Harper & Row, 1962.

Perry, L.R.  "Training," *Education for Teaching.* London: Association of Teachers in Colleges and Departments of Education, Summer 1969, pp. 4–10.

Reisman, F.  *The Culturally Deprived Child.* New York: Harper & Row, 1962.

Rist, R.  "Student Social Class and Teacher Expectations." *Harvard Educ. Rev.,* 40 (1970):411–51.

Roberts, K.  "Entry into Employment." *Sociol. Rev.,* 16 (1968):2, 165–84.

Rosen, B.C.  "The Achievement Syndrome: A Psycho-Cultural Dimension of Social Stratification." *Amer. Sociol. Rev.* 21 (April 1956):203–11.

Schneider, L. and Lysgaard, S.  "The Deferred Gratification Pattern," *Amer. Sociol. Rev.* (April 1953):142–49.

Schwebel, N. and Bernstein, A.J.  "Impulsiveness, Class and Best Performance." *Amer. J. Ortho-psychiatry,* 23 (Fall 1970).

Simon, J.  *The Social Origins of Education.* London: Routledge & Kegan Paul, 1970.

Smith, D.  *Distribution Processes and Power Relations in Education Systems.* Bletchley: Open University, 1973.

Spitzer, S.P.  *The Sociology of Personality.* New York: Van Nostrand Reinhold, 1969.

Stephenson, M.  "Stratification, Education and Occupational Orientation." *Brit. J. Sociol.,* 9 (1958):42–52.

Swift, D.F.  "Meritocratic and Social Class Selection." *Educ. Res.,* 8 (1965) 1; 65–73.

Tressel, R.  *The Ragged Trousered Philanthropists.* London: Panther, 1965.

Turner, R.  *The Social Context of Ambition.* San Francisco: Chandler, 1964.

Veblen, T.  *Instinct for Workmanship.* New York: B.W. Hueback, 1918.

Yee, A.  "Social Interaction in Classrooms." *Sociol. Forces,* 15 (1969):82–97.

# 9

# Changing Patterns of Education and Mobility*

## ROBERT PERRUCCI

A simplified view of the American educational system is one of a series of self-contained stages, with each stage a prerequisite for movement to the next. Moreover, the stages are interconnected to the extent that actions, decisions, and performance undertaken in one stage act as constraints upon actions in a subsequent stage. For our purposes, we may further simplify the model by viewing actions within, and satisfactory completion of, each stage as having a probability value that expresses the likelihood that one will "wind up" in one of the more highly valued positions in the occupational structure. Thus, as one moves from completion of grade school through completion of a graduate degree, the probability of a high status occupation is increased.

Prior to the first part of the 20th century the probability statements generated by such a model would not have been very powerful in predicting future status of persons with various educational backgrounds. Preparation for commercial activities required skills and training that were not necessarily gathered by formal education, and the career of the artisan was often started in the capacity of an apprentice. Even the "older" professions of medicine, law, and the ministry were open to entry through apprenticeship preparation.

Such is not the case in contemporary American society where the revolution in education has paralleled the revolutions in science and technology and their impact upon the occupational structure. Table 1 shows a

* From: On Education: Sociological Perspectives by Donald A. Hansen and Joel E. Gerstl (Eds.). Copyright 1967, John Wiley and Sons. Reprinted by permission of John Wiley & Sons, Inc.

TABLE ONE
Percent of U.S. Population, Aged 5–17 Years,
Attending Public Elementary and Secondary Schools

| 1870 | 57.0 | 1930 | 81.7 |
|------|------|------|------|
| 1880 | 65.5 | 1940 | 84.4 |
| 1890 | 68.6 | 1950 | 83.2 |
| 1900 | 71.9 | 1960 | 82.2 |
| 1910 | 74.2 | 1962 | 84.5 |
| 1920 | 78.3 |  |  |

Source: *Digest of Educational Statistics*, U.S. Department of
Health, Education and Welfare, 1964.

distribution of the proportion of school-age persons in the population who
attended public elementary and secondary schools. The marked increase
in attendance rates occurs primarily between 1870 and 1930. The stable
and slightly irregular fluctuations in rates after 1930 are in large part a
reflection of the changing number of children attending private and religious schools. The rate of increase in attendance in nonpublic schools is
much higher than in public schools between 1940 and 1960 (Statistical
Abstract of the United States, 1963, p. 113). Of course, growth in population during this same period has resulted in a sizable increase in the absolute numbers of children attending both private and public schools. These
relative and absolute increases have also been reflected in the growth in
instructional staff in our primary and secondary schools. In 1870 there
were about 200,000 teachers in public elementary and secondary schools
and this figure had increased to about 1,500,000 by 1962 (Digest of Educational Statistics, 1964).

TABLE TWO
Percentage of Total School Enrollment in High School

| 1870 | 1.2 | 1930 | 17.1 |
|------|------|------|------|
| 1880 | 1.1 | 1940 | 26.0 |
| 1890 | 1.6 | 1950 | 22.7 |
| 1900 | 3.3 | 1960 | 23.5 |
| 1910 | 5.1 | 1962 | 25.0 |
| 1920 | 10.2 |  |  |

Source: *Digest of Educational Statistics*, 1964, p. 10.

In Tables 2 and 3 we can see a more dramatic picture of the changing
pattern of education that has followed the increase in the proportion of
persons attending primary and secondary schools. The increase in the proportion of the total enrollment that is in high school indicates that the general trend of universal public education has been extending the amount of
education being obtained by the growing number of students. Table 3

TABLE THREE
Percentage of Persons 17 Years of Age
Who Graduated from High School

| | | | |
|---|---|---|---|
| 1870 ........ | 2.0 | 1930 ........ | 29.0 |
| 1880 ........ | 2.5 | 1940 ........ | 50.8 |
| 1890 ........ | 3.5 | 1950 ........ | 59.0 |
| 1900 ........ | 6.4 | 1960 ........ | 65.1 |
| 1910 ........ | 8.8 | 1962 ........ | 69.7 |
| 1920 ........ | 16.8 | | |

Source: Adapted from *Digest of Educational Statistics*, 1964,
p. 56.

shows a steady increase in the proportion of persons 17 years old who have graduated from high school.

The trends toward more extensive and intensive use of education have also carried over into higher education. Table 4 shows types of higher degrees earned in selected time periods. Several trends may be observed in this Table. There has been a continuing increase in the proportion of advanced degrees awarded in the last several decades from about six percent to about 20 percent. Most striking is that aspects of the revolution in higher education have been a very recent phenomenon. Over 50 percent of all the doctors' degrees awarded since 1870 have been awarded since 1955. A similar pattern may be observed for other degrees.

The changing patterns of education from high school through graduate work have not occurred in isolation from changes in the occupational structure. Since the turn of the century there has been a steady increase in the proportion of the labor force in those occupations requiring greater amounts of education, while the unskilled and farm occupations have declined. It is difficult to forecast future trends in the occupational structure due to technological change, but it is likely that the decline in farm occupations will soon reach some equilibrium point. Although the full impact of automation in production is still uncertain, its effect should be to increase the need for technicians at the expense of the unskilled occupations.

Glick's (1954) analysis of the 1950 census indicates the connection between changes in the educational system and the occupational structure. Comparing the jobs held by persons who did not complete high school, high school graduates, and college graduates, Glick found that the proportion holding white collar occupations was about 25, 40, and 85 percent, respectively. Given these educational and occupational changes, then, it appears crucial to find out who goes to college—for college graduation has become the main avenue for admission to those occupations that provide the middle class way of life. But going to college represents a complex process of motivation and opportunity. The internal constraints of values and aspirations, and the external constraints represented by the

**TABLE FOUR**
Distribution of College Degrees in United States

| | 1870 | 1880 | 1890 | 1900 | 1910 | 1920 | 1930 | 1940 | 1950 | 1960 | 1962 | 1963 |
|---|---|---|---|---|---|---|---|---|---|---|---|---|
| Bachelor's ...... | 9,371 | 12,896 | 15,539 | 27,410 | 37,199 | 48,622 | 122,484 | 186,500 | 432,058 | 392,440 | 417,846 | 447,662 |
| percent ...... | 100.0 | 93.2 | 93.0 | 93.3 | 93.6 | 90.8 | 87.6 | 86.1 | 87.0 | 82.3 | 81.2 | 81.1 |
| Master's ...... | 0 | 879 | 1,015 | 1,583 | 2,113 | 4,279 | 14,969 | 26,731 | 58,183 | 74,435 | 84,855 | 91,366 |
| percent ...... | – | 6.4 | 6.1 | 5.4 | 5.3 | 8.0 | 10.7 | 12.3 | 11.7 | 15.6 | 16.5 | 16.6 |
| Doctor's ...... | 1 | 54 | 149 | 382 | 443 | 615 | 2,299 | 3,290 | 6,420 | 9,828 | 11,622 | 12,822 |
| percent ...... | 0.0 | 0.4 | 0.9 | 1.3 | 1.1 | 1.1 | 1.6 | 1.5 | 1.3 | 2.1 | 2.3 | 2.3 |
| Total ...... | 9,372 | 13,829 | 16,703 | 29,375 | 39,755 | 53,516 | 139,752 | 216,521 | 496,661 | 476,703 | 514,323 | 551,810 |

Source: Adapted from *Digest of Educational Statistics*, U.S. Department of Health, Education and Welfare, 1964.

social structures one is implicated in, combine to effect the realization of equality of opportunity. One result of the educational revolution has been to make the decisions as well as performance in the eighth or 12th grade among the most crucial determinants of future status.

Thus one of the effects of these educational and occupational changes has been to make higher education the main avenue for mobility. This fact, however, has put an additional burden upon the secondary schools where the decision to go to college is made and where the curriculum prerequisites for entrance either are or are not obtained. The crucial role played by the high schools in sorting out the college bound from the non-college bound has increased in prominence as high school enrollments have increased. In 1870 there were only 16,000 high school graduates and 9,371 college graduates, the latter being about 60 percent of the former. A fair proportion of the relatively few people who graduated from high school were likely to continue on to college, thus relieving a good part of the "quality control" function from the high school. In more recent years we have observed that college graduates are only about 20 percent of high school graduates. Since there are about two million high school graduates, the selection process becomes a much more complex problem.

But it is not only the high school that has been affected by expanding enrollments. Because college education has become the royal road to success, increasing college attendance has had the potential effect of devaluing college education. The adaptation to this possibility has been the "Princeton versus Podunk" pattern that was so well documented in the *Time* magazine study of college graduates (Haveman and West, 1952). What we find here is a growing differentiation in the quality of schools, and more importantly, in the relative success of their graduates (cf. Wilensky, 1964). This increasing differentiation can be interpreted as a transfer of the sorting out process from the high school level to the college level. For as greater and greater numbers of students graduate from high school and continue on to college the quality control function of the high school becomes more difficult to perform effectively. What has been introduced, in effect, is simply another gatekeeper on the road to success. However, this new criterion, namely, the nature of the institution of higher learning one attends, can be viewed as somewhat at odds with normative expectations regarding how avenues of mobility operate in an open class system.

Closely tied to this first set of consequences is our second consideration concerning the effects of these shifting patterns of educational and occupational mobility. Here we face the values and value changes that are associated with mobility, and whether certain value patterns are essential prerequisites for mobility or are a consequence of it. In relatively stable societies with low rates of upward movement the mobility model that is used is one assuming that mobile persons are selected precisely because of their value similarity to the members of their class of destination. The "mobiles" are viewed as holding those values, aspirations, and characteristics that serve to make them highly "visible" among the other members of their class of origin. The mobility heroes of the Horatio Alger type are often presented as already exhibiting those qualities required for success, such as hard work, thrift, and virtue. All that our hero needs, in effect, is a good scrubbing, a suit of clothes, and a position that will give him a chance to "show his stuff" (Wohl, 1953). Within this framework the move into the mobility channel is the problematic condition, and subsequent success is nonproblematic and relatively automatic.

The changes described above, however, suggest that a good bit of the mobility that has occurred in recent decades—both educational and occupational—has been a result of the "structural push" of expanding numbers of high status occupations caused by technological change. A minimum estimate of the number of new jobs created by technical change between 1920 and 1950 is about 8,000,000 (Kahl, 1960, p. 255). Under such conditions of expansion, the stable mobility model of value change or value consonance (in accordance with high status group values) is less likely to be in agreement with the actual mobility process. The great diversity in the ethnic and class origins of persons involved in the upper educational and occupational ranks makes it quite difficult to speak of any kind of value similarity that would play a critical role in the mobility process. An added factor that would tend to support such diversity of basic values is the wide variety of educational programs available as well as the wide variety of occupational destinations for which the mobile person can strive. This does not mean that the educational experience may not lead to greater similarity in values and orientations than existed prior to the educational experience, only that any significant homogenizing effects are more likely to take place within the context of particular colleges and universities. But given the diversity of the schools—created by a combination of the motivations of the students it recruits, the curriculum, the faculty, and the administration—what we would find developing is a certain within-school similarity but between-school diversity. Despite any of these processes, however, the important fact is that the values-mobility sequence has been altered, or at least made a less critical consideration in understanding social mobility.

The important consequence of this shift in the values-mobility sequence, at least from the point of view of this essay, is that the rapid expansion of mobility opportunities has had, above all, the effect of raising expectations concerning the future rewards that higher education will bring. The expectation that higher education will automatically bring money, prestige, power, happiness is probably more appropriate to an age when there were only 16,000 high school graduates a year, and only 9,000 college graduates. Under conditions such as these, higher education would indeed have a very high probability of resulting in success in all its varied forms. It therefore becomes very important to know just how higher education, as the main channel of mobility, operates as a mechanism that either aids or inhibits the free flow of talent to enjoy its "just" rewards.

It is this factor of rising expectations concerning education that brings us to the third effect of the educational revolution. The first two had to do with the instrumental function of stratification, or how people get allocated to positions. Our concern now is with the degree of correspondence between expectations for rewards of occupational and educational mobility and actual rewards realized. Such disparities are important for the integrative function of stratification, for it is under conditions of unfulfilled expectation that the legitimacy of institutional arrangements governing reward structures will be questioned.

There are two different objects or referents for expectations to consider. The first has to do with the distribution of income among various occupational groups. One of the results of the occupational changes described previously has been a growing belief that the upward shift in real income for all groups has been especially pronounced for the blue-collar category, and that such income advances have served to lessen the discrepancy between upper and lower occupational groups. The belief in this shrinking income gap has served as a basis for a number of theories explaining conservative orientations among blue-collar workers who are enjoying both relative and absolute increases in wealth, as well as the anxieties experienced by lower white-collar groups over the status advances of the blue-collar worker. Recent evidence on income distribution among occupational groups suggests that this income gap has not in fact been disappearing as popular belief would have it (Miller, 1962; Hamilton, 1964). Because our estimates of how well we are doing are generally made in relative rather than absolute terms—relative to those groups immediately above or below us whom we may use as standards to evaluate our own income and consumer behavior—the existence of conditions contrary to expectations has the *potential* for inspiring individual and collective dissatisfactions.

The second referent for expectations concerns the view that reward distributions for persons who utilize the legitimate mobility channels will be based on universalistic criteria such as ability and not particularistic criteria such as social origins. Although it is certainly recognized that social origins do affect the likelihood that a person will gain access to the means for mobility, it is often maintained that the negative effects of social origins are "neutralized" among those who manage to complete a higher education. This view has often been expressed in the notion of "careers open to talent," whereby the measure of a man is his ability and performance and his social origins can neither help nor hinder him in the pursuit of such careers. The assumption that the effect of social origins is neutralized in certain careers requires further consideration. This assumption implies that the mobile person does not "carry with him" any of the values and aspirations that are prominently displayed in his class of origin and that might limit his own performance in his career. For this assumption to be valid the values-mobility sequence spoken of earlier would have to mean that mobile individuals are selected because of their value consonance with the class of destination, or that they can easily "shed" the values of the class of origin and "take on" the values of their class of destination. Our earlier discussion of the effects of rapid educational and occupational expansion would suggest that the selection process according to value consonance is not in operation; such a process is much too complex to work effectively according to the "natural" operation of the stratification system.

A second question to be raised concerning the assumption that social origins do not affect movement in certain careers is whether or not the environment in which the mobile person operates is in fact neutral or unaware of the existence of the differences in life experiences, values, and style of life that may exist between the new arrival and the old members. Again, to assume that these differences no longer exist, or that if they do, they make no difference, means that persons evaluate each other solely on the basis of technical skills and abilities. We shall wish to examine the facts that bear upon such assumptions and the implications they might have for the existence of order in the stratification system.

The problems that have been identified and the questions that have been raised concerning the instrumental and integrative functions of a system of stratification will form the framework for the remainder of this paper. In looking at the instrumental function (or how people get allocated to positions) the primary interest will be with those factors that aid or inhibit the mobility process in general, and their persistence in the educational system in particular. This is discussed in the following section. In looking at the integrative function of stratification (or collective responses to the manner in which a society distributes its rewards) the concern will be with the rising expectations concerning the rewards of higher education, and the adaptations of higher education to the influx of students from all social levels. This material is contained in the section on mobility and higher education.

## INTERNAL AND EXTERNAL CONSTRAINTS ON MOBILITY

Social mobility is best viewed as a result of a complex pattern of relationships between the objective opportunity structure of a society, individual values, beliefs, and aspirations concerning elements of the opportunity structure, and the structural settings within which the individual is influenced, and within which his personal views are reinforced, modified, or challenged. Let us begin with an examination of those elements of the self such as values and aspirations that would induce the individual to undertake patterns of activity that are positively related to mobility.

### Values, Aspirations and Personality Patterns

Rather than examine the area of values and aspirations in any general or exhaustive manner, we shall limit our attention to those values and aspirations that have most direct relevance to education as the major means for advancement in our society. The importance of studying the values systems of social classes, which study has a long tradition in sociology, was underscored in an influential paper by Herbert Hyman (1953, p. 426). His efforts in the area of class values and mobility can be taken as a crucial point in the development of a large body of systematic theoretical and empirical work.

> The existence of stratification in American society is well known. The corollary fact—that individuals from lower strata are not likely to climb far up the economic ladder is also known. However, what requires additional analysis are the factors that account for this mobility. Many of these factors of an objective nature have been studied. Opportunity in the society is differential; higher education or specialized training, which might provide access to a high position, must be bought with money—the very commodity which the lower classes lack. Such objective factors help maintain the existing structure. But there are other factors of a more subtle psychological nature which have not been illuminated and which may also work to perpetuate the existing order. It is our assumption that an intervening variable mediating the relationship between low position and lack of upward mobility is a system of beliefs and values within the lower classes which in turn reduces the very *voluntary* actions which would ameliorate their low position.
>
> The components of this value system, in our judgment, involve less emphasis upon the traditional high success goals, increased awareness of the lack of opportunity to achieve success, and less emphasis upon the achievement of goals which in turn would be instrumental for success. To put it simply the lower class individual doesn't want as much success, knows he couldn't get it even if he wanted to, and doesn't want what might help him get success. Of course, an individual's value system is only one among many factors on which his position in the social hierarchy depends. Some of these factors may be external and arbitrary, quite beyond the control of even a highly motivated individual. However, within the bounds of the freedom available to individuals, this value system would create a *self-imposed* barrier to an improved position.

Hyman examined data collected in nationwide surveys concerning class differences in educational values, in motivations for economic advancement, and in perceptions of the opportunity structure. Using a variety of measures of stratification, Hyman finds that the lower socioeconomic groups place less emphasis upon college education as necessary for advancement, and are less likely to desire a college education for their children. He also finds that when adult and young respondents are asked to indicate the most important thing to be considered when choosing a life's work, the lower classes emphasized direct economic considerations such as security and wages, whereas the upper classes stressed the congeniality of the career pattern to the individual's personality, interests, and qualifications. Concerning these differences Hyman (1953, p. 433) states:

> It is our belief that this difference in what would be sought in a career would lead the lower class individuals into occupations that would be less likely to enhance their position. Such desiderata will be achieved in a "good job" but not in such positions as managerial or professional jobs. These latter careers have greater elements of risk and are the very ones that would not mesh with the desire for stability, security and immediate economic benefits, but would mesh with the goal of congeniality to the individual's interest.

Pursuing this line of analysis further, Hyman (p. 441) finds that the lower class individuals are more likely to prefer a low income but secure job, and to have lower aspirations when asked to make projections concerning increased monetary needs. The large body of empirical evidence in which Hyman finds consistent class-based differences is followed by a theoretical coda directed at explaining the cases which do not fit the argument.

> While the evidence thus far presented provides consistent and strong evidence that lower class individuals *as a group* have a value system that reduces the likelihood of individual advancement, it is also clear from the data that there is a sizable proportion from the lower group who do not incorporate this value system. Similarly, there are individuals in the upper classes who do not show the modal tendency of their group. In part, such deviant instances can be accounted for in terms of the crudity of the measurements used. In part, one must recognize that the members of these classes have much heterogeneity in such other social respects as their ethnic, religious, and other memberships and have been exposed to a variety of idiosyncratic experiences.
>
> The value systems would be correspondingly diverse. However, one systematic factor which can be shown to account for the deviant cases which confirms at *a more subtle psychological level* the influence of class factors is that of the reference group of the individual. Some of our lower class individuals may well be identifying themselves with upper groups, and absorbing the value system of another class to which they refer themselves.

Hyman's results concerning class differences in values and aspirations have also been found in a number of other studies conducted in such varied settings as an industrial plant, rural communities, small cities, and urban areas. In a study of high-school-aged adolescents in the middle west in 1941, Hollingshead (1949) found a pattern of vocational choices that roughly corresponded with the job patterns of each class in the adult work world. Sewell, Haller, and Straus (1957) studied the educational and occupational aspirations of a large random sample of public and private nonfarm high school seniors in Wisconsin in 1947. They found a significant association between level of educational and occupational aspirations and social status, with measured intelligence controlled. While their study does not deny the importance of intelligence to aspirations, they do find that status does make an independent contribution. Chinoy (1955) studied the aspirations of automobile workers using data collected by participant observation and prolonged interviews with men employed in one large auto plant. The findings indicate that the auto workers tend to confine their aims to those limited alternatives that seem possible for men with their skills and resources. Of the 62 men interviewed, only eight felt that they had a promising future outside the factory. Within the factory, five men had real hope that they might some day become foremen, while only three semiskilled workers (of a total of 28) felt that it might be possible to move into the ranks of skilled labor. The remaining 46 men restricted their ambitions to such small gains as transfer to a job that pays a few cents more per hour or to one that is easier, steadier, or more interesting. Two interesting patterns observed by Chinoy are the shift of the context of advancement from the occupational sphere to the consumption sphere, and by the moderate tendency to maintain ambitious hopes for their children (cf. Hyman's findings). Chinoy concludes that these automobile workers have retained the form but lost the substance of the American tradition of opportunity.

In addition to the importance of values and aspirations in influencing mobility, there is also the factor of intelligence or ability in undertaking certain mobility-related activities. Intelligence is particularly relevant to mobility within the context of this essay as we are in large part limiting our attention to education as the major means of achieving mobility. In a study of some 3,000 boys in the sophomore and junior years of high school from the Boston area, data were collected which provided estimates of the independent and combined effects of intelligence and social origins upon college aspirations. An examination of these data was undertaken by Kahl, who sought to assess the effects of origins and I.Q. on college plans, and to pursue a question raised earlier by Hyman, namely, what social influences help to explain why students of similar I.Q. and social origins differ markedly in their college aspirations (Kahl, 1960, p. 287–88). Table 5 contains the findings from the questionnaire phase of the mobility project and is followed by Kahl's analysis of the interview data for a specially selected number of cases.

TABLE FIVE
Percentage of Boys Who Expected to Go to College By I.Q. and
Father's Occupation (Boston area, 1950—3348 boys)*

| | I.Q. Quintile (Boys) | | | | | |
| | Low | | | | High | All Quintiles |
| Father's occupation | 1 | 2 | 3 | 4 | 5 | |
| Major white collar | 56% | 72% | 79% | 82% | 89% | 80% |
| Middle white collar | 28 | 36 | 47 | 53 | 76 | 52 |
| Minor white collar | 12 | 20 | 22 | 29 | 55 | 26 |
| Skilled labor and service | 4 | 15 | 19 | 22 | 40 | 19 |
| Other labor and service | 9 | 6 | 10 | 14 | 29 | 12 |
| All occupations | 11 | 17 | 24 | 30 | 52 | 27 |

* From Kahl, 1960, p. 283.

Notice that the combination of I.Q. and social class (in Table 5) successfully predicted college aspiration at the extremes, for a boy with a
Major White-Collar father (lawyer, doctor, executive) who was in the top
quintile or top 20 percent of intelligence had an 89 percent chance of
wanting to go to college, whereas a boy with an Other Labor and Service
father (semi-skilled or unskilled) who was in the bottom quintile in intelligence had only a 9 percent chance. . . .

Fortunately, the Boston study had depth in time, for it collected statistics on the performance of the boys from the first grade in grammar
school up to the time they answered the questionnaire in the middle of
high school. Boys with high I.Q. scores usually had good marks starting
with the first grade, but even more, those with low I.Q. scores had poor
marks. Father's occupation did not affect school performance in the earlier grades, but it began to take effect in the fourth grade, and by the time
of junior high school was slightly more important than I.Q. in predicting
performance.

The pattern is clear: in the earliest years in school a boy performs according to his native talent and, probably, his general emotional adjustment to the classroom situation. . . . But as he grows older, he begins to
shape his performance according to certain values that he learns from his
family and friends. Upper-status boys learn that good, or at least adequate, performance in school is necessary, that they are expected to do
well enough in secondary school to get admitted to college. . . .

By contrast, a boy from a lower status home is taught that college is
either "not for his kind," or at best is a matter of indifference to his parents. The boy's friends are not interested in college nor in high school. . . .
Consequently even a bright boy among them gets discouraged. . . .

What has been said so far concerns boys at the extremes of Table 5;
that is, boys with high intelligence and high social status versus those
with low intelligence and low social status. . . .

However, some boys of high intelligence and low status do head toward college, even though it be a minority of this group (29 percent of the boys in the highest quintile of intelligence from Other Labor and Service homes). Furthermore, if we look again at Table 5, we can notice that boys from Minor White-Collar or Skilled-Labor homes who have high intelligence have almost a 50–50 chance of heading toward college. What differentiates boys in these groups who are interested in college from the majority of their friends who are not?

To explore this problem 24 boys and their parents were interviewed. . . . All had I.Q. scores in the top quintile; all had petty white-collar, skilled or semi-skilled fathers. Yet almost half were college oriented, the rest were not. . . . The motivation (for college) in these exceptional cases came from four directions:

1. If a boy had done well in the early years, *and* had built up a self-conception in which good school performance was important, he would work hard to keep up his record. But the idea that school was important occurred only when that early performance was truly exceptional, or if the importance of his standing to him was reinforced by one or more of the other factors listed below.

2. A boy would sacrifice other pleasures for homework when they were not important to him. If a boy was not good at sports, if he did not have close and satisfying peer contact, or if he had no hobby that was strongly rewarding as well as distracting, then the cost of homework was less and the balance more in its favor. In extreme cases frustration in these alternative spheres motivated a boy to good school performance as compensation.

3. If a boy's family rewarded good school performance and punished poor performance, and the boy was not in rebellion against the family for emotional reasons, he was more likely to give up some play for homework.

4. If a boy had a rational conviction about the importance of schoolwork for his future career, he would strive to keep up his performance. But that conviction never appeared unless the parents emphasized it. . . .

Thus, intelligence and social status account for the major variations in college aspiration, especially at the extremes of the distributions. But in the lower-middle occupational range, and the intelligence range of smart-but-not-brilliant, the prediction is not good, for about half of such boys go to college and half stay away. For those boys the major determining factor is the attitude of the parents regarding the importance of college for occupational success, and the importance of occupational success for personal happiness.

The important question that remains largely unresolved by these studies that show the lower classes as having low aspirations and mobility-inhibiting values is the extent to which these values and aspirations are simply adaptations to objective conditions or a more fundamental part of the lower class youth's personality system. Whether the apparent absence of motivation to get ahead makes its imprint upon the personality in early socialization processes, or whether this is a more or less realistic response to a restrictive opportunity structure for the adolescent or adult is of considerable significance. It is particularly important in situations where attempts to "open up" the opportunity structure, as in education, are being undertaken.

Concern with this question has led to a significant body of work designed to tap the level of aspiration of the different social classes independent of expectations based upon an appraisal of life chances. Stephenson (1956), in a study of about 1,000 ninth grade students in four, semi-industrial, middle-sized cities in New Jersey, sought to determine the occupational plans and aspirations of his subjects, and, in so doing, to separate out the effect of reality factors upon the aspirations of the lower class students. Each student was asked to indicate his occupational plans for the time after he had completed the level of schooling he intended to complete. He was then asked to make a choice of what he would like to do if his circumstances were different and he could do what he really wanted to do. Stephenson found first of all that both occupational plans and aspirations are positively associated with the prestige ranking of father's occupation. At the same time, however, the discrepancy between the student's plans and aspirations also becomes markedly greater with descent in the occupational hierarchy. Under the assumption that plans, as compared with aspirations, represent an adjustment to the constraints of the real world, these data indicate "that while there is a relatively consistent pattern of high occupational aspirations among these youths, their plans tend to conform to their position in the stratification system" (p. 207). Additional evidence in support of the plans-aspirations distinction is found in Stephenson's comparison of the occupational plans and aspirations of Negro and white children of skilled, semiskilled, and unskilled fathers. Although the Negro students tended to have lower occupational plans than their counterparts from each occupational background, their aspirations were as high or higher. This would suggest that the Negro respondents' plans reflected the double burden of being both lower class and Negro (cf. Parker and Kleiner, 1964).

Stephenson's findings clearly support his conclusions that it is important to differentiate between aspirations and expectations when seeking to establish mobility orientation, since "plans or expectations are more definitely class based and, hence, may reflect class differences in opportunity and general life chances" (1956, p. 212). His data, however, do not support his assertion that "aspirations are relatively unaffected by class," since there was a marked decline in occupational aspirations with lower levels of the occupational hierarchy. Even when given an opportunity to make a fantasy choice, the lower class students tended to make more modest selections. Of course, one could argue that lower class students reduced aspirations in light of lowered occupational plans, but this is exactly what

Stephenson tried to avoid in questions asked concerning plans and aspirations. The fact that aspirations are still somewhat related to class origins continues to raise the question of additional class-based factors affecting mobility aspirations.

In discussing class-based aspirations, some consideration should be given to the methodological or theoretical basis of attempts to measure aspirations as a form of a fantasy choice. In other words, should we first seek to establish "reality" choices, and then ask for choices that are based upon very large "ifs"? This does not question the validity of obtaining both reality and fantasy choices in order to show that discrepancies are related to class, as Stephenson did. What is at issue, rather, is whether it is possible to make fantasy choices that do in fact "suspend" the effect of reality plans, and more importantly, even if this assumption is made, whether it is necessary for the theoretical issue under consideration. The problem is not so much to establish that the different social classes have similar aspirations in order to show that their limited educational and occupational attainment is a function of the opportunity structure. Rather, the problem is to establish whether or not the lower classes have any aspirations to move beyond their present situation *regardless of the object of their aspirations*. It is then in the reorganization of an opportunity structure, *not an individual*, that different goal objects are brought into the "reality space" of collections of individuals.

Some of these considerations are to be found in the work of Empey who recognized the importance of avoiding an absolute standard of occupational aspiration as indicative of the desire to "get ahead" (Empey, 1956). Measuring both the relative and absolute aspirations of a state-wide sample of high school seniors, Empey found that while the "lower-class youngsters aspired to get ahead, they aspired to occupations at different status levels than those from higher strata" (1956, p. 708).

Yet while Empey's work was important, its contribution is limited to demonstrating that lower class aspirations did exist if they were measured with reference to their own level as the starting point. The particular *quality* of these aspirations, however, was little explored. Thus, little advance was made toward explaining either the variation in aspirations that occurs among persons with similar values and from similar social strata or the variation that occurs across social strata. The focus upon between-class differences in aspirations resulted in explanatory systems that emphasized a combination of cultural differences and limiting objective conditions. Such explanations proved inadequate in the light of findings of the type obtained by Stephenson, and again by Empey, which did not substantiate the low aspirations of the lower classes. Further inadequacies were revealed when an interest developed in explaining within-class differences, as in the Kahl study.

Much of what has been discussed so far concerning values and aspirations affecting mobility has accounted for only a portion of the variation between the classes. The existence of differential values or levels of aspiration between the classes cannot help to explain the absence of mobility among persons of social classes with values favorable to mobility, nor can it help to explain the presence of mobility among persons in social classes where values unfavorable to mobility predominate. To advance our understanding in this connection we shall have to move beyond values, to a consideration of motivations and behavior patterns that may be a basic part of the personality system. An examination of personality differences, if any do in fact exist among the social classes, will help to determine whether the different social classes have "built-in" mobility-enhancing or inhibiting factors. We assume that the factors that we shall speak of here have a "deeper" and more permanent effect upon behavior than values absorbed through the social structures in which one is involved. The factors we speak of are "deferred gratification pattern" and "achievement motive."

Over a decade ago, Schneider and Lysgaard sought to reconceptualize a variety of isolated and unrelated behaviors found in the middle and lower classes along a single meaningful dimension (1953). Many class-related behaviors reported by other investigators seemed to "cluster" according to whether or not they indicated a tendency to postpone or defer immediate gratifications. Schneider and Lysgaard (1953, p. 143) described this clustering as follows:

> The lower-class-characteristic "impulse-following" (absence of deferred gratification pattern) involves: relative readiness to engage in physical violence, free sexual expression (as through intercourse), minimum pursuit of education, low aspiration level, failure of the parents to identify the class of their children's playmates, free spending, little emphasis on being "well-mannered and obedient," and short-time dependence upon parents. On the other hand, the middle-class-characteristic "impulse renunciation" (presence of deferred gratification pattern) involves the reverse of these traits. . . .

Using a national sample of 2,500 high school students, they sought to measure the distribution of class attitudes toward the various dimensions of the deferred gratification pattern. Their findings indicate general support for the hypothesis of a class-related pattern, with those students who identified themselves as "working class" being less inclined to endorse attitudes and indicate behaviors that are dimensions of the deferred gratification pattern. The important question raised by these findings is the extent to which such normatively defined cultural patterns of gratification postponement have their counterpart in personality patterns. Answers to this type of question would have to be sought through psychological tests that might be able to get at a personality configuration going beyond class-based social roles and culture patterns. Such studies are, of course, fraught with methodological and theoretical difficulties. It is difficult to carry out adequate testing with a sufficient number of subjects to make reliable within-class and between-class comparisons.

One of the earliest attempts to use formal psychological testing in stratification research was undertaken by Bernard Rosen (1956) in a study of male sophomores from two large public high schools in New Haven, Connecticut. Rosen's main concern was to explore both the psychological and cultural factors that affect mobility by influencing the individual's willingness to develop and exploit his talents and opportunities. The central factors for Rosen are achievement motive and achievement value orientation. The personality correlate of achievement called "achievement motive" was measured with a Thematic Apperception Test developed by McClelland and his associates (McClelland et al., 1953). Following standard TAT procedures each subject was asked to tell a story about a set of ambiguous pictures presented to him. The scoring of achievement content in the stories was based upon respondent's story description which discussed an individual's performance in the story within the context of competition with a standard of excellence. That performance is also evaluated by the respondent with a statement showing a positive judgment and approval of the performance in question.

Rosen's findings clearly support his hypothesis that the social classes differ in the strength of the "achievement motive." The mean achievement scores were highest for students in Classes I and II, and declined markedly through Class V (8.40, 8.69, 4.97, 3.40, 1.87. Class I represents the "highest" class and Class V the "lowest." The procedures for classification are reported in Hollingshead and Redlich, 1958). Rosen also reports that over 80 percent of the Class I and II students have high motivation scores, whereas only 23 percent of Class V have high scores. The achievement value orientation scores were also found to decline with social class (4.6, 4.1, 3.8, 3.0, 2.5) and to be quite consistent with the findings of Hyman described earlier. The subjects in higher class groupings were more likely to endorse items showing an activistic, future-oriented, individualistic point of view, which, it is assumed, are most likely to facilitate achievement and social mobility.

Although Rosen clearly established a connection between social class and achievement motive, the hypothesis of a link between achievement motive and mobility remained essentially untested. Since Rosen found some within-class variation in achievement motive, it is possible that this variation is related to the downward mobility of some upper-class individuals and the upward mobility of some lower-class individuals. An exploration of the achievement motive–mobility hypothesis was undertaken by Crockett (1962) in which he closely followed the procedures of Rosen and McClelland in establishing strength of achievement motive. Working with a national probability sample of adult males, Crockett's design allowed for comparisons of high and low achievement motive scores for respondents of four occupational origins (High, Upper-Middle, Lower-Middle, Low) and three mobility levels (occupational prestige below that of father, same as father, and above father). In this way the role of achievement motive can be examined for both upward and downward mobility.

Crockett's findings clearly suggest that achievement motive, as measured by thematic apperception, is an important personality factor related to occupational mobility. Specifically, the findings show "strength of achievement motive clearly related to upward mobility among sons of fathers in the two lower prestige categories but not among sons of fathers in the two higher prestige categories" (Crockett, 1962, p. 203). No relationship was found between strength of achievement motive and downward mobility. Such findings point to the complexities involved in trying to isolate both individual and social factors related to mobility. They suggest that achievement motive may be a multidimensional factor in which different dimensions are operative among different social strata (Kahl, 1965). It certainly makes a good deal of sense that the objective conditions of the relatively lower classes are such that exceptional individual qualities are required to move out of such conditions. It is much like the situation in baseball: there should be no great surprise that the first Negro ballplayer had exceptional talent; the nature of the barriers that he had to hurdle required nothing less.

Before exploring further this possibility of a multidimensional nature for achievement motive, let us first consider the extent to which a number of individual factors related to mobility seem to "hang together." Such efforts at seeking patterns of predictors not only attest to the validity of the individual predictors but also provide for greater continuity in research. We have examined the deferred gratification pattern and achievement motive, suggesting their relationship to social class and mobility. What of the relationship between these factors? Are they two different elements involved in mobility or are they two ways of measuring the same thing?

Straus, in a study of 338 high school juniors and seniors in Wisconsin, sought to examine the link between social class, deferred gratification, and achievement syndrome (Straus, 1962). A prior concern, however, was to retest the Schneider and Lysgaard social-class-deferred gratification hypothesis and to see whether "The deferment of such diverse needs as those for affiliation, aggression, material goods, independence, and sex fall into a *pattern* . . . [such a pattern would] imply that deferment of any one of these needs tends to be correlated with deferment of the others, particularly in the middle class" (Straus, 1962, p. 328).

A Guttman scale was developed for each of the need areas and these scales were intercorrelated, revealing a tendency for the "deferred grati-

fication scales to fall into two clusters, one representing deferment of interpersonal interaction needs, and the other representing deferment of
material needs" (ibid., p. 336). Correlations between deferred gratification and socioeconomic status do not indicate any significant relationships,
contrary to the Schneider and Lysgaard findings.

In looking at achievement, Straus used indicators such as academic
achievement and occupational aspiration rather than the thematic apperception procedures of Rosen and Crockett. Deferred gratification pattern
was found to be related to achievement, as was socioeconomic status. In
fact, the correlation between the DGP scale and achievement was found
to persist independently of socioeconomic status and intelligence. Thus
Straus concludes that "learning to defer need gratification seems to be
associated with achievement at all levels of the status hierarchy . . ." (ibid.,
p. 335).

What, then, may we conclude from the studies relating values, intelligence, aspirations, and achievement motive to social class and social mobility? Beliefs and values that are assumed to have a positive effect upon
social mobility have been found to be class-related. The lower classes are
described by Hyman as placing less emphasis upon success and upon those
patterns of behavior that are likely to result in success. This view would
tend to locate many of the causes of immobility within the individual himself. There are others, however, who have preferred to emphasize similarities in values and aspirations among the social classes while pointing
to the objective conditions that inhibit their attainment (Merton, 1957,
Chap. IV). A recent study by Mizruchi has pointed to the fact that while
the goals of "success" and "education" are equally shared throughout the
class hierarchy, there are different meanings attached to these goals
(Mizruchi, 1964). The classes differ in terms of the symbolic indicators
of success valued, and in terms of their view of education as having intrinsic value or as an instrumental means for advancement.

The *pattern* of the relationship between social class and success found
by Mizruchi—that the same variable (i.e., success) has different meanings
at various levels of class—is similar to that found in other studies discussed
in this section. We found, for example, that intelligence and social status
provide a good prediction for college aspiration; this is especially the case
for both the extremes of intelligence and social status where predictions
regarding college aspirations were best. For persons in the middle status
and middle intelligence groups, however, prediction of college aspirations
on this basis were no better than chance (Kahl, 1960). A similar pattern
is revealed when trying to relate personality variables to social mobility.
Achievement motive, achievement values, and deferred gratification were
all found to be related to social class and to each other. However, when
relating achievement motive to occupational mobility we find strength of
achievement motive related to mobility among the lower strata but not

among the upper strata. In addition, achievement motive is not found to be related to downward mobility.

The "uneven" nature of the findings discussed above attests to the complexity of social data. Simple main effects of one variable upon another neither explain a significant amount of variance nor accurately represent the real world. In explaining social phenomena we often find that two variables in combination (interaction effects) produce consequences that are quite different from each variable taken singly (main effects). In addition, the interaction effect is "uneven," in that it produces certain effects only at specified levels of a variable. Thus, achievement motive was significantly related to mobility at certain levels of social class.

There are several methodological and theoretical steps that can be taken to cope with the apparent complexity of the phenomena of mobility. First of all it appears that many of the things we have been talking about and measuring as achievement orientation and deferred gratification are not unitary but multidimensional phenomena. This is certainly suggested by Straus (1962), who showed that the component parts of the deferred gratification pattern actually form two clusters rather than one, and more recently by Kahl (1965), who factor analyzed achievement-type items from a number of studies. This being the case, it might help to explain some of the inconsistencies in findings from different studies, and in the "uneven" nature of these findings.

With methodological refinement may come theoretical explanations of mobility that are specific to persons located at various levels of the social structure. Youth from upper strata, for example, may not need strong personal motivation for mobility because they often operate in quite structured and determinate careers that are more a function of factors external to the individual. They are, so to speak, carried along by wise decisions, each of which provides an increment to the probability of achievement of high position in the occupational hierarchy. Such decisions as going to college, type of college, type of career, what fraternity, and the like, are more related to the general way of life of one's environment than personal drive. The lower class youth, on the other hand, must learn to make these decisions, and the very process of learning itself may eliminate their possible effectiveness. The "naturalness" of the behavior of the high status person in contrast to the self-conscious striver is well put by Kahl (1965, p. 677):

> Those with more education strive less openly and vigorously, but they have other values that in fact aid them in reaching or maintaining a level of occupational success higher than that obtained by the "striver." They trust in people and are thus able to develop long-term relationships that aid their careers, particularly in bureaucratic structures where the judgments of peers are so crucial. They believe that planning for the future is possible and fruitful; thus not only people but "destiny" can be relied

upon. They are willing to move away from their parents in order to accept career advancement, and in general put efficiency ahead of nepotism. These values are more subtle than open striving, yet are more directly connected with success.

With the general tendency toward greater cultural homogeneity among persons throughout the social structure, as well as the increasing number of persons from low status origins who go on to college and fill high status occupations, research concerning values and motivations related to mobility will have to delve for the more subtle differences and dimensions of values and motivations that have generally remained hidden in earlier efforts.

## WORKS CITED

Chinoy, Ely. *Automobile Workers and the American Dream*. New York: Doubleday and Co., 1955.

Crockett, Harry J., Jr. "The Achievement Motive and Differential Occupational Mobility in the United States," *Am. Sociol. Rev.* 27 (April 1962): 191–204.

Empey, Lamar T. "Social Class and Occupational Aspiration: A Comparison of Absolute and Relative Measurement," *Am. Sociol. Rev.* 21 (1956): 703–9.

Glick, Paul C. "Educational Attainment and Occupational Advancement," in *Transactions of the Second World Congress of Sociology*, International Sociological Association, London, 1954.

Hamilton, Richard F. "Income, Class, and Reference Groups," *Am. Sociol. Rev.* 29 (August 1964):576–79.

Haveman, Ernest, and West, Patricia Salter. *They Went to College*. New York: Harcourt, Brace and Co., 1952.

Hollingshead, August B. *Elmtown's Youth*. New York: John Wiley and Sons, 1949.

Hollingshead, August B., and Redlich, Frederick C. *Social Class and Mental Illness*. New York: John Wiley and Sons, 1958.

Hyman, Herbert H. "The Value Systems of Different Classes: A Social Psychological Contribution to the Analysis of Stratification," in Reinhard Bendix and Seymour M. Lipset (Eds.) *Class, Status and Power*. New York: The Free Press, 1953.

Kahl, Joseph A. *The American Class Structure*. New York: Holt, Rinehart, & Winston, 1960.

———. "Some Measurements of Achievement Orientation," *Am. Jour. Sociol.* 70 (May 1965):669–81.

McClelland, David C., et al. *The Achievement Motive*. New York: Appleton-Century-Crofts, 1953.

Merton, Robert K. *Socail Theory and Social Structure*. New York: The Free Press, 1957.

Miller, Herman P.    "Is the Income Gap Closed? 'No!'," *New York Times Magazine* (November 11, 1962).

Mizruchi, Ephraim A.    *Success and Opportunity.* New York: The Free Press, 1964.

Parker, Seymour, and Kleiner, Robert.    "Status Position, Mobility, and Ethnic Identification of the Negro," *Jour. Social Issues,* 20 (April 1964):85–102.

Rosen, Bernard C.    "The Achievement Syndrome: A Psychocultural Dimension of Stratification." *Am. Sociol. Rev.* 21 (1956):203–11.

Schneider, Louis and Lysgaard, Sverve.    "The Deferred Gratification Pattern: A Preliminary Study." *Am. Sociol. Rev.* 18 (April 1953):142–49.

Sewell, William H., Haller, Archie O., and Straus, Murray A.    "Social Status and Educational and Occupational Aspiration." *Am. Sociol. Rev.* 22 (1957): 67–73.

Stephenson, Richard M.    *Mobility Orientation and Stratification: A Study of One Thousand Ninth Graders,* unpublished doctoral dissertation, Columbia University, New York, 1956.

Straus, Murray A.    "Deferred Gratification, Social Class, and the Achievement Syndrome." *Am. Sociol. Rev.,* 27 (June 1962):326–35.

U.S. Department of Health, Education and Welfare. *Digest of Educational Statistics.* Washington, D.C., 1964.

Wilensky, Harold L.    "Mass Society and Mass Culture: Interdependence or Dependence?" *Am. Sociol. Rev.* 29 (April 1964):173–97.

Wohl, R. Richard.    "The 'Rags to Riches Story': An Episode of Secular Idealism," in Reinhard Bendix and Seymour M. Lipset (Eds.) *Class, Status and Power,* New York: The Free Press, 1953.

# 10

# Programmed for Social Class: Tracking in High School*

WALTER E. SCHAFER, CAROL OLEXA, and
KENNETH POLK

If, as folklore would have it, America is the land of opportunity, offering anyone the chance to raise himself purely on the basis of his or her ability, then education is the key to self-betterment. The spectacular increase in those of us who attend school is often cited as proof of the great scope of opportunity that our society offers: 94 percent of the high school age population was attending school in 1967, as compared with 7 percent in 1890.

Similarly, our educational system is frequently called more democratic than European systems, for instance, which rigidly segregate students by ability early in their lives, often on the basis of nationally administered examinations such as England's "11-plus." The United States, of course, has no official national policy of educational segregation. Our students, too, are tested and retested throughout their lives and put into faster or slower classes or programs on the basis of their presumed ability, but this procedure is carried out in a decentralized fashion that varies between each city or state.

However, many critics of the American practice claim that, no matter how it is carried out, it does not meet the needs of the brighter and duller groups, so much as it solidifies and widens the differences between them. One such critic, the eminent educator Kenneth B. Clark, speculates: "It is conceivable that the detrimental effects of segregation based upon in-

---

* Published by permission of Transaction, Inc. from *Transaction*, Vol. 7, No. 12. Copyright © 1970 by Transaction, Inc.

tellect are similar to the known detrimental effects of schools segregated on the basis of class, nationality or race."

Patricia Cayo Sexton notes that school grouping based on presumed ability often reinforces already existing social divisions:

> Children from higher social strata usually enter the "higher quality" groups and those from lower strata the "lower" ones. School decisions about a child's ability will greatly influence the kind and quality of education he receives, as well as his future life, including whether he goes to college, the job he will get, and his feelings about himself and others.

And Arthur Pearl puts it bluntly:

> . . . "special ability classes," "basic track," or "slow learner classes" are various names for another means of systematically denying the poor adequate access to education.

In this article we will examine some evidence bearing on this vital question of whether current educational practices tend to reinforce existing social class divisions. We will also offer an alternative aimed at making our public schools more effective institutions for keeping open the opportunities for social mobility.

## EDUCATION EXPLOSION

Since the turn of the century, a number of trends have converged to increase enormously the pressure on American adolescents to graduate from high school: declining opportunity in jobs, the upgrading of educational requirements for job entry, and the diminishing need for teenagers to contribute to family income. While some school systems, especially in the large cities, have adapted to this vast increase in enrollment by creating separate high schools for students with different interests, abilities, or occupational goals, most communities have developed comprehensive high schools serving all the youngsters within a neighborhood or community.

In about half the high schools in the United States today, the method for handling these large and varied student populations is through some form of tracking system. Under this arrangement, the entire student body is divided into two or more relatively distinct career lines, or tracks, with such titles as college preparatory, vocational, technical, industrial, business, general, basic, and remedial. While students on different tracks may take some courses together in the same classroom, they are usually separated into entirely different courses or different sections of the same course.

School men offer several different justifications for tracking systems. Common to most, however, is the notion that college-bound students are academically more able, learn more rapidly, should not be deterred in their progress by slower, non-college-bound students, and need courses for college preparation that non-college-bound students do not need. By the same token, it is thought that non-college-bound students are less bright, learn more slowly, should not be expected to progress as fast or learn as much as college-bound students, and need only a general education or work-oriented training to prepare themselves for immediate entry into the world of work or a business or vocational school.

In reply, the numerous critics of tracking usually contend that while the college-bound are often encouraged by the tracking system to improve their performance, non-college-bound students, largely as a result of being placed in a lower-rated track, are discouraged from living up to their potential or from showing an interest in academic values. What makes the system especially pernicious, these critics say, is that non-college-bound students more often come from low-income and minority group families. As a result, high schools, through the tracking system, inadvertently close off opportunities for large numbers of students from lower social strata, and thereby contribute to the low achievement, lack of interest, delinquency, and rebellion which school men frequently deplore in their non-college track students.

If these critics are correct, the American comprehensive high school, which is popularly assumed to be the very model of an open and democratic institution, may not really be open and democratic at all. In fact, rather than facilitating equality of educational opportunity, our schools may be subtly denying it, and in the process widening and hardening existing social divisions.

## TRACKS AND WHO GETS PUT ON THEM

During the summer of 1964, we collected data from official school transcripts of the recently graduated senior classes of two midwestern three-year high schools. The larger school, located in a predominantly middle-class, academic community of about 70,000, had a graduating class that year of 753 students. The smaller school, with a graduating class of 404, was located nearby in a predominantly working-class, industrial community of about 20,000.

Both schools placed their students into either a college prep or general track. We determined the positions of every student in our sample by whether he took tenth grade English in the college prep or the general section. If he was enrolled in the college prep section, he almost always took other college prep sections or courses, such as advanced mathematics or foreign languages, in which almost all enrollees were also college prep.

Just how students in the two schools were assigned to—or chose—tracks is somewhat of a mystery. When we interviewed people both in the high schools and in their feeder junior highs, we were told that whether a student went into one track or another depended on various factors, such as his own desires and aspirations, teacher advice, achievement test scores, grades, pressure from parents, and counselor assessment of academic promise. One is hard put to say which of these weighs most heavily, but we must note that one team of researchers, Cicourel and Kitsuse, showed in their study of *The Educational Decision-Makers* that assumptions made by counselors about the character, adjustment, and potential of in-coming students are vitally important in track assignment.

Whatever the precise dynamics of this decision, the outcome was clear in the schools we studied: socioeconomic and racial background had an effect on which track a student took, quite apart from either his achievement in junior high or his ability as measured by I.Q. scores. In the smaller, working-class school, 58 percent of the incoming students were assigned to the college prep track; in the larger, middle-class school, 71 percent were placed in the college prep track. And, taking the two schools together, whereas 83 percent of students from white-collar homes were assigned to the college prep track, this was the case with only 48 percent of students from blue-collar homes. The relationship of race to track assignment was even stronger: 71 percent of the whites and only 30 percent of the blacks were assigned to the college prep track. In the two schools studied, the evidence is plain: children from low income and minority group families more often found themselves in low ability groups and non-college-bound tracks than in high ability groups or college-bound tracks.

Furthermore, this decision-point early in the students' high school careers was of great significance for their futures, since it was virtually irreversible. Only 7 percent of those who began on the college prep track moved down to the noncollege prep track, while only 7 percent of those assigned to the lower, noncollege track, moved up. Clearly, these small figures indicate a high degree of rigid segregation within each of the two schools. In fact, greater mobility between levels has been reported in English secondary modern schools, where streaming—the British term for tracking—is usually thought to be more rigid and fixed than tracking in this country. (It must be remembered, of course, that in England the more rigid break is between secondary modern and grammar schools.)

## DIFFERENCES BETWEEN TRACKS

As might be expected from the schoolmen's justification for placing students in separate tracks in the first place, track position is noticeably related to academic performance. Thirty-seven percent of the college prep students graduated in the top quarter of their class (measured by grade point average throughout high school), while a mere 2 percent of the noncollege group achieved the top quarter. By contrast, half the noncollege prep students fell in the lowest quarter, as opposed to only 12 percent of the college prep.

Track position is also strikingly related to whether a student's academic performance improves or deteriorates during high school. The grade point average of all sample students in their ninth year—that is, prior to their being assigned to tracks—was compared with their grade point averages over the next three years. While there was a slight difference in the ninth year between those who would subsequently enter the college and noncollege tracks, this difference had increased by the senior year. This widening gap in academic performance resulted from the fact that a higher percentage of students subsequently placed in the college prep track improved their grade point average by the senior year, while a higher percentage of noncollege prep experienced a decline in grade point average by the time they reached the senior year.

Track position is also related strongly to dropout rate. Four percent of the college prep students dropped out of high school prior to graduation, as opposed to 36 percent of the noncollege group.

Track position is also a good indication of how deeply involved a student will be in school, as measured by participation in extracurricular activities. Out of the 753 seniors in the larger school, a comparatively small number of college prep students—21 percent—did not participate in any activities, while 44 percent took part in three or more such activities. By contrast, 58 percent, or more than half of the noncollege group took part in no extracurricular activities at all, and only 11 percent of this group took part in three or more activities.

Finally, track position is strikingly related to delinquency, both in and out of school. Out of the entire school body of the larger school during the 1963–1964 school year—that is, out of 2,565 boys and girls—just over one-third of the college-bound, as opposed to more than half of the non-college-bound committed one or more violations of school rules. Nineteen percent of the college-bound, compared with 70 percent of the non-college-bound, committed three or more such violations. During this year, just over one-third of all the college-bound students were suspended for infractions of school rules, while more than half of all the non-college-bound group were suspended.

Furthermore, using juvenile court records, we find that out of the 1964 graduating class in the larger school, six percent of the college prep, and 16 percent of the non-college-bound groups, were delinquent while in high school. Even though five percent of those on the noncollege track had already entered high school with court records, opposed to only one percent of the college prep track, still more non-college-bound students became delinquent during high school than did college prep students ( 11 percent compared with five percent). So the relation between track position and delinquency is further supported.

We have seen, then, that when compared with college prep students, noncollege prep students show lower achievement, great deterioration of achievement, less participation in extracurricular activities, a greater tendency to drop out, more misbehavior in school, and more delinquency outside of school. Since students are assigned to different tracks largely on the basis of presumed differences in intellectual ability and inclination for further study, the crucial question is whether assignment to different tracks helped to meet the needs of groups of students who were already different, as many educators would claim, or actually contributed to and reinforced such differences, as critics like Sexton and Pearl contend.

The simplest way to explain the differences we have just seen is to attribute them to characteristics already inherent in the individual students, or—at a more sophisticated level—to students' cultural and educational backgrounds.

It can be argued, for example, that the difference in academic achievement between the college and noncollege groups can be explained by the fact that college prep students are simply brighter; after all, this is one of the reasons they were taken into college prep courses. Others would argue that non-college-bound students do less well in school work because of family background: they more often come from blue-collar homes where less value is placed on grades and college, where books and help in schoolwork are less readily available, and verbal expression limited. Still others would contend that lower track students get lower grades because they performed less well in elementary and junior high, have fallen behind, and probably try less hard.

Fortunately, it was possible with our data to separate out the influence of track position from the other suggested factors of social class background (measured by father's occupation), intelligence (measured by I.Q.—admittedly not a perfectly acceptable measure), and previous academic performance (measured by grade point average for the last semester of the ninth year). Through use of a weighted percentage technique known as test factor standardization, we found that even when the effects of I.Q., social class and previous performance are ruled out, there is still a sizable difference in grade point average between the two tracks. With the influence of the first three factors eliminated we nevertheless find that 30 percent of the college prep, as opposed to a mere 4 percent of the noncollege group attained the top quarter of their class; and that only 12 percent of the college prep, as opposed to 35 percent of the noncollege group, fell into the bottom quarter. These figures, which are similar for boys and girls, further show that track position has an independent effect on academic achievement which is greater than the effect of each of the other three factors—social class, I.Q. and past performance. In particular, assignment to the noncollege track has a strong negative influence on a student's grades.

Looking at dropout rate, and again controlling for social class background, I.Q., and past performance, we find that track position in itself has an independent influence that is higher than the effect of any of the other three factors. In other words, even when we rule out the effect of these three factors, non-college-bound students still dropped out in considerably greater proportion than college-bound-students (19 percent vs. 4 percent).

## WHEN THE FORECASTERS MAKE THE WEATHER

So our evidence points to the conclusion that the superior academic performance of the college-bound students, and the inferior performance of the noncollege students is partly caused by the tracking system. Our data do not explain how this happens, but several studies of similar educational arrangements, as well as basic principles of social psychology do provide a number of probable explanations. The first point has to do with the pupil's self-image.

*Stigma.* Assignment to the lower track in the schools we studied carried with it a strong stigma. As David Mallory was told by an American boy, "Around here you are *nothing* if you're not college prep." A noncollege prep girl in one of the schools we studied told me that she always carried her "general" track books upside down because of the humiliation she felt at being seen with them as she walked through the halls.

The corroding effect of such stigmatizing is well known. As Patricia Sexton has put it, "He [the low track student] is bright enough to catch on very quickly to the fact that he is not considered very bright. He comes to accept this unflattering appraisal because, after all, the school should know."

One ex-delinquent in Washington, D.C., told one of us how the stigma from this low track affected him.

> It really don't have to be the tests, but after the tests, there shouldn't be no separation in the classes. Because, as I say again, I felt good when I was with my class, but when they went and separated us—that changed us. That changed our ideas, our thinking, the way we thought about each other and turned us to enemies toward each other—because they said I was dumb and they were smart.
>
> When you first go to junior high school you do feel something inside—it's like ego. You have been from elementary to junior high, you feel great inside. You say, well daggone, I'm going to deal with the *people* here now, I am in junior high school. You get this shirt that says Brown Junior High or whatever the name is and you are proud of that shirt. But then you go up there and the teacher says—"Well, so and so, you're in the basic section, you can't go with the other kids." The devil with the whole thing—you lose—something in you—like it just goes out of you.
>
> *Did you think the other guys were smarter than you?* Not at first—I used to think I was just as smart as anybody in the school—I knew I was

smart. I knew some people were smarter, and I *wanted* to go to school, I wanted to get a diploma and go to college and help people and everything. I stepped into there in junior high—I felt like a fool going to school —I really felt like a fool. *Why?* Because I felt like I wasn't a part of the school. I couldn't get on special patrols, because I wasn't qualified. *What happened between the seventh and ninth grades?* I started losing faith in myself—after the teachers kept downing me. You hear "a guy's in basic section, he's dumb" and all this. Each year—"you're ignorant—you're stupid."

Considerable research shows that such erosion of self-esteem greatly increases the chances of academic failure, as well as dropping out and causing "trouble" both inside and outside of school.

Moreover, this lowered self-image is reinforced by the expectations that others have toward a person in the noncollege group.

*The Self-fulfilling Prophecy.* A related explanation rich in implications comes from David Hargreaves' *Social Relations in a Secondary School,* a study of the psychological, behavioral, and educational consequences of the student's position in the streaming system of an English secondary modern school. In "Lumley School," the students (all boys) were assigned to one of five streams on the basis of ability and achievement, with the score on the "11-plus" examination playing the major role.

Like the schools we studied, students in the different streams were publicly recognized as high or low in status and were fairly rigidly segregated, both formally in different classes and informally in friendship groups. It is quite probable, then, that Hargreaves' explanations for the greater antischool attitudes, animosity toward teachers, academic failure, disruptive behavior and delinquency among the low stream boys apply to the noncollege prep students we studied as well. In fact, the negative effects of the tracking system on non-college-bound students may be even stronger in our two high schools, since the Lumley streaming system was much more open and flexible, with students moving from one stream to another several times during their four-year careers.

## STREAMED SCHOOLS

As we noted, a popular explanation for the greater failure and misbehavior among low stream or non-college-bound students is that they come from homes that fail to provide the same skills, ambition or conforming attitude as higher stream or college-bound students. Hargreaves demonstrates that there is some validity to this position: in his study, low stream boys more often came from homes that provided less encouragement for academic achievement and higher level occupations, and that were less oriented to the other values of the school and teachers. Similar differences may have existed among the students we studied, although their effects have been markedly reduced by our control for father's occupation, I.Q. and previous achievement.

But Hargreaves provides a convincing case for the position that whatever the differences in skills, ambition, self-esteem or educational commitment that the students brought to school, they were magnified by what happened to them in school, largely because low stream boys were the victims of a self-fulfilling prophecy in their relations with teachers, with respect to both academic performance and classroom behavior. Teachers of higher stream boys expected higher performance and got it. Similarly, boys who wore the label of streams "C" or "D" were more likely to be seen by teachers as limited in ability and troublemakers, and were treated accordingly.

> In a streamed school the teacher categorizes the pupils not only in terms of the inferences he makes of the child's class room behavior but also from the child's stream level. It is for this reason that the teacher can rebuke an "A" stream boy for being like a "D" stream boy. The teacher has learned to *expect* certain kinds of behavior from members of different streams. . . . It would be hardly surprising if "good" pupils thus became "better" and the "bad" pupils become "worse." It is, in short, an example of a self-fulfilling prophecy. The negative expectations of the teacher reinforce the negative behavioral tendencies.

A recent study by Rosenthal and Jacobson in an American elementary school lends further evidence to the position that teacher expectations influence student's performance. In this study, the influence is a positive one. Teachers of children randomly assigned to experimental groups were told at the beginning of the year to expect "unusual intellectual" gains, while teachers of the control group children were told nothing. After eight months, and again after two years, the experimental group children, the "intellectual spurters," showed significantly greater gains in I.Q. and grades. Further, they were rated by the teachers as being significantly more curious, interesting, happy, and more likely to succeed in the future. Such findings are consistent with theories of interpersonal influence and with the interactional or labelling view of deviant behavior.

If, as often claimed, American teachers underestimate the learning potential of low track students and expect more negative attitudes and greater trouble from them, it may well be that they partially cause the very failure, alienation, lack of involvement, dropping out and rebellion they are seeking to prevent. As Hargreaves says of Lumley, "It is important to stress that if this effect of categorization is real, it is entirely unintended by the teachers. They do not wish to make low streams more difficult than they are!" Yet the negative self-fulfilling prophecy was probably real, if unintended and unrecognized, in our two schools as well as in Lumley.

Two further consequences of the expectation that students in the non-college group will learn less well are differences in grading policies and in teacher effectiveness.

*Grading Policies.* In the two schools we studied, our interviews strongly hint at the existence of grade ceilings for noncollege prep students and grade floors for college-bound students. That is, by virtue of being located in a college preparatory section or course, college prep students could seldom receive any grade lower than "B" or "C," while students in non-college-bound sections or courses found it difficult to gain any grade higher than "C," even though their objective performance may have been equivalent to a college prep "B." Several teachers explicitly called our attention to this practice, the rationale being that noncollege prep students do not deserve the same objective grade rewards as college prep students, since they "clearly" are less bright and perform less well. To the extent that grade ceilings do operate for non-college-bound students, the lower grades that result from this policy, almost by definition, can hardly have a beneficial effect on motivation and commitment.

*Teaching Effectiveness.* Finally, numerous investigations of ability grouping, as well as the English study by Hargreaves, have reported that teachers of higher ability groups are likely to teach in a more interesting and effective manner than teachers of lower ability groups. Such a difference is predictable from what we know about the effects of reciprocal interaction between teacher and class. Even when the same individual teaches both types of classes in the course of the day, as was the case for most teachers in the two schools in this study, he is likely to be "up" for college prep classes and "down" for noncollege prep classes—and to bring out the same reaction from his students.

A final, and crucial factor that contributes to the poorer performance and lower interest in school of non-college-bound students is the relation between school work and the adult career after school.

*Future Payoff.* Non-college-bound students often develop progressively more negative attitudes toward school, especially formal academic work, because they see grades—and indeed school itself—as having little future relevance or payoff. This is not the case for college prep students. For them, grades are a means toward the identifiable and meaningful end of qualifying for college, while among the non-college-bound, grades are seen as far less important for entry into an occupation or a vocational school. This difference in the practical importance of grades is magnified by the perception among non-college-bound students that it is pointless to put much effort into school work, since it will be unrelated to the later world of work anyway. In a study of *Rebellion in a High School* in this country, Arthur Stinchcombe describes the alienation of non-college-bound high school students:

The major practical conclusion of the analysis above is that rebellious behavior is largely a reaction to the school itself and to its promises, not a failure of the family or community. High school students can be motivated to conform by paying them in the realistic coin of future advantage. Except perhaps for pathological cases, any student can be motivated to conform if the school can realistically promise something valuable to him as a reward for working hard. But for a large part of the population, especially the adolescent who will enter the male working class or the female candidates for early marriage, the school has nothing to offer. . . . In order to secure conformity from students, a high school must articulate academic work with careers of students.

Being on the lower track has other negative consequences for the student that go beyond the depressing influence on his academic performance and motivation. We can use the principles just discussed to explain our findings with regard to different rates of participation in school activities and acts of misbehavior.

## TRACKS CONFORMITY AND DEVIANCE

For example, the explanations having to do with self-image and the expectations of others suggest that assignment to the non-college-bound track has a dampening effect on commitment to school in general, since it is the school that originally categorized these students as inferior. Thus, assignment to the lower track may be seen as independently contributing to resentment, frustration, and hostility in school, leading to lack of involvement in all school activities, and finally ending in active withdrawal. The self-exclusion of the noncollege group from the mainstream of college student life is probably enhanced by intentional or unintentional exclusion by other students and teachers.

Using the same type of reasons, while we cannot prove a definite causal linkage between track position and misbehavior, it seems highly likely that assignment to the noncollege prep track often leads to resentment, declining commitment to school, and rebellion against it, expressed in lack of respect for the school's authority or acts of disobedience against it. As Albert Cohen argued over a decade ago in *Delinquent Boys*, delinquency may well be largely a rebellion against the school and its standards by teenagers who feel they cannot get anywhere by attempting to adhere to such standards. Our analysis suggests that a key factor in such rebellion is noncollege prep status in the school's tracking system, with the vicious cycle of low achievement and inferior self-image that go along with it.

This conclusion is further supported by Hargreaves' findings on the effect of streaming at Lumley:

> There is a real sense in which the school can be regarded as a generator of delinquency. Although the aims and efforts of the teachers are directed

towards deleting such tendencies, the organization of the school and its influence on subcultural development unintentionally fosters delinquent values. . . . For low stream boys . . . , school simultaneously exposes them to these values and deprives them of status in these terms. It is at this point they may begin to reject the values because they cannot succeed in them. The school provides a mechanism through the streaming system whereby their failure is effected and institutionalized, and also provides a situation in which they can congregate together in low streams.

Hargreaves' last point suggests a very important explanation for the greater degree of deviant behavior among the non-college-bound.

*The Student Subculture.* Assignment to a lower stream at Lumley meant a boy was immediately immersed in a student subculture that stressed and rewarded antagonistic attitudes and behavior toward teachers and all they stood for. If a boy was assigned to the "A" stream, he was drawn toward the values of teachers, not only by the higher expectations and more positive rewards from the teachers themselves, but from other students as well. The converse was true of lower stream boys, who accorded each other high status for doing the opposite of what teachers wanted. Because of class scheduling, little opportunity developed for interaction and friendship across streams. The result was a progressive polarization and hardening of the high and low stream subcultures between first and fourth years and a progressively greater negative attitude across stream lines, with quite predictable consequences.

> The informal pressures within the low streams tend to work directly against the assumption of the teachers that boys will regard promotion into a higher stream as a desirable goal. The boys from the low streams were very reluctant to ascent to higher streams because their stereotypes of "A" and "B" stream boys were defined in terms of values alien to their own and because promotion would involve rejection by their low stream friends. The teachers were not fully aware that this unwillingness to be promoted to a higher stream led the high informal status boys to depress their performance in examinations. This fear of promotion adds to our list of factors leading to the formation of anti-academic attitudes among low stream boys.

Observations and interviews in the two American schools we studied confirmed a similar polarization and reluctance by noncollege prep students to pursue the academic goals rewarded by teachers and college prep students. Teachers, however, seldom saw the antischool attitudes of noncollege prep students as arising out of the tracking system—or anything else about the school—but out of adverse home influences, limited intelligence, or psychological problems.

*Implications.* These, then, are some of the ways the schools we studied contributed to the greater rates of failure, academic decline, uninvolvement in school activities, misbehavior, and delinquency among non-college-bound students. We can only speculate, of course, about the generalization of these findings to other schools. However, there is little reason to think the two schools we studied were unusual or unrepresentative and, despite differences in size and social class composition, the findings are virtually identical in both. To the extent the findings are valid and general, they strongly suggest that, through their tracking system, the schools are partly causing many of the very problems they are trying to solve and are posing an important barrier to equal educational opportunity to lower income and black students, who are disproportionately assigned to the noncollege prep track.

The notion that schools help cause low achievement, deterioration of educational commitment and involvement, the dropout problem, misbehavior, and delinquency is foreign and repulsive to many teachers, administrators and parents. Yet our evidence is entirely consistent with Kai Erikson's observation that ". . . deviant forms of conduct often seem to derive nourishment from the very agencies devised to inhibit them."

What, then, are the implications of this study? Some might argue that, despite the negative side effects we have shown, tracking systems are essential for effective teaching, especially for students with high ability, as well as for adjusting students early in their careers to the status levels they will occupy in the adult occupational system. We contend that however reasonable this may sound, the negative effects demonstrated here offset and call into serious question any presumed gains from tracking.

Others might contend that the negative outcomes we have documented can be eliminated by raising teachers' expectations of noncollege track students, making concerted efforts to reduce the stigma attached to noncollege classes, assigning good teachers to noncollege track classes, rewarding them for doing an effective job at turning on their students, and developing fair and equitable grading practices in both college prep and noncollege prep classes.

Attractive as they may appear, efforts like these will be fruitless, so long as tracking systems, and indeed schools as we now know them, remain unchanged. What is needed are wholly new, experimental environments of teaching-learning-living, even outside today's public schools, if necessary. Such schools of the future must address themselves to two sets of problems highlighted by our findings: ensuring equality of opportunity for students now "locked out" by tracking, and offering—to all students —a far more fulfilling and satisfying learning process.

One approach to building greater equality of opportunity, as well as fulfillment, into existing or new secondary schools is the New Careers model. This model, which provides for fundamentally different ways of linking up educational and occupational careers, is based on the recognition that present options for entering the world of work are narrowly limited: one acquires a high school diploma and goes to work, or he first goes to college and perhaps then to a graduate or professional school. (Along the way, of course, young men must cope with the draft.)

The New Careers model provides for new options. Here the youth who does not want to attend college or would not qualify according to usual criteria, is given the opportunity to attend high school part time while working in a lower level position in an expanded professional career hierarchy (including such new positions as teacher aide and teacher associate in education). Such a person would then have the options of moving up through progressively more demanding educational and work stages; and moving back and forth between the work place, the high school and then the college. As ideally conceived, this model would allow able and aspiring persons ultimately to progress to the level of the fully certified teacher, nurse, librarian, social worker, or public administrator. While the New Careers model has been developed and tried primarily in the human service sector of the economy, we have pointed out elsewhere that it is applicable to the industrial and business sector as well.

This alternative means of linking education with work has a number of advantages: students can try different occupations while still in school; they can earn while studying; they can spend more time outside the four walls of the school, learning what can best be learned in the work place; less stigma will accrue to those not immediately college bound, since they too will have a future; studying and learning will be inherently more relevant because it will relate to a career in which they are actively involved; teachers of such students will be less likely to develop lower expectations because these youth too will have an unlimited, open-ended future; and antischool subcultures will be less likely to develop, since education will not be as negative, frustrating, or stigmatizing.

Changes of this kind imply changes in the economy as well and, therefore, are highly complicated and far-reaching. Because of this, they will not occur overnight. But they are possible, through persistent, creative, and rigorously evaluated educational, economic, and social experimentation.

Whatever the future, we hope teachers, administrators, and school boards will take one important message from our findings: what they do to students makes a difference. Through the kind of teaching-learning process they create, the schools can screen out and discourage large numbers of youth, or they can develop new means for serving the interests and futures of the full range of their students.

# 11

# Local Social Structure and Educational Selection*

## NATALIE ROGOFF

This paper is concerned with the way young people are allocated to positions in the social-class structure and the part played by education in the allocating process.

Numerous studies in America, Britain, and western Europe document the fact that youngsters who start life in a given social class vary in the class status they achieve as adults in proportion to the amount of formal schooling they obtain. The more education, the more advantaged the class status. Depending on the starting point, education facilitates either upward social mobility or the maintenance of a favored class position; lack of education brings on downward social mobility, or stability in a disadvantaged class position.

But what are we to make of these facts? Particularly, what is it that sets some youngsters on a path leading ultimately to graduation from college, while others never even complete their secondary education? As usually stated, the facts convey little of a sense of social process, of one thing occurring before another in an identifiable social location, or of one event or status affecting a later event or status through the advent of specific social mechanisms. It is possible that any one or any combination of at least three disparate sets of happenings might bring about the observed relationships. Each of the three, to be proposed here, emphasizes a different key process—one stemming from the effect of schools on individual

* Reprinted with the permission of The Macmillan Company, from *Education, Economy and Society* by A.H. Halsey, Jean Floud, and C. Arnold Anderson, pp. 241–51. © The Free Press, A Division of Macmillan Publishing Co., Inc.

differences in ability, another from the effect of individual family differences in motivation, and the third from differences in community and
school environments. In each case, the social process has a specified mechanism operating in a specified context. That these are extremely divergent
interpretations of the observed correlation should be evident by the following discussion of each.

First, schools, like all formal organizations, develop a system of rewards and punishments as one way of implementing their goals. The acquisition of skills and knowledge by students is clearly one of the goals of
schools. It is certainly not improbable that students who demonstrate the
greatest success in acquiring skills and knowledge should most frequently
receive the rewards that schools have at their disposal—promotion, high
grades, prizes, and scholarships. Since the distribution of marked scholastic ability cuts across the social classes to at least some degree, the reward
and punishment system of the schools would lead to a rearrangement of
students with respect to their potential social achievement: the more able
youngsters, motivated by scholastic rewards, would move further ahead
in school, continue their education longer, and eventually move into more
prestigeful occupational and social positions than the less able. Moreover,
at the end of the school years, a certain amount of social mobility, upward and downward, could be attributed to the encouragement given by
schools to the capable, no matter what their social origins, as well as to
the discouragement given the less able of all social classes. The observed
relationship between educational attainment and adult social-class position might, therefore, be due to the interaction between individual differences in ability and the reward systems of schools.

A second process that would lead to the observed results has its locus
in the family, rather than the school, and hinges on attitudes rather than
aptitude. Some families, valuing achievement, discipline, and social-eco-
nomic success, encourage their children to do as well as possible in school;
the youngster's ability, this interpretation runs, sets only the broadest of
bounds on his school performance. More determining than ability is the
family's attitude toward education—and the distribution of favorable attitudes toward education again cuts across the class structure to some degree. The education and, ultimately, the social-class achievement of youngsters represent family aspirations come true. Note that the school, in this
process, plays essentially a passive role, or at least takes something of a
secondary part. The school actually rewards, not necessarily those who
merit it, but those who *want* to be rewarded, whether or not, in some abstract sense of equitable arrangements, they do merit it. The real locus of
social mobility is the living room, not the classroom.

Finally, the possibility exists that educational attainment and adult class
status are correlated because of processes arising from community and
school structures. Because this idea is less familiar than the others and

because the processes it highlights differ in certain formal ways from the others, it will be developed here at somewhat greater length. First, let it be granted that the various social classes are not randomly distributed among the diverse sizes and types of communities in the United States today. (We defer for the moment the evidence for this assertion.) It follows that each of the social classes will be more heavily concentrated in some kinds of community environments than in others, and that communities will vary in the predominant or average social-class affiliation of their residents. Such structural differences may set in motion both formal arrangements—such as school, library, and general cultural facilities in the community—and informal mechanisms, such as normative climates or modal levels of social aspiration, which are likely to affect *all* members of the community to some extent—parents and children, upper, middle, and working classes.

Many of the studies whose general findings are at issue here have, in fact, covered a wide variety of communities. By pooling the behavior of youngsters living in diverse communities, one of the sources of social mobility may be hidden from view, for it is possible that the formal arrangements and informal norms of the community set both a floor and a ceiling on the ultimate achievements in educational and social-class status of their young residents. For example, when we observe that youngsters from the more favored social origins end up on the average with greater educational attainment, we may in fact be observing the results of the greater concentration of such youngsters in communities that facilitate academic achievement through better schools and through prevailing climates of opinion that nurture and sustain high educational aspiration. Upward social mobility, under these conditions, would result for the lucky minority of working-class youngsters whose families live, by accident or design, in predominantly middle-class communities; and downward social mobility for the unlucky middle-class youngsters living in less favored environments; while stability of class position would be the typical outcome for the majority of youngsters living in towns, villages, or cities where their class status is not a deviant one.

One of the intriguing implications of this idea is that it proposes a continuing but ever-changing link between ecological processes that lead to spatial patterns of residence and work, on the one hand, and the processes through which persons are allocated to positions in the social-class structure, on the other. Socioeconomic position influences the type of community or neighborhood where families will live; their ecological status then affects the life chances of their children, some of whom will maintain the social-class status of the parents, while others will shift in status. Both individual and net shifts of class status in the second generation lead to further changes in ecological patterns, and so on, possibly until some kind of equilibrium is reached.

In sum, three variant interpretations have been offered for a recurrent empirical observation: that young people from given social origins vary in their educational attainment; such variations eventually leading to differences in the social-class status achieved in adulthood. Educational attainment thereby leads to upward or downward social mobility, or to maintenance of parental class status. In effect, the three interpretations can be ordered with respect to the importance they attach to events transpiring in the classroom itself. According to the first, the classroom is the central stage, for it is there that youngsters are rewarded or punished for their scholastic ability and performance, and it is the rewards and punishments they experience that lead to their academic and social attainments. According to the second interpretation, youngsters are carriers of aspirations and attitudes acquired from their families, and it is these states of mind that prevail, although they may be reinforced (unwittingly?) by the reward-and-punishment system of the school. The last interpretation calls attention to the community setting of both schools and families, and suggests that the ecological environment leads to formal and informal arrangements within and outside of the schools, affecting the educational attainment of residents.

None of these interpretations excludes the others. It is not necessary to demonstrate that only one of the social processes can be observed, the others being absent. Instead, a research design is called for that permits us to see whether all three are operative and, if possible, to gauge their relative significance. An empirical study with such a design is currently in process at the Bureau of Applied Social Research of Columbia University. We were fortunate enough to be given access to information gathered by the Educational Testing Service, concerning the college-going and career plans of over 35,000 American high-school seniors, who constituted the entire senior class of 1955 of over 500 public secondary schools. Concerning the schools, which provide a fairly representative sample of the 20,000-odd senior public high schools in the United States, information was collected, at the time of the field work, from their principals. This has now been supplemented by consulting national and state school directories, other published surveys, and census sources describing the towns and counties where the schools are located.

What kinds of information are needed to provide empirical tests of the ideas advanced here? We need to know something about the social origins of the youngsters, something about their future orientations, and their scholastic ability. Finally, we need to introduce some principle for classifying the communities where they attend high school. Specifically, here are the indicators to be used in attempting to compare the proposed types of social processes with the factual evidence. First, we shall see how youngsters who vary in scholastic ability—indicated by their performance on a 20-item test devised especially for this study by the Educational Testing

Service—compare with respect to their plans for going on to college. This will provide the evidence for seeing whether or not the reward-and-punishment system of the schools helps to channel the more capable youngsters into the route of higher education. Moreover, we shall simultaneously trace the effect of the youngster's social background on his college-going orientation. Several criteria have been used to classify the families of orientation of the high-school seniors: their fathers' occupational status, fathers' educational attainment, and the college experience of their older siblings. Combining these three properties of the families with the average college-going propensities of the high-school seniors who belonged to such family types permitted us to construct a set of ranked socioeducational classes, ranging from well-educated professional and managerial families, who clearly imbue their offspring with a desire to go to college, to poorly or uneducated unskilled manual and farm families who are far more indifferent to higher education as a desirable goal. Five such classes were finally discerned, each containing approximately 20 percent of the 35,000 high-school seniors, so that they may be referred to as the socioeducational status quintiles.

One further word about classifying the students according to their scholastic ability. At some of the high schools studied, the vast majority of seniors scored well above the mean, while at other schools, the bulk of the senior class did extremely poorly on the test. While this is in itself a significant result, it also has the following implication: if we were to classify individual seniors according to their absolute scholastic aptitude score, we should be comparing the behavior of youngsters who actually stood at just about all possible relative positions within their own school. Almost any given score represents the top, the middle, and the bottom relative position at one or more of the 518 high schools observed. Therefore, the scores were converted into school-specific quartiles for all those who were in a senior class of 15 or more. (This eliminates about 20 percent of the schools, but less than three percent of the 35,000 students.) Since we want to observe the effect of allocating rewards and punishments by school authorities, we clearly need to compare those who are at the top in their own school with those at the bottom, no matter what the absolute level of scholastic ability is at the school.

Finally, we have used the expressions "scholastic ability" and "scholastic performance" as though they were interchangeable, despite the fact that they are clearly disparate. Fortunately, the principals of about 100 of the high schools were asked to check the school records of each of their seniors and indicate what his class standing was. The correlation between ability, as indicated by the short written test, and class standing, which summarizes the student's performance over a four-year period, is extremely high, although it does vary somewhat among the high schools. Table 1 presents the evidence—which we use as a justification for taking the stu-

**TABLE ONE**
Class Standing and Scholastic Ability

| Scholastic-Ability Quartile* | Percentage Who Are in the Top Half of Their Senior Class, by Grade Average | No. of Cases |
|---|---|---|
| (Top) 4 ............... | 75 | 1,558 |
| 3 ............... | 56 | 1,614 |
| 2 ............... | 40 | 1,689 |
| (Bottom) 1 ............... | 17 | 1,561 |

* Scores on the special aptitude test devised for this study were transformed into school-specific quartiles.

dent's performance on the aptitude test as a fairly good indicator of his behavior in the classroom.

Scholastic ability plays a decisive role in students' plans to continue with their education. Some 61 percent of all high-school seniors in the top quarter of their class planned to go to college; in successive quartiles, the proportion drops to 44 percent, 33 percent, and 24 percent. The preliminary evidence suggests that the high school in effect *does* allocate rewards and punishments in such a way as to encourage the competent and discourage the incompetent. At the same time, there is a marked tendency for students' further educational plans to be influenced by the socioeducational status of their families. Seventy-two percent of those from professional or managerial families plan to attend college; the proportion decreases to 47 percent, 35 percent, 26 percent, and finally 24 percent through the succeeding socioeducational status categories. And, as many other studies have shown, the two social processes reinforce one another. The full picture is given in Table 2, where the proportions planning to attend college are shown at every level of scholastic ability and from each of the five types of social origins simultaneously. College-going propensities vary greatly among the 20 categories of high-school seniors: 83 percent of the brightest youngsters from the most advantaged families plan to attend college, but only 16 percent of the least competent children of skilled and semiskilled workers (category 2) are college-oriented. Both the school and the family play a part in determining who is to gain education beyond high school. Among previous studies, the relative importance of the two has varied greatly; Kahl's study in the suburbs of Boston[1] shows the family to be almost twice as influential as the school, while Sewell's Wisconsin data[2] suggest the school to be almost three times as important as the fam-

[1] J.A. Kahl, "Education and Occupational Aspirations of 'Common Man' Boys," *Harvard Educational Review*, 23 (1953):186–203.

[2] W.H. Sewell et al., "Social Status and Educational and Occupational Aspiration," *American Sociological Review*, 21 (1956):203–11.

TABLE TWO

Percentage of High-School Seniors Planning to Attend College, According to Scholastic Ability (in Quartiles) and Socioeducational Status of the Family

| Scholastic-Ability Quartile* | Family-Status Quintile | | | | | All Quintiles | No. of Cases |
|---|---|---|---|---|---|---|---|
| | (Top) 5 | 4 | 3 | 2 | (Bottom) 1 | | |
| (Top) 4 | 83 | 66 | 53 | 44 | 43 | 61 | (8,647) |
| 3 | 70 | 53 | 37 | 29 | 29 | 44 | (8,709) |
| 2 | 65 | 41 | 31 | 20 | 21 | 33 | (8,696) |
| (Bottom) 1 | 53 | 30 | 22 | 16 | 18 | 24 | (8,509) |
| All quartiles | 72 | 47 | 35 | 26 | 24 | 40 | |
| No. of cases | (6,520) | (6,647) | (6,465) | (8,116) | (6,811) | | (34,561) |

Notes: Students are classified here according to their scholastic-aptitude quartile in their own high school. Family status position, however, is constant for all students coming from a given family background, no matter what the social composition of their high school.

The number of cases on which each of the percentages is based ranges from 963 to 2,505.

ily; our own nation-wide sample falls squarely between the two, with each of the sources playing about an equal role.

So much, then, for the first two social processes leading to the observed correlation between educational attainment and social mobility or stability. What of the third? With the first two, it was clear, both from the logic of the argument and from the guidelines provided by past research, just what indicators to use in order to test the validity of our ideas. The third set of social processes are, we suggested, generated by conditions in the community, which affect the type of educational and cultural facilities the town can provide and which presumably also shape the average social and education aspiration level of the residents. But what types of indicators would most accurately portray such environmental states? This is clearly a major sociological problem and one to which we can make only a limited contribution. Furthermore, we have only begun to probe the data in this study for tentative leads and therefore offer the following evidence with the appropriate reservations.

We start with a principle of classifying communities that derives from a set of frequently used descriptive terms, employed by laymen, educators, social scientists, and just about everyone who has ever given a moments' thought to the varieties of educational experience: the size and type of community—village or small town, suburban or metropolitan—where the schools are located. The temptation is strong to clothe this idea in polysyllabic sociological garb, but in fact the impulse to use such a classification scheme arose from the fact that it is one of the very few environmental properties used frequently enough and over a long enough period of time to warrant a systematic empirical test.

Nine types of communities were discerned, varying in population size and in their relationship to a metropolitan area. Table 3 identifies the types and presents the salient results concerning the college-going propensities of youngsters attending high school in each environment. It is up to the reader to decide whether or not the results confirm his expectations. For example, who would have predicted that the college-going propensities of youngsters attending high school in the very largest cities is almost as low as that of youngsters residing in the smallest towns and villages and is surpassed by that of youngsters from the larger towns and, of course, the suburbs? College-going is apparently affected by the size and type of community where the decision to attend college is made—but hardly in a simple, linear fashion. One note of caution. We were able to observe only those young people who remained in school until the 12th grade, and the tendency to stay in school that long varies among the diverse type of communities. The college-going proportions need to be corrected, therefore, by taking into account those youngsters who will not attend college because they have not completed a secondary education. Community educational-retention rates are positively correlated both with urbanization

TABLE THREE
College-Planning Rates and Social Composition of High-School Senior Classes
in Diverse Community Contexts

| Type of Community | Number of High Schools | Number of Seniors | Percentage Planning to Attend College | Percentage of Seniors in Each Family-Status Quintile | | | | | Total |
|---|---|---|---|---|---|---|---|---|---|
| | | | | (Top) 5 | 4 | 3 | 2 | (Bottom) 1 | |
| Small independent towns: | | | | | | | | | |
| Less than 2,500 .... | 270 | 6,991 | 33 | 9 | 17 | 12 | 20 | 42 | 100% |
| 2,500–9,999 ...... | 85 | 5,451 | 39 | 16 | 20 | 16 | 24 | 24 | 100% |
| 10,000–49,999 .... | 42 | 5,591 | 48 | 21 | 20 | 19 | 24 | 16 | 100% |
| Suburbs: | | | | | | | | | |
| Less than 2,500 .... | 36 | 1,768 | 37 | 17 | 18 | 18 | 26 | 21 | 100% |
| 2,500–9,999 ...... | 15 | 1,085 | 46 | 30 | 18 | 19 | 23 | 10 | 100% |
| 10,000–49,999 .... | 22 | 3,116 | 50 | 34 | 18 | 19 | 21 | 8 | 100% |
| Large towns and cities: | | | | | | | | | |
| 50,000–99,999 .... | 10 | 2,176 | 45 | 22 | 20 | 22 | 23 | 13 | 100% |
| 100,000–499,999 .. | 19 | 3,669 | 37 | 17 | 18 | 24 | 30 | 11 | 100% |
| 500,000 or more ... | 19 | 5,589 | 39 | 20 | 22 | 23 | 24 | 11 | 100% |
| All communities ..... | 518 | 35,436 | 40 | 19 | 19 | 19 | 23 | 20 | 100% |

and with community wealth (median family income), and much more markedly with the latter than the former. Therefore, the wealthy suburbs should have their college-going proportions reduced the least, since most of their youngsters do stay in school through the 12th grade, followed by the larger cities, and finally small towns and rural villages. This would keep the three main types of communities in the same rank order but would increase the gap between the smallest and largest places.

The second part of Table 3 describes the social composition of the student body attending high school in the various types of communities. Note the marked degree of social segregation implied by these distributions— the children of farmers (category 1) concentrated in the smallest villages and towns, the children of professionals and managers in the larger suburbs, and the children of industrial workers (category 2) most heavily concentrated in cities of 100,000–500,000. We cannot here mention more than a few of the major consequences of such ecological segregation.

One of the most interesting consequences concerns the scholastic aptitude of youngsters attending schools situated in diverse community contexts. Table 4 presents the trends, showing median aptitude scores of students coming from families of each of the five socioeducational status types and living in each type of community. Here, of course, we describe students according to their absolute scores on the aptitude test, since we want to evaluate the effect of the environment on scholastic ability. Test scores

TABLE FOUR
Scholastic Ability and College-Planning Rates, by Social Origins and
Community Context

| Type of Community | Family-Status Quintile | | | | | Unweighted Mean of All Quintiles |
|---|---|---|---|---|---|---|
| | (Top) 5 | 4 | 3 | 2 | (Bottom) 1 | |
| A. Median Aptitude Scores | | | | | | |
| Small independent towns: | | | | | | |
| Less than 2,500 ........ | 11.1 | 9.2 | 8.3 | 7.7 | 6.9 | 8.7 |
| 2,500–9,999 .......... | 11.6 | 9.7 | 8.6 | 8.1 | 7.4 | 9.1 |
| 10,000–49,999 ........ | 12.7 | 10.1 | 9.0 | 9.1 | 7.3 | 9.6 |
| Suburbs: | | | | | | |
| Less than 2,500 ........ | 11.9 | 9.8 | 9.0 | 8.2 | 7.2 | 9.2 |
| 2,500–9,999 .......... | *13.0+ | 10.8 | 9.4 | 8.2 | 7.2 | 10.0 |
| 10,000–49,999 ........ | 13.0 | 11.3 | 10.5 | 9.9 | 8.5 | 10.6 |
| Large towns and cities: | | | | | | |
| 50,000–99,999 ........ | 12.0 | 8.8 | 8.0 | 7.1 | *5.0– | 8.0 |
| 100,000–499,999 ...... | 11.8 | 9.5 | 8.4 | 7.7 | 7.0 | 8.9 |
| 500,000 or more ....... | 11.7 | 9.6 | 8.8 | 8.6 | 7.2 | 9.2 |
| B. Percentage Planning to Attend College | | | | | | |
| Small independent towns: | | | | | | |
| Less than 2,500 ........ | 66 | 45 | 35 | 25 | 25 | 39 |
| 2,500–9,999 .......... | 73 | 50 | 33 | 25 | 27 | 42 |
| 10,000–49,999 ........ | 78 | 55 | 42 | 32 | 32 | 48 |
| Suburbs: | | | | | | |
| Less than 2,500 ........ | 69 | 50 | 35 | 25 | 15 | 39 |
| 2,500–9,999 .......... | 74 | 51 | 38 | 22 | 29 | 43 |
| 10,000–49,999 ........ | 77 | 51 | 40 | 26 | 22 | 43 |
| Large towns and cities: | | | | | | |
| 50,000–99,999 ........ | 67 | 44 | 36 | 35 | 37 | 44 |
| 100,000–499,999 ...... | 69 | 45 | 32 | 22 | 20 | 37 |
| 500,000 or more ....... | 64 | 46 | 31 | 28 | 24 | 39 |

* Medians were computed from grouped data, using four score intervals. In these two cases, the medians fell in one of the extreme intervals, and interpolation was not carried out.

ranged from 0 to 20; the mean for all 35,000 seniors to whom it was given is 8.9; the standard deviation, 4.7.

Again, the suburbs stand out as most conducive to pronounced scholastic achievement. For convenience, an unweighted average aptitude score is given for all students attending schools in each community context. This enables us to see the effect that schools exert on their student's academic capacity, without that effect's being obscured by the advantages or disadvantages individual students enjoy by virtue of their family background. It appears that all students, whether in the majority or the minority in the school they attend, enjoy the blessings or pay the price their school affords. From those at the top to those at the bottom of the social-class hierarchy, all students attending large suburban schools emerge from their educational experience relatively better equipped in academic skills, while youngsters who attend school in small villages or large industrial cities emerge from their educational environments less adequately prepared. Note how these trends account for some of the heterogeneity in scholastic aptitude *within* a given social class by the diversity in formal academic training received by the youngsters originating in that class.

The second part of Table 4 shows parallel trends for plans to attend college, according to young people's social origins and the type of community where they attend high school. On the face of it, small towns and suburbs appear to be at a par in producing college-oriented youngsters— but again, we should recall the difference between them in the school retention rates through the 12th grade. After making the appropriate corrections, the suburbs will again rank first in productivity of college students.

The last word has hardly been said on the variety of ways young people may be affected by the community setting where they frame their career and educational goals. Quite the contrary—only after considerably more research effort has been expended will we be ready to make assertions with confidence on the whole matter of broad structural influences on individual behavior.

Specifically, when it comes to schools and social stratifications, the kind of analysis proposed here is carried out in the following spirit: heretofore, when sociologists have investigated the way education and social-class structure relate to one another, relatively scant attention has been accorded the fact that education is a long-term social process, occurring microscopically in the schoolroom and macroscopically in a definite and describable community context. Until now, the challenge of observing these processes has been evaded by the phrase: "Education is the high road to social mobility." No expression could more successfully divert us from the sociological point. The evasion has also directed sociologists to say that the heart of the matter is in the nuclear family, where all of the behavior and all of the attitudes and values are engendered that lead to scholastic achievement, and subsequent social-class achievement, by the members of each new generation. Nothing in our study belies the crucial role of the nuclear family, whose significance is so well recognized that we hardly feel the need to do any proselytizing in its behalf. But that this is all that counts in a bureaucratized, achievement-oriented society, where education is controlled by local communities each with its formally organized school system, is too much to believe. The more we turn in these other directions, the more we will learn about the social structure of our society.

# part FOUR

# The School as a Social Organization

A prominent scholar in the sociology of education has thoroughly explored the nature of schools as social organizations:

> Schools are complex systems of organization. An organization is made up of people in a relatively stable interaction system. The relationships that form in the system constitute its structure, which is the basis of the organization's stability; the structure is comprised of positions which endure as membership changes. Positions, in turn, are composed of systems of norms called roles. A norm is an expectation or a rule as to how people should act toward one another in a particular situation. Organizations, then, are based on norms (and the sanctions for upholding them) which govern the jobs and tasks that members of the organization perform.[1]

According to this definition, it is the relationships that ultimately serve to constitute the structure of the organization. In this regard the school differs substantially from other complex organizations. The school is comprised of a relatively small number of adults—teachers and administrators, and a large number of children or youth. In contrast to other organizations such as manufacturing organizations, armies, hospitals, or research institutes, the vast majority of adults in a school are drawn from one general occupational category—that of teaching. In other types of complex organization there is frequently greater heterogeneity among those who form the major decision-making body within the organization.

Proportionately the greatest numbers involved in schools are the chil-

---

[1] Ronald G. Corwin, A Sociology of Education (New York: Appleton-Century-Crofts, 1965), p. 52.

211

dren or youth. These members are generally systematically graded by age and/or criteria of accomplishment. They are also transient. The students move through the organization on a rather strict time schedule, and each grouping or class is of the same age. Every year the student takes on a new role; last year he was a seventh grader, this year he is in eighth grade, and if it is springtime, in a short time he will be in high school. To the uninformed the difference between these age and grade levels may seem slight and even trivial; to the teacher and student the differences are socially and organizationally analyzable in terms of values, norms, roles, and statuses. Social values produce and shape systems of norms that become the informal rules that govern the behavior of the students as well as the teachers. These sets of behavioral rules determine the roles that students and teachers play in the course of school life.

Roles and statuses are the major concepts sociologists use in analyzing the social relations and behavior of people as they play their parts in the social organizations to which they belong. Students, teachers, principals, counselors, coaches, janitors, clerks, bus drivers, crossing guards, PTA or Home and School officers and other adult activists all play distinct roles and have a place (a status) within the social structure of the school. Roles comprise those informal rules and expectations that regularize behavior within groups and organizations. A teacher is expected to behave in certain ways in carrying out the teaching function; the principal is expected to behave and be concerned and capable of carrying out functions different from teachers; and the fourth grade student is expected to behave in a manner similar, though not identical, to others at his age and grade level. The roles as well as the overall structure of the school can be analyzed from both a formal and informal perspective.

*Formal Structure.* Pictorially, the formal structure of a school is represented by the organization chart. This representation of structure highlights the formal rank or status, of the "chain of command," formal channels of communication and the authority and jurisdiction of the decision-makers within the structure.

*Formal Roles.* The formal or official roles of the members of an organization are the generally expected responsibilities and behaviors that one would find on a job description in the personnel or employment office of the organization. In a sense the formal role is a basic outline of the activities and responsibilities that apply to anyone holding the position (or slot in the organization chart) in question.

*Informal Structure and Informal Rules.* As many people know, there is more to the way an organization works and how its members behave than can be formalized in charts and job specifications. Though all the teachers in a school may have the same official positions, some have greater influence and prestige in the school and community. The same is true for clerks and janitors. Differences in past experience, age, family background, interpersonal relationships with the principal, reputation among parents, students and community influentials contribute to the differences in status and prestige. The manner and style in which an individual, be he teacher or principal, plays his role is of considerable importance in determining his ultimate place in the social organization of the school; that is, each individual goes about being a teacher or janitor in a different way from every other teacher or janitor. The official role requirements are general and indicate a variety of agreed upon behaviors and minimal levels of performance; whereas the specific behaviors that go to make up the role performance of a given teacher vary considerably. The formal or official role requirements may be quite different from the informal role expectations. For example, a baseball coach who is officially hired to coach the high school team may informally be expected to devote a substantial part of each summer vacation to coaching and playing for the town's semi-professional baseball team. An English teacher may be expected to be available to direct plays for a local literary group; and the single female teachers may be informally expected to join a local church and become Sunday School teachers. In other instances, informal roles emerge as a result of background in social relationships. Janitors have been known to be major consultants to principals, possessing substantial influence due to social, political, or economic connections in the community.

Students, like the adult members of the school, are formally expected and required to behave in certain ways, but informal expectations and roles also emerge. The definition of a good student may vary considerably between teachers, adult community influentials, and student peers. To the teacher the role of a good student may include being relatively submissive, working for good grades, and sharing the teacher's values. The good athlete and aggressive leader involved in extracurricular activities may more adequately fit the role definition of "good student" for community people. In addition, the peer group or gang will often prefer role behavior that stresses opposition to the established norms of the school and community.

Within every school there exists an informal peer group structure that has, at times, been characterized as a sub-culture.[2] The informal roles that emerge to form this informal structure govern the behavior and help to determine the values held by the student body. It has been found that work groups in factories and other work settings have a powerful influence in setting and maintaining norms of productivity. In effect, they set the standards for a "fair day's work." Similarly, student peer groups help

---

[2] James S. Coleman, *The Adolescent Society* (New York: The Free Press of Glencoe, 1961).

to determine the norms governing study and other school *work* (or production).[3] Students develop informal rules for how much a teacher ought to expect by way of homework, reading, writing, skill requirements, disciplining actions, as well as the manner in which gestures of friendliness, interpersonal interference, mutual tolerance, and measures of protection from administrators and outside publics ought to be carried out.

The informal status structure extant among students influences teachers, administrators, and students. Popular "right" behaving, prestigious students are informally granted privileges and power not held by the ordinary student; even grades, prizes, and other honors are influenced by the status system of the student sub-culture. The informal structure is maintained by the enforcement of sanctions, which, though unofficial, are frequently known by teachers and administrators. Sanctions may range in severity from physical violence in the school yard or locker room to the use of gossip or the "silent treatment." Not only are the informal rules and expectations for role behavior developed over time, emerging with the authority of precedent and tradition, but the *sanctions* may also attain the force of tradition.

Some of the structural features of large high schools are very similar to other large scale complex organizations, complete with an intricate bureaucratic component. Superficially they evidence many similarities to organizations such as manufacturing concerns, regiments of infantry, department stores, government bureaus, or even prisons. However, in several important respects the school is critically different from other complex social organizations. Two major differences are, as mentioned earlier, that the school is organized in a manner that makes the proportion of adults, teachers and staff, very small compared with the number of students; and that it continually experiences a high turnover of its clientele (students) and its constituents are largely limited to children and youth. From the opposite viewpoint the school has an important element in common with many other social agencies and activities of government. It shares a lack of clear definition of its precise function or what it is specifically supposed to accomplish.

In carrying out its day-to-day activities, the school functions with a great many children compared with the number of adults. This ratio of supervisors to clients makes for a precarious social order in large urban junior and senior high schools. To keep a modicum of order such a ratio of adults to youth requires the imposition of a great many specific rules of behavior. Since many precise rules frequently inhibit individual, innovative, and unique behavior, some of that which the school is supposed to cultivate may be lost. Passion, originality, singleminded drives and ac-

---

[3] George C. Homans, *The Human Group* (New York: Harcourt, Brace and World, Inc., 1950).

tivities, unique work habits, and other idiosyncracies cannot be tolerated within a social structure that must be rule-ridden simply to maintain orderliness and social harmony, or at least, a modicum of peace among its constituents. It is this characteristic that has led some critics to compare the large high school to a prison.

The high turnover of students is a somewhat unique organizational feature of the school. Though a military engagement may change the personnel of a regiment of infantry through casualties, such turnover is not an intricate and planned part of its organizational structure. For example, in the ordinary elementary school at least one-sixth of the population is new every year. Moreover, in the junior and senior high school one-third is turned over every fall. This does not take into account the movement from one school to another that takes place throughout the school year in areas with highly mobile population, such as transitional ghetto areas of metropolitan cities or rural areas using migratory labor.

Each year a whole age cohort leaves and all other age cohorts (classes) move to a new level (grade) in the organization. Everyone gets a new teacher, classroom, all of which demand adjusting to some new norms, values, and expectations. A linear progression, "ever onward and upward," is implied by the organization of the school. Unfortunately this fact of school life is not always consonant with maturation, learning of certain skills and material, nor with personal and family circumstances that are known to affect the individual's life in school.

Finally, the precise function of the school for the community in general and its children and youth in particular is difficult to determine and coherently articulate. Teachers and administrators often find it impossible to meet all of the conflicting demands to which the school is exposed. Although children, somewhat like workers in a factory, may come to school (i.e., work) and perform specific tasks and, if done properly, get rewarded with grades, promotion, social acceptance, and graduation, the potentiality for conflict remains. The choice of what is to be accomplished in school, as well as how it is to be accomplished, is frequently disputed by teachers, administrators, parents, community leaders, organizations such as teachers' unions, and ultimately the children or youth directly involved. As the person charged with carrying out the functions of the school, however vague those functions may be, the teacher is at the center of conflict involving a great many of the hopes, desires, and demands made by individual parents, and organizations like the P.T.A. and Home and School associations. Since both teachers and parents make judgments on the activities and the success of the school experience in meeting a variety of goals, they constitute a relationship fraught with potential conflict. Although there is relatively little conflict over the fact that the school exercises major authority over the children during school hours, there is considerable conflict about what results from the time spent in school.

# 12

# The School Class as a Social System: Some of its Functions in American Society*

## TALCOTT PARSONS

This essay will attempt to outline, if only sketchily, an analysis of the elementary and secondary school class as a social system, and the relation of its structure to its primary functions in the society as an agency of socialization and allocation. While it is important that the school class is normally part of the larger organization of a school, the class rather than the whole school will be the unit of analysis here, for it is recognized both by the school system and by the individual pupil as the place where the "business" of formal education actually takes place. In elementary schools, pupils of one grade are typically placed in a single "class" under one main teacher, but in the secondary school, and sometimes in the upper elementary grades, the pupil works on different subjects under different teachers; here the complex of classes participated in by the same pupil is the significant unit for our purposes.

## THE PROBLEM: SOCIALIZATION AND SELECTION

Our main interest, then, is in a dual problem: first of how the school class functions to internalize in its pupils both the commitments and ca-

* From *Harvard Educational Review*, 29, No. 4 (Fall 1959):297–318. Copyright © 1959 by President and Fellows of Harvard College.

Author's Note: I am indebted to Mrs. Carolyn Cooper for research assistance in the relevant literature and for editorial work on the first draft of this paper.

pacities for successful performance of their future adult roles, and second of how it functions to allocate these human resources within the role-structure of the adult society. The primary ways in which these two problems are interrelated will provide our main points of reference.

First, from the functional point of view the school class can be treated as an agency of socialization; that is to say, it is an agency through which individual personalities are trained to be motivationally and technically adequate to the performance of adult roles. It is not the sole such agency; the family, informal peer groups, churches, and sundry voluntary organizations all play a part, as does actual on-the-job training. But, in the period extending from entry into first grade until entry into the labor force or marriage, the school class may be regarded as the focal socializing agency.

The socialization function may be summed up as the development in individuals of the commitments and capacities which are essential prerequisites of their future role-performance. Commitments may be broken down in turn into two components: commitment to the implementation of the broad *values* of society, and commitment to the performance of a specific type of role within the *structure* of society. Thus a person in a relatively humble occupation may be a "solid citizen" in the sense of commitment to honest work in that occupation, without an intensive and sophisticated concern with the implementation of society's higher-level values. Or conversely, someone else might object to the anchorage of the feminine role in marriage and the family on the grounds that such anchorage keeps society's total talent resources from being distributed equitably to business, government, and so on. Capacities can also be broken down into two components, the first being competence or the skill to perform the tasks involved in the individual's roles, and the second being "role-responsibility" or the capacity to live up to other people's expectations of the interpersonal behavior appropriate to these roles. Thus a mechanic as well as a doctor needs to have not only the basic "skills of his trade," but also the ability to behave responsibly toward those people with whom he is brought into contact in his work.

While on the one hand, the school class may be regarded as a primary agency by which these different components of commitments and capacities are generated, on the other hand, it is, from the point of view of the society, an agency of "manpower" allocation. It is well known that in American society there is a very high, and probably increasing, correlation between one's status level in the society and one's level of educational attainment. Both social status and educational level are obviously related to the occupational status that is attained. Now, as a result of the general process of both educational and occupational upgrading, completion of high school is increasingly coming to be the norm for minimum satisfactory educational attainment, and the most significant line for future occupational status has come to be drawn between members of an age-cohort who do and do not go to college.

We are interested, then, in what it is about the school class in our society that determines the distinction between the contingents of the age-cohort which do not go to college. Because of a tradition of localism and a rather pragmatic pluralism, there is apparently considerable variety among school systems of various cities and states. Although the situation in metropolitan Boston probably represents a more highly structured pattern than in many other parts of the country, it is probably not so extreme as to be misleading in its main features. There, though of course actual entry into college does not come until after graduation from high school, the main dividing line is between those who are and are not enrolled in the college preparatory course in high school; there is only a small amount of shifting either way after about the ninth grade when the decision is normally made. Furthermore, the evidence seems to be that by far the most important criterion of selection is the record of school performance in elementary school. These records are evaluated by teachers and principals, and there are few cases of entering the college preparatory course against their advice. It is therefore not stretching the evidence too far to say broadly that the primary selective process occurs through differential school performance in elementary school, and that the "seal" is put on it in junior high school.[1]

The evidence also is that the selective process is genuinely assortative. As in virtually all comparable processes, ascriptive as well as achieved factors influence the outcome. In this case, the ascriptive factor is the socio-economic status of the child's family, and the factor underlying his opportunity for achievement is his individual ability. In the study of 3,348 Boston high school boys on which these generalizations are based, each of these factors was quite highly correlated with planning college. For example, the percentages planning college, by father's occupation, were: 12 percent for semi-skilled and unskilled, 19 percent for skilled, 26 percent for minor white collar, 52 percent for middle white collar, and 80 percent for major white collar. Likewise, intentions varied by ability (as measured by I.Q.), namely, 11 percent for the lowest quintile, 17 percent for the next, 24 percent for the middle, 30 percent for the next to the top, and 52 percent for the highest. It should be noted also that within any ability quintile, the relationship of plans to father's occupation is seen. For example, within the very important top quintile in ability as measured, the range

---

[1] The principal source for these statements is a study of social mobility among boys in ten public high schools in the Boston metropolitan area, conducted by Samuel A. Stouffer, Florence R. Kluckhohn, and the present author. Unfortunately the material is not available in published form.

in college intentions was from 29 percent for sons of laborers to 89 percent for sons of major white collar persons.[2]

The essential points here seem to be that there is a relatively uniform criterion of selection operating to differentiate between the college and the non-college contingents, and that for a very important part of the cohort the operation of this criterion is not a "put-up job"—it is not simply a way of affirming a previously determined ascriptive status. To be sure, the high-status, high-ability boy is very likely indeed to go to college, and the low-status, low-ability boy is very unlikely to go. But the "cross-pressured" group for whom these two factors do not coincide[3] is of considerable importance.

Considerations like these lead me to conclude that the main process of differentiation (which from another point of view is selection) that occurs during elementary school takes place on a single main axis of *achievement*. Broadly, moreover, the differentiation leads up through high school to a bifurcation into college-goers and non-college-goers.

To assess the significance of this pattern, let us look at its place in the socialization of the individual. Entering the system of formal education is the child's first major step out of primary involvement in his family of orientation. Within the family certain foundations of his motivational system have been laid down, but the only characteristic fundamental to later roles which has clearly been "determined" and psychologically stamped in by that time is sex role. The post-oedipal child enters the system of formal education clearly categorized as boy or girl, but beyond that his *role* is not yet differentiated. The process of selection, by which persons will select and be selected for categories of roles, is yet to take place.

On grounds that cannot be gone into here, it may be said that the most important single predispositional factor with which the child enters the school is his level of *independence*. By this is meant his level of self-sufficiency to relative guidance by adults, his capacity to take responsibility,

---

[2] See table from this study in J.A. Kahl, *The American Class Structure* (New York: Rinehart & Co., 1953), p. 283. Data from a nationwide sample of high school students, published by the Educational Testing Service, show similar patterns of relationships. For example, the ETS study shows variation, by father's occupation, in proportion of high school seniors planning college, of from 35 percent to 80 percent for boys and 27 percent to 79 percent for girls. (From Educational Testing Service, *Background Factors Related to College Plans and College Enrollment among High School Students* [Princeton, N.J., 1957].)

[3] There seem to be two main reasons why the high-status, low-ability group is not so important as its obverse. The first is that in a society of expanding educational and occupational opportunity the general trend is one of upgrading, and the social pressures to downward mobility are not as great as they would otherwise be. The second is that there are cushioning mechanisms that tend to protect the high-status boy who has difficulty "making the grade." He may be sent to a college with low academic standards, he may go to schools where the line between ability levels is not rigorously drawn, etc.

and to make his own decisions in coping with new and varying situations. This, like his sex role, he has as a function of his experience in the family. The family is a collectivity within which the basic status-structure is ascribed in terms of biological position; that is, by generation, sex, and age. There are inevitably differences of performance relative to these, and they are rewarded and punished in ways that contribute to differential character formation. But these differences are not given the sanction of institutionalized social status. The school is the first socializing agency in the child's experience which institutionalizes a differentiation of status on nonbiological bases. Moreover, this is not an ascribed but an achieved status; it is the status "earned" by differential performance of the tasks set by the teacher, who is acting as an agent of the community's school system. Let us look at the structure of this situation.

## THE STRUCTURE OF THE ELEMENTARY SCHOOL CLASS

In accord with the generally wide variability of American institutions, and of course the basically local control of school systems, there is considerable variability of school situations, but broadly they have a single relatively well-marked framework.[4] Particularly in the primary part of the elementary grades (i.e., the first three grades), the basic pattern includes one main teacher for the class, who teaches all subjects and who is in charge of the class generally. Sometimes this early, and frequently in later grades, other teachers are brought in for a few special subjects, particularly gym, music, and art, but this does not alter the central position of the main teacher. This teacher is usually a woman.[5] The class is with this one teacher for the school year, but usually no longer.

The class, then, is composed of about 25 age-peers of both sexes drawn from a relatively small geographical area—the neighborhood. Except for sex in certain respects, there is initially no formal basis for differentiation of status within the school class. The main structural differentiation develops gradually, on the single main axis indicated above as achievement. That the differentiation should occur on a single main axis is insured by four *primary features* of the situation. The *first* is the initial equalization of the "contestants'" status by age and by "family background," the neighborhood being typically much more homogeneous than is the whole society. The *second* circumstance is the imposition of a common set of tasks,

---

[4] This discussion refers to public schools. Only about 13 percent of all elementary and secondary school pupils attend non-public schools, with this proportion ranging from about 22 percent in the Northeast to about six percent in the South. U.S. Office of Education, *Biennial Survey of Education in the United States, 1954–56* (Washington: U.S. Government Printing Office, 1959), Chapter ii, "Statistics of State School Systems, 1955–56," Table 44, p. 114.

[5] In 1955–56, 13 percent of the public elementary school instructional staff in the United States were men. Ibid., p. 7.

which is, compared to most other task-areas, strikingly undifferentiated. The school situation is far more like a race in this respect than most role-performance situations. *Third,* there is the sharp polarization between the pupils in their initial equality and the *single* teacher who is an adult and "represents" the adult world. And *fourth,* there is a relatively systematic process of evaluation of the pupils' performances. From the point of view of a pupil, this evaluation, particularly (though not exclusively) in the form of report card marks, constitutes reward and/or punishment for past performance; from the viewpoint of the school system acting as an allocating agency, it is a basis of *selection* for future status in society.

Two important sets of qualifications need to be kept in mind in interpreting this structural pattern, but I think these do not destroy the significance of its main outline. The first qualification is for variations in the formal organization and procedures of the school class itself. Here the most important kind of variation is that between relatively "traditional" schools and relatively "progressive" schools. The more traditional schools put more emphasis on discrete units of subject-matter, whereas the progressive type allows more "indirect" teaching through "projects" and broader topical interests where more than one bird can be killed with a stone. In progressive schools there is more emphasis on groups of pupils working together, compared with the traditional direct relation of the individual pupil to the teacher. This is related to the progressive emphasis on co-operation among the pupils rather than direct competition, to greater permissiveness as opposed to strictness of discipline, and to a de-emphasis on formal marking.[6] In some schools one of these components will be more prominent, and in others, another. That it is, however, an important range of variation is clear. It has to do, I think, very largely with the independence-dependence training that is so important to early socialization in the family. My broad interpretation is that those people who emphasize independence training will tend to be those who favor relatively progressive education. The relation of support for progressive education to relatively high socioeconomic status and to "intellectual" interests and the like is well known. There is no contradiction between these emphases both on independence and on cooperation and group solidarity among pupils. In the first instance this is because the main focus of the independence problem at these ages is vis-à-vis adults. However, it can also be said that the peer group, which here is built into the school class, is an indirect field of expression of dependency needs, displaced from adults.

The second set of qualifications concerns the "informal" aspects of the school class, which are always somewhat at variance with the formal ex-

---

[6] This summary of some contrasts between traditional and progressive patterns is derived from general reading in the literature rather than any single authoritative account.

pectations. For instance, the formal pattern of nondifferentiation between the sexes may be modified informally, for the very salience of the one-sex peer group at this age period means that there is bound to be considerable implicit recognition of it—for example, in the form of teachers' encouraging group competition between boys and girls. Still, the fact of coeducation and the attempt to treat both sexes alike in all the crucial formal respects remain the most important. Another problem raised by informal organization is the question of how far teachers can and do treat pupils particularistically in violation of the universalistic expectations of the school. When compared with other types of formal organizations, however, I think the extent of this discrepancy in elementary schools is seen to be not unusual. The school class is structured so that opportunity for particularistic treatment is severely limited. Because there are so many more children in a school class than in a family and they are concentrated in a much narrower age range, the teacher has much less chance than does a parent to grant particularistic favors.

Bearing in mind these two sets of qualifications, it is still fair, I think, to conclude that the major characteristics of the elementary school class in this country are such as have been outlined. It should be especially emphasized that more or less progressive schools, even with their relative lack of emphasis on formal marking, do not constitute a separate pattern, but rather a variant tendency within the same pattern. A progressive teacher, like any other, will form opinions about the different merits of her pupils relative to the values and goals of the class and will communicate these evaluations to them, informally if not formally. It is my impression that the extremer cases of playing down relative evaluation are confined to those upper-status schools where going to a "good" college is so fully taken for granted that for practical purposes it is an ascribed status. In other words, in interpreting these facts the selective function of the school class should be kept continually in the forefront of attention. Quite clearly its importance has not been decreasing; rather the contrary.

## THE NATURE OF SCHOOL ACHIEVEMENT

What, now, of the content of the "achievement" expected of elementary school children? Perhaps the best broad characterization which can be given is that it involves the types of performance which are, on the one hand, appropriate to the school situation and, on the other hand, are felt by adults to be important in themselves. This vague and somewhat circular characterization may, as was mentioned earlier, be broken down into two main components. One of these is the more purely "cognitive" learning of information, skills, and frames of reference associated with empirical knowledge and technological mastery. The *written* language and the early phases of mathematical thinking are clearly vital; they involve cognitive skills at altogether new levels of generality and abstraction compared with those commanded by the pre-school child. With these basic skills goes assimilation of much factual information about the world.

The second main component is what may broadly be called a "moral" one. In earlier generations of schooling this was known as "deportment." Somewhat more generally it might be called responsible citizenship in the school community. Such things as respect for the teacher, consideration and co-operativeness in relation to fellow-pupils, and good "work-habits" are the fundamentals, leading on to capacity for "leadership" and "initiative."

The striking fact about this achievement content is that in the elementary grades these two primary components are not clearly differentiated from each other. Rather, the pupil is evaluated in diffusely general terms; a *good* pupil is defined in terms of a fusion of the cognitive and the moral components, in which varying weight is given to one or the other. Broadly speaking, then, we may say that the "high achievers" of the elementary school are both the "bright" pupils, who catch on easily to their more strictly intellectual tasks, and the more "responsible" pupils, who "behave well" and on whom the teacher can "count" in the difficult problems of managing the class. One indication that this is the case is the fact that in elementary school the purely intellectual tasks are relatively easy for the pupil of high intellectual ability. In many such cases, it can be presumed that the primary challenge to the pupil is not to his intellectual, but to his "moral," capacities. On the whole, the progressive movement seems to have leaned in the direction of giving enhanced emphasis to this component, suggesting that of the two, it has tended to become the more problematical.[7]

The essential point, then, seems to be that the elementary school, regarded in the light of its socialization function, is an agency that differentiates the school class broadly along a single continuum of achievement, the content of which is relative excellence in living up to the expectations imposed by the teacher as an agent of the adult society. The criteria of this achievement are, generally speaking, undifferentiated into the cognitive or technical component and the moral or "social" component. But with respect to its bearing on societal values, it is broadly a differentiation of *levels* of capacity to act in accord with these values. Though the relation is far from neatly uniform, this differentiation underlies the processes of selection for levels of status and role in the adult society.

---

[7] This account of the two components of elementary school achievement and their relation summarizes impressions gained from the literature, rather than being based on the opinions of particular authorities. I have the impression that achievement in this sense corresponds closely to what is meant by the term as used by McClelland and his associates. Cf. D.C. McClelland et al., *The Achievement Motive* (New York: Appleton-Century-Crofts, Inc., 1953).

Next, a few words should be said about the out-of-school context in which this process goes on. Besides the school class, there are clearly two primary social structures in which the child participates: the family and the child's informal peer group.

## FAMILY AND PEER GROUP IN RELATION TO THE SCHOOL CLASS

The school age child, of course, continues to live in the parental household and to be highly dependent, emotionally as well as instrumentally, on his parents. But he is now spending several hours a day away from home, subject to a discipline and a reward system that are essentially independent of that administered by the parents. Moreover, the range of this independence gradually increases. As he grows older, he is permitted to range further territorially with neither parental nor school supervision, and to do an increasing range of things. He often gets an allowance for personal spending and begins to earn some money of his own. Generally, however, the emotional problem of dependence-independence continues to be a very salient one through this period, frequently with manifestations by the child of compulsive independence.

Concomitantly with this, the area for association with age-peers without detailed adult supervision expands. These associations are tied to the family, on the one hand, in that the home and yards of children who are neighbors and the adjacent streets serve as locations for their activities; and to the school, on the other hand, in that play periods and going to and from school provide occasions for informal association, even though organized extracurricular activities are introduced only later. Ways of bringing some of this activity under another sort of adult supervision are found in such organizations as the boy and girl scouts.

Two sociological characteristics of peer groups at this age are particularly striking. One is the fluidity of their boundaries, with individual children drifting into and out of associations. This element of "voluntary association" contrasts strikingly with the child's ascribed membership in the family and the school class, over which he has no control. The second characteristic is the peer group's sharp segregation by sex. To a striking degree this is enforced by the children themselves rather than by adults.

The psychological functions of peer association are suggested by these two characteristics. On the one hand, the peer group may be regarded as a field for the exercise of independence from adult control; hence it is not surprising that it is often a focus of behavior that goes beyond independence from adults to the range of adult-*disapproved* behavior; when this happens, it is the seed bed from which the extremists go over into delinquency. But another very important function is to provide the child a source of non-adult approval and acceptance. These depend on "technical" and "moral" criteria as diffuse as those required in the school situation.

On the one hand, the peer group is a field for acquiring and displaying various types of "prowess"; for boys this is especially the physical prowess which may later ripen into athletic achievement. On the other hand, it is a matter of gaining acceptance from desirable peers as "belonging" in the group, which later ripens into the conception of the popular teen-ager, the "right guy." Thus the adult parents are augmented by age-peers as a source of rewards for performance and of security in acceptance.

The importance of the peer group for socialization in our type of society should be clear. The motivational foundations of character are inevitably first laid down through identification with parents, who are generation-superiors, and the generation difference is a type example of a hierarchical status difference. But an immense part of the individual's adult role per-formance will have to be in association with status-equals or near-equals. In this situation it is important to have a reorganization of the motivational structure so that the original dominance of the hierarchical axis is modi-fied to strengthen the egalitarian components. The peer group plays a prominent part in this process.

Sex segregation of latency period peer groups may be regarded as a process of reinforcement of sex-role identification. Through intensive as-sociation with sex-peers and involvement in sex-typed activities, they strongly reinforce belongingness with other members of the same sex and contrast with the opposite sex. This is the more important because in the coeducational school a set of forces operates that specifically plays down sex-role differentiation.

It is notable that the latency period sex-role pattern, instead of institu-tionalizing relations to members of the opposite sex, is characterized by an avoidance of such relations, which only in adolescence gives way to dating. This avoidance is clearly associated with the process of reorgani-zation of the erotic components of motivational structure. The pre-oedipal objects of erotic attachment were both intra-familial and generation-su-perior. In both respects there must be a fundamental shift by the time the child reaches adulthood. I would suggest that one of the main func-tions of the avoidance pattern is to help cope with the psychological dif-ficulty of overcoming the earlier incestuous attachments, and hence to prepare the child for assuming an attachment to an age-mate of opposite sex later.

Seen in this perspective, the socialization function of the school class assumes a particular significance. The socialization functions of the family by this time are relatively residual, though their importance should not be underestimated. But the school remains adult-controlled and, more-over, induces basically the same kind of identification as was induced by the family in the child's pre-oedipal stage. This is to say that the learning of achievement-motivation is, psychologically speaking, a process of iden-tification with the teacher, of doing well in school in order to please the teacher (often backed by the parents) in the same sense in which a pre-oedipal child learns new skills in order to please his mother.

In this connection I maintain that what is internalized through the process of identification is a reciprocal pattern of role-relationships.[8] Unless there is a drastic failure of internalization altogether, not just one, but both sides of the interaction will be internalized. There will, however, be an emphasis on one or the other, so that some children will more nearly identify with the socializing agent, and others will more nearly identify with the opposite role. Thus, in the pre-oedipal stage, the "independent" child has identified more with the parent, and the "dependent" one with the child-role vis-à-vis the parent.

In school the teacher is institutionally defined as superior to any pupil in knowledge of curriculum subject-matter and in responsibility as a good citizen of the school. In so far as the school class tends to be bifurcated (and of course the dichotomization is far from absolute), it will broadly be on the basis, on the one hand, of identification with the teacher, or acceptance of her role as a model; and, on the other hand, of identification with the pupil peer group. This bifurcation of the class on the basis of identification with teacher or with peer group so strikingly corresponds with the bifurcation into college-goers and non-college-goers that it would be hard to avoid the hypothesis that this structural dichotomization in the school system is the primary source of the selective dichotomization. Of course in detail the relationship is blurred, but certainly not more so than in a great many other fields of comparable analytical complexity.

These considerations suggest an interpretation of some features of the elementary teacher role in American society. The first major step in socialization, beyond that in the family, takes place in the elementary school, so it seems reasonable to expect that the teacher-figure should be characterized by a combination of similarities to and differences from parental figures. The teacher, then, is an adult, characterized by the generalized superiority, which a parent also has, of adult status relative to children. She is not, however, ascriptively related to her pupils, but is performing an occupational role—a role, however, in which the recipients of her services are tightly bound in solidarity to her and to each other. Furthermore, compared to a parent's, her responsibility to them is much more universalistic, this being reinforced, as we saw, by the size of the class; it is also much more oriented to performance rather than to solicitude for the emotional "needs" of the children. She is not entitled to suppress the distinction between high and low achievers, just because not being able to be included among the high group would be too hard on little Johnny—however much tendencies in this direction appear as deviant patterns. A

---

[8] On the identification process in the family see my paper, "Social Structure and the Development of Personality," *Psychiatry*, 21 (November 1958):321–40.

mother, on the other hand, must give *first* priority to the needs of her child, regardless of his capacities to achieve.

It is also significant for the parallel of the elementary school class with the family that the teacher is normally a woman. As background it should be noted that in most European systems until recently, and often today in our private parochial and non-sectarian schools, the sexes have been segregated and each sex group has been taught by teachers of its own sex. Given coeducation, however, the woman teacher represents continuity with the role of the mother. Precisely the lack of differentiation in the elementary school "curriculum" between the components of subject-matter competence and social responsibility fits in with the greater diffuseness of the feminine role.

But at the same time, it is essential that the teacher is not a mother to her pupils, but must insist on universalistic norms and the differential reward of achievement. Above all she must be the agent of bringing about and legitimizing a differentiation of the school class on an achievement axis. This aspect of her role is furthered by the fact that in American society the feminine role is less confined to the familial context than in most other societies, but joins the masculine in occupational and associational concerns, though still with a greater relative emphasis on the family. Through identification with their teacher, children of both sexes learn that the category "woman" is not co-extensive with "mother" (and future wife), but that the feminine role-personality is more complex than that.

In this connection it may well be that there is a relation to the once-controversial issue of the marriage of women teachers. If the differentiation between what may be called the maternal and the occupational components of the feminine role is incomplete and insecure, confusion between them may be avoided by insuring that both are not performed by the same persons. The "old maid" teacher of American tradition may thus be thought of as having renounced the maternal role in favor of the occupational.[9] Recently, however, the highly affective concern over the issue of married women's teaching has conspicuously abated, and their actual participation has greatly increased. It may be suggested that this change is associated with a change in the feminine role, the most conspicuous feature of which is the general social sanctioning of participation of women in the labor force, not only prior to marriage, but also after marriage. This I should interpret as a process of structural differentiation in that the same category of persons is permitted and even expected to engage in a more complex set of role-functions than before.

---

[9] It is worth noting that the Catholic parochial school system is in line with the more general older American tradition, in that the typical teacher is a nun. The only difference in this respect is the sharp religious symbolization of the difference between mother and teacher.

The process of identification with the teacher which has been postulated here is furthered by the fact that in the elementary grades the child typically has one teacher, just as in the pre-oedipal period he had one parent, the mother, who was the focus of his object-relations. The continuity between the two phases is also favored by the fact that the teacher, like the mother, is a woman. But, if she acted only like a mother, there would be no genuine reorganization of the pupil's personality system. This reorganization is furthered by the features of the teacher role, which differentiate it from the maternal. One further point is that while a child has one main teacher in each grade, he will usually have a new teacher when he progresses to the next higher grade. He is thus accustomed to the fact that teachers are, unlike mothers, "interchangeable" in a certain sense. The school year is long enough to form an important relationship to a particular teacher, but not long enough for a highly particularistic attachment to crystallize. More than in the parent-child relationship, in school the child must internalize his relation to the teacher's *role* rather than her particular personality; this is a major step in the internalization of universalistic patterns.

## SOCIALIZATION AND SELECTION IN THE ELEMENTARY SCHOOL

To conclude this discussion of the elementary school class, something should be said about the fundamental conditions underlying the process that is, as we have seen, simultaneously (1) an emancipation of the child from primary emotional attachment to his family, (2) an internalization of a level of societal values and norms that is a step higher than those he can learn in his family alone, (3) a differentiation of the school class in terms both of actual achievement and of differential *valuation* of achievement, and (4) from society's point of view, a selection and allocation of its human resources relative to the adult role system.[10]

Probably the most fundamental condition underlying this process is the sharing of common values by the two adult agencies involved—the family and the school. In this case the core is the shared valuation of *achievement*. It includes, above all, recognition that it is fair to give differential rewards for different levels of achievement, so long as there has been fair access to opportunity, and fair that these rewards lead on to higher-order opportunities for the successful. There is thus a basic sense in which the elementary school class is an embodiment of the fundamental American value of equality of opportunity, in that it places value *both* on initial equality and on differential achievement.

---

[10] The following summary is adapted from T. Parsons, R.F. Bates et al., *Family, Socialization and Interaction Process* (Glencoe, Ill.: Free Press, 1955), especially Chapter iv.

As a second condition, however, the rigor of this valuational pattern must be tempered by allowance for the difficulties and needs of the young child. Here the quasi-motherliness of the woman teacher plays an important part. Through her the school system, assisted by other agencies, attempts to minimize the insecurity resulting from the pressures to learn, by providing a certain amount of emotional support defined in terms of what is due to a child of a given age level. In this respect, however, the role of the school is relatively small. The underlying foundation of support is given in the home, and as we have seen, an important supplement to it can be provided by the informal peer associations of the child. It may be suggested that the development of extreme patterns of alienation from the school is often related to inadequate support in these respects.

Third, there must be a process of selective rewarding of valued performance. Here the teacher is clearly the primary agent, though the more progressive modes of education attempt to enlist classmates more systematically than in the traditional pattern. This is the process that is the direct source of intra-class differentiation along the achievement axis.

The final condition is that this initial differentiation tends to bring about a status system in the class, in which not only the immediate results of school work, but a whole series of influences, converge to consolidate different expectations, which may be thought of as the children's "levels of aspiration." Generally some differentiation of friendship groups along this line occurs, though it is important that it is by no means complete, and that children are sensitive to the attitudes not only of their own friends, but of others.

Within this general discussion of processes and conditions, it is important to distinguish, as I have attempted to do all along, the socialization of the individual from the selective allocation of contingents to future roles. For the individual, the old familial identification is broken up (the family of orientation becomes, in Freudian terms, a "lost object") and a new identification is gradually built up, providing the first-order structure of the child's identity apart from his originally ascribed identity as son or daughter of the "Jones." He both transcends his familial identification in favor of a more independent one and comes to occupy a differentiated status within the new system. His personal status is inevitably a direct function of the position he achieves, primarily in the formal school class and secondarily in the informal peer group structure. In spite of the sense in which achievement-ranking takes place along a continuum, I have put forward reasons to suggest that, with respect to this status, there is an important differentiation into two broad, relatively distinct levels, and that his position on one or the other enters into the individual's definition of his own identity. To an important degree this process of differentiation is independent of the socioeconomic status of his family in the community, which to the child is a prior ascribed status.

When we look at the same system as a selective mechanism from the societal point of view, some further considerations become important. First, it may be noted that the valuation of achievement and its sharing by family and school not only provides the appropriate values for internalization by individuals, but also performs a crucial integrative function for the system. Differentiation of the class along the achievement axis is inevitably a source of strain, because it confers higher rewards and privileges on one contingent than on another within the same system. This common valuation helps make possible the acceptance of the crucial differentiation, especially by the losers in the competition. Here it is an essential point that this *common* value on achievement is shared by units with different statuses in the system. It cuts across the differentiation of families by socioeconomic status. It is necessary that there be realistic opportunity and that the teacher can be relied on to implement it by being "fair" and rewarding achievement by whoever shows capacity for it. The fact is crucial that the distribution of abilities, though correlated with family status, clearly does not coincide with it. There can then be a genuine selective process within a set of "rules of the game."

This commitment to common values is not, however, the sole integrative mechanism counteracting the strain imposed by differentiation. Not only does the individual pupil enjoy familial support, but teachers also like and indeed "respect" pupils on bases independent of achievement-status, and peer-group friendship lines, though correlated with position on the achievement scale, again by no means coincide with it, but cross-cut it. Thus there are cross-cutting lines of solidarity which mitigate the strains generated by rewarding achievement differentially.[11]

It is only *within* this framework of institutionalized solidarity that the crucial selective process goes on through selective rewarding and the consolidation of its results into a status-differentiation within the school class. We have called special attention to the impact of the selective process on the children of relatively high ability but low family status. Precisely in

---

[11] In this, as in several other respects, there is a parallel to other important allocative processes in the society. A striking example is the voting process by which political support is allocated between party candidates. Here, the strain arises from the fact that one candidate and his party will come to enjoy all the perquisites—above all the power —of office, while the other will be excluded for the time being from these. This strain is mitigated, on the one hand, by the common commitment to constitutional procedure, and, on the other hand, by the fact that the nonpolitical bases of social solidarity, which figure so prominently as determinants of voting behavior, still cut across party lines. The average person is, in various of his roles, associated with people whose political preference is different from his own; he therefore could not regard the opposite party as composed of unmitigated scoundrels, without introducing a rift within the groups to which he is attached. This feature of the electorate's structure is brought out strongly in B.R. Berelson, P.F. Lazarsfeld and W.N. McPhee, *Voting* (Chicago: University of Chicago Press, 1954). The conceptual analysis of it is developed in my own paper, " 'Voting' and the Equilibrium of the American Political System," in E. Burdick and A.J. Brodbeck (Eds.), *American Voting Behavior* (Glencoe, Ill.: Free Press, 1959).

this group, but pervading school classes generally, is another parallel to what was found in the studies of voting behavior.[12] In the voting studies it was found that the "shifters"—those voters who were transferring their allegiance from one major party to the other—tended, on the one hand, to be the "cross-pressured" people, who had multiple status characteristics and group allegiances that predisposed them simultaneously to vote in opposite directions. The analogy in the school class is clearly to the children for whom ability and family status do not coincide. On the other hand, it was precisely in this group of cross-pressured voters that political "indifference" was most conspicuous. Non-voting was particularly prevalent in this group, as was a generally cool emotional tone toward a campaign. The suggestion is that some of the pupil "indifference" to school performance may have a similar origin. This is clearly a complex phenomenon and cannot be further analyzed here. But rather than suggesting, as is usual on common sense grounds, that indifference to school work represents an "alienation" from cultural and intellectual values, I would suggest exactly the opposite: that an important component of such indifference, including in extreme cases overt revolt against school discipline, is connected with the fact that the stakes, as in politics, are very high indeed. Those pupils who are exposed to contradictory pressures are likely to be ambivalent; at the same time, the personal stakes for them are higher than for the others, because what happens in school may make much more of a difference for their futures than for the others, in whom ability and family status point to the same expectations for the future. In particular for the upwardly mobile pupils, too much emphasis on school success would pointedly suggest "burning their bridges" of association with their families and status peers. This phenomenon seems to operate even in elementary school, although it grows somewhat more conspicuous later. In general I think that an important part of the anti-intellectualism in American youth culture stems from the *importance* of the selective process through the educational system rather than the opposite.

One further major point should be made in this analysis. As we have noted, the general trend of American society has been toward a rapid upgrading in the educational status of the population. This means that, relative to past expectations, with each generation there is increased pressure to educational achievement, often associated with parents' occupational ambitions for their children.[13] To a sociologist this is a more or less classical situation of anomic strain, and the youth-culture ideology which plays down intellectual interests and school performance seems to fit in this context. The orientation of the youth culture is, in the nature of the

---

[12] Ibid.

[13] J.A. Kahl, "Educational and Occupational Aspirations of 'Common Man' Boys," *Harvard Educational Review*, 23 (Summer 1953):186–203.

case, ambivalent, but for the reasons suggested, the anti-intellectual side of the ambivalence tends to be overtly stressed. One of the reasons for the dominance of the anti-school side of the ideology is that it provides a means of protest against adults, who are at the opposite pole in the socialization situation. In certain respects one would expect that the trend toward greater emphasis on independence, which we have associated with progressive education, would accentuate the strain in this area and hence the tendency to decry adult expectations. The whole problem should be subjected to a thorough analysis in the light of what we know about ideologies more generally.

The same general considerations are relevant to the much discussed problem of juvenile delinquency. Both the general upgrading process and the pressure to enhanced independence should be expected to increase strain on the lower, most marginal groups. The analysis of this paper has been concerned with the line between college and non-college contingents; there is, however, another line between those who achieve solid non-college educational status and those for whom adaptation to educational expectations at *any* level is difficult. As the acceptable minimum of educational qualification rises, persons near and below the margin will tend to be pushed into an attitude of repudiation of these expectations. Truancy and delinquency are ways of expressing this repudiation. Thus the very *improvement* of educational standards in the society at large may well be a major factor in the failure of the educational process for a growing number at the lower end of the status and ability distribution. It should therefore not be too easily assumed that delinquency is a symptom of a *general* failure of the educational process.

## DIFFERENTIATION AND SELECTION IN THE SECONDARY SCHOOL

It will not be possible to discuss the secondary school phase of education in nearly as much detail as has been done for the elementary school phase, but it is worthwhile to sketch its main outline in order to place the above analysis in a wider context. Very broadly we may say that the elementary school phase is concerned with the internalization in children of motivation to achievement, and the selection of persons on the basis of differential capacity for achievement. The focus is on the *level* of capacity. In the secondary school phase, on the other hand, the focus is on the differentiation of *qualitative types* of achievement. As in the elementary school, this differentiation cross-cuts sex role. I should also maintain that it cross-cuts the levels of achievement that have been differentiated out in the elementary phase.

In approaching the question of the types of capacity differentiated, it should be kept in mind that secondary school is the principal springboard from which lower-status persons will enter the labor force, whereas those achieving higher status will continue their formal education in college, and some of them beyond. Hence for the lower-status pupils the important line of differentiation should be the one which will lead into broadly different categories of jobs; for the higher-status pupils the differentiation will lead to broadly different roles in college.

My suggestion is that this differentiation separates those two components of achievement which we labelled "cognitive" and "moral" in discussing the elementary phase. Those relatively high in "cognitive" achievement will fit better in specific-function, more or less technical roles; those relatively high in "moral" achievement will tend toward diffuser, more "socially" or "humanly" oriented roles. In jobs not requiring college training, the one category may be thought of as comprising the more impersonal and technical occupations, such as "operatives," mechanics, or clerical workers; the other, as occupations where "human relations" are prominent, such as salesmen and agents of various sorts. At the college level, the differentiation certainly relates to concern, on the one hand, with the specifically intellectual curricular work of college and, on the other hand, with various types of diffuser responsibility in human relations, such as leadership roles in student government and extracurricular activities. Again, candidates for post-graduate professional training will probably be drawn mainly from the first of these two groups.

In the structure of the school, there appears to be a gradual transition from the earliest grades through high school, with the changes timed differently in different school systems. The structure emphasized in the first part of this discussion is most clearly marked in the first three "primary" grades. With progression to the higher grades, there is greater frequency of plural teachers, though very generally still a single main teacher. In the sixth grade and sometimes in the fifth, a man as main teacher, though uncommon, is by no means unheard of. With junior high school, however, the shift of pattern becomes more marked, and still more in senior high.

By that time the pupil has several different teachers of both sexes[14] teaching him different subjects, which are more or less formally organized into different courses—college preparatory and others. Furthermore, with the choice of "elective" subjects, the members of the class in one subject no longer need be exactly the same as in another, so the pupil is much more systematically exposed to association with different people, both adults and age-peers, in different contexts. Moreover, the school he attends is likely to be substantially larger than was his elementary school, and to draw from a wider geographical area. Hence the child is exposed to a wider range of statuses than before, being thrown in with more age-peers whom he does not encounter in his neighborhood; it is less likely that his parents

---

[14] Men make up about half (49 percent) of the public secondary school instructional staff. U.S. Government Printing Office, *Biennial Survey,* chapter ii, p. 7.

will know the parents of any given child with whom he associates. It is thus my impression that the transitions to junior high and senior high school are apt to mean a considerable reshuffling of friendships. Another conspicuous difference between the elementary and secondary levels is the great increase in high school of organized extracurricular activities. Now, for the first time, organized athletics become important, as do a variety of clubs and associations which are school-sponsored and supervised to varying degrees.

Two particularly important shifts in the patterning of youth culture occur in this period. One, of course, is the emergence of more positive cross-sex relationships outside the classroom, through dances, dating, and the like. The other is the much sharper prestige-stratification of informal peer groupings, with indeed an element of snobbery that often exceeds that of the adult community in which the school exists.[15] Here it is important that though there is a broad correspondence between the prestige of friendship groups and the family status of their members, this, like the achievement order of the elementary school, is by no means a simple "mirroring" of the community stratification scale, for a considerable number of lower-status children get accepted into groups including members with higher family status than themselves. This stratified youth system operates as a genuine assortative mechanism; it does not simply reinforce ascribed status.

The prominence of this youth culture in the American secondary school is, in comparison with other societies, one of the hallmarks of the American educational system; it is much less prominent in most European systems. It may be said to constitute a kind of structural fusion between the school class and the peer-group structure of the elementary period. It seems clear that what I have called the "human relations" oriented contingent of the secondary school pupils are more active and prominent in extracurricular activities, and that this is one of the main foci of their differentiation from the more impersonally- and technically-oriented contingent. The personal qualities figuring most prominently in the human relations contingent can perhaps be summed up as the qualities that make for "popularity." I suggest that, from the point of view of the secondary school's selective function, the youth culture helps to differentiate between types of personalities which will, by and large, play different kinds of roles as adults.

The stratification of youth groups has, as noted, a selective function; it is a bridge between the achievement order and the adult stratification system of the community. But it also has another function. It is a focus of prestige that exists along side of, and is to a degree independent of, the

15 See, for instance, C.W. Gordon, *The Social System of the High School: A Study in the Sociology of Adolescence* (Glencoe, Ill.: Free Press, 1957).

achievement order focussing on school work as such. The attainment of prestige in the informal youth group is itself a form of valued achievement. Hence, among those individuals destined for higher status in society, one can discern two broad types: those whose school work is more or less outstanding and whose informal prestige is relatively satisfactory; and vice versa, those whose informal prestige is outstanding, and school performance satisfactory. Falling below certain minima in either respect would jeopardize the childs' claim to belong in the upper group.[16] It is an important point here that those clearly headed for college belong to peer groups that, while often depreciative of intensive concern with studies, also take for granted and reinforce a level of scholastic attainment necessary for admission to a good college. Pressure will be put on the individual who tends to fall below such a standard.

In discussing the elementary school level it will be remembered that we emphasized that the peer group served as an object of emotional dependency displaced from the family. In relation to the pressure for school achievement, therefore, it served at least partially as an expression of the lower-order motivational system *out* of which the child was in process of being socialized. On its own level, similar things can be said of the adolescent youth culture; it is in part an expression of regressive motivations. This is true of the emphasis on athletics despite its lack of relevance to adult roles, of the "homosexual" undertones of much intensive same-sex friendship, and of a certain "irresponsibility" in attitudes toward the opposite sex—e.g., the exploitative element in the attitudes of boys toward girls. This, however, is by no means the whole story. The youth culture is also a field for practicing the assumption of higher-order responsibilities, for conducting delicate human relations without immediate supervision and learning to accept the consequences. In this connection it is clearly of particular importance to the contingent we have spoken of as specializing in "human relations."

We can, perhaps, distinguish three different levels of crystallization of these youth-culture patterns. The middle one is that which may be considered age-appropriate without clear status-differentiation. The two keynotes here seem to be "being a good fellow" in the sense of general friendliness and being ready to take responsibility in informal social situations where something needs to be done. Above this, we may speak of the higher level of "outstanding" popularity and qualities of "leadership" of the person who is turned to where unusual responsibilities are required. And below the middle level are the youth patterns bordering on delinquency, withdrawal, and generally unacceptable behavior. Only this last level is

---

16 J. Riley, M. Riley, and M. Moore, "Adolescent Values and the Riesman Typology" in S.M. Lipset and L. Lowenthal (Eds.), *The Sociology of Culture and the Analysis of Social Character* (Glencoe, Ill.: Free Press, 1960).

clearly "regressive" relative to expectations of appropriate behavior for the age-grade. In judging these three levels, however, allowance should be made for a good many nuances. Most adolescents do a certain amount of experimenting with the borderline of the unacceptable patterns; that they should do so is to be expected in view of the pressure toward independence from adults, and of the "collusion" which can be expected in the reciprocal stimulation of age-peers. The question is whether this regressive behavior comes to be confirmed into a major pattern for the personality as a whole. Seen in this perspective, it seems legitimate to maintain that the middle and the higher patterns indicated are the major ones, and that only a minority of adolescents comes to be confirmed in a truly unacceptable pattern of living. This minority may well be a relatively constant proportion of the age-cohort, but apart from situations of special social disorganization, the available evidence does not suggest that it has been a progressively growing one in recent years.

The patterning of cross-sex relations in the youth culture clearly foreshadows future marriage and family formation. That it figures so prominently in school is related to the fact that in our society the element of ascription, including direct parental influence, in the choice of a marriage partner is strongly minimized. For the girl, it has the very important significance of reminding her that her adult status is going to be very much concerned with marriage and a family. This basic expectation for the girl stands in a certain tension to the school's curricular coeducation with its relative lack of differentiation by sex. But the extent to which the feminine role in American society continues to be anchored in marriage and the family should not be allowed to obscure the importance of coeducation. In the first place, the contribution of women in various extra-familial occupations and in community affairs has been rapidly increasing, and certainly higher levels of education have served as a prerequisite to this contribution. At the same time, it is highly important that the woman's familial role should not be regarded as drastically segregated from the cultural concerns of the society as a whole. The educated woman has important functions *as wife and mother*, particularly as an influence on her children in backing the schools and impressing on them the importance of education. It is, I think, broadly true that the immediate responsibility of women for family management has been increasing, though I am very skeptical of the alleged "abdication" of the American male. But precisely in the context of women's increased family responsibility, the influence of the mother both as agent of socialization and as role model is a crucial one. This influence should be evaluated in the light of the general upgrading process. It is very doubtful whether, apart from any other considerations, the motivational prerequisites of the general process could be sustained without sufficiently high education of the women who, as mothers, influence their children.

## CONCLUSION

With the general cultural upgrading process in American society that has been going on for more than a century, the educational system has come to play an increasingly vital role. That this should be the case is, in my opinion, a consequence of the general trend to structural differentiation in the society. Relatively speaking, the school is a specialized agency. That it should increasingly have become the principal channel of selection as well as agency of socialization is in line with what one would expect in an increasingly differentiated and progressively more upgraded society. The legend of the "self-made man" has an element of nostalgic romanticism and is destined to become increasingly mythical, if by it is meant not just mobility from humble origins to high status, which does indeed continue to occur, but that the high status was attained through the "school of hard knocks" without the aid of formal education.

The structure of the public school system and the analysis of the ways in which it contributes both to the socialization of individuals and to their allocation to roles in society is, I feel, of vital concern to all students of American society. Notwithstanding the variegated elements in the situation, I think it has been possible to sketch out a few major structural patterns of the public school system and at least to suggest some ways in which they serve these important functions. What could be presented in this paper is the merest outline of such an analysis. It is, however, hoped that it has been carried far enough to suggest a field of vital mutual interest for social scientists on the one hand and those concerned with the actual operation of the schools on the other.

# 13

# Open-Space Schools: The Opportunity to Become Ambitious*

ELIZABETH G. COHEN

The fundamental peculiarity of the occupation of public elementary school teaching is the flatness of the reward structure. Whether teachers are more or less committed to their profession or more or less skillful in performance has little effect on the rewards they receive. Tenure and salary relate mainly to years of service rather than to skill and commitment. Indeed, evaluation by organizational superiors is infrequent for all but probationary teachers.

There are relatively few opportunities for professional advancement in elementary school teaching. Ambitious classroom teachers cannot look forward to an increase in responsibility and influence without somehow leaving the classroom. They may leave education altogether; they may return to schools of education in search of credits or advanced degrees; or they may move into the field of school administration. At this time, however, the possibility of moving into administration appears as a viable alternative to the small number of male elementary school teachers, but not to the female teachers who wish to have a wider impact on education. Examination of state directories of education reveals comparatively few women in the field of school administration; and graduate students in school administration are almost all male; indeed, very few women apply to such programs.

From *Sociology of Education*, vol. 46 (Spring 1973):143–61. Reprinted by permission.

* This research is supported by funds from the United States Office of Education, Department of Health, Education and Welfare. The opinions expressed in this publication do not necessarily reflect the position, policy, or endorsement of the Office of Education. (Contract No. OEC 6–10–078, Project No. 5–0252–0307.)

Lortie (1969) argues that teachers are not powerful figures in the organization of the school, being restricted to classrooms as "small universes of control." Teachers have few participation rights in school-wide decisions. Studies (cf. Corey, 1970) show that the limits of teachers' responsibility and influence are as important a source of teachers' dissatisfaction with work as are more obvious questions of salary.

Informal peer rewards for the elementary school teacher are as few and weak as are those available within the formal organization of the school. In most elementary schools, teachers are socially isolated from their colleagues; they do not see or hear each other in the act of teaching; they rarely meet for the purposes of planning or evaluation of teaching tasks. Indeed, there are very few mutual or common tasks. The traditional isolation of elementary school teachers is such that there are norms against visiting a fellow teacher while she is working with the children in the classroom. Teachers talk to one another, but their conversation rarely occurs in a formal occupational context where decisions are being made on school policies, discipline, curriculum, or evaluation of the teaching process.

The effect of not being able to see and hear each other at work is profound; teachers have almost no basis for supporting and rewarding each other in the process of instruction. There is no opportunity for one teacher to tell another that she has carried out a lesson well, handled a difficult child with skill, or planned a clever curriculum unit. There are few opportunities for teachers to earn professional respect from other teachers on the basis of proven skill in teaching or skill in planning and evaluation within a collaborative teacher group.

Little visibility has still further effects on opportunities for teachers to make an impact on anyone but their own group of students. Without a chance to see and hear each other at work, teachers cannot form any sensible idea of who is relatively skilled and should act as a leader and model for other teachers. Even if teachers have no formal organizational rights to evaluate and control one another's behavior, they might still be able to function as highly influential in a colleague group. But, without a process of decision-making in collaborative teacher groups, there is no way to convince colleagues of the efficacy of one's techniques or curriculum ideas. If one teacher is unusually successful in planning small group work in classrooms, there is no way for her to influence other teachers to plan with her techniques.

In review, the elementary school is a formal organization giving few rewards for competence and loyalty to the teacher; there are few opportunities for promotion; and pay is rarely related to competence. In addition, the teacher has very little power and authority outside her particular classroom. The same may be said of opportunities for playing an influential role or receiving professional rewards in the informal work organization; there is little chance to receive praise, respect and support from other teachers or for controlling the behavior of colleagues through a process of influence on professional matters.

The open-space school, an innovative form of school architecture, represents significant change in both the formal and informal organization of elementary school teaching. This paper reports partial results of a study of organizational innovation by the Environment for Teaching program, at the Stanford Center for Research and Development in Teaching. The larger study (Meyer, Cohen et al., 1971) compared teachers from teams working in open-space elementary schools with teachers in conventionally organized schools.

The "open-space" school should not be confused with the concept of the "open classroom." A relatively recent innovation in school architecture, the "open-space school" lacks interior partitions, visual and acoustical separation between teaching stations and classroom areas is limited or eliminated.[1] The most common practice has been to create instructional areas by forming "pods," "classroom clusters," or "big rooms" that accommodate a definite number of teachers and class groups usually ranging from the equivalent of two to nine classrooms. According to a survey of 43 state directors of school planning, over 50 percent of all new schools constructed within the last three years have been of open design.[2]

## RESEARCH QUESTIONS ON AMBITION

Suspicion that the reward structure and powerlessness of elementary school teaching helps to drive out some of its most desirable members has often been voiced in educational literature (cf. Bush, 1970, p. 112). A major question of this analysis was the relationship between ambition in teachers and job dissatisfaction. Was it true that more committed teachers were more dissatisfied than less committed and ambitious teachers? At the start of the larger study, we could not know what changes in formal organization these open-space schools entailed beyond delegation of decision-making powers to a team of teachers and the factor of increased visibility of a teacher's work to her colleagues. Nevertheless, we wished to examine the effect of working in open-space schools on the relationship of ambition to dissatisfaction. Would team teaching in open-space schools represent a major change for ambitious teachers, so that ambition might be positively associated with job satisfaction in the new setting? The third question was theoretical: If the relationship between ambition and job satisfaction changed in the open-space schools, what particular features

---

[1] School Planning Laboratory, School of Education, *Open-Space Schools* Project Bulletin No. 1, March 1970 (Stanford, California: Stanford University).

[2] Ibid., p. 5.

of the new setting and organization of work were associated with this change? "Open-space school" is not a theoretical concept but an architectural term: we need to know how to abstract and characterize organizational sources of critical changes in the teacher's role.

As the study progressed, it became apparent that the open-space schools in the sample did not represent changes in the formal rewards available to competent teachers or increased opportunities for promotion to higher paying positions such as team leader. Principals' evaluations of teachers were infrequent in both types of schools. It was true that the authority structure of the two types of schools was different; the power to plan for and to schedule large groups of children had been delegated to teams in the open-space schools. But the teams were, formally speaking, equal status teams, so that the increase in decision-making power was a characteristic of the group rather than a competitive opportunity for an ambitious teacher.

What *had* changed radically was the nature of the interaction between teachers and their opportunity to teach in full view of each other. Unless the portable partitions were up, teachers in the open-space schools could see and hear each other at work. Time was usually set aside for team meetings where planning, decision-making and discussion of "problem" children and curriculum problems took place. In addition, teachers in open-space schools frequently conferred during the course of a working day.

Overall survey results revealed that interaction on the team is a necessary but not sufficient condition for an increased sense of influence and autonomy on the part of team teachers. For some teachers, the chance to become influential in a group of peers appears to lead to a general increase in a sense of autonomy and influence. Teachers in open-space schools were far more likely to perceive themselves as influential and autonomous than teachers in conventional schools.

Teams in open-space schools not only report increased interaction opportunities and an increased sense of influence, observations revealed that the teachers provided a source of reward and support to each other within team meetings. In the team situation, a teacher who reports the success of a classroom technique or the handling of a child who is defined by the team as a "problem" can and does receive the warm approbation of team members.

In discussions of curriculum decisions, the ideas of each teacher on at least some of the many tasks are likely to be agreed upon and favorably evaluated by peers. There are many chances for praise and social support. All favorable evaluation does not necessarily flow to one influential teacher (although some teams are dominated by one teacher): interaction patterns may vary over different meetings and different tasks (Molnar, 1971).

For the purposes of the analyses of this paper, then, the distinction between the open-space school and the conventional school becomes a rough indicator of differences in the probability of receiving praise and support from colleagues and differences in the probability of playing an influential role among colleagues. The architectural and work situation difference is *not* an indicator of a difference in the chance of favorable formal evaluation and possible reward based on competence, nor a difference in the availability of upward mobility within the ranks of the school.

The open-space school has provided a chance to examine the relationship between teacher morale and an increased perception of teacher power and efficacy. Under conditions of organizational change, there is a marked rise in the perception of teachers as influential and in the tendency to see oneself as autonomous. And those teachers who respond to the new setting with perceptions of influence and autonomy are likely to be satisfied with their job. In other words, if teachers are made to feel more powerful as a result of changes in the organization of work, they will have higher morale.

The second feature of elementary school teaching, lack of differential reward for competence, was studied in the responses of teachers who felt sufficiency competent for demonstration teaching and supervision. There is a surprising increase in the percentage of professionally ambitious women in the open-space schools as compared with the traditional schools. Moreover, in the open-space schools, professional ambition was positively associated with job satisfaction, while in self-contained classrooms, the more ambitious a woman was, the more dissatisfied she was likely to be.

The increased occurrence of professional ambition and its associated improvement in teacher morale could not have occurred because of a formal change in the rewards and evaluation system—there were no such changes. Rather, these findings may indicate a *growth* of ambition and job satisfaction in response to certain informal rewards in the group interaction setting offered by the teaching team.

A final feature of elementary school teaching is the lack of opportunities for promotion into administration for women. Women who were oriented toward advancement, recognition, and supervisory responsibilities were markedly more dissatisfied than unambitious women in both settings. The inference can be made that the lack of opportunity for upward mobility is very frustrating to these ambitious teachers and may well drive them out of the profession. If we could find a school organization truly offering promotion opportunities to women, this relationship between ambition and dissatisfaction should change markedly.

Elementary school teaching is a traditional haven for women who work: rarely is this occupation used as an example of sex discrimination. Yet, most school administrators are men. And for women who have no wish to leave the classroom, but who are highly professionally oriented, there is a lack of reward and reinforcement for professional merit. There are many women in this sample who could be described as "ambitious" in an absolute sense by our attitude indices; they were typically highly dissatisfied with teaching. The structure of elementary school teaching may well drive some of these women out of the profession. Even if sex discrimination in school administration were eliminated, the dilemma of the professionally ambitious teacher would not be solved. More fundamental changes in the evaluation of teaching and rewards for competence will be necessary to alter the uniformly low status of women in elementary school teaching.

From a practical point of view, these findings suggest that if the status of teachers is raised by means of increasing their influence within the organization of the school, there will be an increase in job satisfaction among women teachers. Increased morale is of special concern because of the marked dissatisfaction among the more committed and ambitious teachers in the study, women likely to have desirable orientations toward children. Looking to the future, a most interesting question may be the long-range outcome of this kind of innovation with an attendant increase in professionally ambitious women and an increasing sense of teacher efficacy. Will team activities continue to provide gratification for these women as the years pass or will they desire larger fields of operation such as influence over teacher trainees, shared power in school-wide decision-making, and more voice in school districts? A planned longitudinal study of the organizational innovations will examine longer-range consequences of increased ambition and efficacy among women teachers.

## REFERENCES

Bush, R.N. "The Status of the Career Teacher: Its Effect upon the Teacher Dropout Problem." In T.M. Stinnett (Ed.), *The Teacher Dropout*. Itasca, Ill.: Peacock Publishers, 1970.

Corey, A. "Overview of Factors Effecting the Holding Power of the Teaching Profession." In T.M. Stinnett (Ed.), *The Teacher Dropout*. Itasca, Ill.: Peacock Publishers, 1970.

Lortie, D.C. "The Balance of Control and Autonomy in Elementary School Teaching." In A. Etzioni (Ed.), *The Semi-Professional and Their Organization*. New York: The Free Press, 1969.

Meyer, J., and Cohen, E. et al. "The Impact of the Open-Space School upon Teacher Influence and Autonomy: The Effects of an Organizational Innovation." Stanford, California: Stanford Center for Research and Development in Teaching, Technical Report No. 21, 1971.

Molnar, S. "Teachers in Teams: Interaction, Influence, and Autonomy." Stanford, California: Stanford Center for Research and Development in Teaching, Technical Report No. 22, 1971.

School Planning Laboratory. *Open Space Schools*. Project Bulletin No. 1, Stanford, California: Stanford University, March 1970.

# 14

# The Character of Bureaucracy in Urban Schools*

## RAYMOND C. HUMMEL and JOHN M. NAGLE

In his study of the organizational society, Robert Presthus describes a bureaucratic model that seems particularly relevant to urban school systems.[1] According to that model, a bureaucracy is characteristically so *large* that none of its members can interact face to face with more than a relative few of all the others. Although big organizations need not be bureaucratic, bureaucracies are large by definition. Closely related to their size is their dependence on *specialization of labor;* that is, as the size of an organization increases, so too do the complexity of its operations and the need for a greater number and variety of specially qualified personnel. As any organization becomes more bureaucratic, the number of generalists in it decreases while the number of specialists increases. Theoretically, the increased specialization of the work to be done by any one member of the organization leads to greater organizational effectiveness and efficiency; but it also leads to tension between the specialists and generalists in the organization. Administrators in a bureaucracy not only are required to prove their legitimacy as generalists in an organization of specialists, but must also mediate between competing specialized units of the organization.

A third characteristic of a bureaucracy is its hierarchical structure. Typically, this structure is depicted as a triangle, with the highest positions in

* From *Urban Education in America: Problems and Prospects* by Raymond C. Hummel and John Nagle. Copyright © 1973 by Oxford University Press, Inc. Reprinted by permission.

[1] Robert Presthus, *The Organizational Society* (New York: Vintage Books, 1962), pp. 27–58.

the organization at the apex and the lowest positions at the base. This hierarchy of positions determines the *status* accorded each member of the organization—that is, the allocation of prestige, authority, income, deference, rights, and privileges. As one moves down the hierarchy, the number of positions increases, the relative degree of status decreases.

The hierarchy of positions also governs the channeling of communication in a bureaucracy—that is, who talks to whom and about what. Because information is a prerequisite to participation in decision-making, and because the design of the hierarchy is triangular, the few individuals at the top have considerable power to manipulate and control both the issues that are raised for consideration and the information available to those who resolve them. Ultimate authority and control in a bureaucracy are thus held by a small number of its members. Presthus suggests that this tendency toward *oligarchy*—rule by the few—is almost inevitable to bureaucracy:

> When organizations become large, communication is difficult and the power of decision tends to be restricted to a few leaders. Some elites enhance their power by concealing information; but in any event the problems of disseminating information and providing for widespread participation present almost insuperable obstacles. The pressure of demands for quick decisions often makes consultation impracticable. The highly technical character of many decisions tends furthermore to limit participation to those who have the requisite skills and knowledge—this despite the fact that the ramifications of the decision may extend throughout the organization. Thus the intensity of oligarchy probably increases in some sort of geometric ratio to organizational size.[2]

Related closely to the oligarchic tendency of bureaucratic organization is the function of *cooptation*, the process by which those in power designate their successors. By placing high value on seniority, loyalty, and cooperation, cooptation leads inevitably to a "sameness" in the behavior of organization members and thus to a kind of inbreeding.

Finally, a bureaucracy is characterized by *rationality and efficiency* and, at least in principle, by *freedom from conflict*. Rationality may be defined as the capacity for objective, intelligent action; it is sought in a bureaucracy by the imposition of rules and procedures that limit diffusion of the decision-making process, and provide for recruitment and assignment of personnel on an objective and systematic basis. In principle, rationality leads to increased efficiency in the allocation and use of available resources; and because each component of the bureaucracy has clearly defined functions to perform and its own unique role to play in the total organization, there is, in theory, minimal room for conflict among components.

---

[2] Ibid., p. 40.

In summary, the structural characteristics of Presthus' bureaucratic model include size, specialization, hierarchy, status, authority, oligarchy, cooptation, rationality, efficiency, and freedom from conflict. These characteristics produce a distinctive work environment. Expected behavior is clearly prescribed. Interpersonal relations and the flow of information are governed by refined distinctions of authority, status, and rank, thus reducing ambiguity or uncertainty about what is expected of each member. And the organization's posture toward its environment is deliberately designed to protect personnel from rather than involve them with hostile and competing forces.

## BUREAUCRACIES IN URBAN EDUCATION

The nation's big-city school systems exhibit to a considerable degree the organizational characteristics described in Presthus' bureaucratic model. The number of students they enroll, personnel they employ, and dollars they expend each year indicate clearly that as organizations urban school systems are undeniably large and complex. Their size and complexity preclude face-to-face interaction among more than limited segments of their total membership, and likewise inhibit the development of meaningful school–community relationships. Urban school personnel, particularly those at the school and neighborhood level, thus face constituents who frequently feel, and usually are, unable to influence decisions regarding the education of their children; and frustration leads many of these constituents to develop negative, or even openly hostile, attitudes toward the "system" and those who control it.

Specialization of labor is a second major organizational characteristic of urban school systems. In any school district, some employees teach young children, others teach adolescents; some teach reading, others teach science; still others serve as counselors, librarians, supervisors, or principals; some drive buses or care for buildings; some function within a single building, others have authority throughout a district; some make policy, others implement it; and so on. Because of its magnitude and complexity, an urban school system requires not only a high degree of specialization, but also a large number of individuals to fulfill each role.

Perhaps ironically, it should also be noted that despite the creation of specialized roles in urban schools in recent decades, those of teacher and building principal have changed little and are still rather roughly defined. As their responsibilities have grown and their tasks have become more and more complex, teachers and principals have increasingly experienced "role overload," the burdening of an individual with so many tasks that none can be performed well. Even in the most modern urban school facilities, the time and energy of most teachers and principals are taken up by an astounding variety of instructional and noninstructional tasks.

While some distinctive roles have been created—guidance counselor, librarian, nurse, custodian, remedial reading teacher, supervisor—most schools boast a principal, two or three specialists, and twenty or thirty classroom teachers. The teachers prepare their classrooms, operate duplicating machines, telephone parents, conduct classes, write examinations, grade papers, select library books, supervise students, diagnose learning problems, counsel students, conduct assemblies, keep records, monitor cafeterias, and otherwise perform as if they had no help. The principal and his assistant (if he has one) schedule classes, oversee the budget, interview candidates, telephone parents, attend school and community meetings, supervise custodians and cafeteria workers, solve bus problems, and, if they find time, work with teachers to improve curricula and classroom instruction.[3]

Hierarchy is a third organizational characteristic of big-city school systems—with a school board at the apex of the triangle and students constituting its base. Between the two, in descending order of authority and status, are the district's administrative staff, its building principals, and its teachers. As in any bureaucracy, the hierarchy determines the status of each individual in the school district, and with it the degree of authority, earnings, and information received, privileges enjoyed, and deference and prestige accorded. The triangular structure of the hierarchy sets up an oligarchy among administrative school personnel: nearly all critical decisions are made at its highest levels, and by a relatively few individuals—the school board, the superintendent, and a half dozen administrative personnel in the central office. One important result is that local school personnel typically believe it is impossible to influence school policy except through the central office. The centralized control that typifies urban systems is a major source of complaint from those both within and outside those systems.

In urban school systems, cooptation is also evident. Standardization, attention to detail, maintenance of the status quo, and dedication to the system are rewarded; those who raise questions about the system, who evaluate its performance and work to bring about change are not. Promotion "through the ranks" to higher and higher positions in the organizational hierarchy—from teacher to counselor to vice-principal to building principal to central office administrator—thus usually favors school personnel who have not deviated along the way, and who have not questioned either the philosophy of the system or the adequacy of its current operations.

Studies have shown that administrators favor teachers who maintain orderly classrooms, keep accurate records, and maintain stable relations with

---

[3] U.S. Office of Education, "Targeted Program in Research and Development: The Organization and Administration of Elementary and Secondary Schools," in draft form, June 1970 (mimeographed), 76.

parents and the community. Other studies reveal that middle managers in the educational system, such as principals and supervisors, tend to be recruited from among teachers who demonstrate these orderly qualities. Because they are rewarded for maintaining the system, administrators are not likely either to challenge it or to reward subordinates who do.[4]

That urban school systems became bureaucratic as they developed is understandable and was, to a degree, even desirable. In part, as Callahan trenchantly notes, the new vocation of school administration that developed in the early 1900s over-identified itself with the new science of industrial management and its worship of efficiency and economy. But bureaucratic practices also grew out of the need, around the turn of the century, to protect public schools—particularly those in large cities—from the inroads of political patronage and pressure by special interest groups. To assure their separation from political influence, school systems created their own administrative structures, notably including impersonal rules on hiring, promotion, and tenure for professional personnel. These bureaucratic practices have benefited both the educational process and the operation of urban schools, since they have given teachers protection against formal reprisals for innovation or for challenging existing conditions. They also have protected administrators from the pressure to make decisions for solely political reasons; and they have given all school personnel an equal opportunity for advancing their careers.

In another sense, however, many of the bureaucratic reforms instituted in the first half of the century—even including some advocated by progressive reformers—now prevent urban school systems from responding effectively to changing needs and conditions both within their organizational boundaries and in the larger community. Most bureaucratic practices help to protect the system; they encourage organizational inbreeding, they tend to reduce differences among personnel in values and styles of action, they encourage buck-passing and thereby centralize authority. They reward passivity, conformity, caution, smoothness, and superficial affability rather than boldness, creativity, and innovation. They breed a stronger loyalty to the organization than to professional principles or to human needs, encouraging personnel to place extrinsic rewards above the intrinsic satisfactions of teaching.

Ultimately, as one critic has suggested, the bureaucratic model is inconsistent with the kind of organizational structure required for maximum learning and creative teaching:

> . . . in virtually every important respect, the behaviors and attitudes appropriate for bureaucracies are quite the opposite of those appropriate for education. Educational relationships are diffuse, the student is treated

---

[4] John I. Goodlad, "The Schools vs. Education," *Saturday Review* (April 19, 1961), p. 61.

as a "whole" person, but the hallmark of bureaucratic interaction is its specificity; education best proceeds in personal settings, through "primary" contacts, but bureaucracies are formal and impersonal; educational behaviors are consummatory, motivation is "intrinsic," but bureaucratic activities are entirely instrumental; education is responsive to the needs of the student, instruction is "individualized," but bureaucracies are first and always agencies of control; and so on. For schools which seek to educate through personal and responsive methods, then, a bureaucratic organizational structure is highly inappropriate and, theoretically speaking, perhaps the worst imaginable.[5]

## RESISTANCE OF URBAN SCHOOL SYSTEMS TO CHANGE

An earlier chapter in this book contained excerpts from a report on the effort to introduce extensive resources from New York University into a ghetto school—an effort that a year later ended in failure. The National Teacher Corps, created ostensibly to prepare teachers for inner-city schools, has not produced a substantial effect on the operation of those schools. Even an apparently successful pilot project in New York, Higher Horizons, failed when it was expanded into the More Effective Schools Program. The list of projects that have produced "no significant results" is discouragingly long. As one observer has noted, "Most attempts to reform large urban school systems have seemed to end in failure. Whether reform is initiated inside the system, as are most programs of compensatory education, or outside, like the thousands of short-term institutes and workshops set up by universities, little or no large-scale system-wide change seems to occur. . . . Most school children in the inner-city are affected not at all; the large systems stand unmoved."[6] Another observer, after interviewing personnel from over 100 schools in a number of major metropolitan areas of the country, also concluded: "It is dangerous to generalize about something as large, complex, and presumably diverse as schooling in the United States. . . . As far as our sample of schools is concerned, however, we are forced to conclude that much of the so-called educational reform movement has been blunted on the classroom door."[7]

A voluminous literature on organizational change has been produced in the past decade. In school systems throughout the country, funds for innovation have been provided by Title III of the Elementary and Secondary Education Act. It would be unfeasible to examine here all the hundreds of projects that have been conducted in urban school programs.

---

[5] Buford Rhea, "The Large High School in Its Social Context," *The Bulletin of the NASSP*, 331 (November 1968):37.

[6] George B. Thomas, "Tension: A Tool for Reform," *Saturday Review* (July 19, 1969), p. 50.

[7] Goodlad, "The Schools," p. 60.

Among the noteworthy projects are model schools such as the John Dewey School in New York, the Parkway School in Philadelphia, and the John Adams School in Portland, Oregon. The history of these and similar innovative projects is still too recent to permit a judgment of their long-term worth. If past experience is any indicator, however, they will all gradually wither with the departure of their original leadership, and as other interests in the school district compete for funds. Even more to the point is the question of how much in these innovations programs can be successfully incorporated into the regular programs of school systems. The fate of such experiments has in general been quite discouraging.

The multiple factors in this resistance to change, which tend to reinforce the basic conservatism of most urban school systems, include the following: (1) the organizational structure of most urban school systems, (2) the nature of their personnel, (3) the lack of incentives, and (4) the lack of educational planning.

Ultimately, the most serious obstacle to change is the complexity of the problems to be solved. Often, the effort toward an innovative solution aggravates them and puts new stresses on the organization. Edward C. Banfield claims this dynamic in the War on Poverty; that many training, employment, and housing programs associated with it left their clients worse off than before.[8] The military efforts by the United States in South Vietnam during the past decade may be seen as a colossal instance of this dynamic.

## DECADENT ORGANIZATIONAL STRUCTURES

It is estimated that over 100 additional functions have been assumed by the nation's public education system within the past several decades. Yet most of its urban school systems were designed to meet the educational needs of an earlier era: that is to supply "uniform instruction in basic skills at a minimum level of quality and at a low per pupil cost to the mass of the population at a time when farming and simple factory work occupied most of the people." Even today, ". . . the graded school of the past, with its ten-month year, five-hour day, 30-pupil classes, technologically primitive classrooms, undifferentiated staffing, and continuously talking teachers is still the American standard."[9]

In most urban schools, despite their size, the definition of who does what, when, and to whom is little different today from what it was 60 years ago. The predominant reason for this maintenance of the status quo is, of course, the bureaucratic design of urban schools. Their hierarchies

---

[8] Edward C. Banfield, *Unheavenly City: The Nature and the Future of Our Urban Crisis* (Boston: Little, Brown, 1970).

[9] U.S. Office of Education, "Targeted Program . . . ," p. 73.

so inhibit lateral and vertical communications among personnel that decisions made at the top, except on purely administrative matters, rarely affect operating practices to any notable degree. In addition, centralized administrative controls discourage independence, experimentation, and idiosyncrasies of style and attitude; and building principals, who might most logically put innovation into effect, are frequently inhibited by a central office staff at the district level, which "gives the orders on teacher assignment, controls the flow of substitutes, shapes the curriculum, dispenses the budget, promulgates 'circulars' by the hundreds, and demands reports in equal volume."[10] Rewards are given not for performance but for seniority or for pursuing university courses that may be only remotely related to work in an urban school. Finally, promotions within the hierarchy encourage uniformity. As a result, most urban schools, along with most other public schools, are still geared to processing students through the standardized format of an industrial assembly line.

## RESISTANCE AMONG PROFESSIONAL EDUCATORS

Educators have worked for decades to establish their professional status and to achieve appropriate social recognition and pay; in the process, they have blocked interference in their domain by nonprofessionals. Thus, schools of education operate to indoctrinate potential members; accreditation agencies, professional organizations, and teachers' unions monitor curriculum development, hiring practices, and working conditions; certification laws control entry into the profession. Education, as Michael Katz notes, "acquired a core of career professionals—high school principals and administrators—that would expand in size until it controlled all aspects of local school affairs. . . . Soon teachers would have a machine so large that they would be able to talk only to each other."[11] And "professional organizations" of educators have now developed a political arm strong enough to thwart any move to diminish their newly acquired status and power.

The organizational behavior of most urban school personnel, particularly administrators and supervisors, is typically self protective. The culture of urban schools seems to forbid the admission of error or failure. An urban school administrator rarely questions his own competence, and regards those who criticize either him or the system as misguided enemies of public schools. The previously mentioned study of building principals reported "an angry defense of the virtues of the school system, of the difficulties of dealing with ghetto children, and the absurdity of letting 'un-

---

10 Bernard Bard, "New York City Principals: On the Razor's Edge," *Saturday Review* (January 24, 1970), p. 72.

11 Michael B. Katz, *The Irony of Early School Reform: Educational Innovation in Mid-Nineteenth Century Massachusetts* (Cambridge: Harvard University Press, 1969).

qualified,' politically motivated insurgents take over the schools from those who have had a lifetime of service, experience, and commitment in public education."[12]

Martin Mayer, who served for five years as chairman of a subdistrict school board in New York City, has described the self-protective behavior of most urban school administrators as a kind of deafness:

> When a working mother suggests that it might be a good idea to open a school at 8 rather than 8:30 so women like herself could leave their children in a supervised place before going to work, the answer is that there's no budget for that. When mothers whose children ride a disorderly bus to and from school volunteer to take turns keeping peace on the vehicle, the answer is that the system's insurance policy covers only children supervised by licensed personnel. These are supposed to be real answers, but what they mean, obviously, is that nobody's listening.
>
> Parents don't realize that teachers get the same sort of answers. At one of our meetings, a junior high teacher came forward to complain that she had spent the summer working at a university on the problems of teaching illiterate 13-year-olds to read. Now she had a class of illiterate 13-year-olds, and her principal wouldn't let her give her children the books she had learned to use; he said they weren't on the Board of Education's "approved list" of materials that could be bought for the classrooms. The teacher, who had been conditioned to obeying silly rules, was prepared to accept this answer, but she was puzzled about why the books hadn't been approved. When she checked up, she found that they really were on the approved list, but they were new and her principal had an old list. Then the principal told her all the money was spent, so she still couldn't have the books that she was sure would help her desperate class.[13]

## LACK OF INCENTIVES FOR CHANGE

A third obstacle to innovation in urban schools is simply the lack of effective incentives for change. One reason for this is that the power of the bureaucracy to use its reward system to control behavior and maintain the status quo is considerable, as this observation suggests:

> So long as members of the school staff know that the principal source of approval and promotion is at the central headquarters, it is to that "community" that they will look for appraisal and recognition. As the typical city system now operates, there is little incentive for a principal or a teacher to be deeply concerned about what his local community expects of him. So far as his professional progress is concerned, that community possesses neither carrot nor stick. The lines of authority, stimulation, and reward now center at a single point. Until that situation is altered and the

---

[12] Ibid., p. 58.

[13] Martin Mayer, "What's Wrong with Big-City Schools," *The Saturday Evening Post* (September 1967), p. 21.

local community is given a larger voice in setting expectations for the professional staff and rewarding their attainment, most other schemes for placing the control of schools in the hands of local citizens will remain exercises in futility and largely an illusion.[14]

A second condition that reduces the incentives to change is that salaries paid to school personnel are often unrelated to the quality of their work. It is not student performance but seniority in the district and/or course work at a university, that governs increases. And those with tenure are virtually assured of their jobs for as long as they want them, regardless of the harm or good they do in the classroom.

Third, urban school personnel are without meaningful models or systematic training that would encourage innovation. Proposals for change are typically co-opted out of existence; in-service training is sporadic, usually consisting of one- and two-day workshops; and efforts at organizational reform are generally superficial.

Finally, any change at all is somewhat threatening to everyone concerned because of the uncertainty it brings. Human beings have a strong inclination to avoid uncertainty. Only when continuation of things as they are becomes more painful than rewarding are human beings likely to change their ways. For most urban schoolmen, this shift in the balance does not yet seem to have occurred.

## POVERTY OF EDUCATIONAL PLANNING

Most urban school systems have failed to develop processes for managing information or planning for change. It is typical of school districts generally to carry out their activities in relative isolation. Rarely, for example, does a district testing program address itself to specific classroom objectives as teachers themselves define them; rarely does the budgeting process take account of the data collected by the testing program; and rarely is there close coordination of district-wide goals, curriculum guides, and individual lesson plans. Neither the separate activities within a typical public school district nor those affecting the district as a whole are systematically carried out. In urban school districts, this lack of systematic planning is especially unfortunate.

Underlying the poverty of educational planning in urban schools is, first of all, the lack of any real system for managing the information that is generated in such massive quantities. Computers are typically used as nothing more than sophisticated accounting machines—for scoring tests,

---

14 John H. Fischer, "Urban Schools: Issues in Responsiveness and Control," *Decentralization and Racial Integration,* Carroll F. Johnson and Michael D. Usdan (Eds.), a Report of the proceedings of a Special Training Institute on Problems of School Desegregation, July 10–12, 1968 (New York: Teachers College, Columbia University, 1968), p. 24.

recording attendance, preparing payrolls, and printing report cards—rather than as aids for data-analysis, planning, and decision-making. Second, planning itself is still primitive in most urban school systems. Usually it

> . . . is limited to simple linear extrapolation and the use of formulas to compute needs: 100 more students equals three new teachers; next year's budget equals this year's budget plus 8 percent for salary raises and other rising costs; five school buses become seven years old and thus need to be replaced; the maintenance schedule calls for the auditorium to be painted every ten years, and so on. Alternative arrangements are rarely generated, priced, and rated in terms of their probable effect.
>
> Few schools have planning processes for coping with serious shifts in the social setting: erosion of the tax base, the arrival of bilingual students, rising teacher militancy, or the sale of drugs on campus. Plans for handling emergencies—violence, for example—are outdated or nonexistent.[15]

Third, the complexity and rigidity of budget-making discourage the financing of innovation, given the diversity of special interest groups to which an urban school district must listen and respond, and the pressure to minimize costs that is integral to the process of preparing annual budgets in any public school district. In addition, a number of the simplifications that have been developed over the years to facilitate the preparation of urban school budgets have had the undesirable effect of rigidifying the entire process of allocating resources. As budgetary decision-making has been increasingly centralized, the opportunities for building principals to make instructional and administrative changes at their own level have been reduced. Formulas for allocating various items in the budget among schools have standardized the process still further. For example, teachers are usually allotted on the basis of expected student enrollment, custodians on the basis of square footage, and supplies on the basis of expected average daily attendance. Because it is generally difficult to adjust these formulas from one year to the next, it is likewise difficult to develop alternative expenditure allotments to support desirable instructional and administrative changes.

An enormous amount of energy is expended in urban school systems simply to maintain the status quo. This resistance to change is exacerbated by decadent organizational structures, self-protectiveness among professional employees, a lack of incentives for innovation, and inadequate procedures for planning and decision-making. . . .

---

15 U.S. Office of Education, "Targeted Program . . . ," p. 84.

# part FIVE

# Social Processes and Classroom Interaction

Although a dominant emphasis in the sociology of education concerns the structure and organization of classes and schools, considerable work has been done in the social psychology of the classroom. The interpersonal relations that originate and develop in the everyday life of the classroom give rise to many unspecified and subtle attitudes, evaluations, self-images, and internalized modes of conduct. This is as true for the teachers as it is for the children.

The emergence and development of a particular social climate along with its attendant patterns of interaction has a powerful influence on the attitudes and perspectives of the students. The students' view of school, family, neighborhood, friends, and future prospects are influenced and shaped by the social interaction and social psychological processes that take place or originate in the classroom.

The teacher is a key factor in the development of the social climate of the classroom. Despite the development of the "open" school stimulated by A.S. Neill and the unique school called Summerhill, the basic relationship between teacher and pupil is one of dominance and submission. Although the approach of A.S. Neill is to wait for the inner development in the child before initiating certain formal aspects of instruction, the ultimate relationship is one in which the pupil must be willing to accept the teacher as someone who may teach him and for that to happen certain conditions must be met. One of these conditions is the ability to accept and function in some form of dominance and submissive relationship. Needless to say, the vast majority of schools require an *immediate* acceptance of the teacher as the dominant authority. It is quite apparent that many children find this extremely problematic. Moreover, the nature of this relationship is partially reordered every time a pupil gets a new teacher or moves to a different class.

Every class is comprised of students who differ in attitude toward school, ability to do school work, social, psychological and physical maturity, physique, appearance, temperament, and personal and social background. They are confronted with a teacher who brings personal perspectives on education, attitude toward the job, ambitions, biases, fears, inadequacies, and capacity for concern and affection for school children with him into the classroom. On the basis of these varied and unique factors human interaction takes place and patterns of relationships or roles emerge. These roles give structure and form to life in the classroom and determine the potentialities and limits of the learning that will occur.

Although the dominant force in the classroom is the teacher, he or she cannot fully control the social life of the class. Rather the teacher has the *most* influence in determining what sort of classroom it will be. In the elementary grades the teacher has considerable influence in ordering and managing the development of norms and values, but the social and psychological characteristics of the class and the attitudes and requirements of other teachers and administrators also influence the direction and development of interpersonal relations in the classroom.

It is readily understood that a teacher's expectations can and will affect the students' performance in school. Shaw's *Pygmalion* is based on the critical nature of the phenomena of expectations. Eliza Doolittle observed that "the difference between a lady and a flower girl is not how she behaves, but how she is treated. I shall always be a flower girl to Professor Higgins, because he always treats me as a flower girl, and always will; but I know I can be a lady to you, because you always treat me as a lady, and always will." As Silberman points out, a social climate of low expectations for performance in school can have devastating results. "In most slum schools, the children are treated as flower girls. One cannot spend any substantial amount of time visiting schools in ghetto or slum areas, in fact, be they Black, Puerto Rican, Mexican American, or Indian American, without being struck by the modesty of the expectations of teachers, supervisors, principals, and superintendents have for the students in their care."[1] In effect, the level of teacher-student expectations may result in social and psychological conditions that virtually obviate the principle of equal opportunity in education. The persistent differences in the achievement levels between majority and minority group children seems to support a charge of inequality.

The Coleman Report has revealed that the differences in academic

---

[1] Charles E. Silberman, *Crisis in the Classroom* (New York: Random House, 1970), p. 84.

achievement between black and white school children could not be attributed to the differences in the quality of the schools. There were only minor differences between black and white schools on such factors as average class size, library facilities, number of textbooks, age of school buildings, and teachers' education and background. Differences in achievement seem to be most closely related to such factors as the students' own family background and the backgrounds of their fellow students, rather than the objective quality of the school. To carry the analysis one step further and relate it back to our discussion of the importance of expectations, the background of the students has considerable influence on the nature of teachers' expectations. Being treated as "flower girls" is frequently a function of differences in socioeconomic background. In this instance the differences in class and status background between students and teachers is a crucial factor. Teachers with either middle class backgrounds or a middle class orientation tend to have low expectations for lower class children, be they black or white. Thus the objective qualities of a school may be equal while the socioeconomic differences bring the "pygmalion effect" into play resulting, in part, for the persistent lower achievement of black and Spanish-speaking slum children.

A perspective of low expectations held by middle strata teachers serves to protect and even reinforce support for traditional methods of teaching and management of the classroom. Prejudging that children of poor backgrounds in ghetto schools will be unable to perform with the regular classroom methods has fastened a reliance on compensatory and remedial approaches. This perspective, in turn, has led to the development of new or experimental efforts such as Head Start, special teachers and special schools (which are segregated by ability and special problems).

The well-known Head Start program of pre-school education was based on the assumption that poor children suffered so much deprivation that it was mandatory that some form of compensatory education take place. Although it was called "radical," it did little to change the structure and function of the typical classroom into which Head Start pupils would eventually enter. Despite the great publicity given the program, it generally failed.[2] Riessman argues that, instead of using a compensatory approach, one utilizing relevant and familiar aspects of the life of black slum children would be much more effective. He suggests the "use of hip language of the youngsters, role playing, the helper technique, team learning —all based on utilizing the low-income youngster's style and strength. . . ."[3] His major indictment of the compensatory approach is that it con-

---

[2] Frank Riessman, "The New Pre-School Mythology: Child-Centered Radicalism," in Patricia Cayo Sexton, *Readings on the School in Society* (Englewood Cliffs, N.J.: Prentice-Hall, Inc., 1967), p. 214.

[3] Ibid., p. 214.

centrates on weaknesses and deficits incurred from deprivation rather than emphasizing and using the skills and strengths possessed by the children.

The interplay of expectations is at the core of the consequences that flow from classroom interaction in the school. A constant reiteration, no matter how subtle, of expectations for learning and other behavior associated with success in school is obviously of great import in whatever consequences flow from interaction in the classroom.

An important aspect of life in school has been referred to as the social climate.[4] This has been characterized as comprising several different behavioral orientations, one of which is described as involving an authoritarian or democratic type of leadership and group organization; another involves an orientation toward a climate of competition or cooperation as the dominant mode of interpersonal relationships within the classroom and school. The analysis of social climate in terms of these two polar typologies is immensely complicated by the fact that American society possesses a range of variations on all four of these types. For example, although Americans possess a fairly strong commitment to a democratic ideology, many areas of American life exhibit decided authoritarian behavior patterns. The school itself is usually organized and administered in a rather authoritarian fashion. The same is true of most aspects of workaday life within the large private and public bureaucracies that dominate the life of a large proportion of the adult population. The traditional role of the teacher has also typically leaned in the direction of authoritarian leadership.

A social climate of autocracy seems to have definite consequences for the social and psychological development of young children. Group life organized around a dominant leader, whether in or out of the classroom, tends to affect a child's social development by generating greater hostility and tension than democraticly or cooperatively led groups. The very definition and basic nature of democratic social arrangements require that a functioning member of such groups be given the opportunity to learn and adopt the give-and-take of the democratic mode of organization. The school is, obviously, one of the places where this might take place. This becomes all the more critical when we are reminded of a fact pointed out by Kurt Lewin. He "emphasized the idea that democracy has to be *learned,* while autocracy is *imposed* on the individual."[5]

Interpersonal relations described by the typology of competition—co-

---

[4] Wilbur B. Brookover, A *Sociology of Education* (New York: American Book Co., 1955), pp. 317–37.

[5] Kurt Lewin, *Resolving Social Conflicts* (New York: Harper and Bros., 1948), p. 82, cited in Brookover, *Sociology of Education,* p. 330; emphasis provided by the editor.

operation are another important element in the analysis of social climate in school and classroom. The values of the school regarding these value patterns are very ambiguous in contrast to those regarding autocracy or democracy. Unlike the dominant ideology of democracy, but fraught with the actuality of much authoritarianism, the proscriptions regarding competition and cooperation seem hopelessly ambiguous. Both competition and cooperation are viewed as positive modes of behavior. Although in some areas of social life competition is viewed negatively and even at times destructively. In the arena of economics, competition is assumed to be the underlying basis for American affluence and economic progress. The social process of competition is also seen as a bulwark in the maintenance of individual freedom and development. On the other hand, cooperation is extolled as a basic requirement in the functioning of complex social organizations—ranging from families to giant bureaucracies. In effect, American values insist on the acceptability and efficacy of both behavioral modes. Thus the schools must function within a cultural context that creates a continuously shifting approach to common values governing interpersonal relations.

The observation has been made that the competitive nature of the reward and punishments—the grading system—of the school constitutes one of the most rigorously competitive areas of American life. The grading system with its strong emphasis on *individual* achievement and publicly acknowledged ranking system offers little or no escape for those who, for a variety of reasons, are unable to meet the prevailing criteria of merit. In social and psychic terms a system rigidly based on merit of a particular kind often yields much by way of tension, frustration, feelings of failure, antagonism, conflict, and rejection. Although recent recognition of the social costs of unmitigated competition has led to the abolition of grades in some schools, few rewards for cooperation—the counterpart of competition—have been incorporated into school life.

In a general sense the expectations for interpersonal behavior in most schools are ambiguous and shift from one mode to another. Despite the resulting apparent confusion, this fact has been considered as an acceptable approach in preparing youth for life in adult society. At least by operating along such lines the schools cannot be charged with teaching about and describing an ideal world only to have their graduates confronted with a harsh and unknown reality when they move on into the world of work and adult responsibility. The schools have been charged with failing, not only of teaching adequately how to function democratically, but of failing to expose and analyze the many areas of autocracy that are clothed as though democratic procedures and decision-making were the rule rather than the exception.

It is a well known truism that schools tend to reflect the culture of which they are a part. It is, therefore, not surprising that the heterogeneity and rapid social change that characterize modern industrial society have resulted in ambiguity and shifting value patterns. Moreover, the apparent and real social problems continually confronting various segments of society has stimulated a search for solutions. For decades the school has been at the head of the list of solutions. Being at the focal point of serious attention has led to much innovation as well as superficial rearranging. Some of the innovation has been directed at changing the social and psychological climate of the classroom. The "open classroom," "individualized instruction," and "ungraded school" are all attempts to take cognizance and act upon the fact that many children do not develop intellectually, socially, and psychologically in schools where traditional teaching techniques and orientations predominate. Mass education has brought almost *all* children into the formal school. Thus, the educational institution has felt the brunt of the diversity and heterogeneity of the society as a whole.

# 15
# Which Pupils Do Teachers Call On?*

THOMAS L. GOOD


Johnny's performance in the classroom seems to be determined, largely, by what Teacher expects of Johnny. So some researchers contend.

Robert Rosenthal (Rosenthal, 1968, p. vii) outlined a brief explanation of what is at work here:

> To a great extent, our expectations for another person's behavior are accurate because we know his past behavior. But there is now good reason to believe that another factor increases our accuracy of interpersonal predictions or prophecies. Our prediction or prophecy may in itself be a factor in determining the behavior of other people.

Rosenthal (Rosenthal, 1968, pp. vii–viii) describes his work in this way:

> To anticipate briefly the nature of this new evidence it is enough to say that 20 percent of the children in a certain elementary school were reported to their teachers as showing unusual potential for intellectual growth. The names of these 20 percent of the children were drawn by means of a table of random numbers, which is to say that the names were drawn out of a hat. Eight months later these unusual or "magic" children showed significantly greater gains in IQ than did the remaining children who had not been singled out for the teachers' attention.

Bloom (Bloom, 1968, p. 1) describes a self-fulfilling prophecy in this way:

> Each teacher begins a new term (or course) with the expectation that about a third of his students will adequately learn what he has to teach.

* From: *Elementary School Journal*, 70 (January 1970):190–98. Copyright © 1970 by the University of Chicago Press.

He expects about a third of his students to fail or to just "get by." . . . This set of expectations, supported by school policies and practices in grading, becomes transmitted to the students through the grading procedures and through the methods and materials of instruction. This system creates a self-fulfilling prophecy such that the final sorting of students through the grading process becomes approximately equivalent to the original expectations.

Jackson (1968, p. 6) describes the student's fate in this way:

He must learn how the reward system of the classroom operates and then use that knowledge to increase the flow of rewards to himself. . . . Most students soon learn that rewards are granted to those who lead a good life. And in school the good life consists, principally, of doing what the teacher says.

Do teachers distribute a variety of maps routing different approaches to the "good life," encouraging some children to compete in the classroom but giving other pupils the idea that they should remain silent? It is commonly agreed that teachers control the "opportunity roulette wheel." Does the wheel stop at random, or do teachers call some "numbers" with significantly greater frequency than others?

Much research evidence suggests that the wheel of opportunity does not operate randomly in the classroom. Teachers treat pupils differently. Pupils do not get equal classroom opportunities, nor do they get equal amounts of praise from the teacher. Charters (1968), describing the work of Davis and Dollard, suggested that lower-class children gather most of the teacher's corrections while higher-class children reap rewards. Becker, who interviewed 60 teachers in the Chicago school system, noted that they voluntarily made evaluations of their pupils and the evaluations were based on the pupil's social status (1952).

There is literature indicating that inequalities in the ratio of teacher–pupil contact cannot be explained fully by the social class of the pupil. Hoehn (1954) failed to substantiate a relationship between the amount of teacher contact and the pupils' social class. His data did suggest that pupils who were low achievers had a greater proportion of conflictive and dominative contacts with teachers and that teachers typically directed their promotive and supportive acts at pupils who were higher achievers. Lahaderne suggested, as Hoehn had earlier, that the kind of pupil–teacher interaction, as well as the absolute and relative frequency of interaction, differed with achievement (Lahaderne, 1967). Thompson (1962) reported that sixth-grade pupils who received the largest amounts of teacher approval during a school year were the best scholars.

Jackson and Lahaderne (1966, pp. 13 and 15) vividly describe the wide differences between teacher–pupil contacts in the same classroom:

For at least a few students, individual contact with the teacher is as rare as if they were seated in a class of a hundred or more pupils, even though there are actually only 30 or so classmates present. . . . This observation calls into question the conventional view of looking upon each classroom as a unit whose participants have shared a common educational experience.

If the teacher's expectancy does have an important effect on pupils, the mechanisms at work must be elevated from mysterious abstractions to a clear statement. The statement would reveal the overt teacher behaviors that communicate teacher expectancies to pupils, leading them to perform in a manner which confirms the teacher's original expectancies. The classroom may be looked upon as a roulette table, where the teacher can place bets on pupils' performance and then has the power to manipulate forces that will allow her forecast to be realized.

Do teachers call on pupils perceived as high achievers significantly more than they call on pupils perceived as low achievers? It is not difficult to understand the processes that subtly prod the teacher to call on some groups of pupils more often than on other groups. A teacher who solicits responses from pupils does not haphazardly pose questions and randomly focus on one of the many waving hands. The teacher has a reason for asking questions, and she tries to call on pupils who are capable of satisfying this purpose.

Unfortunately, many expectancies teachers have stack the deck against pupils who are low achievers and lessen their chances for opportunities to respond. A teacher who wants to motivate or to encourage the class does not call on a pupil who consistently provides inappropriate responses.

Teachers who are seeking reinforcement occasionally call on a pupil for evidence that they are doing a good job. It seems reasonable to assert that when teachers want reinforcement they do not call on pupils of low academic ability.

Finally, teachers may reduce the number of opportunities for slow pupils to respond in the hope of reducing their anxiety and removing them from criticism by their peer group. As Jackson noted (1968, p. 20) the teacher is not the only classroom evaluator in elementary schools: "At other times the evaluation occurs without any urging from the teacher, as when an egregious error elicits laughter. . . ."

Subjects for the study reported here were selected from four first-grade classrooms in two predominantly white, working-class neighborhoods. Pupils in the sample had not participated in special programs during the year. The four classroom teachers were women who had taught for at least three years.

To assess the effect of the teacher's expectancy on opportunities for pupils to respond, it was necessary to focus on the teacher's assessment of her pupils' achievement. Teachers who took part in the study were asked to provide the investigator with a seating chart and a list of pupils ranked in order of achievement.

Teachers were told that the researcher was observing pupils to identify behavioral characteristics of the pupils associated with distinct levels of achievement. Teachers expressed a desire to cooperate fully and said they understood that the observer did not want to see special activities but wanted to witness child behavior in normal and routine classroom events. Teachers were told that their ranking of pupils on the basis of achievement would guide an observer in viewing and classifying pupil behavior. Finally, teachers were told that their observations of behavior and performance throughout the year should be the chief criteria in preparing their academic rankings. The study was conducted in April and May, to assure that the teachers' assessments of pupils' achievement would be relatively stable; hence, conditions were most favorable to testing the hypothesis that teachers do treat children differently.

Teachers' rankings of achievement were used to select pupils to be observed. The first four pupils on the teachers' achievement lists were classified as "high observation groups." The last four pupils on the lists were classified as "low observation groups." The middle four students were those at midpoint in the ranking of pupils by achievement.

The Good Opportunity Observation Device, which was used in this study, required that the names of the 12 pupils selected for observation be listed. Each time the teacher provided one of these pupils an opportunity to respond an observer entered a tally beside that pupil's name. A tally was also entered each time a teacher provided positive or negative feedback to one of these pupils. Data on feedback will be presented in another report. Messages directed to more than one pupil (a competitive response situation) were ignored. Pilot activities indicated overwhelmingly that to include opportunities for competitive response would inflate the number of opportunities to respond recorded for high achievers. For example, the question, "Class, can anyone remember a word beginning with a long *e?*" presents an opportunity for a collective response. The winners of such collective or competitive opportunities were rarely low achievers. An opportunity for individual response (not pupil responses) was the unit of analysis. If the teacher called on a pupil, the act was coded as an opportunity to respond whether or not the pupil responded.

Pupils' opportunities to answer questions were divided into two major and independent areas: academic opportunities and reading opportunities. Any opportunity to respond presented to one of the pupils selected for observation outside the reading period was classified as academic. Pilot activities suggested a need to divide pupils' responses into these two classifications, for first-grade reading activities provided a more nearly equal opportunity for pupil participation than other classroom activities did. This finding is not surprising, since reading groups are designed to allow teachers to work with small groups of similar ability. The researcher hypothesized that teachers' bias would be more forcefully represented when they were dealing with the class as a whole.

Data on reliability were collected by having a second observer make simultaneous and independent recordings for one complete day of observation. To help assure objectivity, the sample classroom for the reliability study was selected before the investigator had observed the teacher of this classroom in a teaching role. The second observer knew only the names and the seating locations of the 12 pupils selected for observation. He had no information about their achievement. The reliabilities for pupils' opportunities to respond were excellent. Inter-observer reliabilities using Pearson's product-moment coefficient of correlation were .94 for reading responses and .93 for academic responses.

The investigator spent two complete days in each class viewing and recording opportunities for pupils to respond and teachers' reinforcement of pupils' behavior. In all, ten hours of instructional proceedings were observed in each classroom. Observation days were scheduled to avoid days when student teachers had the class and days when there were assembly programs or other special activities that would significantly shorten or alter a regular instructional day. In short, only normal classroom activities conducted by the teacher were observed.

A major advantage of the Good Opportunity Observation Device is its simplicity. The few categories are easy to manage. They give an observer time to make a record of the opportunities to respond and the type of feedback of a reasonably large number of pupils in the same class. In this study, pupils to be observed were selected from lists in which pupils were ranked in order of achievement as judged by the teacher. It would be possible, however, to identify pupils to be observed on the basis of intelligence quotient, achievement score, creativity measures, sex, and status in the peer group. The chief advantage of this instrument is that it allows researchers to study the behavior of individual pupils. The data can be used to describe differences in the classroom.

Because of extreme non-normality of the data, the Kruskal-Wallis one-way analysis of variance by ranks was used to test the hypothesis. Siegel (1956) rates the Kruskal-Wallis analysis as the most efficient of the non-parametric tests for independent samples. It has a power efficiency of 95.5 percent when compared with the $F$ test.

As Table One clearly shows, the opportunities to respond were closely related to pupil achievement as rated by the teacher. The high achievers received a greater number of opportunities to respond than the low achievers did.

TABLE ONE
Number of Opportunities To Respond Teachers Extended to First-Graders Ranked as High, Middle, or Low in Achievement

| Type of Opportunity | Sum of Ranks | | | H |
| | High | Middle | Low | |
|---|---|---|---|---|
| Reading Response .......... | 503 | 403 | 270 | 8.7* |
| Academic Response ........ | 628.5 | 337.5 | 210 | 29.2† |

\* P .02.
† P .001.

**TABLE TWO**
Number of Opportunities To Respond Received by Pupils During
Two Days of Observation

|  | Rank | | |
| --- | --- | --- | --- |
| Response Opportunity | High | Middle | Low |
| Class I Mean Response Opportunity ............. | 40.5 | 26.3 | 15.5 |
| Class II Mean Response Opportunity ............ | 23.3 | 10.5 | 3.3 |
| Class III Mean Response Opportunity ........... | 33.3 | 11 | 12 |
| Class IV Mean Response Opportunity ........... | 22.8 | 20.8 | 9.8 |
| Total Mean Response Opportunity .............. | 29.9 | 17.1 | 10.1 |
| Range of Pupil Response Opportunity .......... | 17–53 | 7–37 | 1–21 |
| Total Number of Response Opportunities ........ | 479 | 274 | 162 |

Table Two makes it possible to reconstruct the opportunities to respond provided to pupils by achievement level. As Table Two shows, for pupils at any given level of achievement, the opportunity to respond varies from class to class, but high achievers consistently received more opportunities to respond than pupils in other achievement groups did.

To view more broadly the relation between teachers' judgment of pupils' achievement and pupils' opportunity to respond, a series of Spearman rank coefficients of correlations was computed between pupil achievement and opportunities to respond extended by the teacher. Siegel writes that the Spearman rho has a power-efficiency of 91 percent when compared with the most powerful parametric coefficient of correlation, the Pearson rho (Siegel, 1956). Table Three shows the relation between op-

**TABLE THREE**
Spearman Rho, by Classes, Between Pupils'
Opportunity To Respond and
Pupils' Achievement

| Class | Academic R | Reading R |
| --- | --- | --- |
| Class 1 ........ | .89* | .82† |
| Class 2 ........ | .93* | .97* |
| Class 3 ........ | .66‡ | .45 (N.S.) |
| Class 4 ........ | .68‡ | .60‡ |

* P .001.
† P .01.
‡ P .05.

portunity to respond and pupils' achievement. The data reported in Table Three demonstrate that opportunity to respond is closely related to pupils' achievement. In every classroom there was a close relationship between pupils' achievement and the opportunity to respond.

An analysis of opportunities to respond offered to certain pupils at distinct levels of achievement showed that teachers created discussion "stars" by extending to high achievers significantly more opportunities to respond. An analogy can be made between first-grade classrooms and baseball teams. Both have a hard core of performers who field most opportunities, and both are directed by a manager who occasionally allows a reserve to pinch hit or to run for a regular. The especially important finding in this study is that low achievers were deprived of opportunities to respond in competitive, non-reading, classroom situations.

What are the effects of classroom life on low achievers who daily march to a factory that isolates them and affords them limited compensations and rewards? We do not transform young and insecure violin players into confident and capable performers by contriving situations that assure their continual failure and by excessively limiting their practice time. It is strange educational strategy that attempts to transform low achievers, whose language skill is usually underdeveloped, into successful classroom participants by ignoring them. The low achievers have limited skills and short attention spans. If limited opportunity to respond and negative feedback are the classroom prescription, the treatment will surely fail to help low achievers overcome their deficiencies. The treatment is more likely to sustain inadequacies and contribute to an educational demise.

The consistency of the findings in each of the four classes as well as in the pilot classes buttresses the contention that in first grades taught by women teachers in working-class schools the low achievers receive significantly less opportunity for classroom response than the high achievers do. In going beyond this small sample to a larger one, it would be mandatory to collect data in a variety of locations and conditions.

The most damaging weakness of the findings is the inability to parcel out the effects of a classroom observer on teacher behavior. Does a teacher, threatened by the presence of an observer, alter her normal classroom routine? In an effort to impress the visitor, does the teacher try to call only on pupils who will respond in an impressive fashion? It is impossible to answer these questions intelligently. The effect of an observer on teacher behavior is a concern in all observational studies. The investigator tried to create a positive and secure relationship with each teacher. It was felt that the teachers were not especially concerned about having an observer in the room and that normal classroom behavior was not excessively changed by his presence.

Teachers consistently gave high achievers significantly more chances to speak in the classroom than low achievers. The difference in opportunities to respond separates low achievers from classroom life and militates against their educational progress. Pupils who have a low achievement record continue to show less achievement than their classmates. Teachers' actions may contribute substantially to the vicious circle. Teachers "know" that low achievers cannot provide the answer and do not call on them.

The large differences in teacher-pupil contacts in the same classroom suggest that major research efforts should center on patterns of interaction between the teacher and individual pupils. Schedules used to observe interaction in classroom research generally use the classroom as the unit of analysis for studying teacher behavior, ignoring differences within the classroom and consequently masking highly important data. If researchers are to identify constructive behaviors associated with pupil growth, attention must be focused on differences within the classroom. In short, in studies of classroom life and teacher behavior, the unit of analysis should be the individual pupil or groups of pupils in the classroom.

## REFERENCES

Becker, H.S. "Social Class Variations in the Teacher–Pupil Relationship," *Journal of Educational Sociology*, 25 (April 1952):451–65.

Bloom, Benjamin S. "Learning for Mastery," *Evaluation Comment* 1 (May 1968):1.

Charters, W.W., Jr. *Handbook of Research on Teaching*. Edited by N.L. Gage. Chicago: Rand McNally and Company, 1963.

Hoehn, A.J. "A Study of Social Status Differentiation in the Classroom Behavior of Nineteen Third-Grade Teachers," *Journal of Social Psychology*, 39 (May 1954):269–92.

Jackson, Philip W. *Life in Classrooms*. New York: Holt, Rinehart, and Winston, 1968.

Jackson, Philip W., and Lahaderne, Henriette M. "Inequalities of Teacher-Pupil Contacts." Expanded version of a paper delivered at the American Psychological Association Convention, New York City, September 3, 1966.

Lahaderne, Henriette M. "Adaptation to School Settings: A Study of Children's Attitudes and Classroom Behavior." Unpublished doctoral dissertation. Chicago: Department of Education, University of Chicago, 1967.

Rosenthal, Robert, and Jacobson, Lenore. *Pygmalion in the Classroom: Teacher Expectation and Pupils' Intellectual Development*. New York: Holt, Rinehart, and Winston, 1968.

Siegel, Sidney. *Nonparametric Statistics: For the Behavioral Sciences*. New York: McGraw-Hill Book Company, 1956.

Thompson, George G. *Child Psychology: Growth Trends in Psychological Adjustment*. 2nd ed. Boston: Houghton Mifflin Company, 1962.

# 16

# The Hidden Curriculum and the Nature of Conflict*

## MICHAEL W. APPLE

## CONFLICT AND THE HIDDEN CURRICULUM

The fact that schools are usually *overtly* insulated from political processes and ideological argumentation has both positive and negative qualities. The insulation has served to defend the school against whims and fads that can often have a destructive effect upon educational practice. It also, however, can make the school rather unresponsive to the needs of local communities and a changing social order. The pros and cons of the school as a "conservative" institution have been argued fervently for the last ten years or so, at least. Among the most articulate of the spokesmen have been Edgar Z. Friedenberg and the late Jules Henry. The covert teaching of an achievement and marketplace ethic and the probable substitution of a "middle-class" and often "schizophrenic" value system for a student's own biographical meanings are the topics most usually subject to analysis. A good deal of the focus has been on what Jackson (1968) has so felicitously labeled the "hidden curriculum"—that is, on the norms and values that are implicitly, but effectively, taught in schools and that are not usually talked about in teachers' statements of ends or goals. Jackson (pp. 3–37), for instance, deals extensively with the way students learn to cope with the systems of crowds, praise, and power in

---

* From: *Interchange* 2, No. 4 (1971):27–40.

Michael W. Apple is Associate Professor of Curriculum and Instruction at The University of Wisconsin, Madison. He has written monographs and articles on ideology and curriculum, the hidden curriculum, and student rights. Among his recent publications are *Educational Evaluation: Analysis and Responsibility* and *Schooling and the Rights of Children.*

classrooms: with the large amount of waiting children are called upon to experience, with the teacher as a child's first "boss," and how children learn to falsify certain aspects of their behavior to conform to the reward system extant in most classrooms.

These critiques of the world-view being legitimated in the schools have been incisive, yet they have failed to focus on a prevailing characteristic of current schooling that significantly contributes to the maintenance of the same dominant world-view. There has been, so far, little examination of how the treatment of *conflict* in the school curriculum can lead to political quiescence and the acceptance by students of a perspective on social and intellectual conflict that acts to maintain the existing distribution of power and rationality in a society. The topic of conflict is crucial for two reasons. How it is dealt with helps to posit a student's sense of the legitimate means of gaining recourse within industrial societies. This is particularly important, and will become more so, in urban areas. It may be rather imperative that urban students develop positive perspectives toward conflict and change, ones that will enable them to deal with the complex and often repressive political realities and dynamics of power of their society in a manner less apt to preserve current institutional modes of interaction (cf. Eisinger, 1970). Also, there may well be specific programmatic suggestions that can be made and instituted fairly readily in ongoing school programs that may alleviate some of the problems.

We can learn a bit about the importance of tacit or hidden teaching from the literature on political socialization. It is beginning to be clear that "incidental learning" contributes more to the political socialization of a student than do, say, civics classes or other forms of deliberate teaching of specific value orientations (Sigel, 1970, p. xiii). Children are taught how to deal with and relate to the structures of authority of the collectivity to which they belong by the patterns of interaction they are exposed to to a certain extent in schools.

Obviously, it is not only the school that contributes to a student's "adjustment to authority." For instance, peer groups and especially the family, through its child-rearing practices and its style of interpersonal interaction, can profoundly affect a child's general orientation to authority (Sigel, p. 105). However, there is a strong suggestion in recent research that schools are rather close rivals to the family as significant agents of political socialization. As Sigel (p. 316) puts it:

> [There] is probably little doubt that the public schools are a choice transmission belt for the traditional rather than the innovative, much less the radical. As a result, they facilitate the political socialization of the mainstream young and tend to equip them with the tools necessary for the particular roles they are expected to play in a given society. One may wish to quarrel with the differential roles the government and the schools assign

to students, but it would probably be considerably more difficult to deny the school's effectiveness.[1]

It should be stated that the negative treatment given to the uses of conflict goes far beyond the way with which it is overtly dealt in any one subject, say, social studies, the area in which one usually finds material on and teaching about conflict situations. Rather, the negative and quite unrealistic approach seems endemic to many areas, and especially to science, the area usually associated with objectivity and noninterpersonal conflict.

It has become increasingly evident that history books and social studies texts and materials have, over the years, presented a somewhat biased view of the true nature of the amount and possible use of internecine strife in which groups in this country and others have engaged. Our side is good; their side is bad. "We" are peace loving and want an end to strife; "they" are warlike and aim to dominate. The list could be extended considerably especially in racial matters (Gibson 1969; Willhelm 1970). Yet, we must go beyond this type of analysis, often even beyond the work of the revisionist historians, political scientists, students of political socialization, and educators to get at many of the roots of the teaching of this dominant orientation. We examine here two specific areas—social studies and science. In so doing, we point out that the presentation of these two areas (among others) in schools both mirrors and fosters an ideology that is oriented to a static perspective: in the social studies, on the positive and even essential functions of social conflict; and in science, on the nature of scientific work and argumentation and on what has been called "revolutionary" science. The view presented of science, especially, in the schools is particularly interesting since it is essentially an archetype of the ideological position on conflict we wish to illuminate.

Two tacit assumptions seem to be prominent in teaching and in curricular materials. The first centers around a negative position on the nature

---

[1] Such a statement is both realistic and rather critical. In a way, critics of the schools (and the present author to a large extent) are caught in a bind. It is rather easy to denigrate existing "educational" structures (after all, everyone seems to do it); yet, it is not quite as easy to offer alternative structures. The individual who attempts to ameliorate some of the more debilitating conditions runs the risk of actually helping to shore up and perpetuate what may very well be an outmoded set of institutional arrangements. Yet, not to try to better conditions in what are often small and stumbling ways is to neglect those real human beings who now inhabit the schools for most of their pre-adult lives. Therefore, one tries to play both sides of the battle often. One criticizes the fundamental assumptions that undergird schools as they exist today and, at the same time, paradoxically attempts to make these same institutions a bit more humane, a bit more educative. It is an ambiguous position, but, after all, so is one's total situation. Our discussion of the fundamental glossing over of the nature and necessity of conflict and the tacit teaching that accompanies it shows this ambiguity. However, if urban education in particular is to make a difference (and here we should read politically and economically), then concrete changes must be effected now *while* the more basic criticisms are themselves being articulated. One is not an excuse for the other.

and uses of conflict. The second focuses on man as a recipient of norms mainly by coping with the day-to-day encounters and tasks of classroom life. The fact that these norms that students learn penetrate many areas of later life is critical since it helps document how schooling contributes to individual adjustment to an ongoing social, economic, and political order. Schooling, occupation, and politics in the United States are well integrated for Dreeben (pp. 144–45). The former acts as a distributor of a form of rationality that, when internalized by the student, enables him to function in and, often, accept "the occupational and political institutions which contribute to the stability of an industrial society."

Social studies and science as they are taught in the large majority of schools provide some of the most explicit instances of the hidden teaching. We have chosen these areas for two reasons. First, there has been built up a rather extensive and important literature concerned with the sociology of the disciplines of scientific endeavor. This literature deals rather insightfully with the "logic-in-use" of scientists (that is, what scientists seem actually to do) as opposed to the "reconstructed logic" of scientists (that is, what philosophers of science and other observers say scientists do) that is normally taught in schools (Apple in press). Second, in social studies the problems we discuss can be illuminated rather clearly by drawing upon selected Marxian notions (ideas, not necessarily dogma) to show that the common-sense views of social life often found in the teaching of social studies are not inevitable. Let us examine science initially. In so doing, we propose an alternate or, rather, a broader view of scientific endeavor that should be considered by educators and, especially, curriculum workers, if they are, at the very least, to focus on the assumptions inherent in much that is taught in our educational institutions.

## CONFLICT IN SCIENTIFIC COMMUNITIES

One of our basic theses is that science, as it is presented in most elementary and a large proportion of secondary classrooms, contributes to the learning by students of a basically unrealistic and essentially conservative perspective on the usefulness of conflict. Scientific domains are presented as bodies of knowledge ("thats" and "hows"), at best organized around certain fundamental regularities as in the many discipline and inquiry-centered curricula that evolved after the "Brunerian revolution," at worst as fairly isolated data one masters for tests. Almost never is it seriously examined as a personal construction of human beings. Let us examine this situation rather closely.

A science is not "just" a domain of knowledge or techniques of discovery and formulating justifications; it is a *group* (or rather, groups) of individuals, a *community* of scholars in Polanyi's (1964) terms, pursuing projects in the world. Like all communities, it is governed by norms, values, and principles that are both overtly seen and covertly felt. By being made up of individuals and groups of scholars, it also has had a significant history of both intellectual and interpersonal struggle. Often the conflict is generated by the introduction of a new and usually quite revolutionary paradigm that challenges the basic meaning structures that were previously accepted by the particular body of scientists, often, thereby, effectively dividing the scholarly community. These struggles have been concerned with the modes of gaining warranted knowledge, with what is to be considered properly scientific, with the very basic foundations upon which science is based. They have also been concerned with such situations as conflicting interpretations of data, with who discovered what first, and many more.

What can be found in schools, however, is a perspective that is akin to what has been called the *positivist ideal* (Hagstrom, 1965, p. 256). In our schools, scientific work is tacitly always linked with accepted standards of validity and is seen (and taught) as always subject to empirical verification with no outside influences, either personal or political. "Schools of thought" in science do not exist or, if they do, "objective" criteria are used to persuade scientists that one side is correct and the other wrong. Just as is evident in our discussion of social studies instruction, children are presented with a *consensus theory of science*, one that underemphasizes the serious disagreements over methodology, goals, and other elements that make up the paradigms of activity of scientists. By the fact that scientific consensus is continually exhibited, students are not permitted to see that without disagreement and controversy science would not progress or would progress at a much slower pace. Not only does controversy stimulate discovery by drawing the attention of scientists to critical problems (Hagstrom, p. 264) but it serves to clarify conflicting intellectual positions. More is mentioned about this point later in our discussion.

A point that is also quite potent is that it is very possible that the standards of "objectivity" (one is tempted to say "vulgar objectivity") being exhibited and taught in school may often lead to a detachment from political commitment. That is, it may not be neutrality as it is overtly expressed, but it may mirror a rather deep fear of intellectual, moral, and political conflict (Gouldner, 1970, pp. 102–3), and the personally intense commitment that coheres with the positions taken (Polanyi, 1964). The focus in educational institutions on the student/scientist (who is often a passive observer in many classrooms despite the emphasis being placed on inquiry by theorists and curriculum specialists) as an individual who objectively and rationally tests or deduces warranted assumptions or makes and checks hypotheses or what have you critically misrepresents the nature of the conflicts so often found between proponents of alternative solutions, interpretations, or modes of procedure in scientific communities. It cannot enable students to see the political dimension of the process by which one alternative theory's proponents win out over their competitors. Nor can such a presentation of science do more than systematically neglect the power dimension involved in scientific argumentation.

Not only is the historical and continuing conflict between competing theories in scientific domains ignored, but little or no thought has evidently been given to the fact that hypothesis-testing and the application of *existing* scientific criteria are *not sufficient* to explain how and why a choice is made between competing theories. There have been too many counter-instances that belie this view of science (Kuhn 1962).[2] It is much more perceptive to note that science itself is not necessarily cumulative, nor does it proceed according to a basic criterion of consensus, but that it is riven by conceptual revolutions that cause groups of scientists to reorganize and reconceptualize the models by which they attempt to understand and manipulate the world.

> The history of science has been and should be [seen] as a history of competing research programs (or, if you wish, "paradigms"), but it has not been and must not become a succession of periods of normal science: the sooner competition starts the better for progress. (Lakatos, 1970, p. 155)[3]

We are not trying to make a case here for a view of science that states that "objectivity" and "neutrality," hypothesis-testing and inquiry procedures are not of paramount importance. What we are saying is that scientific argumentation and counter-argumentation are a major part of the scientific enterprise and that the theories and modes of procedure ("structures of disciplines," if you will) act as norms or psychological commitments that lead to intense controversy between groups of scientists (Apple, in press; Mulkay, 1969). This controversy is central to progress in science, and it is this continuing conflict that is hidden from students.

Perhaps this point can be made clearer by delving a bit more deeply into some of the realistic characteristics of scientific disciplines often hidden from public view and almost never taught in schools. We have been discussing conflict in scientific domains, yet it is difficult to separate conflict from competition.[4] One of the more important oversights in schools is the lack of treatment whatsoever of the "problem" of competition in

---

[2] Kuhn's seminal work is subjected to rather acute analysis, and discussed with rebuttal and counter-rebuttal in Lakatos and Musgrave (1970). The entire volume is devoted to the issues, epistemological and sociological, raised by Kuhn's book.

[3] Normal science refers to that science that has agreement (consensus) on the basic paradigms of activity to be used by scientists to interpret and act on their respective fields. See Kuhn (1962, 1970) for an intensive analysis of normal and revolutionary science.

[4] It is important to distinguish between conflict and competition, however. While conflict seems to stem from a number of the conditions we have examined or will examine—new paradigms, disagreements over goals, methodology, etc.—competition seems to have its basis in the exchange system of science. See, for example, Storer's (1966) interesting examination of the place of professional recognition and commodity exchange in the scientific community.

science. Competition over priority and recognition in new discoveries is a characteristic of *all* established sciences (Hagstrom, 1965, p. 81). One need only read Watson's (1968) lively account of his race with Linus Pauling for the Nobel Prize for the discovery of the structure of DNA to realize how intense the competitiveness can be and how very human are scientists as individuals and in groups.

Competition also can be seen quite clearly between specialties in a discipline (Hagstrom, 1965, p. 130), not necessarily on the "frontiers" of knowledge as in Watson's case. Here, as in football, the "commodity" (if I may speak metaphorically) is top-notch students who can be recruited to expand the power and prestige of an emerging specialty. There is continuous, but usually covert, competition among subdisciplines in science for what seem to be limited amounts of prestige available. The conflict here is crucial. Areas whose prestige is relatively high tend to recruit members with the most talent. Relatively lower prestige areas can have quite a difficult time gaining adherents to their particular interests. Realistically, a prime factor, if not *the* most important factor, in high quality scientific research is the quality of student and scientific "labor" a specialty can recruit. Prestige has a strong influence in enticing students and the competition over relative prestige can be intense, therefore, because of these consequences (Hagstrom, p. 173).

My point here is decidedly not to denigrate competition in science, nor is it to present a demonic view of the scientific enterprise in all its ramifications. Rather it is to espouse a more realistic perspective on this enterprise and the *uses of conflict among its practitioners.* Conflict and competition themselves are quite functional. They induce scientists in each area to try to establish a domain of competence in their subjects that is specifically theirs. Competitive pressures also help to assure that less popular research areas are not neglected. Furthermore, the strong competitive element in the scientific community encourages members to take risks, to outdistance their competitors, in effect, thereby increasing the possibility of new and exciting discoveries (Hagstrom, pp. 82–83).

Conflict is also heightened by the very normative structure of the scientific community itself. In fact, it may be a significant contributing agent in both conflict and competition. Among the many norms that guide the behavior of scientists, perhaps the most important for our discussion here is that of organized skepticism. Storer (1966, pp. 78–79) defines it as follows:

> This norm is directive, embodying the principle that each scientist should be held individually responsible for making sure that previous research by others on which he bases his work is valid. He cannot be excused if he has accepted a false idea and then pleads innocence "because Dr. X told me it was true," even if privately we cannot accuse him of willfully substituting error for truth; he should have been properly sceptical of Dr. X's work in the first place. . . .

The scientist is obligated also by this norm to make public his criticisms of the work of others when he believes it to be in error. . . . It follows that no scientist's contribution to knowledge can be accepted without careful scrutiny, and that the scientist must doubt his own findings as well as those of others.

It is not difficult to see how the norm of organized skepticism has contributed to the controversies within scientific communities.

Other examples of conflict abound. Perhaps the one most important for our own topic is the existence of "rebellious" subgroups in scientific communities. Specialities that revolt against the goals and/or means of a larger discipline are quite common within the scientific tradition. These rebellious groups of researchers are alienated from the main body of current scientific discourse in their particular areas and sparks may very well fly because of the argumentation between the rebels and the traditionalists. Here, often added to this situation, even the usual arguments that we associate with science—that is, arguments among groups and individuals over substantive issues such as warranted knowledge and the like—blend with arguments over goals and policies (Hagstrom, 1965, pp. 193–94).[5] Even more importantly today, it is becoming quite common (and in my view, happily so) for there to be heated discussion and dissension over the political stance a discipline should take and over the social uses of its knowledge.

So far we have been documenting the rather important dimension of conflict in scientific communities. We have been making the point that scientific knowledge as it is taught in schools has, in effect, been divorced from the structure of the community from which it evolved and which acts to criticize it. Students are "forced," because of the very absence of a realistic picture of how communities in science apportion power and economic resources, to internalize a view that has little potency for questioning the legitimacy of the tacit assumptions about interpersonal conflict that govern their lives and their own educational, economic, and political situations. Not only are they presented with a view of science that is patently unrealistic, but, what is more important for our own position, they are not shown how critical interpersonal and intergroup argumentation and conflict have been for the progress of science. When this situation is generalized into a basic perspective on one's relation to the economic and political paradigms of activity in a society, it is not difficult to see how it can serve to reinforce the quiescence of students or lead them into "proper channels" for changing these structures.

## CONFLICT IN SOCIETY

The second area of schooling in which one finds hidden curricular encounters with and tacit teaching of constitutive assumptions about con-

---

[5] Statistics is an interesting example.

flict, and that we have chosen to explicitly focus upon, is that of social studies. As in our discussion of science, in delving into this area we propose an alternative or broader view on conflict in society. We also document some of the social uses of intellectual and normative conflict, uses that are ignored in most of the curricular encounters found in schools.

An examination of much of the literature in social studies points to an acceptance of society as basically a cooperative system. Observations in classrooms over an extended period of time reveal a similar perspective. The orientation stems in large part from the (perhaps necessarily unconscious) basic assumption that conflict, and especially social conflict, is *not an essential* feature of the network of social relations we call society (Dahrendorf, 1959, p. 112). More often than not, a social reality is pictured that tacitly accepts "happy cooperation" as the normal if not the best way of life. Now it must be made clear that the truth value of the statement that society is a cooperative system (if only everyone would cooperate) *cannot* be determined empirically. It is essentially a value orientation that helps determine the questions that one asks or the educational experiences one designs for students. And the educational experiences seem to emphasize what is fundamentally a conservative perspective.

The perspective found in schools leans heavily upon how all elements of a society, from the postman and fireman in first grade to the partial institutions in civics courses in high school, are linked to each other in a functional relationship, each contributing to the ongoing *maintenance* of society. Internal dissension and conflict in a society are viewed as inherently antithetical to the smooth functioning of the social order. *Consensus* is once more a pronounced feature. This orientation is also evident in the implicit emphasis upon students (and man in general) as value-transmitting and value-receiving persons rather than as value-creating persons in much of their school experience (Gouldner, 1970, p. 193).

The fact that there are a number of paradigmatic ways one can perceive the social world has long been noted. However, it is also important to note that each posits a certain logic of organization upon social activity and each has certain, often strikingly different, valuative assumptions that underlie it. The differences between the Durkheimian and the more subjectivistic Weberian perspectives offer a case in point. The recent analysis of structural-functional social theories, especially those of Parsons, by Gouldner offers a more current example. His examination, one that has a long intellectual history in the sociology of knowledge, raises intriguing questions about the social and political consequences of contemporary social thought—that much of its background of assumptions is determined by the personal and class existence of the thinker, that it presents a "very selective, one-sided picture of American society," one geared to "the avoidance of political tensions" and aimed at a notion that political stability, say, "would be achieved if efforts at social change prudently stopped short of changing established ways of allocating and justifying power"

(p. 48). In short the underlying basis of such a social "paradigm" used to order and guide our perceptions is fundamentally oriented to the legitimation of the existing social order. By the very fact that it seeks to treat such topics as social *equilibrium* and system *maintenance,* for example, there is a strong tendency toward conformity and a denial that there need be conflict (pp. 210–18).

Opposed to the structural-functional type of reasoning, Gouldner advocates a different "paradigm," one that is rooted in the individual's search to transform himself and his activity, and one that sets not existing society as measure but rather the possibility of basic structural change through an individual's passionate commitment and social involvement. The question of legitimation, hence, becomes less a process of studying how institutional tensions evolve and can be "settled," and more an attempt to link institutions with their historical development and their need for transformation according to explicitly chosen principles based on political and moral argumentation. The perspective on conflict of the latter position is quite different from that of the school of thought Gouldner criticizes.

In its analysis of the background assumptions of Parsonian social thought, for example, Gouldner's examination documents the place of moral argumentation and value conflict, which are at the heart of the human sciences and their understanding of society. He thereby considerably expands the boundaries of possible conflict. This situation is perhaps most evident in his criticism of the inordinate place Parsons gives to a socialization process that implicitly defines man as primarily a recipient of values (p. 206). He censures Functionalist social theories for being incapable of dealing with "those who oppose social establishments actively and who struggle to change its rules and membership requirements." Gouldner opposes this view with a focus upon human beings as engaged in a dialectical process of receiving, creating, and recreating values and institutions (p. 427; Berger and Luckmann, 1966). The continual recreation of values in a society is a difficult process and often involves conflict among those of disparate valuative frameworks. It is this type of conflict, among others, to which Gouldner attempts to give a place.

By their very nature, social "paradigms" themselves are constantly changing. In fact, Gouldner's recent work can be seen to mirror and be a part of this change. However, they leave behind reifications of themselves found in both elementary and high school curricula. This may be particularly true in the case of the models of understanding of social life we find in schools today.

There is, perhaps, no better example of the emphasis upon consensus, order, and the absence of any conflict in social studies curricula than that found in one of the more popular sets of educational materials, Science Research Associates' economics "kit," *Our Working World.* It is designed to teach basic concepts of disciplined economics to elementary school students. The primary-grade course of study subtitled "Families at Work" is organized around everyday social interaction, the likes of which children would be familiar with. Statements such as the following pervade the materials.

> When we follow the rules, we are rewarded; but if we break the rules, we will be punished. So you see, dear, that is why everyone does care. That is why we *learn* customs and rules, and why we *follow* them. Because if we do, we are all rewarded by a nicer and more orderly world. (Senesh, 1963, p. 22)

The attitude exhibited toward the *creation* of new values and customs and the value placed on an orderly, nonconflicting world seem to be indicative of a more constitutive set of assumptions concerning consensus and social life. When one realizes that students are inundated with examples of this type throughout the day, ones in which it is rather difficult to find any value placed upon disorder of any significant sort, it makes one pause.

Even most of the inquiry-oriented curricula, though fruitful in other ways to be sure, show a signal neglect of the efficacy of conflict and the rather long and deep-seated history it has held in social relationships. For example, the basic assumptions that conflicts are to be "resolved" within accepted boundaries and that continuing change in the framework and texture of institutional arrangements is less than desirable can be seen in the relatively sophisticated discipline-centered social science curricula that are being developed currently. One of these curricula (Center for the Study of Instruction, 1970) overtly offers a "conceptual schemes" approach that puts forward a hierarchy of generalizations that, ideally, are to be internalized by the student through his active participation in role-playing and inquiry. These levels of generalizations range from rather simple to fairly complex and are subsumed under a broad "descriptive" generalization or "cognitive scheme." For example, subsumed under the organizing generalization "Political organization (government) resolves conflicts and makes interactions easier among people" are the following subgeneralizations. They are listed in ascending complexity.

1. The behavior of indviduals is governed by commonly accepted rules.
2. Members of family groups are governed by rules and law.
3. Community groups are governed through leadership and authority.
4. Man's peaceful interaction depends on social controls.
5. The pattern of government depends upon control by participation in the political system.
6. Stable political organization improves the quality of life shared by its citizens. (p. T-17)[6]

---

[6] It is questionable whether many blacks in the ghettos of the United States would support this "description."

Coupled with these "descriptive" generalizations, which the students are to be led up to, are such "supporting concepts" as "Rules help to maintain order" and "Rules help protect health and safety" (p. T-26). Now, few will quarrel with these statements. After all, rules do help. But, like the assumptions prevalent in the economics material, children are confronted with a tacit emphasis once again on a stable set of structures and on the maintenance of order.

What is intriguing is the nearly complete lack of treatment of or even reference to conflict as a social concern or as a category of thought in most available social studies curricula or in most classrooms observed. Of the more popular materials, only those developed under the aegis of the late Hilda Taba refer to it as a key concept. However, while the Taba Social Studies Curriculum overtly focuses on conflict, and while this focus in itself is a welcome sight, its orientation is on the serious consequences of sustained conflict rather than on the many positive aspects also associated with conflict itself. Conflict again is viewed as "dysfunctional," even though it is pictured as being ever present (Durkin, Duvall, and McMaster, 1969, p. v).

As we noted previously, to a large extent society as it exists, in *both* its positive and negative aspects, is held together by implicit common-sense rules and paradigms of thought. Social studies materials such as this (and there are many others to which we have not referred) can contribute to the reinforcing and tacit teaching of certain dominant basic assumptions and, hence, a pro-consensus and anti-dissension belief structure.

This view is being countered somewhat by a portion of the content now being taught under the rubric of Black Studies. Here, struggle and conflict on a communal basis are often explicitly and positively focused upon (Hare 1969; Wilcox, 1969, pp. 20–21). While many curriculists may find such overt espousal of community goals somewhat antithetical to their own inclinations, the fact that there has been an attempt to present a comparatively realistic outlook on the significant history and uses of conflict in the progress of social groups, through the civil rights and black power movements for instance, must be recognized. Even those who would not applaud or would applaud only a rather safe or conservative view on this subject should realize the potency and positive value of just such a perspective for developing a group consciousness and a cohesiveness not heretofore possible. This point is made again in our more general discussion of the uses of conflict in social groups.

To say, however, that most Black Studies curricula exhibit this same perspective would be less than accurate. One could also point to the by now apparent presentation of black historical material where those blacks are presented who stayed within what were considered to be the legitimate boundaries (constitutive rules) of protest or progressed in accepted economic, athletic, scholarly, or artistic fields. Usually, one does not find reference to Malcolm X, Marcus Garvey, or others who offered a potent critique of existing modes of activity. However, it is the *massiveness* of the tacit presentation of the consensus perspective that must be stressed, as well as its occurrence in the two areas examined in this paper.

It is not sufficient, though, for our purposes to "merely" illuminate how the hidden curriculum obligates students to experience certain encounters with basic rules. It is essential that an alternative view be posited and the uses of social conflict that we have been mentioning be documented.

It is possible to counter the consensus orientation with a somewhat less consensus-bound set of assumptions, assumptions that seem to be as empirically warranted, if not more so, as those to which we have raised objections. For instance, some social theorists have taken the position that "society is not primarily a smoothly functioning order of the form of a social organism, a social system, or a static social fabric." Rather, continuous change in the elements *and* basic structural form of society is a dominant characteristic. Conflicts are the systematic products of the changing structure of a society and by their very nature tend to lead to progress. The "order" of society, hence, becomes the regularity of change. The "reality" of society is conflict and flux, not a "closed functional system" (Dahrendorf, 1959, p. 27). It has been stated that the most significant contribution to the understanding of society made by Marx was his insight that a major source of change and innovation is internal conflict. This crucial insight can be appreciated without the necessity of accepting his metaphysical assumptions (Walker, 1967, pp. 217–18). In essence, therefore, conflicts must be looked at as a basic and often beneficial dimension of the dialectic of activity we label society.

An examination of positions within and closely allied with this general orientation can help to illuminate the importance of conflict. One of the more interesting perspectives points to its utility in preventing the reification of existing social institutions by exerting pressure upon individuals and groups to be innovative and creative in bringing about changes in institutional activities. Coser (Dahrendorf, 1959, p. 207) puts it well:

> Conflict within and between groups in a society can prevent accommodations and habitual relations from progressively impoverishing creativity. The clash of values and interests, the tension between what is and what some groups feel ought to be, the conflict between vested interests and new strata and groups demanding their share of power, have been productive of vitality.

Yet one is hard pressed to find anything akin to this orientation in most of the materials and teaching exhibited in schools. The basic rules of activity that govern our perception tend to cause us to picture conflict as primarily a negative quality in a collectivity. However, "happy cooperation" and conflict are the two sides of the societal coin, neither of which is wholly positive or negative. This outlook is forcefully put by Coser (1956, p. 31):

> No group can be entirely harmonious for it would then be devoid of process and structure. Groups require disharmony as well as harmony, dissociation as well as association; and conflicts within them are by no means altogether disruptive factors. Group formation is the result of both types of processes. The belief that one process tears down what the other builds up, so that what finally remains is the result of subtracting the one from the other, is based on a misconception. On the contrary, both "positive" and "negative" factors build group relations. Conflict as well as cooperation has social functions. Far from being necessarily dysfunctional, a certain degree of conflict is an essential element in group formation and the persistence of group life.

The basic rule of activity that constitutes the unconscious negative value associated with conflict tends to lead to the designing of experiences that focus on the "law or rule breaking" dimension of conflict, yet it should be made clear that conflict leads not "merely" to law breaking but is, in effect, law *creating* as well (Coser, p. 126).[7] It performs the considerable task of pointing to areas of needed redress. Furthermore, it brings into conscious awareness the more basic rules that govern the particular activity over which there is conflict but that were hidden from view. That is, it performs the unique function of enabling individuals to see the hidden imperatives built into situations that act to structure their actions, thereby partially freeing individuals to create relevant patterns of actions to an extent not usually possible. These law-creating and expanding-awareness properties of conflict situations offer, in combination, a rather positive effect. Since conflict brings about inherently new situations that to a large degree are undefined by previous assumptions, it acts as a stimulus for the establishment of new and possibly more flexible or situationally pertinent norms of activity. By literally forcing conscious attention, issues are defined and new dimensions can be explored and made clear (Coser, pp. 124–25).

Documentation of the positive effects of conflict would not be even nearly adequate if a major use were to go unmentioned, especially given our own commitment to making urban education, in particular, more responsive to the needs of the community it serves. Here we are speaking of the importance of conflict for both creating and legitimating a conscious and specifically ethnic experience. It is now well known that one of the

---

[7] Perhaps the best illustration of material on the law-breaking dimension of conflict is a primary-grade course of study, "Respect for Rules and Law" (New York State Bureau of Elementary Curriculum Development, 1969). One set of curricular materials does take some interesting and helpful steps in allowing for a more honest appraisal of conflict. See Oliver & Newmann (1968).

primary ways groups define themselves is by perceiving themselves as struggling with other groups and that such struggle both increases members' participation in group activities and makes them more conscious of the bonds that tie them together (Coser, p. 90). That the black and other ethnic communities have, to a significant extent, defined themselves along these in-group/out-group lines is of no small moment since it enables a greater cohesiveness among the various elements within their respective communities. By drawing upon "primordial sentiments" such as race, a communal meaning structure is created that makes plausible an individual's and a group's continued and separate existence (Berger, 1967, pp. 24–25; Geertz, 1963, p. 118). Just as conflict seems to be a primary means for the establishment of individual autonomy and for the full differentiation of personality from the outside world (Coser, 1965, p. 33),[8] so too is it effective for the full differentiation of community autonomy. Respect for pluralistic societies may require a greater acceptance of this perspective.

We have been proposing an alternative outlook on the presence and uses of conflict in social groups. It is feasible for it to be used as a more objective foundation for designing curricula and guiding teaching so that the more static hidden curriculum students encounter can be counterbalanced to some extent. The explicit focusing on conflict as a legitimate category of conceptualization and as a valid and essential dimension of collective life could enable the development by students of a more viable and potent political and intellectual perspective from which to perceive their relation to existing economic and political institutions. At the least, such a perspective gives them a better understanding of the tacit assumptions that act to structure their own activity.

## PROGRAMMATIC CONSIDERATIONS

There are a number of programmatic suggestions that can be made that could at least partially serve to counterbalance the hidden curriculum most evident in science and social studies. While these are by their very nature still rather tentative and only partial, they may prove important.

A more balanced presentation of some of the espoused values of science is essential, especially that relating to organized skepticism. The historical importance to the scientific communities of the overriding skeptical outlook needs to be recognized and focused upon.

The history of science can be seen as a continuing dialectic of controversy and conflict between advocates of competing research programs and paradigms, between accepted answers and challenges to these "truths." As such, science itself could be presented with a greater historical orien-

---

[8] This is perhaps one of Piaget's most fruitful insights.

tation documenting the conceptual revolutions necessary for significant breakthroughs to occur.

Rather than adhering to a view of science as truth, the balanced presentation of science as truth-until-further-notice, a process of continual change, could prevent the crystallization of attitudes (Apple and Popkewitz, 1971). In this connection also, the study of how conceptual revolutions in science have proceeded would contribute to a less positive perspective on consensus as the only mode of progress.

To this point can be added a focus upon the moral uses and dilemmas of science. For example, personalizing the history of science through cases such as Oppenheimer, Watson, and, intriguingly, the controversy surrounding the Velikovsky case (cf. Mulkay 1969), would indeed be helpful. When taken together, these suggestions would help to eliminate the bias of present curricula by introducing the idea of personal and interpersonal controversy and conflict.

In the social studies, a number of suggestions can be made. The comparative study of revolution, say the American, French, Russian, and Chinese, would serve to focus upon the properties of the human condition that cause and are ameliorated by interpersonal conflict. This suggestion is made more appropriate when coupled with the fact that in many countries revolution is the legitimate (in a quite real sense of the word) mode of procedure for redressing grievances.

A more realistic appraisal and presentation of the uses of conflict in the civil rights movement of blacks, Indians, and others would no doubt assist in the formation of a perspective that perceives these and similar activities as legitimate models of action. The fact that laws *had* to be broken and were then struck down by the courts later is not usually focused upon in social studies curricula. Yet, it was through these types of activities that a good deal of progress was and is made. Here community and "movement" studies by urban students of how changes have been effected is an interesting process, one that should prove of considerable moment.

Finally, the comparison of different paradigmatic views on social life and the differing value assumptions of each would be helpful. While the normative implications of many paradigms of social thought may serve to limit their usefulness as models of action, and in fact may make them totally unacceptable on occasion, the presentation and analysis of alternative conceptions to those now dominant could still be effective.

Beyond these suggestions for specific programmatic changes, one further area should be noted. Sociological "paradigms" also attempt to account for the common-sense reality in which students and teachers dwell. Schools are integrally involved in this reality and its internalization. It might be wise to consider engaging students in the articulation and development of paradigms of activity within their everyday lives at school. Such involvement could enable students to come to grips with and amplify crucial insights into their own conditionedness and freedom. Such insights could potentially alter the original paradigm and the common-sense reality itself. It would also make possible to a greater degree a concrete and meaningful educational encounter for students with the process of value and institutional recreation.

## CONCLUSIONS

Research on political socialization of children seems to indicate the importance of the president and the policeman as points of contact between children and the structures of authority and legitimacy in a society (Easton and Dennis, 1969, p. 162). For instance, there is a strongly personal initial bond between the child and these representatives of the structures of authority. As the child matures, these very personal ties are transferred to more anonymous institutions such as a congress or to political activities such as voting. The tendency to lift impersonal institutions to high esteem may be quite an important source of the relative stability and durability of the structures of authority in industrial societies (pp. 271–76).

Yet it is not quite certain that this formulation really answers the questions one could raise concerning political and social stability. The foundation of political (broadly conceived) leanings and relations to political and social structures is in a belief system that itself rests upon basic patterns of assumptions. Such rules for activity (and thought as a fundamental form of this activity) are probably more important to a person's relation to his life-world than we realize. We have been examining one of these constitutive assumptions.

It is our contention that the schools systematically distort the functions of social conflict in collectivities. The social, intellectual, and political manifestations of this distortion are manifold. They may contribute significantly to the ideological underpinnings that serve to fundamentally orient individuals.

Students in most schools and in urban centers in particular are presented with a view that serves to legitimate the existing social order since change, conflict, and man as creator as well as receiver of values and institutions are systematically neglected. We have pointed to the massiveness of the presentation. Now something else must be stressed once again —the fact that these meaning structures are obligatory. Students receive them from persons who are "significant others" in their lives, through their teachers, other role models in books and elsewhere. To change this situation, students' perceptions of to whom they are to look as holders of "expert knowledge" must be radically altered. In ghetto areas, a partial answer is, perhaps, instituting a more radical perspective in the schools. This change can be carried out only by political activity. It may very well be that to divorce an educator's educational existence from his political existence is to forget that as an act of influence, education is also an inherently political act.

One of the primary tasks of this analysis has been to present lenses that are alternatives to those that normally legitimate many of the activities and encounters curriculists design for students. The curriculum field has limited its own forms of consciousness so that the political and ideological assumptions that undergird a good deal of its normal patterns of activity are as hidden as those that students encounter in schools (Huebner, 1962, p. 88). We have pointed to the possibilities inherent in a more theoretically realistic approach to the nature of conflict as one alternative "form of consciousness." Yet when all has been said, it is still possible to raise the question of whether such theoretical investigations are either heuristically, politically, or programmatically helpful.

One of the difficulties in seeking to develop new perspectives is the obvious and oft pointed to distinction between theory and practice or, to put it in common-sense language, between "merely" understanding the world and changing it. This distinction is rooted in our very language. Yet it is crucial to remind ourselves that while, say, Marx felt that the ultimate task of philosophy and theory was not merely to "comprehend reality" but to change it, it is also true that according to Marx revolutionizing the world has as its very foundation an *adequate understanding* of it. (After all, Marx spent most of his lifetime *writing Das Kapital* —Avineri, 1968, p. 137).

The significant danger is not that theoretical thought offers no mode of critiquing and changing reality, but that it can lead to quietism or a perspective that, like Hamlet, necessitates a continuing monologue on the complexity of it all, while the world tumbles down around us. It would seem important to note that not only is an understanding of existing reality a necessary condition for changing it (Avineri, p. 148) but it is a major (and perhaps the major) step in actually effecting this reconstruction. However, with this understanding of the social milieu in which curriculists operate, there must also be a continual attempt to bring to a conscious level those hidden epistemological and ideological assumptions that help to structure the decisions they make and the environments they design (Huebner, 1962).[9] These fundamental assumptions can have a significant impact on the hidden curriculum in which students tacitly dwell.

Without an analysis and greater understanding of these latent assumptions, educators run the very real risk of continuing to let values work

---

[9] The common-sense assumptions that seem to posit a rather static logic upon curriculum design also seem to cohere with a type of bureaucratic rationality that has had a long tradition in curriculum thought. For an excellent analysis of this tradition, see Kliebard (1971).

through them. A conscious advocacy of a more realistic outlook on and teaching of the dialectic of social change would, no doubt, contribute to preparing students with the political and conceptual tools necessary to deal with the dense reality they must face. I do not think it is necessary to enumerate the possible consequences if this self-evaluation should not occur.

## REFERENCES

Apple, M.W.   "Community, Knowledge, and the Structure of Disciplines." *The Educational Forum*, in press.

Apple, M.W., and Popkewitz, T.S.   "Knowledge, Perspective and Commitment: An Essay Review of Thomas Kuhn and Alvin Gouldner." *Social Education*, 35 (1971):935–37.

Avineri, S.   *The Social and Political Thought of Karl Marx*. New York: Cambridge University Press, 1968.

Berger, P.L.   *The Sacred Canopy*. New York: Doubleday, 1967.

Berger, P.L., and Luckmann, T.   *The Social Construction of Reality*. New York: Doubleday, 1966.

Center for the Study of Instruction.   *Principles and Practices in the Teaching of the Social Sciences: Teacher's Edition*. New York: Harcourt, Brace and World, 1970.

Coser, L.   *The Functions of Social Conflict*. New York: Free Press, 1956.

Dahrendorf, R.   *Class and Class Conflict in Industrial Society*. Stanford: Stanford University Press, 1959.

Dahrendorf, R.   *Essays in the Theory of Society*. London: Routledge & Kegan Paul, 1968.

Dreeben, R.   *On What Is Learned in School*. Reading, Mass.: Addison-Wesley, 1968.

Durkin, M.C., Duvall, A., and McMaster, A.   *The Taba Social Studies Curriculum: Communities Around Us*. Reading, Mass.: Addison-Wesley, 1969.

Easton, D., and Dennis, J.   *Children in the Political System*. New York: McGraw-Hill, 1969.

Eisinger, P.K.   "Protest Behavior and the Integration of Urban Political Systems." Unpublished paper, Institute for Research on Poverty, The University of Wisconsin, Madison, Wisc., 1970.

Garfinkel, H.   *Studies in Ethnomethodology*. Englewood Cliffs, N.J.: Prentice-Hall, 1967.

Geertz, C.   "The Integrative Revolution: Primordial Sentiments and Civil Politics in the New States." In C. Geertz (Ed.), *Old Societies and New States*, pp. 105–57. New York: Free Press, 1963.

Gibson, E.F.   "The Three D's: Distortion, Deletion, Denial." *Social Education*, 33 (1969):405–09.

Gouldner, A.W.   *The Coming Crisis of Western Sociology*. New York: Basic Books, 1970.

Hagstrom, W.O.   *The Scientific Community*. New York: Basic Books, 1965.

Hare, N.    "The Teaching of Black History and Culture in the Secondary Schools." *Social Education,* 33 (1969):385–88.

Huebner, D.    "Politics and the Curriculum," in A.H. Passow (Ed.), *Curriculum Crossroads,* pp. 87–95. New York: Teachers College Press, 1962.

Jackson, P.    *Life in Classrooms.* New York: Holt, Rinehart & Winston, 1968.

Kliebard, H.M.    "Bureaucracy and Curriculum Theory." In V. Haubrich (Ed.), *Freedom, Bureaucracy and Schooling,* pp. 74–93. Washington: Association for Supervision and Curriculum Development, 1971.

Kuhn, T.S.    *The Structure of Scientific Revolutions.* Chicago: University of Chicago Press, 1962.

————.    *The Structure of Scientific Revolution.* 2nd ed. Chicago: University of Chicago Press, 1970.

Lakatos, I.    "Falsification and the Methodology of Scientific Research Programmes." In I. Lakatos and A. Musgrave (Eds.), *Criticism and the Growth of Knowledge,* pp. 91–95. New York: Oxford University Press, 1970.

Lakatos, I., and Musgrave, A. (Eds.)    *Criticism and the Growth of Knowledge.* New York: Oxford University Press, 1970.

McClure, H., and Fischer, G.    "Ideology and Opinion Making: General Problems of Analysis." Unpublished paper, Bureau of Applied Social Research, Columbia University, July 1969.

Mulkay, M.    "Some Aspects of Cultural Growth in the Natural Sciences." *Social Research,* 36 (1969):22–52.

New York State Bureau of Elementary Curriculum Development.    *Respect for Rules and Law.* Albany: New York State Dept. of Education, 1969.

Oliver, D., and Newmann, F.    *Harvard Social Studies Project: Public Issues Series.* Columbus, O.: American Education Publications, 1968.

Polanyi, M.    *Personal Knowledge.* New York: Harper & Row, 1964.

Senesh, L.    "Recorded Lessons," in L. Senesh (Ed.), *Our Working World: Families at Work.* Chicago: Science Research Associates, 1964.

Sigel, R. (Ed.)    *Learning about Politics.* New York: Random House, 1970.

Storer, N.W.    *The Social System of Science.* New York: Holt, Rinehart & Winston, 1966.

Walker, J.L.    "A Critique of the Elitist Theory of Democracy." In C.A. McCoy and J. Playford (Eds.), *Apolitical Politics,* pp. 199–219. New York: Cromwell, 1967.

Watson, J.D.    *The Double Helix.* New York: Atheneum, 1968.

Wilcox, P.    "Education for Black Liberation." *New Generation,* 51 (1; 1969): 17–21.

Willhelm, S.M.    *Who Needs the Negro?* Cambridge, Mass.: Schenkman, 1970.

Wittgenstein, L.    *Philosophical Investigations.* New York: Macmillan, 1958.

# 17

# Language as Curriculum Content and Learning Environment*

## COURTNEY B. CAZDEN

## LANGUAGE AS CURRICULUM CONTENT

Language poses multiple problems for education because it is both curriculum content and learning environment, both the object of knowledge, and a medium through which other knowledge is acquired.[1]

Usually, education in the institutions we call schools imparts knowledge about something without considering the context in which that knowledge is to be used. Language poses a particular challenge to curriculum designers because it is not certain that teaching knowledge about language helps us in any way. The unclear role of knowledge entails two further curriculum problems: inciting motivation and providing opportunities for practice. I will discuss these related questions with reference, in turn, to first languages, second languages, and dialects.

Communicative competence[2] implies a knowledge of both linguistic and sociolinguistic rules: a knowledge, in other words, both of language (in the narrow sense of phonology, syntax, and semantics), and of the social world in which it must be used.

To date, we know far more about the child's acquisition of linguistic

* Reprinted by permission of *Daedalus:* Journal of the American Academy of Arts and Sciences, Boston, Massachusetts. Summer 1973, *Language as a Human Problem.*

[1] I am grateful to Betty H. Bryant for critically reviewing this paper from a black perspective. Not all her criticisms have been met, but the paper is better for her sharp comments.

[2] D. Hymes, "Competence and Performance in Linguistic Theory," *Language Acquisition: Models and Methods,* R. Huxley and E. Ingram (Eds.) (New York: Academic Press, 1971), pp. 3–28.

rules than about his acquisition of sociolinguistic rules, and the two processes may be quite different. About the acquisition of linguistic rules, we know that, during the most dramatic language learning period from two to five years old, children are not taught syntax directly. Parents correct erroneous labels and factual inaccuracies, and they try to teach what they think of as speech etiquette (a matter of sociolinguistic rules) by censuring taboo words and admonishing the child to say "please" or to be quiet; but they do not correct immature grammatical forms. One may, after the fact, conjecture about what information on language structure is conveyed by parental utterances.[3] But parents themselves talk without any intent to teach language structure, and the child's immature grammatical forms assume a transparency through which parents and children engage in reciprocal communication from the very beginning.

Somehow, by means of the speech they engage in or overhear, children do internalize abstract rules. One example of these rules can stand for many: the contrasting meanings of English indefinite and definite articles, "a" and "the," investigated experimentally by Maratsos.[4] A child was seated at a table with a group of identical toy cars in front of him. The experimenter sat facing the child across the table. At the experimenter's request, the child handed him one of the cars. The adult then asked one of the two questions:

"Do you have a car?"

"Do you have the car?"

The questions were asked in random order, with normal intonation. To the first question, most children as young as three years old answered "yes" or nodded their heads; to the second question they said "no" or shook their heads. Somehow, many children, at least by the time they are three, have learned the contrast in meaning between what we label "definite" and "indefinite," a very abstract distinction which no one tries to teach a child directly.

Furthermore, all the evidence[5] shows that teaching grammatical rules in school has no effect on students' actual performance in speech or writing. In other words, grammatical performance seems to be based on implicit grammatical knowledge, which is unaffected by explicit teaching. One reason, therefore, why language is such a difficult subject for curric-

[3] Cf. C.E. Snow's study of the speech of college-educated mothers, "Language Acquisition and Mothers' Speech to Children," *Child Development*, 43 (1972):549–65; and C. Ward's study of the speech of mothers in the ex-plantation community of Rosepoint, Louisiana, *Them Children: A Study in Language Learning* (New York: Holt, Rinehart and Winston, 1971).

[4] M.P. Maratsos, "The Development of Definite and Indefinite Reference." Unpublished doctoral dissertation, Harvard University, 1972.

[5] J. Moffett, *Teaching the Universe of Discourse* (Boston: Houghton Mifflin, 1968).

ulum planners is that we do not understand the relationship between what is in some way *learned* and what can be *taught*. Polanyi's distinction between two kinds of awareness may be helpful. When hammering in a nail, we see the nail as the *focal* point and the hammer as a mere *subsidiary* instrument.

> Subsidiary awareness and focal awareness are mutually exclusive. If a pianist shifts his attention from the piece he is playing to the observation of what he is doing with his fingers while playing it, he gets confused and may have to stop. This happens generally if we switch our focal attention to particulars of which we had previously been aware only in their subsidiary role. . . . All particulars become meaningless if we lose sight of the pattern which they jointly constitute.
>
> When we use words in speech or writing we are aware of them only in a subsidiary manner. This fact is usually described as the *transparency* of language.[6]

In Polanyi's scheme, *maxims*—rules about aspects of a skill—can play a role:

> Maxims are the rules, the correct application of which is part of the art which they govern. The true maxims of golfing or of poetry increase our insight into golfing or poetry and may even give valuable guidance to golfers or poets; but these maxims would instantly condemn themselves to absurdity if they tried to replace the golfer's skill or the poet's art. Maxims cannot be understood, still less applied by anyone not already possessing a good practical knowledge of the art.[7]

If we accept Polanyi's view, it does not follow that maxims of effective communication cannot be taught, but only that the maxims selected should be at the level of functional effectiveness and style, not at the level of grammar. It may be argued, of course, that English teachers have always given style some consideration. But it is all too easy to ignore Polanyi's insistence on intentionality. Neither practice for practice's sake, nor maxims for maxims' sake will suffice. Both must serve a personal purpose, an intentionailty that alone binds the parts into a whole.

Thus, to realize the goals of language as curriculum content, it is necessary to design a particular kind of environment for language use, one in which the contrast between language as curriculum content and as learning environment is reduced. We must create environments in which (1) each individual is motivated by a powerful communicative intent, (2) to use language in ways which extend his repertoire beyond what he uses

---

[6] M. Polanyi, *Personal Knowledge: Towards a Post-Critical Philosophy* (New York: Harper Torchbooks, 1964), pp. 56–57.

[7] Ibid., p. 31.

out-of-school, and in which he can receive (3) feedback on the effectiveness of his efforts in speech or writing, and even (4) generalizations (Polanyi's maxims) that go beyond the individual case.

Critical problems in designing such environments vary according to the age of the learner. For young children, consistency of adult-child relationships, distribution of adult talking time, and the character of the adult-child interaction seem to be important;[8] for older children and adults, the problem of motivation probably overwhelms all others.[9]

Traditionally, we have believed that a second language was learned by a different process from a first language; recently that belief is being questioned. Dulay and Burt review the evidence[10] that, at least for young children, first and second language learning processes are very similar.

Consider just one interesting comparison. Brown[11] has described some nine basic kinds of two-word utterances used by monolingual children at about two years of age around the world. One kind, for example, indicates *possession* ("Mommy sweater" or "My ball"), another *location* ("Sweater chair" or "Pencil cup"). But time relations, which could also be expressed in two-word utterances like "Fall yesterday," do not appear.

By contrast, Dodson, Price and Williams report[12] on five-year-old children, initially monolingual in English, who attended the reception class of a Welsh Infant School where they spent two hours in a Welsh-speaking environment each afternoon. These children also went through a period of using two-word utterances, in this case in Welsh. One of the relationships expressed by these five-year-olds is time:

> Shirley wedyn        "Shirley afterwards"

This is as it should be if, as Brown argues, conceptual complexity as opposed to grammatical complexity determines order of acquisition at this early stage. Children learning a first language are at this stage at about age two. The Welsh children were five and their age shows. Five-year-olds should be thinking in terms of time as well as space.

Dodson, Price, and Williams also separated these children's utterances into those in which correct Welsh is structurally different from English

---

8 C.B. Cazden, "Two Paradoxes in the Acquisition of Language Structure and Functions," *The Development of Competence in Early Childhood*, J.S. Bruner and K.J. Connolly (Eds.) (New York: Academic Press, forthcoming).

9 C.B. Cazden, *Child Language and Education* (New York: Holt, Rhinehart and Winston, 1972), Ch. 10.

10 H. Dulay and M.K. Burt, "You Can't Learn without Goofing (an Analysis of Children's Second Language Errors)," *Error Analysis—Perspectives in Second Language Acquisition*, J. Richards (Ed.) (London: Longmans, forthcoming).

11 R. Brown, *A First Language, the Early Stages* (Cambridge: Harvard University Press, forthcoming).

12 C.J. Dodson, E. Price, and T.I. Williams, *Towards Bilingualism: Studies in Language Teaching Methods* (Cardiff: University of Wales Press, 1968).

and those which are a direct translation and found that: "This association with or discrimination from the mother tongue had little effect on the children's response, and they seemed to use the apparently more difficult patterns as readily as the easier ones."[13] Examples of the children's Welsh utterances expressing possession are:

| *esgidiau Dadi* | "Daddy's shoes" |
| *blodyn gwyn Karen* | "Karen's white flower" |
| *cadair y babi* | "the baby's chair" |

It is visually clear that in Welsh the possessor is named last, rather than first as in English. The children were evidently able to learn the reversed order without confusion.

On the basis of scanty evidence to date, it seems likely that the nature of second language learning changes with age, and that younger learners resemble first language learners more than older ones do. But the age of that turning point, or even whether there is only one, is a matter of controversy. At Geneva, H. Sinclair and her student, Margarite Levalée, suggest that a change takes place between five and seven years.[14] Lenneberg's work[15] would suggest that it takes place at the onset of adolescence. It is undoubtedly no coincidence that the two ages suggested coincide with the change in Piaget's developmental progression to concrete and formal operations respectively. But exactly how language learning, in this case second language learning, interlaces with other aspects of cognitive development is not yet clear.

What is clear is the supremely important role of attitude in second language learning. How can we create educational environments that activate the natural language learning abilities all children have? Here, probably, is the source of the problems some foreign language speaking minorities have in learning English.

At least that seems to be the implication of one success story of second language learning in school. Lambert, Just, and Segalowitz[16] describe two classes of monolingual English children in Montreal who received their first years of schooling entirely in French. The kindergarten program, which the authors think may be crucial, "conducted almost entirely in French by two very skilled and experienced teachers from Europe, stressed vocabulary development and listening comprehension through art, music,

---

13 Ibid., p. 42.

14 H. Sinclair and Margarite Levalée, personal communication, 1971.

15 E.H. Lenneberg, *Biological Foundations of Language* (New York: John Wiley, 1967).

16 W.E. Lambert, M. Just, and N. Segalowitz, "Some Cognitive Consequences of Following the Curricula of the Early School Grades in a Foreign Language," *Twenty-first Annual Round Table: Bilingualism and Language Contact*, J.E. Alatis (Ed.) Monograph Series on Languages and Linguistics, No. 23 (Washington, D.C.: Georgetown University Press, 1970), pp. 229–62.

and play, and encouraged spontaneous verbal expression in French."[17] French was the only language used from first grade on, and the children achieved dramatically both in languages and in mathematics. Furthermore, the children transferred what they had learned about reading from French to English with little trouble.

Ervin-Tripp asks the obvious question: Why does being taught in a foreign language work for these Montreal children and fail for Chicano, Puerto Rican, and Navajo children in the United States? In her words, "the differences are social."[18] In commenting on the same contrast, Haugen agrees:

> We need to think in terms of dominant and nondominant, but these are terms we don't like to talk about because they are ultimately political. . . . Children are sensitive to the pressure of society through their parents and their peers. I think the opposition of dominant and nondominant is so important that I wonder if Lambert's good results may not be accounted for by the fact that he is teaching the members of a dominant group a nondominant language which has potentialities of dominance, while in Texas or New Mexico we are teaching a dominant language to a nondominant group. This alters the educational picture totally.[19]

The same conclusions about the importance of attitudes was reached by Tax and his colleagues in the Carnegie Corporation Cross Cultural Education Project of the University of Chicago[20] which was concerned with raising the literacy level of Cherokees in eastern Oklahoma. Cherokee history is particularly interesting because in the 19th century 90 percent of the Cherokees were literate in their native language—using a writing system developed in 1819 by Sequoyah, a Cherokee with no formal education—and they were more literate in English than the whites in neighboring communities in Texas and Arkansas. Walker suggests what it would take for them to regain this status:

> It seems clear that the startling decline during the past sixty years of both English and Cherokee literacy in the Cherokee tribe is chiefly a result of the recent scarcity of reading materials in Cherokee and of the fact that learning to read has become associated with coercive instruction, particularly in the context of an alien and threatening school. . . . For the Cherokee community to become literate once again, Cherokees must be con-

---

[17] Ibid., p. 233.

[18] S. Ervin-Tripp, "Structure and Process in Language Acquisition," *Twenty-first Annual Round Table: Bilingualism and Language Contact*, p. 314.

[19] E. Haugen, *Twenty-first Annual Round Table: Bilingualism and Language Contact*, p. 310.

[20] S. Tax and R.K. Thomas, "Education for American Indians: Threat or Promise," *The Florida FL Reporter*, 7 (1; 1969):15–19 ff.; W. Walker, "Notes on Native Writing Systems and the Design of Native Literacy Programs," *Anthropological Linguistics* (1969):148–65.

vinced that literacy does not imply the death of their society, that education is not a clever device to wean children away from the tribe. This is not a uniquely Cherokee situation. Identical attitudes toward education and the school no doubt can be found in Appalachia, in urban slums, in Afro-Asia, and indeed, in all societies where the recruitment of individuals into the dominant society threatens the extinction of a functioning social group.[21]

Children learn to speak like the people important to them in their home community. On some nonconscious level, children pick their parents and later their peers as language models despite the fact that they listen, during long periods of watching television, to standard American patterns of pronunciation and grammar. Around the world, people retain their speech patterns as expressions of self-identity and community solidarity, despite the potentially homogenizing effect of the mass media.

This selection of speech patterns, and the linguistic pluralism that results, is a source of both potentialities and problems: potentialities because rich alternative forms of expression are available to their users; problems because if speech patterns are a form of self-identification, they can be used for discriminatory purposes in a discriminatory society. Unlike the grammatical immaturities of young children, dialect features are not transparent. Quite the opposite. They are often so opaque that true reciprocal communication is impossible as judgments are formed about the educability of a child or the employability of an adult.

In the long run, these problems produce the "Pygmalion effect" and the pressure to include instruction in Standard English in the curriculum. There is no empirical evidence (only heated arguments) that dialect differences *per se* have any direct adverse affect on a child's educability.

But there is empirical evidence of an indirect adverse effect—the effect of a child's speech on his teacher's attitudes toward him, and thereby on the learning environment that is created by the teacher. Seligman, Tucker, and Lambert,[22] for example, report that a recorded speech pattern had more influence on third grade teachers' ratings than the quality of a child's composition or drawing.[23] Here a curriculum on language is sorely needed —but for teachers, not children.

Whether schools should attempt to teach standard English is a matter

21 W. Walker, "An Experiment in Programmed Cross-cultural Education: The Import of the Cherokee Primer for the Cherokee Community and for the Behavioral Sciences," Mimeo (Middletown, Conn.: Wesleyan University, March 1965), p. 10.

22 C.R. Seligman, G.R. Tucker, and W.E. Lambert, "The Effects of Speech Style and Other Attributes on Teachers' Attitudes toward Pupils," Language in Society, 1 (1972):131–42.

23 F. Williams, J.L. Whitehead, and L. Miller, "Relations between Language Attitude and Teacher Expectancy," American Educational Research Journal, 9 (1972): 263–77; F. Williams et al., Explorations of the Linguistic Attitudes of Teachers (Austin: University of Texas, 1972).

of values—whether parents wish to maintain their distinctive culture, encourage their children to learn the standard speech patterns of the larger society, or both. Despite our current American failure to teach standard English effectively in school, Fishman and Lueders-Salmon[24] offer a convincing description of how such language pluralism is achieved in another country—the area around Stuttgart, Germany. There, where standard German is taught successfully, teachers and students are often members of the same speech community, the teachers respect the children's home dialect, accept its spontaneous use in classroom discussions, and emphasize both in their own speech behavior and in their language instruction the functional value of being able to shift among varied verbal repertoires.

## LANGUAGE AS LEARNING ENVIRONMENT

Since language is the medium of instruction for most curriculum content, including itself, it is a large part of any learning environment. School language may differ in function from that used outside; for example, language in school is used more often to refer to nonperceptible people, events, and relationships. School language may differ from other language even when used for functions that are also common outside school, such as influencing the behavior of others.[25]

Two criteria for analyzing the role of language in learning environments will be applied here: situational appropriateness and functional effectiveness. (One could well add another: aesthetic taste, a criterion raised too rarely by curriculum planners. Despite its importance, however, the matter of aesthetics will be omitted here because I feel unqualified to give more than opinions.)

We know that all speakers of a language can speak in more than one way and unconsciously shift their style of speaking to adapt to different situations. They switch pronunciation, syntax, and word selection. Even in a seemingly homogeneous speech community, such code selection occurs. For example, Fisher[26] discovered switching between "-ing" and "-in'" in a semirural New England village. Children from three to ten years old varied their pronunciation, depending on the formality of the setting, the change in their mood as they became more relaxed within a single inter-

24 J.A. Fishman and Erika Lueders-Salmon, "What Has the Sociology of Language to Say to the Teacher? On Teaching the Standard Variety to Speakers of Dialectal or Sociolectal Varieties," Functions of Language in the Classroom, C.B. Cazden, V.P. John and D. Hymes (Eds.) (New York: Teacher's College Press, 1972), pp. 67–83.

25 Functions of Language in the Classroom; H. Mehan, "Language Using Abilities," Language Sciences (Bloomington: Indiana University Research Center for the Language Sciences, 1972).

26 J.L. Fisher, "Social Influence in the Choice of a Linguistic Variant," Word, 14 (1958):47–56. Reprinted in Language in Culture and Society, D. Hymes (Ed.) (New York: Harper & Row, 1964), pp. 483–88.

view, and even (for one boy) the connotations of specific verbs: "reading" and "criticizing" versus "swimmin'" and "punchin'." Children can also shift their styles of interacting from peer groups, where no one controls who talks when, to mixed groups where children are expected to respond only to adults or to be seen but not heard.[27]

Yet there is evidence that such shifts do not always occur where they would be appropriate and beneficial to the speaker. Three problems stand out: cultural conflict between the norms of interaction at home and those at school, failure to transfer apparent classroom learning to performance on tests, and probable differences between the learning of linguistic and sociolinguistic rules.

Consider first possible conflicts between home and school. "Those brought together in classrooms, even though having the language of the classroom in common, may not be wholly members of the same speech community. They may share a speech situation, but bring to it different modes of using its language and of interpreting the speech that goes on there."[28] The styles of language use children learn at home may inhibit their participation in the learning environment of the school or, to describe it in the reverse way, the learning environment of the school may repress rather than maximize the participatory skills of children or may favor some (even a majority) at the cost of others.

The work of two anthropologists is illustrative. Laura Lein, an anthropology student of Claudia and Keith Kernan's at Harvard, has been living in upstate New York with black families from Florida who migrate north every summer as farm laborers. In studying selected aspects of the language used by these migrant children, in the migrant camp and at school, she became interested in how the children respond to commands. Responses to parents are of two kinds. "Reasonable" commands, such as "You can't go outside now, it's dark," are immediately obeyed. But commands without obvious justification, like "Wipe that smile off your face," or "Come stand over here by me," are treated differently. The children understand the latter quite correctly as invitations to engage in a routinized verbal game in which the children resist, the adults repeat, with escalating insistence until the adults appeal to higher status members of the family or community to enforce the command. The game often lasts 15 to 20 minutes, and everyone understands it as such. One can easily imagine what Lein found in school. The children thought that the situation for this game was defined by the content of the commands and did not understand that it was defined also by the setting (home but not school). Thus, they resisted playfully when their teachers gave the meaningless commands

---

[27] Ward, *Them Children.*

[28] D. Hymes, "Introduction," *Functions of Language in the Classroom,* p. xxxvii.

which teachers are apt to give, were labeled "defiant" by the teachers, and never understood the source of the problem.[29]

Philips[30] studied the speech patterns of children on the Warm Springs Indian Reservation in Oregon, both in and out of the classroom. Philips refers to structural arrangements of interaction as "participant structures." In the public school classrooms on the Warm Springs Reservation, teachers use four participant structures:

> In the first type of participant structure the teacher interacts with all of the students. . . . And it is always the teacher who determines whether she talks to one or to all, receives responses individually or in chorus, and voluntarily or without choice. In a second type of participant structure, the teacher interacts with only some of the students in the class at once, as in reading groups. In such contexts, participation is usually mandatory rather than voluntary, individual rather than chorus, and each student is expected to participate or perform verbally.
>
> A third participant structure consists of all students working independently at their desks, but with the teacher explicitly available for student initiated [and private] verbal interaction.
>
> A fourth participant structure, and one which occurs infrequently in the upper primary grades, and rarely, if ever, in the lower grades, consists of the students being divided into small groups which they run themselves.[31]

Outside the home, in the Warm Springs communities, social (speech) events are open to all: each individual decides the degree, form, and time of participation for himself, and there is no leader who has the right to enforce the participation of one person in the presence of others. It is not surprising that, under these contrasting conditions, teachers label Indian children as "shy."

The relationship between eliciting context, sociolinguistic rules, and valid inferences is critical in all education—in everyday classroom events in which children's words are taken as indicators of what they have learned, and even more in the special situations we call "tests," whether administered by experimenters or teachers. After viewing videotapes of psychological experiments, Emanuel Schegloff suggested that such situations are "interactionally impoverished."[32]

Children are differently prepared—by age or experience in home and school—to cope with the special interaction requirements of tests. Shapiro,

---

[29] Lein, Language seminar, Harvard Graduate School of Education, 1971.

[30] S.U. Philips, "Acquisition of Rules for Appropriate Speech Usage," *Functions of Language in the Classroom*, pp. 370–94.

[31] Ibid.

[32] Emanuel Schegloff, personal communication.

concerned that first grade children who were clearly learning in the classroom were not responding well on tests, puts the problem this way:

> Since situations are sociologically and psychologically apprehended, their sociological and psychological parameters must be described and specified. . . . Specifically, for studies like the present one, the relevance and appropriateness of the classroom and the test situation as locations for studying the impact of schooling on children requires re-evaluation. Each can supply useful information, but in both instances the evidence is situation-bound.
>
> Determining the appropriate timing for the evaluation of impact demands that we know when [at what age] it is plausible and valid to expect children to be able to function readily and competently in a variety of situations, to switch from one form of communication to another, to be able to produce on demand. At what point and as a consequence of what kinds of experience does the restrictive influence of situational factors become less crucial?[33]

An important contrast implicit in this paper must be made explicit, even if it cannot be explained: that between linguistic and sociolinguistic interference in learning. According to Labov:

> The development of formal rules of discourse is a necessary ingredient in the analysis of subcultural differences. . . . Where subcultures differ in such rules, the consequences for personal interaction can be strong. Though native speakers of a given dialect show an extraordinary ability to interpret the grammatical rules of another dialect, they do not necessarily show the same ability in dealing with the broader aspects of communicative competence. The rules of discourse tend to differ not in obligatory sequencing rules, but in the interpretation of the social significance of actions—differences in the forms of politeness, ways of mitigating or expressing anger, or of displaying sincerity and trust. This is an area where ethnographic and linguistic description has an important role to play.[34]

This is also an area where we need to know more about the learning processes involved. The way we learn about appropriate and effective language use may be quite different from the way we learn language structure. Perhaps here an explicit sociolinguistic curriculum could be valuable.

Lest we despair of the possibilities, it may be a healthy antidote to academic obsessions to be reminded how quickly changes in people's lives can produce changes in their behavior, sociolinguistic behavior included.

---

[33] E. Shapiro, "A Pilot Study of a Bank Street Follow Through Program for First Grade Children in Three Geographic Regions," Final Report to Project Follow Through, U.S. Office of Education, 7 (New York: Bank Street College of Education, December 1971), pp. 8–10.

[34] W. Labov, "The Place of Linguistic Research in American Society," *Linguistics in the 1970s* (Washington, D.C.: Center for Applied Linguistics, 1970), pp. 64–65.

Fanon, a black French psychiatrist assigned to an Algerian hospital, analyzes the "new attitudes adopted by the Algerian people in the course of the fight for liberation with respect to a precise technical instrument: the radio."[35] According to Fanon, before 1945, when the only station available was Radio-Alger, the voice of France in Algeria, 95 percent of all receivers were in the hands of European settlers, and hundreds of Algerian families who could easily afford radios did not have them. Fanon describes one reason that was given for this passive resistance to radios, one which has an authentic sociolinguistic ring:

> Pressed with questions as to the reasons for this reluctance, Algerians rather frequently give the following answer: "Traditions of respectability are so important for us and are so hierarchical, that it is practically impossible for us to listen to radio programmes in the family. The sex allusions, or even the clownish situations meant to make people laugh, which are broadcast over the radio cause an unendurable strain in a family listening to these programmes.
>
> The ever possible eventuality of laughing in the presence of the head of the family or the elder brother, of listening in common to amorous words or terms of levity, obviously acts as a deterrent to the distribution of radios in Algerian native society. . . .
>
> Here, then, at acertain explicit level is the apprehension of a fact: receiving sets are not readily adopted by Algerian society. By and large, it refuses this technique which threatens its stability and the traditional types of sociability.[36]

Fanon then goes on to show "how artificial such a sociological approach is, what a mass of error it contains." At the end of 1956, a new station went on the air: Voice of Free Algeria. In less than twenty days the entire stock of radio sets in Algeria was bought up and battery-operated receivers were in great demand in the rural regions of the country.

> Traditional resistances broke down and one could see in a dewar groups of families in which fathers, mothers, daughters, elbow to elbow, would scrutinize the radio dial waiting for the Voice of Algeria. Suddenly indifferent to the sterile, archaic modesty and antique social arrangements devoid of brotherhood, the Algerian family discovered itself to be immune to the off-colour jokes and the obscene references that the announcer occasionally let drop.
>
> Almost magically—but we have seen the rapid and dialectical progression of the new national requirements—the technical instrument of the radio receiver lost its identity as an enemy object [and] Algerian society made an autonomous decision to embrace the new technique and thus

---

[35] F. Fanon, *A Dying Colonialism* (Middlesex, England: Penguin Books, 1970), p. 53.

[36] Ibid., p. 54.

tune itself in on the new signalling systems brought into being by the Revolution.[37]

It is probably harder to change the way people act than the way they respond, the way they speak than the way they listen. Even when feelings of self-identity change, well-practiced habits may make new forms of behavior difficult to maintain. But the two factors implicit in Fanon's report of a change in listening habits—a dramatic shift in the symbolic value of a stimulus that comes from a change in the underlying social reality, and strong support for change from within the speaker's reference community—probably apply to changes in ways of speaking too.

We cannot, of course, evaluate learning environments solely on the basis of whether the home and the school have the same expectations for children.

Take Ward's ethnographic study of language learning in Rosepoint, Louisiana as a case in point. She compares the language learning of young children—such as Mark—with the children studied by Roger Brown. A few quotes convey the quality of the language environment in Rosepoint:

> Speaking is often equated with the quality "bad." A twelve-month baby sat absolutely still on the couch for an hour. His mother commented that her baby was "good": he could not yet talk. When babies learn to talk they are "bad children."
>
> Mark [28 months old] has never been rewarded for verbal advances; no one expects him to say more than the bare minimum. . . . In fact, as the conversations indicate, the children hold their parent's attention longer *if they say nothing.* [emphasis in the original]
>
> A child's requests for information are not treated as a demand for knowledge (which adults are expected to supply) or as an attempt to open the lines of communication. . . . A child actively seeking information will be treated as a noisy child, not as an inquiring, curious one.[38]

We have all seen or read of classrooms where the same kind of sociolinguistic rules obtain, in which quiet passivity is valued over active inquiry.

In considering these learning environments, we need to know not only whether the home and school function consistently—as they may for Ward's children but do not for Lein's playful migrant children or for Philips' shy Indian children—but also whether that functioning is conducive to learning. Speaking for myself—and in this value-laden area I can do no more—I would want to remove home-school discontinuities for Philips' children by making the interactional setting of the school more like that of the home, whereas I would be reluctant to accept the same solution for Ward's children. Admittedly such decisions imply definite

---

[37] Ibid., p. 67.
[38] Ward, *Them Children,* pp. 29, 46–47, 52.

notions about what experiences promote maximum mental functioning. In making decisions about whether or how to "intervene," an outsider must remember that any system functions as a whole, in terms both of the relationship among its parts and of its relationship to some larger social unit. Robert L. Munroe of the Child Development Research Unit in Nairobi, Kenya, reported an open discussion following the presentation of research data on traditional child rearing practices. When Munroe suggested that some of these practices might have the effect of depressing the development of what we call "intelligence" in children, a Ghanian colleague replied that even if that were true, he would be unwilling to attempt to change to more "western" styles at the price of a decrease in courtesy and obedience—qualities more important in tribal life than the "intelligence" which westerners value so highly.[39] The Ghanian did not want to disrupt the internal cohesiveness of his culture.

Emanuel Jackson, Director of the Martin Luther King Family Center in Chicago's West Side, focused on the relationship of black family life to the larger world:

> My concern would be, if a kid's not talking, to understand why and why not before one goes in and undermines defenses that are very necessary. Some little kids are hostile, they're suspicious, they're alert, and it's diagnosed as pathology. In our community, if you're not suspicious and alert, you're not going to live. . . .
>
> We're trying to understand what it is about language and Black people that may make Black people seem more non-verbal. Maybe Black people need to be more non-verbal. When my Mother tells me "Now don't you tell the teacher this" and "Don't you tell the teacher that," we get a message about talking. I'm saying that the world makes my Mother have to tell me to shut up or she'll be done in.[40]

Advisors and supervisors working with teachers are also aware of how the teacher's behavior—e.g., how much child activity and talk she allows in her classroom—is affected by the system of which she is a part. Perhaps all that we as outsiders can do is what Munroe did—point out the possible implications as we understand them, suggest alternatives, and do all we can to help work out the ensuing problems for those who do wish to change.

---

[39] Munroe, personal communication, 1971.

[40] Emanuel Jackson, Colloquium at the Harvard Graduate School of Education, 1971.

# part SIX

# The Teacher

Teaching is generally defined as a profession. However, full recognition as a professional is frequently denied to the individual teacher. The lack of clear definition of the status and role of the teacher is a powerful factor in shaping the sociology of the school. Many elements contribute to lack of clarity in the status of teachers as well as education itself in the social scheme of modern society. Some of the ambiguity in the occupational status of teachers stems from the size and heterogeneity of the occupation. In 1972 over 2,300,000 public and private teachers taught almost 46 million school children. Only engineers of all kinds comprise as large a group as teachers.

The heterogeneity of the system can be judged by the great variety of ethnic communities, status communities, villages, towns, and cities that comprise the thousands of counties and the 50 states. Vast differences are exhibited in the variations in expenditures per pupil as well as teachers salaries. In 1973–74 New York spent $1,809 per pupil while Alabama spent $716.[1] Teachers' salaries ranged from an average of $16,053 in Alaska to $7,854 in Mississippi. In addition to the great range in financial resources of schools and the size of the monetary rewards for teaching, security of tenure may vary from one school to another.

Professional status, usually, not only includes reasonable security of tenure, but also insures substantial individual autonomy, implies commitment, and provides substantial social prestige. Security of tenure is still far from being the norm for many teachers. Most schools have many ways of getting rid of an unwanted teacher. In the larger school systems formal rules of procedure are usually required for terminating a teacher, but

---

[1] *New York Times,* July 2, 1974.

almost any kind of behavior can be used as a reason for denying re-appointment to a teacher if important persons in the school or the community want a particular teacher removed, irrespective of how long the accused has been employed in the system. In large metropol-itan school systems in which strong teachers' unions are formally recog-nized as bargaining agents and effective contracts are in force, tenure is quite secure. But these circumstances are the exception rather than the rule.

Personal autonomy is another element of professionalism that has a checkered history in the teaching profession. Although a considerable degree of autonomy is possible within the confines of the classroom, many of the other areas of decision-making relative to teaching are frequently challenged or usurped by administrators, school board members, parents or community leaders. For example, the development and choice of the various elements that make up curriculum, as well as the choice and as-signment of reading material is frequently done without the involvement of the classroom teacher. Even when the choice of reading is left to the teacher, the assignment of a controversial book can lead to severe strain and even loss of employment. Outside of the classroom a teacher's auton-omy varies greatly, frequently by the size of community. In the city the teacher usually has considerable autonomy and can live a life that is much less apt to be under the constant scrutiny of the community than is the case in small towns and rural areas. In smaller communities where the teacher is readily known and recognized the local populace frequently expects him or her to contribute to the community, outside of school ac-tivities. Coaches may be expected to play baseball for the town team, while female teachers are "favored" with explicit invitations to teach Sun-day or Vacation School for one of the local churches. Although these expectations have decreased in recent years, they serve as an example of the kinds of roles teachers may be expected to play in the local commu-nity. In general, a teacher's private life is expected to exemplify the preva-lent ideals of middle class morality. In some instances the teacher is ex-pected to serve as a better model than the parents themselves.

Like some members of the more prestigious professions, an unknown proportion of teachers honestly view their work as a "calling" in the full Weberian sense. That is, their commitment is supported by a set of strong moral values and norms that provide them with the belief that they are doing work of a very worthwhile kind and that their occupation is much more than simply a job from which they earn a living. At the other end of the varied range of teacher perspectives are those who view teaching as a more or less acceptable white collar job that gives them some respectabil-ity with a medium level income. Unfortunately, the numbers that fall in or near this end of the continuum is quite large. Empirically the substan-tial size of this category is suggested by the fact that the average stay in the teaching profession is approximately five years.[2] Of course, this is partly accounted for by the entry of large numbers of young women into the profession. Nevertheless, this fact also tends to illustrate the temporariness and low level of continuity created by the constant turnover of occupational membership.

An important element in weakening the professional status of teachers is the uncertainty and variability of the teacher's esteem and prestige. In most instances teachers are accorded high prestige by their charges. This is especially true of the young children in elementary schools. This is also generally true for junior high and high school students in working class and lower middle class schools. In upper middle and upper class schools high school students, particularly, may be contemptuous of their teachers; they are quite aware that their own family socioeconomic level is much higher than that of the vast majority of their teachers.

The status level of teachers in American schools has undergone considerable change in the last few decades. Prior to the 1920s teachers were recruited largely from urban middle class families and from the lower to upper middle class families in small towns and rural areas.[3] Teaching was viewed as a respectable occupation for women, although this generally applied only to those who were unmarried, and those men who, in turn, were frequently categorized by the old adage that "those that can, do; those that can't, teach." In recent years the social origins of teachers has shifted more and more from the broad middle classes to the lower working classes. This is especially true in the large urban school systems. This shift in social origins has meant that entrance into the teaching profession signaled substantial social mobility for members of blue collar families. Achievement of middle class socioeconomic status has posed a problem for those who hold newer perspectives regarding the necessity of having teachers who can easily identify and even evidence behavior that is common to children who come from lower class and poverty-ridden families. This problem results from the social psychological consequences of the upward mobility achieved by the teacher with lower class origins. It is seen in the over-identification with the means which led to mobility, that of formal education. Furthermore, the high value placed on education by the mobile person is frequently coupled with a strong adherence to middle class life styles. This may manifest itself in a reluctance to behave in ways acquired in childhood and characterized as lower class, even to the point of not wanting to be put into a position of having to admit to one's true social origins.

---

[2] Theodore R. Sizer, "The Schools in the City" in James Q. Wilson (Ed.), *The Mertopolitan Enigma* (Cambridge, Mass.: Harvard University Press, 1968), p. 323.

[3] Wilbur B. Brookover, *A Sociology of Education* (New York: American Book Co., 1955), p. 276.

Not only is the teacher, who is an example of success gained through education, not willing to utilize identifiable lower class styles of speech and behavior in gaining rapport with lower class students, but he or she may overemphasize the importance of education and begin to assume that advanced education is the correct behavior pattern to be followed by all "worthwhile" young people of lower class background, irrespective of interest or intellectual ability.

Sociologists have found important relationships between social origins and the role behavior of teachers. Though important in understanding the performance of teachers, socioeconomic background by itself explains very little; it must be viewed in conjunction with relevant personality characteristics, as well as the organizational structure of school and community.

It is a truism that education has been a primary occupation of women. About 66 percent of all teachers are women; this is especially true in the nation's elementary schools. In contrast to past concerns about the predominance of women teachers, Brophy and Good indicate that the assumed negative social consequences of "feminization" of the school is open to debate.[4] They point out that the general expectations associated with the academically oriented role of student fits more closely with the general female role than with the male role. Brophy and Good conclude that hiring more male teachers, without changing the expectations of the student role, as well as both of the general roles of males and females, will have little effect in changing the differential behavior and performance of the sexes in American schools. Although the dominance of female teachers may not greatly affect the variation in the ways boys and girls respond to school, it has had the effect of skewing the distribution of male and female teachers in the organization of schools. Men who have gone into teaching are almost expected to teach only long enough to manage their entry into the ranks of administration. While women may have done most of the teaching, men have moved into the positions of power over women teachers. To what degree the new programs (e.g., Affirmative Action) of insuring equity in hiring, firing, and promotion will change the situation remains to be seen.

The same currents of social change that have led toward equity for women and minorities have stirred considerable controversy in improving the schools, particularly those that serve the urban poor. It has been argued that the schools do not adequately prepare students for life in a pluralistic society. It is interesting to note that a few years ago the social commentators were inveighing against the great conformity and sameness in American culture. The current concerns center on the school's role in deal-

---

[4] Jere E. Brophy and Thomas L. Good, "Feminization of American Elementary Schools," *Phi Delta Kappan* 54 (April 1973):564–66.

ing with the present and potential ("alternative") life styles reflected in the social backgrounds of school children in large systems of mass education. A question of values emerges. Does the teacher readily accept the values of the child's parents as expressed and exemplified in school behavior?[5] Or does the teacher impose his or her own conception of acceptable values? What about values that lead to rebellion and confrontation with norms and values viewed as oppressive to groups at the lower socioeconomic levels? To what extent do the new approaches expressed by the concepts of "individualized instruction" and the "open classroom" mean that the public school is moving to the full recognition of pluralism, alternative life styles, and the social change that might occur were these precepts followed in actual practice.

The concern over the quality of inner city schools has generated a movement toward making teachers more specifically "accountable" in reference to the skills and knowledge that they presume to impart. This has indirectly led to new concerns over the professional status of the teaching profession. Any kind of publicly understood measures of the success or failure of a teacher would make teachers highly vulnerable to the shifting concerns and values of persons outside of the profession. Any system that allowed the laymen to make basic decisions as to specific outcomes of educational experiences would be a severe blow to the present level of long fought for professionalism. The professional autonomy and educational judgments of trained and experienced teachers could be easily manipulated by the shifting of a few points on the various achievement measures used to judge teacher effectiveness. It is ironic that the potential dangers to the profession along these lines are the result of heavy investments in research and professional expertise in the area of testing and measurement, a powerful sector of the broad educational profession.

During the past decade or so the unionization of large numbers of teachers has become a reality and most major urban school systems have unions of varying strength, with a substantial number serving as the legal bargaining agents for all teachers. One of the major concerns of the teacher's unions is the maintenance and enhancement of the professional status of teachers. They are in the forefront of the discussions and plans regarding the push for teacher accountability. Although there is a wide range of opinion on professionalism, there are few who contest the importance of union efforts toward gaining higher salaries, more equitable tenure rules, and teacher involvement in matters of curriculum and instruction. There seems little evidence to indicate that teachers will back away from the long term establishment of some kind of organized efforts to maintain the meager professional status they have thus far attained.

The necessity for protecting past gains is presently augmented by the

---

[5] Sizer, "Schools in the City," p. 321–22.

decline in the need for teachers. The passing of the results of the baby boom of the 1950s has meant a decline in enrollments throughout the nation's educational systems. The current recruiting of prospective students by teacher training institutions has been sharply curtailed and in some areas there are large numbers of education graduates who cannot find teaching positions. With the fertility rate of the current crop of potential mothers at a very low level—zero growth for 1973—the need for teachers will continue to decline in the near future. This demographic fact will have numerous social consequences. The geographic mobility of ambitious teachers, including those who must move with mobile spouses, will find it more difficult to affect a satisfactory change. Teachers who lack adequate academic or other credentials will be more apt to be left out and even pushed out in favor of more qualified applicants. Administrators who hold power over hiring and firing will gain greater influence and power as the number of teaching positions declines in relation to the number of applicants available.

The restriction on mobility from one school to another resulting from the oversupply of teachers may take away one of the few means by which teachers can seek to improve their position by getting a new and more satisfying position every so often. The status differences between teachers in their work milieu are very slight. The lack of differentiation of both formal and informal roles within the ranks of teachers are so slight that there is little chance of movement in terms of financial rewards, prestige, authority or responsibility. (This is more thoroughly discussed in the article in this section authored by the editor.) Few professional level occupations which are carried on in bureaucratized organizations offer such slight opportunities for upward mobility or promotion. In general, seniority and related salary differences are frequently the only differences between teachers, and even in this area the range between beginner and veteran is quite small. There are few ways in which the talented, dedicated, and effective teacher can be accorded recognition for merit. As stated, moving to a new and hopefully "better" school may be the only substitute for social mobility within the profession.

# 18

# The Teacher's Role—
# A Sociological Analysis*

## BRYAN R. WILSON

### HISTORICAL ANTECEDENTS

In the true sense of the word, teachers exist as a specialist profession only in advanced societies. In static societies values, techniques, skills and what are taken to be "facts" are transmitted from father to son. If specialist activities are developed at all, their skills and the mystique that accompanies them is learned from practitioners not from teachers, and the learners are apprentices rather than pupils. Teachers exist as specialists in their own right only where the diffusion of knowledge is an accepted social goal—hence only in dynamic societies.

Certainly in traditional societies there is often a distinctive intellectual élite, but they are not so much teachers as guardians of knowledge, and knowledge is esoteric, sacred, aristocratic. It is frequently the knowledge of the gods, revealed to inspired seers; its guardians are priests or literati. In such a society knowledge advances—if it advances at all—by the elaboration of its own internal coherence. It is challenged only when a charismatic figure emerges who propounds new knowledge and new moral precepts. Knowledge in such a society tends to be recondite, literal, sacred —a knowledge of holy texts, of the ancient. The literati do not transmit new ideas, but rather keep pure old dogmas: they are not teachers and disseminators, but custodians of the sacred. Their intellectual institutions are closed—segregated seminaries set in remote places, preserving a shrine-like quality of apartness. They function according to a holier dis-

* From: *The British Journal of Sociology* (#1), 13 (March 1962):15–32.

pensation than that which prevails in the wider society. They are not centers from which knowledge is disseminated, but places where it is preserved and stored to be only slowly and carefully transmitted, and then only to the initiated. The approved recipient is marked by the tonsure and the sacred vestment, not by the examination certificate; his knowledge is not to be acquired through routinized courses. The literati discipline new knowledge, which means that they suppress it if it stems from outside sources, since knowledge is exclusive, treasured because of the sacred source from which it stems, not for its practical utility.

Such a system is appropriate to a traditional and static society where the natural and social orders are accepted rather than understood, and where because these orders of things are sacred, nothing is challenged or challengeable.

Teachers, as distinct from literati, really emerge as specialists only in societies where knowledge is secularized. This type of knowledge develops at certain places—particularly at points where there is interchange of produce and ideas. Cultural diffusion is the process whereby new ideas are evolved, and the agency by which secularization begins.[1] When knowledge is to be transmitted and used it ceases to be the exclusive monopoly of the intelligentsia. Much of such knowledge is initially practical and consequently it tends to be fostered and transmitted in classes different from, and sometimes hostile toward, the literati. This type of knowledge is diffused, and its bearers are characterized by their inquisitiveness rather than by their passive receptivity of ideas from established authorities. Whereas the wisdom of the literati is arcane, vast, and unassailable, embracing all that is to be known, the new knowledge is practical, piecemeal, and there is an admission of what men do not know. Knowledge ceases to be a secret hoard which a few men store up and invest with sacred quality —it becomes a circulating specie, the influence of which grows as it is circulated. There is an awareness of the enormity of human ignorance as well as of the profundity of human knowledge. Knowledge becomes commonplace, available to increasing numbers until the right of men to knowledge is gradually accepted as self-evident. Its character also changes and it becomes more changeable—it is imported, exported, borrowed, transmitted, and adapted.

The social changes which lie behind this change in knowledge do not concern us here: what matters is the growth of new attitudes toward knowledge and its role in society. The new attitudes are attitudes of inquiry, of willingness to interchange ideas, the acceptance of critical stan-

---

[1] See on this subject the penetrating article by Robert Redfield and Milton Singer, "The Cultural Rôle of Cities," *Economic Development and Cultural Change*, 3 (October 1954):54–73.

dards and desirability of challenging discussion. Doubt replaces faith as
the test of knowledge, and the learner's task is made more difficult because, while he must learn facts and values, he also has to learn to acquire
an open and challenging mind and a critical faculty rather than to learn
blind trust, simple faith, and good memory. The educational task is thus
transformed, and it is made in many ways more delicate because while
data has to be transmitted so has the liveliness of mind that challenges
every interpretation of data. Where as the literati could invoke authority
and exert authority, and could ultimately discipline to the point of death
those who failed to accept their wisdom, the teacher must cultivate some
spirit of heresy within certain bounds in those to whom some more-or-less
established information must nonetheless be transmitted. Their own authority must always be tempered and restricted if the right critical spirit
is to be drawn forth in the pupils. And yet there is still something in the
teacher's role which demands that certain social values be preserved and
inculcated. In seeking to cultivate attitudes of mind the teacher is necessarily involved in propounding certain values, setting standards for personal behavior and decorum, in eliciting respect and establishing ideals
of personal discipline as behavior patterns approved of in society. At the
lowest level these standards are necessary as the determinants of the climate within which teaching can occur.

In Britain this development of the teacher's role has been radically
affected by a set of unique historical circumstances. Before the extension
of secondary education in the early years of the present century, the upper
classes had already developed a system of education for their children.
These schools sought especially to inculcate the particular virtues prized
among the aristocracy and the gentry. Their emphasis was less with learning and more with leadership. This was an entirely appropriate schooling
for those destined to undertake leadership roles in a society where military, gentlemanly, and aristocratic behavior was explicitly demanded in
the ruling groups. The formation of a certain type of character, rather
than the cultivation of rarified intellect was the educational aim. The
schools reflected the values of the social strata from whom their clientele
was predominantly drawn. The absence of social revolution in England
allowed this model to persist unchallenged as the entrenched ideal of education, in both the public schools and the universities. When secondary
education was extended for a wider population, it was this model that
influenced the character of the new and revived grammar schools. Some
of those who were concerned with these schools—national and local politicians as well as headmasters—had themselves received the gentlemanly
education of public school and ancient university: for them it was self-
evident that the educational aim was exactly what their own schools had
sought to do—these were the best models. Social emulation is a powerful

force, and particularly so in a society where there is a strong traditionalist ethic, a well-entrenched upper class, and a growing middle class seeking social acceptance for their expanding pretensions.

Thus it was that the shibboleths of education for gentlemen were transferred to the sons of traders, shopkeepers, and artisans—the clientele of the expanded system of secondary education. Character-building on the aristocratic model became a predominant motive of the schools, and ideals of social honor, team-spirit and inner discipline were very much their concern, fostered as they were by team games, house loyalty and house rivalry, and regulated competition. The ideal diverges conspicuously from that of the continent, where social revolution had eliminated the aristocratic ideal, and where intellect had become the well-entrenched major concern of the schools;[2] and from that of the American educational system where the necessity of forging an ethnically diversified clientele into one nation imposed on the educational system a concern for "adjustment" that is evident to this day.

As society grows more complex and comes to rely on more elaborated technical means of production it is necessary for certain basic skills—numeracy and literacy—to be diffused throughout the society, and some more specialist skills to be cultivated in smaller sections of the society. The teacher's role grows more significant as this process occurs, and teaching becomes a process to which all must be exposed as a social necessity, rather than a process extended by the whim of charity to only a proportion. The teacher learns increasingly in order to teach, but he becomes more than a mere transmitter of knowledge, and must increasingly cultivate a spirit of inquiry: the educational trend has been from "telling them" to "encouraging them to find out." Whereas the literati transmitted exact knowledge and relied on the closed character of the institution to socialize the acolyte into the scholar, the teacher helps the child to discover knowledge. Because he has lost the support of the closed institution with its rigorous routines, a greater onus is thrown upon the teacher to stimulate the child to respond to, and accept, certain social values. As the educational process extends, society becomes increasingly more aware of the need for children to acquire certain value-orientations from their school experience. A salient shift is that whereas the literati rely on the social control established in the seminary, the teacher, without such institutional support, must do more to socialize the child—to build in these controls as part of the child's developing personality structure. A further problem arising in the creation of this value-context is the fact that the kind of knowledge society increasingly demands tends to be in itself in-

---

[2] See *Special Reports on Educational Subjects*, 8 (1902); cd. 835, Paper 13 (pp. 481 ff.) on Hungarian Education by Catherine Dodd, and the illuminating appendix to this report by Dr. Emil Reich, pp. 531–32.

trinsically further removed from concern with values. Whereas the knowledge of the literati was suffused with social values—a knowledge of religious texts and moral precepts—modern knowledge is increasingly of a more objective and scientific character. Thus the values the teacher must transmit become in some sense extrinsic to the knowledge he is assisting young people to acquire. As long as education rested in an essentially sacred matrix this divorce could not occur: the secularization of knowledge implies the loss, or at least the reduction of specific intrinsic value-commitment. Even those subjects that stem more directly from the concerns of the literati—the literary and humanistic subjects—become more scientifically handled, and subject to more precise critical appraisal. And yet, paradoxically, as this acceptance of the relativity of knowledge grows, as doubt is enhanced, so the awareness grows that society needs for its continuance, and individuals need for their own careers, a certain value-commitment. Increasingly schools and teachers are expected to inculcate social values in young people and to socialize them. Men become aware that scientific knowledge outstrips moral, spiritual, and political wisdom and there are periodic demands for more concentration on these aspects of education. And to this may be added the significance of the concern for character that modern education has inherited from upper-class models. It becomes the case that the school is expected to provide for all children what the family used to provide for the more favored strata. The content of aristocratic education was largely the humanities, which lend themselves much more readily to the transmission of values than do the sciences: character could be formed in the appreciation of the heroes of literature and history. One consequence of acceptance of these models was the in-building of disdain for the practical and useful arts. The humanities were preserved in the top strata of society—the sciences necessarily had their fullest development in the new classes that challenged the older order. Here lies the historical and sociological root of the "two cultures." Aristocratic education could afford, from its position of superiority, and in training the "natural" leaders of society, to disdain the sciences and technology: it did not need the work of Daniel Defoe or Samuel Smiles —which was written for different social groups. But in the long run these disciplines were to be of more account to industrial society than the training for leadership and character of the older system. It was precisely the entrenchment of these newer educational ideals that produced the phenomenal technical developments in Germany, and subsequently in Russia and America. In England the neglect of technical education for so long was the consequence of accepting the public school model. The other consequence has been the growth of technology—when it did occur—without humanistic commitment. A type of reciprocal contempt is evident whereby the technologies today disdain the arts. This is readily evident in the universities and probably builds back to the schools. The vast majority of the most intelligent children are channeled into the sciences, which, in a highly specialized educational system, means that they lose almost all contact with the humanities. The sciences and technologies are moving into the position of dominance in the educational field as an increasing proportion of money is available for their extension. It is in part a consequence of this process that we find the recurrent demand for teachers to transmit social values to young people—a more imperative demand now that the specific content of education has so largely passed from the arts to the sciences.

## SOCIAL SELECTION AND SOCIALIZATION

In a complex industrial society with a wide diversity of social roles, where basic education is obligatory for everyone, social selection—the allocation of individuals to particular occupations within society—occurs within the educational system rather than, as in the case of traditional societies, before education is embarked upon. This means that the teacher becomes also a social selector, preparing people in the capacities in terms of which selection will occur. Increasingly selection is made in objective terms of intellect and knowledge, rather than in terms of character and life-style. It is this occupational mobility—imperative in advanced society —that makes the teacher's role indispensable. In traditional societies, in which occupational succession prevails, fathers teach sons and mothers teach daughters: but in our society, son's occupation will not be father's, and we do not even consider that home-making and motherhood are the primary tasks for which girls should be trained. Thus, if the child is to be prepared for some social role other than that of its father or mother (and indeed, in our sort of society, even if for that same type of role), it is the teacher who is largely responsible for the preparation. Clearly the child brings with it, to the teaching situation, certain equipment derived from home, and this equipment will positively or negatively influence its further development. But the specific terms in which selection must occur, and the process of selection itself, are the concerns of the teacher's role.

We have already seen that, perhaps, because of this dominant intellectual stress, the teacher has taken over from the parent some of the activities of socializing the child. The teacher becomes a social weaning agent— helping the child to acquire new attitudes of mind, new values, new knowledge, and new motivations, which are not forthcoming in the home context for most children. Social selection—the knowledge of opportunities, which may be the first necessity for inducing adequate motivation, and the knowledge of how to take advantage of opportunities—has itself become a specialist task, and it is the task of the teacher and not of the parent. The teacher, then, has to help the child towards social mobility. He has to transmit personal standards, orientations, ideals of attainment, which diverge from those learned in the home. If he is to help the child to "get on," he must also help the child to "move on"—which means to move away from the values and assumptions of parents. The teacher must extend the horizons of the child, diversify its knowledge of opportunity, raise its threshold of aspiration, and induce it to exercise its talents so that it may find a place in the social structure different from—and not contingent upon—the roles of its parents.[3]

Since our society demands continual reallocation of intellectual resources while people are young enough to be trained, it is essential that bright young people be adequately motivated—and it is in this task of inducing motivation that the teacher's role becomes crucial. Thus a considerable part of the socializing task—performed by parents in earlier times—has now passed to the teacher. Teachers already supervise meals; supervise play; give religious instruction; give training in hygiene; inculcate ideals of fair play; give instruction about sex ethics, public safety, moral obligation: they transmit values appropriate to the stratum in society to which the brighter child will move. Educating for these ends is not done by rote learning: the process demands an empathic commitment on the part of the teacher—a basic sympathy with children that is not dissimilar to that of parents. Increasingly the child depends on the teacher —particularly at that stage at which it needs new models for behavior, some new type of ego-ideal hero. Parents are inadequate to its vision and the teacher is frequently held up to parents as a model of higher standards. The mirror of the teacher can supply a new self-image and self-interpretation for the child. Inevitably this process is not accomplished without strains: two different people with rather different stakes in the socialization of the child may readily experience rivalries. Certainly at a rather earlier period—in the 1930s—there appear to have been many tensions between teachers with lower-middle or middle-class ideals and the working-class parents of their pupils. Today, increased acceptance of social mobility has done much to reconcile parents to the teacher's influence on the child.[4] The relation of parents and teachers is necessarily muted, but the condition of symbiosis that prevails in contemporary England is not the only way in which this relationship has been regulated. As parents recognize the growing importance of the teacher's role for the child, so they may increasingly demand to control teachers and their activities. Thus, in the United States, where the ideal of social mobility is more or less universally accepted, there has developed a strong movement by par-

---

[3] The importance of the differential threshold of aspiration is brought out in J.E. Floud, A.H. Halsey and F.M. Martin, *Social Class and Educational Opportunity* (Heinemann, London, 1956).

[4] On the extent to which social mobility is accepted as an ideal see the interesting discussion in S.M. Lipset and R. Bendix, *Social Mobility in Industrial Society* (Heinemann, 1959), pp. 76 ff.

ents towards control of the teachers through the Parent Teachers Association. Alternatively in the U.S.S.R., where teachers are seen as the agents of the state and as the loyal inculcators of the state's official ideology teachers are accorded a higher degree of autonomy, and greater freedom from parental interference: the teachers are seen as vital socializing agents, and the school is held as a counter influence to the family.

If the teacher is to act as a socializing agent, and to remedy the omissions of the home, he must be in a position to foster a sustained relationship with the child. He must occupy a place in the child's scheme of things, which makes the transmission of values, standards, and attitudes of mind one that can occur easily and naturally. Such relationships cannot be prescribed by any blue-print of institutional organization: they cannot be written into a contract. They must occur in a favorable climate where the teacher can cultivate children in this way. This particular facet of the teacher's role is frequently neglected, although its consequences—the sensitive imagination, the appreciation of scholarly values, and the well-rounded, sensible good citizen—are demanded perhaps more vociferously than ever before. While this is the case, it is also true that in an age of specialization the teacher's role, like other social roles, has become more routinized, more impersonalized, more exposed to the time-calculation and the achievement orientation of our society. The wider social climate would appear to have increased the difficulty of drawing forth any high personal commitment of the kind which appears indispensable to the teaching role.

## DIFFUSENESS AND DIVERSITY

Roles that involve the provision of personal services are difficult to define briefly: the very debate about what teaching is or should be illustrates this difficulty. When we say that a role is specific we mean that

(1) there are set tasks that can be defined in terms of the exact manipulations involved; a set time these operations take; there is a precise content change in the material handled, which results from the role performance;

(2) the role-player has a specialized and easily defined expertise;

(3) there is a formal limitation to the competences the role-player exercises in his role (any other competences and capabilities and character-values being incidental and gratuitous);

(4) the role-player's commitment is delimited.

But the business of socializing children—of motivating, inspiring, and encouraging them, of transmitting values to them, awakening in them a respect for facts and a sense of critical appreciation—all of this is unspecific. It implies "what a man is" as much as "what a man does." The role obligation is diffuse, difficult to delimit, and the activities of the role are highly diverse.

If we compare other professional roles—those of the doctor and the lawyer, for example—we find that their roles are easier to define. But they, too, must be certain sorts of people. Their relationship with their client must also be one of confidence, since their services cannot be examined beforehand. The professional man is trusted to give a quality of service that cannot be quantified and therefore cannot be specifically stated or contracted for. He gives his personality.[5] His commitment is moral. This moral commitment to the professional role is less evident in other types of work. Because the tasks and the means of performing them cannot be precisely specified, there is discretion and autonomy for the role-player. Consequently there have to be some safeguards for the clientele. This safeguard is found in the professional ethic, which is voluntarily accepted and internalized by the members of the profession. The ethic defines what type of man the professional is—and the ethic is regulated by and within the profession, with expulsion for breaches.[6]

In the case of the doctor and the lawyer there is, however, a definable expertise: the objective body of medical knowledge, or the objective body of law (though both are, inevitably, subject to controversy at the margins). There is for the teacher what appears initially as a parallel—the objective body of mathematical, historical, musical, or some other knowledge. But the symmetry of the analogy is not exact. The doctor and the lawyer are applying the rules of their expertise: they are not attempting to inculcate it: they are not socializing by building up attitudes of mind. Doctors and lawyers make *patients* out of persons, and *cases* out of clients. Whereas for the teacher the child must, of necessity, remain a whole person. For the doctor and lawyer there is an end of their concern with the "cure effected," "the operation performed," the "case won." The "examination passed" is again not a symmetrical analogy. When the pupil does not get through, the *good* teacher's concern does not end—nor does that of the educational system end. Failure cannot be counted in terms of examinations alone otherwise the system would cease to be interested in 75 percent of children at the age of 11. Educating is implicitly recognized throughout all educational institutions as something immensely bigger than examination-passing.

To refer to the *good* teacher begs questions. But the fact that one can refer to a *good* teacher when one does not qualify "doctor" or "lawyer" in

---

[5] For a discussion of the professions and the nature of the fiduciary relationship see T.H. Marshall, "The Recent History of Professionalization in Relation to Social Structure and Social Policy," *Canadian Journal of Economics and Political Science*, 5 (13; August 1939): 325–40.

[6] See Everett C. Hughes, "The Sociological Study of Work," *American Journal of Sociology*, 57 (5; 1952):423–27.

this way implies the moral commitment of the teacher's role—a moral commitment that passes beyond the formulation of a professional ethic. In itself, this usage illustrates the difficulty of defining the teacher's role —and the further difficulty of doing so without making value-judgments. This is so because we are ultimately concerned with the quality of the values the teacher transmits. There are—of necessity—value-judgments implicit in the doctor's role and the lawyer's role, but they are much less exposed value-judgments, and they are allowed to go more or less unchallenged. Who doubts that sick people *ought* to be made better, and that the accused should have proper defense and the guilty be detected?

The teacher's role is more diffuse than the doctor's or lawyer's because their concern is limited to areas of deviation or abnormality within the system—sickness, injury, crime, or dispute. These items are not part of our usual experience—they are contrary to our widely accepted normative expectations in society. They are items we accept should be put right— items needing adjustment, regulation, or restoration. Because they are departures from the accepted norms there is much less dispute about what should be done, and doctors and lawyers have built up a professional expertise that gives them the exclusive knowledge of just how it shall be done. But since the teacher is a socializer, concerned with the whole child and its normal self as a social entity, his involvement is necessarily more enduring, slower, steadier. He is not concerned with the pathological aspects of the person. His role appears, in consequence, to be less urgent, less dramatic, even though in fact it is no less vital. Because it is less urgent and less dramatic it receives less social respect, and carries less salary. We confer gratitude and rewards on those who put things right when they go wrong rather than on those who quietly keep things right. The element of the supererogatory is much more evident in the dramatic situation of the doctor's client or the lawyer's client than in the teacher's client where supererogatory acts must be more sustained if they are to achieve their end.

Because teaching is a stable, normal need of society it requires more agents than do the law and medicine, which is, of course, another factor influencing social prestige and the conferment of rewards. There is no objective reason to believe that the special skills of the lawyer and of the doctor are particularly scarce in society. The abilities employed are probably potentially more abundant than those of a teacher. But these professions maintain a monopoly of training and keep lawfully recognized practitioners deliberately scarce. Of course, society needs fewer doctors and lawyers than teachers. The expansion of education has meant that whether people have high abilities for teaching or not they have to be accepted because large numbers of teachers are needed. As a profession it has never been in a position to choose whom it will have. Teacher training colleges rarely fail people; and graduates, merely by being graduates, are thought to be equipped to teach. There is no explicit professional ethic, no professional control of members and no expulsions—because there have never been conditions in which adequate selectivity has been possible. Thus society accepts as dramatic and even glamorous those professional roles that "put things right" and accepts the myth that these abilities are scarce because the need for them is limited. It tends to disparage diffuse roles constantly and universally in demand, because a standard of performance is difficult to establish. This is so because the task is defined in terms of the general ends desired rather than in terms of the precise activities involved.

Because a teacher is concerned with a whole person over a prolonged period of time—and not merely with his delictual acts or his disturbed health—so *he* tends to become involved as a whole person. Since his role is difficult to define in terms of its action-content so it is difficult to delimit the extent to which his purely personal virtues are involved in it. The fact that the teacher employs his whole person in his role gives rise to unparalleled satisfactions, but equally to intense frustrations. A total commitment necessarily imposes strains—it means "living the job." And this is increasingly uncommon and uncalled for in our type of society in which specificity, time-calculation, and contractual obligations are the rule. The diffuse role means diffuse involvement. The teacher carries his work around with him—because he has to "re-create" his role continually, to re-interpret, re-enact, re-structure relationships and behavior patterns. He is the model for the child at a formative period and we know, and most teachers know in their work situation, that a child can be seriously disturbed if he discovers shortcomings in his model. The teacher has to be virtually beyond reproach. It is only because demand is great and selection limited that society has to put up with the uncommitted teacher. Thus there is no way of delimiting the role either in terms of the person dealt with or in terms of the role-performer himself.

Because our society is a society in which specialization continually increases, prestige increasingly attaches to the specialist. But there are distinct limits to the extent of specialization in teaching because the role is diffuse. Again, because our society relies on increasing technologization, it is instrumental roles that win social approval—in which clearly defined operations are undertaken and means are manipulated to achieve proximate ends, which in turn become means to further ends. In some measure, increasingly higher rewards are given to those whose roles involve them in the use of elaborate equipment—both technical and organizational. But the teacher's role is not directly instrumental—it is concerned with ends, with values. It is, of its nature, personal and direct. The results achieved are not dramatic achievements issuing from complex manipulation of elaborate mechanical or human machinery. They are imperceptibly gradual—and even when they are recognized the teacher's part in their achievement may not be credited—the boy was a bright boy, anyway! Results are always more manifest in instrumental roles and the process —the equipment, jargon, tools, formulae, mystique—is impressive; but teaching has little of all this. Thus, diffuse roles tend to lack the prestige of specific, instrumental roles. The same process has diminished the social prestige of the religious functionary. The process does not occur, of course, where the teacher is regarded as a vital agent of consciously-sought social change in accordance with an entrenched ideology—as is the case in the Soviet Union.

## THE AFFECTIVITY OF THE ROLE

Since the teacher is totally involved, warmth of personality, and affective concern for children are implicit in the role. Role-performance is a living process in which the establishment of rapport, the impact of personality, are necessary to the stirring of the imagination and the awakening of enthusiasm involved in the learning process. Affection is the first language man understands, and it becomes the lever by which all other languages can be initially learned. The teacher must engage the sympathy of his class; he must attain a certain contentment in order to teach and to create the atmosphere of learning. And yet this process has to occur in a society in which a limited investment of the self is all that is expected in most roles—an investment of skills, know-how, time and energy, but not of affection, which is a private affair. The strictly professional attitude—to remember that one's clients are just cases—so much stressed in medicine, law, and social work is simply not possible in teaching.

Paradoxically, in a world in which most roles are affectively neutral the positive affectivity of the teacher's role increases in importance. The teacher has to pry the child loose, in some respects, from the values of its family, and the teacher must employ the same agency of socialization as does the kinship group. In our society the individual's relationships tend to be impersonal, anonymous, dominated by role obligations and status expectations. Only kinship, friendship, courtship, and marriage stand out as the obvious exceptions to the affective neutrality of most of our daily relationships, and even these relationships are attenuated in significance and comprise a smaller part of our total relational activity. But individuals still need an affective context in which to gain assurance, support, and a sense of identity. And since the family in contemporary society is structurally smaller, functionally more restricted to basic essentials, associationally in decline, and afflicted by divergent value ideals social and occupational mobility imposes, and the growing separation of the generations, it is other socializers who must satisfy these needs. The teacher becomes willy-nilly a type of parent—a person whom the child, however much he may deviate from the teacher's ideals, can nonetheless trust. And because the rest of society is so dominated by contractual and role relationships so there is necessarily greater reliance on this relationship of trust. To take the paradox a stage further it might be said that the family itself has become a highly specialized agency for affection.[7] It has lost the other types of social activity that were once so much of its activities—the workplace, the dance hall, the youth club, and other institutions have taken over its economic and recreational functions, and its political and religious functions were lost long ago. Even the service-agency aspects of the family have declined now that more meals are consumed in schools and canteens, new materials have all but eliminated stitching and darning. What remains to the family is the mutuality of affection. And yet, if the family has lost so many of its shared activities on what can these emotional orientations rest besides the biological base? Affection needs activities and commitments on which to grow. The family has become an over-specialized agency in affection and has lost the sustaining concerns in which affection develops. In the educative task affection has a real context—a context of common interest, activity, and the cultivation of shared attitudes of mind. But the family is less and less supported as a social entity —as children grow it is increasingly exposed to cross-cutting pressures. It has lost its mystery, its permanence, its persisting meaning, and its appropriateness as a context in which the individual is identifiable. The generations are pulled apart in a mobile, rapidly changing society, so that the young quickly grow apart from their families and especially in adolescence reject identification with them and their values. But the school has ongoing concerns for young people, and these are concerns in which affectivity has a context and a necessary function.

## ROLE-CONFLICTS AND INSECURITIES

All roles in which there is a high commitment to other people are subject to considerable internal conflicts and insecurities. The most obvious ones—with which we are not concerned here—are the conflicts arising from one person's performance of several roles some of which may be, at some times, contradictory of each other. But the conflicts that concern us are those intrinsic to the teacher's role and the circumstances in which it is performed. These conflicts and insecurities might be grouped in six broad categories: (1) those inherent in the role because of its diverse obligations; (2) those that derive from the diverse expectations of those whose activities impinge on the role—now referred to as "the role-set"; (3) those arising from circumstances in which the role is marginal; (4) those arising from circumstances in which the role is inadequately supported by the institutional framework in which it is performed; (5) those

---

[7] For this point I am indebted to my friend Norbert Elias.

arising from conflict between commitments to the role and commitments to the career-line; (6) those arising from divergent value-commitments of the role and of the wider society. We shall now turn to each of these categories.[8]

(1) Diffuse roles are likely to embody internal role-conflicts because of the absence of clear lines of demarcation whereby the role-player knows when he has "done his job." Because the teacher's work—like all socializing tasks—is unending he must continually ask himself whether he has fully discharged his obligations. There is a tendency for the teacher to overextend himself in his role—even though he also knows that adequate role-performance really requires constant refreshing with outside interests and activities. In few roles is the need for creative and alternative activity so necessary. When the teacher is given a heavy teaching load and little inducement to keep alive his own mind the quality of teaching deteriorates.

A second conflict that inheres in the role is the problem of authority in the teaching role. The teacher is both the affective agent and the disciplinary agent; he is the advocate of a pupil, but also in considerable measure the objective assessor. He must win approval and respect, but he must also maintain standards. The conflict has been noticed by teachers in respect to headteachers where the role becomes somewhat modified. Headteachers have higher authority and less opportunity for affectivity, a more prestigious but perhaps less directly satisfying role. As teacher is to parent, headmaster is to grandparent—the "soft disciplinarian" who seeks the affective contact from which his role removes him.[9]

(2) The conflicts associated with the role-set have been set forth by the originator of the term, Robert K. Merton.[10] These conflicts are essentially the diverse expectations of a given role that are made manifest by all those affected by the role-performance—headmasters, the governors, and local education authority; colleague groups; the clientele—both parents and children; and manifold external agencies that put pressure on teachers and criticize teaching. Again, the role-set of the teacher is especially formidable because the role is diffuse and because everyone in contemporary society has ready opinions about what the teacher does and should do.

(3) This particular type of role-conflict arises for certain teachers but it is a type of conflict that is probably growing: it arises for the teacher whose role is marginal—the humanist in the technical college is a case in

---

[8] For a rather different analysis of role-conflicts see Jackson Toby, "Some Variables in Role Conflict Analysis," *Social Forces*, 30 (March 1952): 323–27.

[9] This suggestive analogy is employed by Miss Margaret Phillips in an unpublished manuscript she has kindly permitted me to see.

[10] Robert K. Merton, "The Role Set: Problems in Sociological Theory," *British Journal of Sociology*, 8 (2; June 1957): 106–20.

point. To a lesser extent the whole arrangement of day-continuation teaching may impose somewhat similar insecurities. The humanist in the technical college is the vendor of precarious values: the material in which he deals has little or no prestige within the context in which he performs his role. His values are imposed by the Ministry on reluctant hosts. His subject is thought of—by colleagues and clientele alike—as a trimming, a piece of ministerial whitewash with no significance for the real business of the institution. Even in the universities this type of marginality is not unknown. Clearly the teaching role can be adequately performed only if insecurity is reduced by the provision of adequate institutional support.[11]

(4) Role-conflicts and insecurities arise from the vulnerability of the institutions in which the teacher's role is performed. The school is subject to political pressure: ultimately it is laymen who determine the character of the school. Of all professions, teachers have least control of the institution in which their role is performed. Because the role is diffuse the institutional arrangements supporting the role influence its performance. Lawyers determine very much more completely the character of the courts in which, or in relation to which, they perform their role. Doctors do not run hospitals but have an exalted position within them. In universities it is the professors who—at least theoretically—make the decisions about the institution itself. But schools are much more exposed to public pressure than any of these institutions. This is because the process that is occurring is socialization, which in its own nature is not an esoteric process. Teachers perform in public—their role is unprotected from observation. Indeed it is deliberately exposed to inspection. They cannot protect their role by jargon, or by the use of dead language as doctors and lawyers do. The children whom they serve are a public who have less automatic trust than the clients of lawyers and doctors; their dependence is less dramatic and less urgent, and the processes less special and less apparently essential. The clientele too, is a clientele in only a partial sense: behind it stand the parents as interested parties in the role-performance of teachers, and capable of being mobilized in criticism. The institution itself is hierarchic, and ultimately, beyond the school, the highest echelon is laic. The teacher is exposed to much more authority than are other professional role-players, and yet he too must wield authority. There is continual dispute about his authority—as for instance in the matter of corporal punishment—which is an indication of the diversity of opinion that exists about just what is necessary for adequate role-performance.

An associated type of conflict arises from the growth of size of schools, which makes more difficult the affective elements of the teacher's role.

---

[11] This type of analysis is developed by Philip Selznick: see, for example, "Institutional Vulnerability in Mass Society," *American Journal of Sociology*, 56 (January 1951):320–32. See also Burton Clark, "Organizational Adaptation and Precarious Values," *American Sociological Review*, 21 (June 1956): 327–36.

Economic argument suggests that the provision of new equipment for schools—laboratories, mechanical visual aids, facilities of all kinds—can be supported only when the clientele are concentrated in large numbers. But if increase of school size implies a more impersonal atmosphere, a diminished opportunity for sustained personal contacts, a growth of rational specialism in the staff, then it reduces the affective commitment of the teacher. This may make the formal process of lecturing easier, but it may make the business of teaching much harder. Much of the satisfaction of the role is lost for the teacher when the circumstances in which he can actively stimulate and encourage individuals is lost. If schools are to be very large there is the likelihood of producing the mass atmosphere in which the quality of teaching is sacrificed for the quantity of instruction. It may mean, too, that instead of teachers socializing children we shall see children socializing children.

(5) Because of the diffuse, affective character of the teaching role there is, in contemporary society, a most significant role-conflict arising from the divergence of role-commitment and career-orientation.[12] The teacher is—like everyone in contemporary society—exposed to the pressure to "get off." Achievement and social mobility are the accepted cultural goals of our society, and there are well-structured systems of inducement to motivate men to these ends. Yet the teaching role demands the cultivation of sustained relationships with particular children, and this necessarily means a continued commitment to a particular situation. But the teacher, and particularly the young teacher, ought to want to "move on to a better job," according to our widely accepted social values. If this is not a possibility he should want to improve himself in other ways—to move to more congenial schools. There is a considerable horizontal mobility as well as vertical mobility in the teaching profession.[13] Teachers prefer better surroundings, more teachable and brighter children, fewer problems of discipline, and yet the need for committed people as teachers, and as models, is evident. If teachers are "on the move" the affective aspects of their role are less well performed, they become impersonal transmitters of skills, who do not know their children and whose children do not know them—sometimes not even by name! The damage done by high teacher turnover has not been assessed and yet a frequent excuse by children and headteachers for poor performance is the fact that there has been a change of teachers. Often, the least attractive schools, with the need for the highest commitment, suffer most. Thus it is that the career-line the young

---

[12] This type of role-conflict is examined in a different context of analysis in Melvin Seeman, "Role Conflict and Ambivalence in Leadership," American Sociological Review, 18 (August 1953):373–80.

[13] A study of horizontal mobility in America is made by Howard S. Becker, "The Career of the Chicago Public Schoolteacher," American Journal of Sociology, 57 (5; March 1952):470–77.

teacher is expected to desire is in fact a career-line that cuts across the commitment to his role. It means reduced loyalty to the institution of which he is a part, to the clientele whom he serves—especially so since his service is of its very nature particularistic. But it is evident that colleagues and the world at large judge the individual in terms of his career-line rather than in terms of the care, concern and commitment that are involved in role-performance. These are largely unseen, and in a highly mobile society are likely to be seen less and less. There is an inducement in this situation to make right impressions on the significant people rather than significant impressions on the right people—the children. Financial security, social prestige, one's own self-esteem, once these values have been completely internalized, are reflected more and more in the capacity to "get on," rather than to do the job well. Indeed, inability to do well in the role may itself be an inducement to further mobility: the less role-committed can become the more career-oriented, and the less adequate teachers can accept the incentive to get ahead more easily than the intensely role-committed. In an inner-directed society the satisfactions of good performance of the role would be sufficient; once men are "other-directed" they become more concerned with success as acknowledged by others rather than with their own knowledge of their good performance. Thus it is that there is structurally in-built tension in the teacher's role in a society that places a high premium on social mobility.

There is a further implication of a paradoxical kind associated with this particular conflict. The dedication to achievement and the striving for social mobility has its impact on the school at the 11-plus examination —the first step in the allocation of intellectual resources to suitable training. But intellectual ability is not manifested without motivation, and the teacher's task is thus to motivate his pupils to high achievement. Yet he himself is torn between achievement-orientation and role-commitment! His means for inspiring children is essentially affective. The pupils must be won over to accept the inducements of the system, and the teacher's part in this is to use a positive affective approach to strengthen the structure of values that prevail in our society—values that are themselves affectively neutral, impersonal and achievement-oriented—the pursuit of a career. So the teacher must represent to the child values, which, in the nature of his own role, he must in some measure eschew, and some of the consequences of which he must also, in his moral capacity, more or less condemn.[14]

(6) Finally there is the conflict of a role that implies specific value-commitments performed in a society where these values are, at best, only

---

[14] See the very cogent discussion on the value consequences of social mobility by Melvin M. Tumin, "Some Unapplauded Consequences of Social Mobility in Mass Society," *Social Forces*, 36 (1; October 1957).

partially supported. It might be asserted that the wider society manifests a considerable confusion in the realm of values, and the different sections of society show a highly differential acceptance of the values which are implicit in the teacher's role. The teacher has been described as someone who expresses value-consensus.[15] The conflict of his role is clear in a society where such consensus is no longer a reality. Traditionally he represents moral virtues, integrity of mind, honest criticism, tolerance, loyalty, sensitivity, appreciative imagination, consideration for others—but in a society with an intense achievement-orientation, with the commercial exploitation of what were once manifestations of personal relationships, these values are frequently under attack. Children are exposed to television and other mass media for almost as much of their time as they are in school, and generally the values which the mass media present are not those of the teacher. Frequently, too, these alternative values, are presented through agencies that confer specially significant weight—highly technical media presenting a readily acceptable, largely escapist, type of material, and providing the fantasy of vicarious success by quick methods, rather than by slow hard work. The message of the media is presented by young people, and is frequently presented in terms of the values of youth against those of age—and the teacher is clearly represented as the voice of the past. This circumstance creates conflict in the teacher's role, but it is a conflict that passes beyond it into the very structure of contemporary society.

---

[15] This point is made in a highly suggestive article by Kaspar Naegele, "Clergymen, Teachers and Psychiatrists," *Canadian Journal of Economics and Political Science*, 22 (1; February 1956):46–62.

# 19

# Authority, Conflict, and Teacher Effectiveness*

## WILLIAM G. SPADY

The sources of conflict in schools appear to reside in three overlapping arenas: the goals and functions of public schools, the nature of the roles that are defined by these functions, and the manner or style in which these roles are played out. This analysis will attempt to link all three.

In virtually all Western societies schools are expected to play a major role in preparing the young to assume adult roles and responsibilities. This is done through two general functions of schooling: instruction and socialization. The instructional function of the school involves those activities that increase the information base and cognitive and physical skills of the child. These include the development of literacy, computational, conceptual, and manual skills plus the accumulation of often less "practical" kinds of information. Socialization involves developing in the child the expectations, attitudes, values, and beliefs that enable him to interact compatibly with others in his society and to utilize his cognitive and physical skills in effective (socially approved) ways. This, argued Durkheim (1961), is the most important function of the public school in any "modern" society.

Beyond these two general functions school systems typically perform at least three other functions that are seldom stated as a part of their formal rationale or goals but whose outcomes are often more demonstrable

* From: *Educational Researcher*, 2 (January 1973):4–10. Reprinted by permission of William Spady, Sr. Research Sociologist, National Institute of Education, Washington, D.C. 20208.

An expanded version of this paper entitled "The Authority System of the School and Student Unrest: A Theoretical Exploration" will be published in the National Society for the Study of Education's 1974 *Yearbook of Education*, edited by C. Wayne Gordon.

than those of the socialization and instructional functions themselves. These are: custody-control, certification, and selection. These functions interact and overlap both with each other and with the socialization and instructional functions in such a way that they induce some of the most severe and persistent strains in school system activity.

The custody-control function of the school is a product of universal compulsory attendance laws in most Western countries. These laws compel young people to attend school usually well into their teens (middle adolescence), whether they care to or not. This function is imposed on the school by the society and, in Bidwell's (1971) terms, creates an organization whose clients are *involuntary* members. The school's most challenging task is to establish a set of social control mechanisms through which the involuntary and coercive aspects of the custody-control function are minimized.

The consequences of the school's custody-control function are so pervasive that they impinge directly on its certification function as well. Since academic standards tend to be highly variable across schools within the same system, the school diploma typically certifies both the student's *minimum* proficiency in the required curriculum and his capacity to endure compliantly 12 years of compulsory schooling without having flagrantly undermined the system.

Furthermore, the school's monopoly on basic certification clearly impinges on the social and economic life-chances of students because diplomas open doors of opportunity that ability and limited experience cannot do. Certification is important because of its relation to social selection processes.

*The criteria and mechanisms that the school uses for evaluating the performance of its clientele become central to the relation between its instructional and socialization functions on the one hand and its certification and selection functions on the other.* Since learning ultimately involves the cooperation and interest of the learner, in the final analysis students govern what is learned within the formal curriculum of the school (i.e., its instructional function). What they do not control, however, are the particular aspects of their learning that are eventually evaluated; what the criteria, standards, conditions, and mechanisms of evaluation are; and the uses to which the evaluation is put. In effect, students are compelled both to attend school and to live with the long-term consequences of the evaluation, certification, and selection mechanisms that operate within them. These constraints on student choice make control an overriding feature of school life.

## MECHANISMS OF SOCIAL CONTROL

Control exists, according to Bachrach and Baratz (1963), when one party gains compliance from another in an interactional setting. This compliance may be arrived at either involuntarily (when power or force is required) or voluntarily, either through persuasion (influence) or authority.

*Power.* According to Weber (1958), power is the probability of carrying out one's will in a social situation despite resistance from others. In such situations, compliance (control) is achieved because the dominant party is perceived to be capable of manipulating critical resources in such a way that the other party believes he cannot sustain his present state of affairs (such as employment, reputation, or physical well-being) without enduring some intolerable loss. In effect, the party who can monopolize and manipulate the greatest number of critical resources can restrict the options or alternatives of the other party and, thereby, gain some measure of control over (i.e., apply sanctions against) him. Etzioni (1964) uses the term *coercion* to describe essentially the same phenomenon. Here compliance is achieved by means of either the *threat* or the direct use of sanctions.

Given that such compliance is essentially involuntary, the resulting condition is usually an uneasy, short-term truce the subordinate party accepts with resentment and hostility, making stable and cooperative social arrangements between parties highly unlikely. Furthermore, coercion alone will not produce learning. Therefore, if instruction is really to be the most important function of the school, some other mechanism of social control besides power must be used to realize that goal.

*Persuasion.* Persuasion rather than power is a more desirable alternative since compliance (student engagement in prescribed learning activities) will be based on the subordinate's judgment and voluntary cooperation. In persuasion situations the subordinate party voluntarily complies because he sees that certain alternatives will inherently enhance his welfare, not because negative sanctions will be applied by the dominant party if he does not.

Most humanists argue that persuasion should be the *only* mechanism of control used in schools because it neutralizes many of the inherent status differences between staff and students, opens the conditions of school life to negotiation and change, and assures the voluntary participation of students in learning activities. However, relying on persuasion forces the teacher to negotiate his every step and to justify the terms under which classroom activity will take place. This places an enormous demand on the teacher's influence and persuasiveness and can lead to a lack of efficiency and predictability in school operations.

The solution to this dilemma, if any, appears to rest on the use of *authority* as a guiding principle of social control in schools. According to Weber, authority differs from power in two important respects: first, people comply with the requests (demands) made of them *voluntarily* rather than involuntarily; and second, they *withhold judgment* regarding the legitimacy of these demands at the time they are made. In simple terms, *people willingly obey directives whose wisdom they do not question.* Although this suspension of judgment presumably occurs at the moment of interaction, it is not "blind," for it is based on experiences and prior judgments that are reflected in one's set of basic values. Compliance appears to occur "automatically" because the request being made is congruent with values that indicate which conditions take priority in the subordinate's life. Whereas persuasion is necessary in situations involving parties with discrepant values and goals, the subordinate party in an authority relationship *grants legitimacy* to the dominant party because the latter embodies attributes that the former regards as consistent with his own goals and as valuable in promoting his general welfare.

In other words, the key condition for suspension of judgment and voluntary compliance is the *legitimacy* (respect) that the dominant party possesses in the eyes of the subordinate. Legitimacy, respect, and deference are *granted* by the subordinate on the basis of the dominant party, in his eyes, having *earned* them. This makes the "cardinal rule" of many teachers and administrators—i.e., "walk in and *establish* authority immediately"—false by definition. The *power* to *grant authority* lies with the students!

## THE NATURE OF LEGITIMACY

In his original conceptual treatment of this topic, Weber discussed three major kinds of value orientations that legitimate the exercise of control: beliefs in charisma, tradition, and rational-legal processes. *Charismatic authority* is based largely on respect for extra-ordinary gifts of body or spirit embodied in dynamic leaders and believed to be inaccessible to most people. Charisma is usually associated with a great sense of mission, and its strength depends on the congruence between the mission being undertaken and the *needs* of the people being served. The charismatic leader maintains his recognition by *continuing to prove himself* (i.e., "deliver the goods") to his constituents *by using extra-ordinary means to improve their welfare*. In this sense he must have demonstrable capacities for outstanding performance that are recognized as *relevant* and *beneficial* by his constituents. "Meeting the needs" demands being *sensitive* and *empathetic* to what the needs are.

*Traditional authority* primarily rests on a legitimacy base that has its roots in *strong attachments to and reverence for established customs and institutions.* Authority is legitimatized by the sanctity of tradition when the present social order (and the system of privileges embodied in it) is viewed as sacred and inviolable. This authority mode clearly tends to perpetuate the existing social order and encourages a resistance to innovation and social change.

Weber's third type of authority, *rational-legal,* was originally conceptualized to account for the emergence of "modern" social institutions, particularly large-scale organizations. It rests primarily on a belief in the supremacy of the law in governing social arrangements. Weber assumed that the law is rational in the sense that it reflected social norms intended to channel conduct in the efficient pursuit of specified goals. He considered this to be prototypic of the model bureaucracy; hence, this legitimating mode is often referred to as *bureaucratic authority*. Since rules that are presumably formulated to maximize the efficient use of resources are often counter-productive and therefore retard it, we should differentiate between beliefs in the primacy of *rules* or *law* on the one hand and in *rationality* or *expertise* on the other. *Legal authority* depends on one's allegiance to codified sets of social arrangements, while *expert authority* depends on a strong respect for the demonstrated competence and technical resources of individuals, regardless of their formal status or characteristics.

These four modes of legitimacy (charismatic, traditional, legal, and expert) form a typology that can be defined by two major frames of reference, one social-structural and the other normative (i.e., value-based —see Figure 1). Essentially *traditional* and *legal* authority are based on values and loyalties that emphasize the primacy of social *institutions*, while *charismatic* and *expert* authority reflect primarily on the attributes of particular *individuals*. The normative or value-orientation dimension distinguishes between loyalties based primarily on a combination of mystical and emotional criteria (tradition and charisma) from those based on what Weber refers to as secular and rational (legal and expert).

**FIGURE ONE**
**Four Modes of Authority Based on Their Social Structural and Normative Dimensions**

|  |  | SOCIAL-STRUCTURAL DIMENSION | |
|  |  | Institutional | Personal |
| NORMATIVE DIMENSION | Mystical, Emotional | Traditional | Charismatic |
|  | Secular, Rational | Legal | Expert |

This typology reflects purely idealized or ideal-type theoretical constructions that have few unambiguous manifestations in the real world because most compilance-control situations involve subtle mixtures of power, persuasion, and authority. Nonetheless, this typology provides an important vehicle for understanding the nature of social control in schools, for it provides a greater degree of precision in dealing with the concept of authority than is found elsewhere. Also, it suggests that students may comply voluntarily and automatically with requests from teachers or administrators when the latter embody some characteristic, such as expertise, which is congruent with student values or needs in situations in which that criterion is deemed relevant to the nature of the request. If the teacher or administrator lacks credibility with respect to that criterion, he may still have some degree of legitimacy based on the other three.

Given that the legitimacy of a staff member's behavior may be nonproblematic in the eyes of a majority of students, those whose compliance is not automatic and voluntary can probably be "handled" by means of coercion and/or persuasion as *individual cases*. However, the situation changes when large numbers of students fail to grant legitimacy to staff. Then the manipulation of single individuals becomes impossible and alternative modes of control, such as persuasion, must be tried; but if the discrepancy in values is severe enough, even persuasion will not work. That leaves only power or force as alternatives, with the consequence being some form of confrontation between staff and students with its attendant use of sanctions and hostile reactions.

Although this underscores the importance of the teacher's legitimacy in the eyes of students, it does not explain how legitimacy is developed. The answer is trust and experience. If a person is to suspend judgment and comply voluntarily with requests, he must believe that complying will not work to his disadvantage. This level of trust is itself acquired from experience. Experience tells the individual whether or not he is likely to be treated positively or negatively in similar situations. Hence, his willingness to comply voluntarily under conditions when manifestations of tradition, law, charisma, or expertise are operative depends on what he believes the consequences of his compliance will be. If he does not automatically comply, he may have to be persuaded or compelled to respond.

The implications for the classroom teacher are explicit: if the dominant mode of classroom organization is to be legitimate rather than persuasive or coercive, the teacher must earn the respect and trust of each student. Unless other fortuitous conditions are met, this will only be accomplished by treating him fairly and compassionately over a sustained period of time.

## LEGITIMACY AND ACHIEVEMENT

Given that the instructional mission of the school is universally endorsed, one major concern of the teacher is to improve the skills of students. When these skills are channeled into productive activities and performance standards are met we call them achievements. Kemper (1968) suggests that three basic reference group functions must be operating for an individual to be a consistent performer (achiever).

First, he requires a *normative reference group;* that is, at least one individual who sets (high) *expectations* for performance and who possesses the capacity to mete out *negative sanctions* if these standards are not met. Normative groups demand and attempt to enforce conformity to group norms. Second, he requires a *role model* (one of the four kinds of comparison group functions in Kemper's framework), someone who *exemplifies* and demonstrates the *skills* necessary for high performance by means of his own achievements. Third, high level performance also requires an *audience group*, at least one individual to whom the child *attributes* the ability to provide meaningful *positive rewards* for his endeavors. As a result he tries to *capture their attention and approval* by behaving in a way that he *believes* they will find attractive. Since the absence of negative rewards is not equivalent to the presence of positive rewards, the assumption is made that the child will consistently undertake the risk of failing to meet normative standards only when abundant positive approval is perceived to be available.

Therefore, consistent high performance (achievement) is regarded here as the product of (1) confronting expectations (2) with a clear notion of how one goes about meeting them (3) in view of the positive rewards that are probably available.

There is also a tendency for the role model and audience group functions to coexist so that master performers are viewed as major rewards and/or positive rewarders soon become emulated as role models. This natural compatibility of comparative and audience group functions is further reinforced in that neither role implies a controlling function that might ultimately require legitimation. Being a skillful performer and having the potential for providing approval and positive rewards do not require legitimation: people are completely free to observe and emulate one's performance or to accept his rewards.

But the normative reference group function, which involves setting standards of performance and reinforcing them with the threat of sanctions, is inherently troublesome since the latter is characteristic of control achieved by means of power or coercion. If these threatened sanctions are not to breed hostility and resentment, their potential use must be accepted as legitimate by the subordinate party. This requires that the subordinate have a set of values that supports both the importance of high level performance in given activities and the legitimacy of reinforcing substandard performance with negative sanctions.

If the teacher is to operate effectively as a normative reference group for students, the students must believe in both the importance of achievement and the right of the teacher to give them poor grades or curtail other privileges if they do not do well. Of these two orientations, the second is by far the more problematic since it operates contrary to the natural self-interest of the student. It is compounded when evaluation is done on a comparative basis such that a certain proportion of students always receive poor evaluations. Few students will be able to accept a continual

bombardment of this form of punishment without making some accommodation to it. This response might include rejecting grades as legitimate
indices of one's performance, rejecting competition as a context for academic involvement, or even rejecting achievement as a desirable goal. In
each case the disaffection of the student results from a deterioration of the
legitimacy of some important component of the achievement-evaluation
system. This disaffection, in turn, provides the basis for withdrawing support from the major values and structures of the school and leads to one
or more manifestations of what can be called "alienation."

## MAXIMIZING TEACHER EFFECTIVENESS AND LEGITIMACY

How, then, can the teacher minimize the alienation of students and
maximize their achievement? Maslow's (1954) theory of the hierarchy of
human needs provides a useful framework for seeking an answer.

Maslow suggests that human behavior can be interpreted as an attempt
to satisfy a number of physiological and psychological needs that reflect
themselves in a consistent hierarchy of priorities. Man's most fundamental
needs involve physical survival and safety. Only after he has solved these
basic problems can he turn his attention to meeting the need for psychological security and affection, and then, in turn, the needs for recognition
and self-esteem. For our purposes, however, the most important aspect of
Maslow's theory is that men will be incapable of fully realizing their
achievement and creative potentials until these more basic needs for security, love, and esteem are themselves satisfied. In other words, the risks
involved in deferring immediate gratifications to meet longer term achievement expectations will probably be too great for an individual with unmet
security and esteem needs.

In terms of the foregoing discussion, the major implication of Maslow's
theory for the authority system of the classroom is that the imposition of
achievement expectations by the teacher must be preceded by a sufficient
period of supportive and affirmative behavior. Only in this way can the
necessary rapport, confidence, and feelings of security between student
and teacher be established that enable the child to react positively to demands for high performance. The child must feel secure, adequate, and
respected before he can consistently be expected to meet expectations to
achieve, and this sense of adequacy and worthiness is clearly facilitated
by the positive expression of affect and approval by the teacher. Perhaps
the most important component of the teacher's repertory of abilities, in
other words, is the capacity to establish a sense of rapport with students
by caring about them as individuals in order to aid them in developing a
sense of security and confidence. This establishes for the teacher a sound
basis for serving an audience group function for the class, enhances the
probability that he will serve as a role model, and satisfies the basic con-

ditions necessary for students to trust him and grant him legitimacy to serve in a normative reference group capacity as well.

When combined with Stinchcombe's (1970) analysis of the teaching role, this entire set of factors can be synthesized into a model of the teacher's role that would appear to maximize both his legitimacy and effectiveness in facilitating student achievement. According to Stinchcombe, the central task of the teacher involves capturing the attention of students and channeling it toward sets of informative instructional activities. It is, in other words, a performance role defined almost entirely in terms of the quality of the interaction that takes place within the classroom. To be a good teacher, one has to be effective at capturing and sustaining students' interests in learning activities. Although the following points may reflect the biases of a "teacher-centered" classroom, these ideas suggest that the truly effective teacher must (1) have something of substance and interest to say, (2) be capable of saying it clearly and accurately, (3) be capable of saying it in a stimulating and exciting fashion, and (4) base this communication directly on a concern for the personal welfare of each student. These four conditions or attributes can be grouped in pairs: the first two, referring to the teacher's subject matter expertise and pedagogical skills, underlie a general "expertise" dimension; the third and fourth define a "charismatic personality" dimension consisting of an exciting and inspiring, yet empathetic, manner of relating to others and their personal needs.

Assuming for the moment that teachers vary on each of these four dimensions, these variations can be portrayed by a general classification scheme such as that in Figure 2. To do so, it is necessary to reduce each presumably continuous dimension into two categories, high and low. The

**FIGURE TWO**
A Classification Scheme for Attributes to Maximize Teacher
Legitimacy and Effectiveness.

| CHARISMATIC DIMENSION | | | | EXPERTISE DIMENSION | | | | |
|---|---|---|---|---|---|---|---|---|
| | | | | Subject Matter Expertise | | | | |
| | | | | Low | | High | | |
| | | | | Pedagogical Expertise | | Pedagogical Expertise | | |
| | | | | Low | High | Low | High | |
| Stimulation, Excitement | High | Empathy, Concern | High | 4 | 3 | 2 | 1 | |
| | | | Low | 9 | 7 | 6 | 5 | |
| | Low | Empathy, Concern | High | 12 | 11 | 10 | 9 | |
| | | | Low | 16 | 15 | 14 | 13 | |

horizontal dimension of the figure contains the two major components of expertise: mastery of a significant body of knowledge and expertise in exercising what Dreeben (1970) calls the technology (i.e., methodology) of teaching. Its vertical dimension contains the two major components of charisma: concern with the personal needs of students coupled with an inspiring and stimulating way of communicating (i.e., leading classroom activities). According to this scheme, the ideal teacher is one who clearly embodies each of these attributes in the classroom (cell #1 in Figure 2); i.e., he is high on all four dimensions. The Type 1 teacher serves as an optimum role model because of his expertise and an optimum audience group because of his charismatic qualities. The remaining 15 cells represent presumably less effective combinations of these four attributes, with cell #16 describing the archetypal disaster of the educational world: the Type 16 teacher who is low on all of these important charismatic or expert qualities.

There is also a definite parallel between the three basic components of professionalism found in Dreeben's (1970) analysis of the teaching role, and three of the four dimensions in this model. Dreeben implies that a "professional" teacher will emphasize: (1) competence and personal performance, (2) the use of effective techniques, and (3) a concern for meeting the needs of his clientele. The respective elements in this model are subject matter expertise, pedagogical expertise, and empathy and concern. Whereas the real key to teacher effectiveness in Dreeben's view is pedagogy, *the critical variable in this analysis appears to be empathy and concern.* For the teacher who is empathic toward his students has a better chance of meeting their basic security and esteem needs, serving an effective audience group role, and developing among students the trust that ultimately underlies his legitimacy.

## THE BREAKDOWN OF LEGITIMACY

The ideal conditions just described are symbolized by the Type 1 teachers in Figure 2, but numerous educational critics doubt that many of these "professional paragons" exist. Instead, schools are criticized for their rigid, inhibiting, and authoritarian tactics that pay greater homage to the welfare of the system than to the welfare of its clientele. In effect, teachers and administrators are often stereotyped in terms that are polar opposites of those suggested by the "professional paragons." To the extent that they have any legitimacy at all, these Type 16s must depend not on a combination of charisma and expertise but of tradition and respect for rules. According to the criteria established in Figure 1, authority based on these two principles derives its legitimacy essentially from institutional rather than personal sources. Operationally this means that the authority of the Type 16 teacher is based not on characteristics implicit in the performance of the instructional role but on the mere occupation of a position that the institution attempts to invest with legitimacy. As they find themselves incapable of meeting instructional demands, their grounds for legitimacy shift from an essentially personally-based professional pattern characterized by charisma and expertise to a more institutionally-grounded "bureaucratic" pattern typified by a formalization of adult status privileges into local laws and school rules. In effect, this represents a major shift away from achievement as the dominant feature of the classroom to an emphasis on control itself.

The earliest period in the child's schooling career is usually characterized by high degrees of emotion and strong identification with the teacher. This is very naturally facilitated by the dominant legitimacy mode of the classroom: charisma. To the young child the capacities and stature of virtually *all adults* appear to be exciting, exceptional, and often beyond their powers of understanding. This aura of mystery and seeming omnipotence that surrounds adults is the ideal condition for enabling children to grant charismatic (as well as expert) legitimacy to the teacher, particularly when these teachers channel their activities toward the basic interests and needs of their students. Except for cases in which they have already acquired a suspicion of adults, most young children also have no experiential base for not trusting their teachers.

However, within a period of a few years, the perceptive and rational capacities of children mature to an extent that enables them to evaluate the behavior of adults more realistically and objectively. As a result, behavior that once looked exceptional and even awesome at times becomes both more routine and comprehensible with time. In effect, teachers, like most adults, lose a considerable degree of their glamour and appeal as a simple function of the increased awareness of the child. This, in turn, erodes their natural power base, charismatic appeal, and in some cases their legitimacy as experts.

This implies that the older and wiser students become the greater are the demands they make on the personal (charismatic and expertise) resources of the teacher and on the instructional mission of the school. At the same time the character of classroom activity becomes decidedly less affective and expressive and more instrumental and impersonal. In addition, performance standards and their implications for certification and placement become more serious matters. The paradox is that as the school intensifies its performance demands and hints at the negative future consequences that will result if (constantly increasing) standards are not met, students judge teachers more exclusively in terms of their unquestioned ability to deliver the goods.

Since teacher charisma and expertise always depend on the level of development and expectation of the students, *teachers are constantly being challenged to maintain a specific degree of advantage over their students or else risk losing their personal authority base by failing to meet these rising performance expectations.* Only when the legitimacy of this base is defined in institutional as well as personal terms can the teacher risk occasional "lapses" in performance without precipitating such a loss, but when these lapses are lengthy or permanent the criteria on which his legitimacy depends shift dramatically away from personal performance to institutionalized forms. This shift symbolizes a breakdown in the instructional mission of the school and the emergence of custody and control as primary goals.

Student respect for the overriding principles of law does give the teacher a final alternative authority base, beyond that of tradition, but as Waller (1932) illustrates, legal authority has limitations. This figurative appeal of last resort has legitimacy to the extent that society and the rules of the school invest the teacher with the right to hold out performance expectations for students and to enforce them by means of grades. However, since legitimacy in this case no longer resides in the teacher's performance or in the honor associated with adulthood, the instructional mission and validity of the role are severely undermined. Because their ability to control students becomes increasingly associated with the tenability of their institutional rather than their personal role, bureaucratic teachers devote most of their loyalty to the system that, in effect, protects them. They place a premimum on strict adherence to customs, established practices, and school rules among both their students and their colleagues; and they elevate order to the position of being an end in itself rather than a means of facilitating higher priority instructional objectives.

## REFERENCES

Baratz, M.S. and Bachrach, P. "Decisions and Nondecisions: An Analytical Framework." *American Political Science Review* 57 (1963):632–42.

Bidwell, C.E. "Students and Schools: Some Observations of Client-Serving Organizations." In W.R. Rosengren and M. Lefton (Eds.), *Organizations and Clients: Essays in the Sociology of Service.* Columbus: Charles E. Merrill, 1970, pp. 37–70.

Dreeben, R. *The Nature of Teaching: Schools and the Work of Teachers.* Glenview, Illinois: Scott-Foresman, 1970.

Durkheim, E. *Moral Education: A Study in the Theory of the Sociology of Education.* New York, Free Press of Glencoe, 1961.

Etzioni, A. *Modern Organizations.* Englewood Cliffs, N.J.: Prentice-Hall, 1964.

Kemper, T.D. "Reference Groups, Socialization, and Achievement." *American Sociological Review* 33 (1968):31–45.

Maslow, A. *Motivation and Personality.* New York: Harper, 1954.

Stinchcombe, A. "Review Symposium: *On What is Learned in School,* by Robert Dreeben." *Sociology of Education* 43 (1970):218–22.

Waller, W. *The Sociology of Teaching.* New York: Wiley and Sons, 1932.

Weber, M. *From Max Weber: Essays in Sociology.* H. Gerth and C.W. Mills (Eds.) New York: Oxford University Press, 1958.

# 20

# Teaching the Teacher*

ESTELLE FUCHS

Ideally, the public schools exist to provide equal educational opportunity for all, and to provide opportunity for each to develop according to his capacity. The following excerpts, which follow the experience of a first-grade teacher and her class through the first semester, illustrate the way in which the bureaucratic structure of the school frustrates the attainment of ideal goals. This case indicates the way in which, through both informal and formal mechanisms, the teacher comes to accept the mores of the slum school, which tend to project the cause of school failure upon the children or their families and away from the school.

*October 26.* Mrs. Jones, the sixth-grade teacher, and I went on to discuss the problems of reading. I said, "I wonder about my children. They don't seem too slow; they seem average. Some of them even seem to be above average. I can't understand how they can grow up to be fifth- and sixth-grade children in school and still be reading on the second-grade level. It seems absolutely amazing."

Mrs. Jones explained about the environmental problems that these children have. "Some of them never see a newspaper. Some of them have never been on the subway," she said. "The parents are so busy having parties and things that they have no time for their children. They can't even take them to a museum or anything. It's very important that the teacher stress books."

Mrs. Jones tells her class, "If anyone asks you what you want for Christmas, you can say you want a book." She told me that she had a 6/1 class last year and it was absolutely amazing how many children never even

* Reprinted from Estelle Fuchs *Teachers Talk*, Doubleday Anchor Books, 1969, Garden City, N.Y., pp. 172–184. Copyright © 1967, 1969 by Estelle Fuchs. Reprinted by permission of Doubleday & Company, Inc.

saw a newspaper. They can't read Spanish either. So she said that the educational problem lies with the parents. They are the ones that have to be educated.

It's just a shame that the children suffer. I guess this problem will take an awful lot to straighten it out. I guess it won't take one day or even a year; it will take time.

*December 14.* Here I am a first-grade teacher. I get a great thrill out of these children being able to read, but I often wonder, "Am I teaching them how to read or are they just stringing along sight words that they know?" I never had a course in college for teaching phonetics to children. In this school we have had conferences about it, but I really wish that one of the reading teachers would come in and specifically show me how to go about teaching phonics. I have never gotten a course like this and it is a difficult thing, especially when there is a language barrier and words are quite strange to these children who can't speak English. How can they read English? So we have a great responsibility on our shoulders, and teachers should take these things seriously.

*January 4.* Something very, very important and different has happened to me in my school. It all happened in our last week before the vacation, on Tuesday. Mr. Frost, our principal, came over to me and asked me if I would be willing to take over a second-grade class starting after the vacation. Well, I looked at him and I said, "Why?"

He told me briefly that the registers in the school have dropped and according to the Board of Education the school must lose a teacher. Well, apparently he was getting rid of a second-grade teacher and he wanted to combine two of the first-grade classes. The registers on the first grade were the lowest in the school, I believe. Anyway, he told me that he was going to all the afternoon first-grade teachers asking if any of them would be willing to change in the middle of the term. He said that he thought perhaps someone really would want it and, instead of his just delegating a person, it would be better if he asked each one individually.

I was torn between many factors. As you know, I enjoyed my class very, very much and I enjoy teaching the first grade. But because I was teaching afternoon session (our school runs on two different sessions) I was left out of many of the goings on within the school, as my hours were different, and it also sort of conflicted with my home responsibilities. Well, with these two points in mind, I really felt that I would rather stay with my class than to switch over in the middle of the term. But he explained further that some of the classes would not remain the same because there would be many changes made. So, being the type of person that I am, I felt that, even though I did want to stay with my class and the children and the first grade, if something had to be done in the school, there was no way of stopping it and I might as well do it. I explained to Mr. Frost that even though I wouldn't want to change in the middle—after all, it would be a whole new experience, two classes of children would be suffering by the change—but if it had to be done I would be willing to take on the new responsibility.

With that, Mr. Frost said, "Thank you," and said he would go around to the other teachers to see if anyone really wanted to change. Well, already I felt that it was going to be me, but I wasn't sure.

A little later on in the day I was taking my class to recess and we were lining up. We had just gotten into the hall. I had spoken to Miss Lane, another teacher, about what had happened. He had also spoken to her. She told me that she didn't quite understand what Mr. Frost was talking about, so I explained it to her in more detail. At that point Mr. Frost came over and spoke to me and told me that he was sorry but that I had been the one elected. Well, I said that I hoped that I would be able to do a good job, and that was that.

From that point on there was an awful lot of talk in the school. Everybody was talking about it, at least, everyone who knew something about the matter. So all the afternoon first-grade teachers and all the morning first-grade teachers knew and many of the new teachers (those that I came into the school with), and apparently there was a lot of business going on that I can't begin to describe because I don't know how the whole thing started in the first place. However, from the office I did find out that it wasn't Mr. Frost's fault or anything that the second-grade teacher was going to be dismissed. It was a directive from higher up that stated he would lose a teacher. How he chose this particular teacher to let go I really can't say. I understand that they really didn't get along too well and neither of them was too happy in the school working together.

Everything went so quickly and everybody was talking to me. Mrs. Parsons spoke to me. She is my assistant principal. She was supervisor of the first grade and she will be in charge of the second grade also. I was told that I would have to take over the new class on January 2, the first day that we return from the vacation. I really felt terrible about my children, but it was something that had to be done and I did it.

Thursday, Mr. Frost talked to the other afternoon teachers and myself. He referred to me as the hero and he said, "Now it is your turn to be heroes also." He asked the afternoon first-grade teachers if they would be willing to have their registers become higher by having my twenty-seven children split up among the four remaining afternoon classes, or did they think he should have them split up among all the first-grade classes, some of which met in the morning.

He was straightforward, saying that he didn't think it would be a good idea for the children to be split up among all the first-grade teachers. I agreed with him. He felt that it would be trying on the parents and on the children to have a whole new schedule worked out. After all, if you're used to going to school from 12 to four, coming to school from 7:30 to 12 is quite a difference. It would be very, very hard on the parents. Especially in this neighborhood, where sometimes you have a few children in the same grade, a few in different grades. These parents do bring them to school and take them home. So I agreed with Mr. Frost. The other teachers didn't seem too happy about the idea, but they said they would go along with it.

Mr. Frost and Mrs. Parsons worked out a plan whereby the 1/1 class register would go up to 35, which is generally what a 1/1 class has (34 or 35, I can't remember exactly), and the 1/3 class register would go up to 32 or 33. And so forth down the line. Class 1/5 (my class) would be erased, and then came 1/7. Their register would go up to about 30; and then came 1/9, which would go up to about 26 or so. The teachers didn't think it was so bad then, but we all did have added responsibilities.

Mr. Frost then added that if at this time we had any children in our classes that we felt did not belong, this was our chance to have them changed, since there would be many interclass transfers in order to make more homogeneous classes and he would be willing to grant these changes now. So we all had to sit down and think—"Who belongs? Who doesn't belong?"—and I, of course, had to decide where 27 children would belong. I went through my class and divided them into groups to the best of my ability. I put them where I felt they would belong. In the 1/1 class, I put Joseph R., who scored the highest on the reading readiness test, and as a result of his score on the test and his work in class I felt Joseph did belong in the 1/1 class. Then again, I looked further and Lydia A., who I believe is a very smart girl and who wasn't really working as well as she could in my class, I felt she belonged in the 1/1 class. Lydia scored second highest on the reading readiness test. In the 1/1 class I also put Anita R. Anita is a bit older than the rest of the children, but she has caught on most beautifully to most phases of school work even though she just came to the United States last March. Also, she scored the same as Lydia on the reading readiness test.

Then I looked further and I decided that I would put Robert M. in the 1/1 class. I felt strongly that Robert was by far the best child in my class. Robert did every bit of the work ever assigned. He caught on very, very quickly to all phases of work besides doing his work well, quickly, efficiently, and neatly. Even though on the reading readiness he only scored in the 50th percentile, I felt he really stood out and *I also felt that once you're in a "1" class, unless you really don't belong, you have a better chance. For some reason the "1" class on the grade is really the only class that you could term a "good" class.* [Author's emphasis] So those four children I recommended for the 1/1 class.

Then I went down the line, and for the 1/3 class I picked nine children, really good children who on the whole listened and did their work. Most of them scored in the 50th and 40th percentile on the reading readiness and they were coping with school problems very, very well. In the 1/7 class I put the slower children, and in the 1/9 class, of course, which is Mrs. Gould's, I put all the children that really weren't doing well in schoolwork at all. I think I should tell you some of the children that I placed in that class. First, of course, Alberto. Alberto is still not able to write his name, so he was in that class. Then I put Beatrice, Stella, Pedro, and several others who really were not working as well as the other children in the class.

I know that the other teachers do have a big job before them because whichever class these children are placed in will not have been doing exactly the same work. The children either have much to catch up on or they might review some of the work and the teachers will have to be patient either way. On the whole, I really don't think anyone will have serious discipline problems except perhaps in the 1/1 class where Lydia and Anita have been placed.

The time came when I had to tell the children that I would not be their teacher any more. Well, as young as they are I think that many of them caught on immediately and before I could say anything, faces were very, very long and the children were mumbling, "But I wanted you for a teacher."

That was all I needed! I felt even worse than I felt when I found out that I wouldn't be with them any more. So I continued talking and I told them that it's just something that happens and that I would still be in the school and maybe next year they would get me when they go to the second grade. I told them that I would miss them all, that they would have a lot of fun in their new classes and they would learn a lot. And, of course, I said, "You know all the other teachers. Some of you will get Mrs. Lewis. Some will get Miss Lane, some will get Miss Taylor, and some will get Mrs. Gould."

To my astonishment, Anita kept saying over and over, "But I want you for a teacher. But I want you for a teacher."

I looked around the room. Most of the children were sitting there with very, very long faces. Joseph C. was sitting there with the longest face you could imagine and Robert G. said he didn't want another teacher and all of a sudden Joseph started crying and just didn't stop. He cried all the way out into the hall when we got dressed to go home. I spoke to him softly and said, "Joseph, wouldn't you like Miss Lane for a teacher?" She was standing right near me and finally he stopped crying.

I said goodbye to them and that I would see them all. And that was the end of my class. . . .

. . . Good schools. Poor schools. What is a good school? Is a good school one that is in a good neighborhood, that has middleclass children? Is that a good school? Is a poor school one in a depressed area where you have

Negro and Puerto Rican children? These are common terms that people refer to all the time. They hear your school is on Wolf Street—"Oh, you must be in a bad school."

I don't really think that that is what a good or a bad school is. I think a good school is a school that is well run, has a good administration, has people that work together well, has good discipline, and where the children are able to learn and also, of course, where there are numerous facilities for the children and the teachers. In my estimation a poor or a bad school would be one in which the administration and the teachers do not work together, are not working in the best interests of the children, and where learning is not going on. Also, a poor school is one where you don't have proper facilities. I am not acquainted with many of the public schools and I really can't say that the ones that I know are better or worse. I believe my school is a pretty good school. It isn't in the best neighborhood. There are many, many problems in my school, but on the whole I think that the teachers and the administration work together and I do believe that they are doing the best they can with the problems that are around.

*You have to remember that in a school such as ours the children are not as ready and willing to learn as in schools in middle class neighborhoods.* [Author's emphasis]

## DISCUSSION

Although the human being is born with the capacity to function within a social group, his position within it and the forms of behavior and beliefs appropriate to his particular culture have to be learned. Socialization is the name given to the process by means of which the individual is integrated into his society. It is through this process that the individual adapts to fellow members of his group and is assigned or achieves the various status positions he will assume during his lifetime. These can vary with sex, age, kinship, etc.[1]

Man must do an enormous amount of learning to achieve competency and acceptability in his culture. The process of learning the behavior and beliefs appropriate to the culture and to the position of the individual within it has been termed enculturation.[2] It is through this process that the individual's behavior falls well within the limits of tolerance established by the culture, for the individual internalizes the values and beliefs, becomes possessed of the necessary skills and techniques to function within the society, and becomes capable of adjusting and adapting to his physical and social environment.

---

[1] Melville J. Herskovitz, *Man and His Works* (New York: Alfred A. Knopf, 1949), p. 38.

[2] Ibid., pp. 39–40.

Enculturation proceeds throughout one's lifetime, for although by adulthood one has usually learned the culture so well that he need give it little thought, an individual has continually to learn the behavior and attitudes appropriate to the new situations in which he finds himself. Thus, although already socialized and learned in the ways of the culture as a student in college, the potential teacher must learn principles, methods, and an ideal role in regard to teaching. As a teacher within a school, he or she must learn the appropriate behavior, attitudes, and skills required in the new situation. Much of this learning is conscious. Some of it is not. What is significant is that, while on the job, the teacher is also socialized (i.e., she is integrated into the ongoing society of the school), and, in addition, the teacher is learning the values, beliefs, and attitudes which in reality govern the functioning of the institution.

The saga of class 1/5 illustrates the manner in which one teacher internalized the cultural characteristics of the slum school in which she is working, coming to accept its organization and the prevailing rationale for pupil failure. There are many lessons here for administrators of inner-city schools. If they wish to change the pattern of failure in schools in order to equip inner-city youngsters with the education to enable them to participate equitably in the opportunities provided by American society, they must become increasingly aware of the values and attitudes prevailing in the school milieu, as well as the educational implications of the organizational structure, for these conditions play a crucial role in the education of children.

The teacher of class 1/5 has warm, friendly relations with her youngsters. She respects and admires their abilities and is troubled by what she foresees in the future for them as she surveys the large amount of educational failure by the sixth grade evident in her school.

Very early in her teaching career, however, this new teacher is indoctrinated by a more experienced teacher in the belief, widely held, that the children come from inferior backgrounds and that it is the deficits in their homes—expressed here as being lack of newspapers and parental care— that prevent educational achievement. That the teachers and the school as an institution also operate as agents to ensure the failure of the children is never even implied or understood as a possible cause.

The beginning teacher, in her description of what happens to class 1/5, provides some insight into the genesis of failure that appears to be an almost inevitable consequence for most of the youngsters in the class.

First, their actual instruction should be examined. Early in her career, this new, very sincere teacher is painfully aware of her own deficits as a teacher. Unclear concerning her teaching of so fundamental a subject as reading, she raises serious questions about how effectively she is providing instruction. As yet, she has not internalized the notion that the failure of children stems from gaps in their backgrounds. She is too sensitive concerning her own inadequacies and expresses a desire for professional growth in the teaching of reading. Although no consensus exists concerning reading methodology, the teacher is telling us that there are serious weaknesses in evaluation and feedback, so that she is unable to know what the children have really been taught and have learned.

By the end of the term, however, all this has changed. By that time, the prognosis for failure is positive. The school practically ensures the failure of the children, and the teacher has been socialized to rationalize this in terms of pupil inadequacy.

An examination of the case will give insight into how this takes place. First, as a result of the drop in school register, the principal loses a teacher, which means the loss of a class, leading to the distribution of one class of children among other classes. The principal and the teachers have little control over this phenomenon. They are themselves manipulated by forces outside their direct control. Education budgets, tables of organization, or directions from headquarters, create conditions without regard for the views and advice of those people in closest relation to the children themselves.

A drop in pupil registers would seem to imply the opportunity to provide for a higher adult-pupil ratio and, consequently, the opportunity for more individualized instruction and pedagogical supports for the youngsters and teachers in this school. Instead it led to the loss of a teacher, higher registers, and, perhaps most important, increased time spent by the administrator and his staff on the mechanics of administration rather than on educational supervision—less time spent on professional growth of teachers and on the education of the children. Why one teacher rather than another was released is unclear, though the substitute status and lower rank of the dismissed teacher was probably involved. As a result of this situation, many classes are disrupted, several first-grade class registers increase, time for instruction is lost, and concern is felt by teachers and pupils alike.

Another even more significant clue to possible eventual failure for the children is described in poignant detail by our teacher when she tells how the youngsters in her class will be distributed among the other first-grade classes. All educators have learned about different maturation rates for children, differential rates of learning readiness, and the developmental differences between boys and girls relevant to learning. To determine the educational outcome for youngsters at this early stage of their development, without due provision for understanding of these normal growth variations, would seem to be a travesty of the educational process. Yet here, in the first half of the first grade, a relatively inexperienced young teacher, herself keenly aware of her own deficiencies as an educator, is placed in the position of literally deciding the educational future of her charges. A few are selected for success—"I felt that once you're in a '1' class, unless you really don't belong, you have a better chance. For some reason the '1' class on the grade is really the only class that you would term a 'good' class." Several children are placed in a class labeled "slow." The other youngsters are relegated to a state of limbo, and the middle range does not carry with it the hope of providing a "better chance."

Thus, before these youngsters have completed four months of schooling, their educational futures have been "tracked," for all through the grades the labels of their class placement will follow them, accompanied by teacher attitudes concerning their abilities. Some youngsters are selected very early for success, others written off as slow. The opportunity to move across is limited, for differential teaching occurs and helps to widen the gap between children. In addition, the children too become aware of the labels placed upon them. Their pattern for achievement in later years is influenced by the feelings of success or failure in these early school experiences.

As she reflects upon what a "good" school or a "bad" school is, our teacher continues to include the learning by children as a significant criterion, together with good relations between staff and administration. The children in the school in which she works do not achieve academically. When describing whether or not her own school is "good" or "bad" she stresses the good relations between the administration and the teachers. That the children do not learn does not now seem so important, for ". . . the children are not as ready and willing to learn as in schools in middle-class neighborhoods."

How well the teacher has internalized the attitude that child deficits explain the failure of children to succeed in school. How normal she now considers the administrative upheavals and their effects upon teachers and children. How perfectly ordinary she considers the tracking of youngsters so early in their school years. The teacher of class 1/5 has been socialized by the school to accept its structure and values. She is not likely to effect much change in the prognosis of failure for most of the children in this school, because she has come to accept the very structural and attitudinal factors which make failure nearly certain. In addition, with all the good intentions in the world, she has come to operate as an agent in the process of determining the life chances of the children in her class by distributing them as she does among the ranked classes on the grade.

This teacher came to her position with very positive impulses. She thought highly of her youngsters and was disturbed that, with what appeared to be good potential, there was so much failure in the school in the upper grades. She looked inward for ways in which she might improve her professional effectiveness in order to forestall retardation, and was not repelled by the neighborhood in which she worked. There is every indication that she had the potential of becoming a very desirable teacher of disadvantaged youngsters. However, her impulses were not enough. Unarmed with the strength that understanding the social processes involved might have given her, as well as having little power within the school hierarchy, this young teacher was socialized by the attitudes of those around her, by the administration and by the availability of a suitable rationale to explain her and the school's failure to fulfill ideal roles. As a result she came to accept traditional slum school attitudes toward the children, and traditional attitudes toward school organization as the way things have to be. She gives every indication of being a pleasant, flexible, cooperative young woman to have on one's staff. But at the same time, she has learned to behave and think in a way that perpetuates a process by which disadvantaged children continue to be disadvantaged.

# 21

# The Professional Prestige of Classroom Teachers: A Consequence of Organizational and Community Status*

## HOLGER R. STUB

Ever since the rise of mass education the public school classroom teacher has been faced with a status dilemma,[1] a fact that has contributed to certain problems currently facing American education. The persistent debate over whether the teacher is a professional, the continued preponderance of females in teaching, the large number of persons who leave

* This study was supported by a grant-in-aid from the Faculty Research Committee of Temple University.

[1] This is only a small selection of the large number of works dealing with the status of teachers: Willard Waller, *Sociology of Teaching* (New York: John Wiley & Sons, 1932); Wilbur B. Brookover, *A Sociology of Education* (New York: American Book Co., 1955); Ronald G. Corwin, *A Sociology of Education* (New York: Appleton-Century-Crofts, 1965); Myron Lieberman, *Education as a Profession* (Englewood Cliffs, N.J.: Prentice-Hall, 1956); Mary Vlick, "Historical Status of the Teacher," *Educational Forum*, 22 (March 1958):341–48; Willard E. Goslin, "Forces Undermining Professional Status," *Childhood Education*, 34 (February 1963):272–73; Patrick J. Groff, "The Social Status of Teachers," *Journal of Educational Sociology*, 36 (September 1962):20–25; Donald Walkout, "The Teacher Image in America," *Journal of Higher Education*, 32 (January 1961):31–36; S. Rettig and B. Passamanick, "Status and Job Satisfaction of Public School Teachers," *School and Society*, 87 (March 14, 1959): 113–16; G.G. Gordon, "Conditions of Employment and Service in Elementary and Secondary Schools: Teacher Status and Role Expectations," *Review of Educational Research*, 33 (October 1963):382; Hazel Davis et al., "Economic, Legal, and Social Status of Teachers," *Review of Educational Research*, 33 (October 1963):398–414; National Education Association, *The Status of the American Public School Teacher* (Washington, D.C.: NEA, 1957).

teaching after a short stay, the lower academic abilities of many who became teachers, and inconsistencies in the public attitude toward teaching as an occupational choice are illustrative of the problems involving the teacher's role and status.

A number of underlying social and sconomic factors are involved in these problems of status. Some of these factors are closely related to the organization of the school and its consequences for the status and prestige of the teacher in the community. This paper will attempt to analyze the relationship between the teacher's status within the organized structure of the school and in the community itself.

The following definitions will be used in analyzing the relationship between these two statuses.[2] In general, the concept of status refers to (1) one's position relative to others in a social context, (2) the deference or prestige granted by others within that context. Status is thus defined both in structural and social-psychological terms.[3] The teacher's role will be viewed in terms of two analytically different statuses. Community status will refer to the teacher's status and prestige in the community.[4] An empirical referent of this status involves others' opinions of teaching as an occupation (occupational prestige) and its place relative to other occupations held by community members. The term organizational status will refer to the teacher's position and prestige within the organized structure of the school.[5]

Status "on the job" is a significant determinant of status in the community, in that occupation has become a critical variable in shaping one's social norms, self-definition, and expectations for the behavior of others. Caplow considers occupation crucially important in modern societies; he

---

[2] These definitions are similar to the two types of status relations defined by Burleigh Gardner and David G. Moore, *Human Relations in Industry* (Homewood, Ill.: Richard D. Irwin, Inc., 1955), pp. 103 ff. They distinguish one kind of status involving not only differences in rank, but also the right to give orders (organizational status). The other type of status does not involve this right, but expresses relative rank or superiority and inferiority (community status).

[3] The theoretical basis for the present use of this concept is derived from Linton on one hand, and from Weber on the other.

[4] The concept of community is another ambiguous and difficult term, but hopefully the context of the present paper will provide the necessary referents for this discussion.

[5] Barnard uses a similar distinction in his concept of *functional status*, which is a general attribute and refers to such groups as "different callings, trades, crafts, métiers, division of labor, specialization, and professions." This kind of status does not depend on authority and jurisdiction and is generally what I mean by community status. Scalar status (Barnard's term) is similar to my use of organizational status. It refers to position in an organizational hierarchy wherein amount of formal authority is the criterion of one's position in the structure. According to Barnard, scalar status is "determined by (1) the relationship of superordination or subordination in a chain of command or formal authority and (2) by jurisdiction." See Chester I. Barnard, "Functions and Pathology of Status Systems in Formal Organizations," in William F. Whyte (ed.), *Industry and Society* (New York: McGraw-Hill Book Co., 1946), pp. 48–49.

states that occupation serves "as a measure of a man."[6] A critical aspect of the teacher's occupational role is revealed in the recurrent debate over whether teaching can be called a profession. This issue has important ramifications for the teacher's community and organizational status.

## THE TEACHER AS A PROFESSIONAL

Both teachers and nonteachers are apparently unsure of the teacher's position vis-à-vis traditional professions. A recent survey investigated whether the members of a particular community considered high school teachers as professionals. The results are strongly in the affirmative—over 96 percent of the population views high school teaching as a profession. Nevertheless, other evidence indicates that teaching may not qualify as a profession. For example, frequently those who say they regard teaching as a profession do not seriously consider it as an acceptable occupational choice for their children.[7] This discrepancy may stem, in part, from the fact that most teachers are severely limited in their occupational autonomy and are ignored in the determination of school policy.

> Teachers have virtually no control over their standards of work. They have little control over the subjects to be taught; the materials to be used; the criteria for deciding who should be admitted, retained, and graduated from training schools; the qualifications for teacher training; the forms to be used in reporting pupil progress; school boundary lines and the criteria for permitting students to attend; and other matters that affect teaching.[8]

The lack of status inherent in certain aspects of the teacher's role is further illustrated by the NORC study of occupational prestige. Reiss analyzed the findings from the NORC study and noted that, in contrast to most of the professional or semiprofessional occupations listed in the study, school teaching is most devalued by those with the highest socioeconomic background.[9] Respondents at the lowest socioeconomic level assign the highest percentages of negative evaluations to most of the other occupations in the same category, whereas prosperous and middle-class persons vary slightly one way or the other. Thus, only at the lower socioeconomic levels does teaching have the prestige accorded other professions. However, the greater value assigned by the lower strata to teaching seems to

---

[6] Theodore Caplow, *The Sociology of Work* (Minneapolis: University of Minnesota Press, 1954), p. 31.

[7] Lieberman, *Education*, p. 465.

[8] Corwin, *Sociology of Education*, p. 241.

[9] Albert Reiss, *Occupation and Social Status* (Glencoe, Ill.: Free Press, 1961), pp. 276, 295. Additional data is presented in Robert W. Richy, William H. Fox, and Charles E. Fauset, "Prestige Ranks of Teaching," *Occupations*, 30 (October 1951):33–37.

be based primarily on the fact that this occupation offers a feasible avenue of social mobility for lower class individuals. Its prestige as an occupation is therefore relative to its place in the job market.

The problem of professional status for teachers is intensified by the fact that teachers are trained to view themselves as professionals. But the new teacher quickly learns that there are few rewards for behaving in a manner consistent with his professional training.[10] According to Gerstl,

> the greatest fact of life of teaching is . . . likely to strike as a culture shock: the recognition that the teacher is an employee. The demands of pedagogy must be placed against (and often subservient to) those of bureaucracy —the world of Delany cards, attendance sheets, supply requisitions, toilet passes, and fire drill regulations.[11]

The activities that constitute the teaching occupation occur under circumstances that affect the attainment of professional status. The work of the school teacher is under constant neighborhood and community surveillance. Parents receive continuous information (both accurate and distorted) from their children. Parents must contend with the rules of the school in managing their home life—this is especially true for mothers of elementary school children. However, in return the school does free the mothers from responsibility for their children for a few hours a day. The mothers of a community are some of the key judges of teachers, and it is they who can confer or deny prestige or deference to a given teacher and to teachers generally. When problems arise, mothers are the ones who must be impressed or defended against, depending upon the observer's perspective. Mothers are particularly important since they provide their children with opinions and attitudes about teachers from kindergarten well into junior high school.

The handiwork of the teacher and school is much more visible on a continuous basis than that of other professional occupations. Although visible, the teacher's work is not necessarily understood. Gerver and Bensman point out that the process by which members of an occupation gain recognition as experts is related to social visibility and distance.

> Experts do not arrive in society spontaneously but are the result of a complex process of institutional development, claims for recognition as experts, and the granting of social recognition is the *social visibility* of those claiming expertness and the *social distance* of the conferring groups from the alleged experts. The more distant groups (i.e., those least technically qualified) grant recognition which is based not upon a knowledge of ex-

---

[10] Chandler Washburne, "The Teacher in the Authority System," *Journal of Educational Sociology*, 30 (May 1957):394.

[11] Joel E. Gerstl, "Education and the Sociology of Work," in Donald Hansen and Joel E. Gerstl (Eds.), *On Education—Sociological Perspectives* (New York: John Wiley & Sons, 1967), p. 247.

pert procedures, methods and information, but instead upon the imputed consequences of expert action. . . . The recognition of expertness, then, varies with the social distance of the conferring groups and their criteria of recognition.[12]

In terms of social visibility and distance, teachers apparently occupy a particular place relative to receiving recognition as experts. School teachers are highly visible to almost all the status conferring groups in the community.[13] Although the least educated families may feel socially distant from teachers, their own school experience provides them with a range of information and opinions about teachers, which is not true for other experts in our society. Although many Americans do feel competent to judge some aspects of the teacher's work, they are uncertain about the consequences of the "expert action" of teachers. The traditionally high levels of anti-intellectualism, the strong emphasis on experience, and the attributing of success to one's personal characteristics, makes the teacher's expertness open to question. The so-called "school of hard knocks" has received some of the credit that might otherwise have been accorded the teaching profession. The apparent ineffectiveness of education in bettering the lives of those most socially distant from teachers (the lower socioeconomic strata) does not help to promote high status for teachers.

The recent success of teachers in winning better salaries and working conditions, commensurate with a professional image, has resulted partly from a recognition that the expert actions of teachers may have important consequences. The teacher's community and organizational status has probably been enhanced by a growing awareness of educational achievement as an increasingly critical variable in social mobility.

A client seeking services among the established professions is much freer in his choice of a professional than in education. Consequently, the level of surveillance or visibility of the established professions is decreased. The relative lack of information about the inner workings of law, medicine, and similar professions can facilitate the promotion of illusions, myths, and favorable professional images. However, high visibility prevents public school teachers from utilizing certain kinds of image-enhancing techniques. With respect to gaining status and prestige for teachers, one might argue that educators should not be overly concerned with

---

[12] Israel Gerver and Joseph Bensman, "Toward a Sociology of Expertness," *Social Forces,* 32 (March 1954):226–27.

[13] Teachers "are the sanctioning agents for the young, the guardians of morals, the arbiters of conduct, and it is in this status that they are remembered by all adults from their own childhood. In truth, teachers constitute a kind of conscience in society, and their status is that of the conscience—recognized as fundamentally important, but neglected as much as possible." Frederic W. Terrien, "The Occupational Role of Teachers," *Journal of Educational Sociology,* 29 (September 1955):14–20. See also J.W. Getzels and E.G. Guba, "The Structure and Role Conflict in the Teaching Situation," *ibid.,* p. 30.

informing parents about the latest pedagogical theories and the development of new strategies, such as the "new math." However, if the teacher must rely on parents to augment the educational process, then sufficient information and knowledge to meet educational goals must be shared. There is considerable evidence showing that parental behavior can facilitate the educational process, but whether such behavior includes technical aspects of pedagogy is questionable.

The conditions imposed by lay control of American schools also increase the teacher's difficulties in attaining full professional status. Most public schools are characterized by relatively low tolerance for variation in behavior within the school. A substantial share of the demand for conformity is a result of external pressures for a standardized product. Coser notes that external pressures on a group or organization tend to reduce internal tolerance, a fact which not only affects the student's life, but also narrows the teacher's range of "individual autonomy."[14]

Educators have written and implied that local lay control inhibits the professionalization of school teachers. Intuitively, this seems reasonable, in terms of the school's place in society. The fact that the school system is "open" at the top and bottom makes internal professional controls very difficult to enforce. At the top of the structure are the laymen on the school boards, and at the bottom are the children, who also in a sense, represent the community. Thus, external intrusions at either end of the school structure can potentially be extreme and create conditions of unpredictability. Such a situation can in turn be detrimental to the development of professional norms and values. In general, the school board end of the school hierarchy structure apparently poses less of a threat to the formation of a viable set of internal professional norms and values than we could expect. In a recent article Kerr argues that school boards may actually function more as agencies of legitimation than as controlling and innovating bodies representing the community.[15] School administrations, headed by the superintendent, are apparently not wholly ineffective in coopting school board members. The size and complexity of many school systems place the superintendent and his immediate staff in the position of experts, which implies considerable influence over the lay board. This type of situation can favor the development of professionalism within the school. This situation probably only holds true in relatively large and complex systems.

However, the literature contains some discordant notes on school administration in general and on superintendency in particular. Many books

---

[14] Lewis Coser, *The Function of Social Conflict* (Glencoe, Ill.: Free Press, 1956), p. 103.

[15] Norman D. Kerr, "The School Board as an Agency of Legitimation," *Sociology of Education*, 38 (Fall 1964):34–59.

dealing with the role of the superintendent overlook the fact that the superintendent should function in a social context involving other professionals (i.e., the teaching staff). One recent textbook referred to superintendents with the rather euphemistic title of "status leader." The author found it necessary to justify the use of an authority system headed by the superintendent in the otherwise democratically oriented structure of the American school. The following characteristics were given in describing this authoritative role of "status leader":

1. He is employed by an individual, a board, or a company.
2. He is responsible to his employer for getting defined work done.
3. This work is done by others responsible to him.
4. He is usually chosen by an employer who places him over other workers.
5. His continued employment rests upon the judgment of the employer.
6. His authority comes from his employer.
7. His authority, selection, and continuance are wholly or in major part beyond the control of the group responsible to him.
8. He has a large measure of authority in selecting those who work for him, in determining how their work shall be done, and in determining whether or not they shall remain at work.[16]

These characteristics could just as easily describe the authority position of the executive head of a private corporation; they come close to describing the position of commanding officers of military units. There is no mention either of authority based on expertise or professional training and competence, or of the shared authority and need for consensus implicit in a collegial structure.[17] In one instance the professionalization of superintendents was discussed, but no reference was made to the profession of teaching.[18] Whether this implies that the former are professionals and the latter are not, or that there are two different types of professionals in the public schools was not made clear.

The concern over the professional status of teachers has led some educators to note that such status depends partially on the degree to which teachers participate in the social affairs of the community.[19] However, amount of social participation is probably more a *consequence* than a

---

[16] Van Miller and Willard B. Spalding, *The Public Administration of American Schools* (Yonkers-on-the-Hudson: World Book, 1958), p. 494.

[17] Max Weber, *The Theory of Social and Economic Organization,* translated and edited by A.M. Henderson and Talcott Parsons (New York: Oxford University Press, 1947), pp. 392 ff.

[18] H.A. Moore, Jr., *Studies in School Administration* (Washington, D.C.: American Association of School Administrators, 1957).

[19] L.W. Drabick, "Teacher's Day: Analysis of Professional Role Perceptions," *Educational Administration and Supervision,* 45 (November 1959):329–36; Roy C. Buck, "The Extent of Social Participation Among Public School Teachers," *Journal of Educational Sociology,* 33 (April 1960):311–19.

cause of low status.[20] Promoting community participation to enhance the teacher's status reflects a common approach to certain problems—the treatment of symptoms rather than causes. Other professionals participate in social affairs to the degree determined by their status, particular style of life, and the traditional community expectations regarding social involvement. There is probably a minimum level of necessary social participation for any particular occupational group that effectively claims professional standing. However, there is no one-to-one relationship between high status and participation in community affairs. For example, the type and amount of social participation is substantially different for doctors and scientists, although both areas are associated with high professional status.

## BUREAUCRATIZATION AND THE TEACHER AS A PROFESSIONAL

The status dilemma of the teacher is closely related to the fact that schools, of necessity, have become more bureaucratically organized. According to Corwin, the recent past has seen a dual evolution of professional and bureaucratic principles in education. Despite the development of some aspects of professionalism,

> the employee status of teachers has been reinforced, first by a strong tradition of local, lay control over education, and then by the subsequent growth of complex school systems, which have required more administrative control to maintain coordination.[21]

Bureaucratization is also occurring in medicine and law, but under different circumstances. The professional status of doctors and lawyers was fully established before the onset of bureaucratization and thus had to be fully taken into account in introducing new bureaucratic principles of organization and conduct. As a result, new types of bureaucratic structures have evolved, especially designed for the professional and his activities. In education, however, the new bureaucracies have not been adapted to a teaching corps already possessing full professional rights and responsibilities. For this reason bureaucratic principles have sometimes taken precedence over emerging professional principles among teachers.

Despite many of the presumably negative consequences of bureaucratization for the professions, the process may actually have produced some positive results for the professionalization of teachers. In a recent study,

---

[20] Madaline K. Remmhein, Marth L. Ware, and Jean Flanigan, "Economic, Legal and Social Status of Teachers," *Review of Educational Research*, 28 (June 1958): 242–55.

[21] Ronald G. Corwin, "Professional Persons in Public Organizations," *Educational Administration Quarterly*, 1 (Autumn 1965):4

teachers in school systems defined as high in bureaucratic characteristics report a greater "sense of power" with respect to influencing school policy than do teachers employed in school systems rated low in bureaucracy. The study concludes that "bureaucracy provides the teacher with an understandable and predictable ethos in which to pursue his profession."[22]

Although certain features of bureaucratic structure may aid the process of professionalization, the teacher must gain what has been called "individual authority"[23] in order to qualify as a professional. He must be free to make professional decisions based on his own expert judgment rather than on the basis of directives issued by his superiors in the bureaucratic structure. Such authority is of the collegial type; it is characterized by Goss's discussion of how professional norms function in authority structures within the medical profession:

> When both supervisor and supervised are physicians, the control-oriented behavior of each is largely predetermined by established professional norms and values which both know and accept in advance. Relatively little mutual adjustment of role expectations is therefore required on the part of either person. . . .[24]

## THE STATUS OF THE TEACHER WITHIN THE SCHOOL

Since bureaucratization in the public school has occurred under conditions that deemphasize the professional status of teachers, a hierarchical- rather than collegial-type authority system has developed. This situation is exemplified by the mode of instituting and following rules within the school, as well as by many teachers' perceptions of authority figures.

Systems of rules govern much of the behavior of professionals and employees, but rules that ordinarily apply to professionals are more diffuse and abstract. Regulations for employees are frequently unconditionally binding, whereas those applicable to professionals are stated or perceived as alternatives. Teachers are frequently subject to apparently unconditional rules:

> For example, rules stating that personnel [teachers] may not leave the building until 3:30 and that they may not leave the premises without permission of the administration defines them as employees.[25]

---

[22] Gerald H. Moeller, "Bureaucracy and Teachers' Sense of Power," *School Review*, 72 (Summer 1964):152.

[23] Logan Wilson, *The Academic Man* (New York: Oxford University Press, 1942), p. 73; L. Vrick (Ed.), *Dynamic Administration: The Collected Papers of Mary Parker Follett* (New York: Harper & Bros., 1940), pp. 227–81.

[24] Mary E.W. Goss, "Influence and Authority Among Physicians in an Out-Patient Clinic," *American Sociological Review*, 26 (February 1961):50.

[25] Corwin, "Professional Persons," p. 238.

There is evidence that classroom teachers *view* themselves as employees in a hierarchical and authoritarian structure. In a recent study a teacher is quoted as saying:

> After all, he's the principal, he is the boss, what he says should go, you know what I mean. . . . He's the principal and he's the authority, and you have to follow his orders; that's all there is to it.[26]

Becker characterizes the authority structure of the school as a "small, self-contained system of social control."[27] This small world containing principal and teachers results in a structure more predictable (and hence, more satisfactory) than a structure involving several ranks of teachers along with the administrative ranks of principals and assistant principals. It is implied that this simple two-rank structure protects the teacher and the administrator from lay persons in the community. The major functionary in the protective relationship is the principal. However, the principal often fails to support fully the action of a teacher. In this case, the teacher lacks sufficient authority and prestige to ward off or effectively counter an attack from an offended parent or disturbed citizen.[28]

In many ways the teacher's status position in the school can be compared to that of a foreman in a factory. Like the foreman, the teacher is the "man in the middle," subject to conflicting social demands from above and below. Both teacher and foreman are key functionaries in implementing organizational goals, and both hold positions quite distant from the level of large-scale decision making in the two types of structures. The two occupational roles require the utilization of considerable social skill in interpersonal relations, to gain close cooperation on one hand, and to maintain the status of expert and authority on the other. The teacher and foreman both lack the unambiguous status necessary for maintaining a consistent degree of autonomy, yet both roles demand a measure of independence in order to be effectively fulfilled.

One factor involved in creating these status dilemmas for the teacher is reflected in the conception of power and decision making held by many Americans. Clayton cogently discusses the relationship between the professionalization of teachers and current premises underlying conceptions of power. He refers to Lynd and Galbraith, and states that Americans in general have refused to deal adequately with problems of power. "We Americans," says Professor Lynd,

---

[26] Howard S. Becker, "The Teacher in the Authority System of the Public School," in A. Etzioni (Ed.), *Complex Organization* (New York: Holt, Rinehart, and Winston), p. 46.

[27] Becker, "Teacher in the Authority System," p. 251.

[28] This may be further reflected in the fact that the type of principal is a crucial variable in determining the quality of the school. See Edward Gross, "Sociological Aspects of Professional Salaries in Education," *Educational Record*, 41 (April 1960):137.

have an uneasy awareness that organized power, as we know it and use it, and democracy as we profess it, do not fit well together. And this leaves us for the most part busy with, but reticent about, power.

This orientation seems to result in

the refusal to recognize power while jealously guarding it, the use of euphemisms to disguise the possession of power, the vagueness and equivocation that cover up who is responsible for what, and the consequent exposure of the society as a whole to the risks of legerdemain when the control of power is short circuited. . . . [Consequently,] when power is wielded over others and covered up by equivocation, there is no way to reduce its arbitrary character. It becomes power to manipulate and to sustain the practice of manipulation rather than power to engage in and extend a professional activity.[29]

The decision-making process found in the public school system has suffered from this kind of malaise, at least since the rise of mass education.

## THE STATUS AND AUTHORITY STRUCTURE OF THE SCHOOL

The ambiguity surrounding the professionalization of teachers, the exposure to criticism and intervention because of high visibility and local lay control, the occurrence of bureaucratization before teachers had realized full professional status, and current conceptions of power in American society have all contributed to the development of schools with authority structures inimical to the professionalization of teachers. As noted earlier, teachers have little or no control over most major aspects of the educational process. Power is wielded by ex-teachers who have become administrators, and classroom teachers are virtually powerless as a group. The situation has resulted in a rather drastic polarization of two major groups—teachers versus administrators. This polarity is reflected in the increasing militancy and unionism among teachers in an effort to achieve higher salaries.

This polarity, which has been spurred by the awareness that power lies in teacher solidarity and common action, results partly from the simple two-level status structure of the school. When virtually all the major functionaries in a polarized status structure—namely, teachers—are on the same status level, the *informal* status system assumes added significance. The teacher's lack of opportunity for promotion, as well as the availability of other formal means of recognition for merit and achievement, tends to

---

[29] A. Stafford Clayton, "Professionalization and Problems of Power," *Journal of Teacher Education,* 16 (March 1965):72–73. [The reference made is to Robert S. Lynd, "Power in American Society as Resource and Problem," in Arthur Kornhauser (Ed.), *Problems of Power in American Democracy* (Detroit: Wayne State University Press, 1957), p. 7.]

direct status demands along other lines. This process eventuates in the elaboration of the informal system of relationships found in all organized structures.

In the school the informal system has become the major device for achieving status. Within this informal system status can be achieved, for example, by assignment to a more prestigeful school (i.e., a school that contains students from high-status families). This constitutes a status gain through horizontal movement within the system.[30] Personal contacts and friendships with a high-status teacher, building custodian, principal, superintendent, or school board member can also lead to the influence and privileges symbolic of higher status.

The earlier reference to the positive relationship between schools with a high level of bureaucratization and teachers' "sense of power" illustrates the relationship between bureaucratization and the informal status system in the school.[31] Moeller notes that in low-bureaucracy schools nearly everyone—including teachers, parents, and interested laymen—has equal access to the superintendent, access based primarily on friendship and informality. Such unstructured arrangements tend to devalue access to the top authority as a major avenue of influence, and lend a degree of ambiguity and unpredictability to the authority system. This type of situation can lead to an atmosphere of intrigue and manipulation.

Although a bureaucratized school does not preclude the development of an informal system, it does routinize the degree of access to authority figures. Only individuals with rank (both formal and informal) have ready access to the top executive. Within the more bureaucratically structured school, teachers can ascertain those with rank in the *informal* system by determining who has access to the individuals in authority. By this means, teachers can make some kind of systematic judgment about their own current status and their future prospects for status and influence. The importance of the informal status system results from the lack of a formal system.

According to certain equalitarian ideas, teachers and those in other "dedicated" occupational groups should be unconcerned with matters of status. However, it is quite evident that "nearly all members of formal organizations may be observed to be much preoccupied with matters of status."[32] Reliance on an informal status system is conducive to the wielding of power based on personal and semiprivate dealings among adminis-

[30] Robert E. Herriot and Mary Hoyt St. John, *Social Class and the Urban School* (New York: John Wiley & Sons, 1966), p. 9 [cited from: Bobby J. Chandler, Lindley J. Stiles, and John I. Kitsuse, *Education in Urban Society* (New York: Dodd, Mead & Co., 1962), pp. 3–35]; Helen E. Amerman, "Perspective for Evaluating Intergroup Relations in a Public School System," *Journal of Negro Education*, 26 (1957):108–20; and Hermine I. Popper, *How Difficult Are Difficult Schools?* (New York: Public Education Association, 1959).

[31] Moeller, "Bureaucracy," pp. 153–56.

[32] Barnard, "Function and Pathology," p. 50.

trators, lay people, and individual teachers. As noted earlier, authority systems of such a nature readily lead to the kind of arbitrary and manipulative behavior that are contrary to the type of power wielding inherent in professional and collegial structures.

The status system of an organization provides rewards and incentives, which have, in turn, a direct effect on the problem of variation in abilities among teachers. It is a truism that teachers do not all have equal ability. Although the lay public may have difficulty in assessing the abilities of teachers, other teachers and administrators can evaluate these abilities to some extent, on the basis of shared criteria. The problem of cooperation among persons with unequal ability faces all kinds of complex organizations. Barnard states that

> . . . individuals of superior ability and those of inferior ability can comfortably work together only on a basis of physical or social segregation. If no formal segregation is established, either friction and noncooperation occur or there is spontaneous informal segregation. . . .

Some of the consequences for the individuals concerned are that:

> To be lumped with inferiors in ability seems an unjust withholding of recognition, an injury to the integrity of the person. Their escape from this position will probably be more individualistic than those of inferior abilities who must more often resort to group solidarity. One escape or attempt to escape for the superior individual is to try and organize the group, to adopt a function of leadership, or to dominate without authority. Another is to leave the group. . . .[33]

The lack of variability of status positions for classroom teachers may account partially for the emergence of group solidarity. Solidarity does aid in pressuring school boards; however, it may reflect in part what Barnard characterizes as the mode of response of teachers who cannot adequately meet the demands of organizational roles, as well as of superior teachers seeking informal leadership in school affairs. Escape from the group— leaving the field of teaching altogether—is apparently another response of some potentially superior teachers.[34]

The foregoing discussion underlines the ambiguity of rewards characteristic of the status system of the school. There is evidence that the breadth of the status system ( e.g., the "opportunity for promotion") is an important element in making one school more desirable than another. An analysis of the individual's status situation both inside and outside the organized work structure must consider the relationship between "need"

---

[33] Ibid., pp. 61–62.

[34] Robert L. Thorndike and Elizabeth Hagen, "Men Teachers and Ex-Teachers: Some Attitudes and Traits," *Teachers College Record*, 62 ( January 1961):306–16. This study indicates that of the male teachers and ex-teachers who took aptitude tests for the Air Force in 1943, the ex-teachers were significantly superior to those still in teaching in the areas of mathematics, arithmetic reasoning, and reading comprehension. In addition, the ex-teachers had a 25 percent greater income.

(or motivation) for achievement and the prestige of the occupational role. Research supporting Barnard's assertions indicates that persons with strong motivation for achievement tend to be attracted to activities that can provide an unambiguous indication of their competence.[35] A study of scientists in a large research center shows that recognition and rewards (through promotion and other means) constitute very important incentives, both in fostering further achievement and in job satisfaction.[36] In the field of teaching the criteria of excellence and the system of granting rewards are extremely ambiguous. Since such ambiguity has important consequences for the self-definition of teachers, it implies that those with a strong desire for achievement will find the field unsatisfactory.[37]

Some critical observations can be made in comparing school administrators with teachers. For example, Lieberman notes that

> . . . [salary] differentials between administrators and teachers are greater than the differentials between administrators and practitioners in any other profession. . . . in many professions the differentials either do not exist at all or exist in favor of the practitioners rather than the administrators. Doctors often receive several times the income of their hospital administrators.[38]

At present, there are no opportunities for teachers to attain salaries that are comparable to those of other professionals—unless they abandon the classroom for administrative posts. Since size of salary is an important status symbol, this situation undeniably acts to hinder professionalization among teachers.

## THE STATUS SITUATION OF COLLEGE PROFESSORS VERSUS SCHOOL TEACHERS

In the literature on the status of the teacher, one rarely encounters comparisons of college professors and school teachers, despite the apparent logic for making such comparisons. It is possible that the teacher's perception of the status of the college professor is less favorable than that of the

[35] David C. McClelland et al., *The Achievement Motive* (New York: Appleton-Century-Crofts, 1953); Eugene Burnstein, Robert Moulton, and Paul Liberty, Jr., "Prestige vs. Excellence as Determinants of Role Attractiveness," *American Sociological Review*, 28 (April 1963):213.

[36] Barney G. Glaser, *Organization Scientists: Their Professional Careers* (New York: Bobbs-Merrill, 1964), chaps. 1, 3.

[37] Raymond Kuhler and Wilbert Dipbrze, *Motivational and Personality Factors in the Selection of Elementary and Secondary Teaching as a Career* (Washington, D.C.: United States Department of Health, Education and Welfare, Office of Education, Cooperative Research Project [Syracuse, N.Y.: Syracuse University], 1959). This study indicates that prospective public school teachers do, in fact, exhibit *lower* needs for achievement, autonomy, and change than other professionally directed groups.

[38] Lieberman, *Education*, p. 403.

"free" professions, and thus does not serve as a very desirable model for comparisons. Lieberman comments on the inability of college professors to gain the status honor and attendant privileges (particularly higher income) commensurate with full professional status. He claims that public school teachers can be criticized for being too much like college professors.[39] He is probably right with respect to winning income and developing impregnable professional organizations. However, there is still a great difference in occupational prestige between professors and school teachers—a level of prestige apparently not wholly contingent upon high income.

Some differences in the community status of professors and school teachers are related to differences in the organizational status of both types of teachers. The professor's position in a college or university usually provides a considerable amount of individual autonomy in his performance as teacher, scholar, counselor, surrogate parent, and administrator. He has professional status at the same time that he functions within an organized structure. He has rank *as a professor* within the academic structure, a fact of substantial consequence with respect to such important status criteria as income, tenure, special privileges (e.g., offices, telephones, a private library, etc.), and authority within the decision-making system of the faculty. Part of the professor's status and prestige is based on the fact that the administrative officers of the university or college exercise only limited control over the faculty. Students soon learn that faculty members have important professional prerogatives, especially when the students try to bring administrative pressure to bear, or when they see that important decisions are made by committees of faculty members. Of course, having a few intellectual celebrities on a faculty contributes both to organizational and community status.

Compared with that of the public school, the status system (or reward and incentive system) of the college is structurally similar to the reward systems used in dealing with other professionals within complex organizations. It provides the incentives asociated with the "opportunity for promotion." Many lawyers, clergymen, "organizational" scientists, and professional experts working in government, church bureaucracies, and industrial organizations function within structures that provide a range of rank and status differences, based on merit and achievement.

The lack of infallible criteria for measuring teaching ability in public schools[40] and colleges is not sufficient reason to eliminate all other criteria of teacher role performance in the two educational settings. The common

[39] Lieberman, *Education*, pp. 506 ff.

[40] Walter H. Worth, "Can Administrators Rate Teachers?" *Canadian Administration*, 1 (October 1961):1–6; A.S. Barr, "Wisconsin Studies of the Measurement and Prediction of Teacher Effectiveness, Summary of Investigation," *Journal of Experimental Education*, 30 (September 1961):5–156.

argument for automatic salary increases based on time in service and number of graduate credits apparently grows out of the lack of precision in judging teaching merit. This argument has some validity, but it should not exclude using imprecise criteria for judging teaching ability *plus* criteria for evaluating additional important aspects of teachers' roles. If teachers are to assume professional rights and privileges, some of them must lead others, develop new methods and techniques, write new textbooks, conduct educational experimentation and research, administer supplementary programs, select appropriate books and teaching aids, determine pupil composition of classes and special groupings, take on extracurricular activities (which must be done by persons with talent rather than by those who primarily need additional money), and be involved in numerous other nonclassroom *teaching* functions.

The argument for eliminating all criteria for judging and rewarding merit is based primarily on the real and/or apparent capriciousness of some school boards and administrators in dispensing rewards in the past, as well as on the difficulties inherent in developing an equitable reward system in large, complex school systems. The obvious hiatus in income, prestige, and authority between school administrators and teachers is an important factor in mobilizing teachers to demand (and in some instances to effect) a reward system that prevents certain kinds of inequities. But, in this process another inequity is introduced—namely, that merit and achievement cannot be adequately rewarded.

Clearly, the types of reward systems found among professionals in many large organizations, including colleges and universities, are rarely observed in the public schools. This difference apparently has important implications for the status dilemmas that have plagued public school teachers for a long time. Barnard emphasizes the use of a status system in developing incentives and responsibility. He states that

> the scarcity of effective incentives calls for the use of many kinds of incentives; and their wise use requires, especially in larger organizations, their systematic use.

The only status system that differentiates superior and inferior teaching performance in the contemporary public school is an informal reward system, which, by its very nature, cannot be systematically used to provide incentives. Formal status provides

> . . . prestige for its own sake, as a reinforcement of the ego, as security for the integrity of the person. . . . a status system is a strong and probably an indispensable developer of the sense of responsibility and therefore, of stability and reliability. . . . the function of status in creating and maintaining dependable behavior is probably indispensable.[41]

All of these qualities are fundamental to an effectively functioning school.

[41] Barnard, "Function and Pathology," pp. 68–69.

## CONCLUSIONS

The previous discussion suggests that the present narrow, essentially two-level, status structure of the American public school is inadequate for the further development of teaching as a profession. A change in the status system could have a number of important consequences for the teacher's organizational and community status. A considerable body of theory and research indicates that the teacher's status, both in the school and community, would be indirectly enhanced by an expansion of the internal status arrangements of the school. This expansion would eliminate identical official rank for all classroom teachers and establish a variety of official ranks. The educational literature provides some support for this approach.[42] However, the most relevant and available model of such an existing status system is to be found in American universities and colleges. It is possible that ranks comparable to instructor, assistant professor, associate professor, and professor could be introduced into the public school structure. For example, the following labels might be used: associate teacher (noncertified), teacher (beginning certified teacher), career teacher (major category of experienced teachers with tenure), and master teacher (those with great teaching abilities and other special skills).

At this point we can briefly explore some of the possible practical consequences of expanding the status structure of the school to include several official levels of status and of developing a concomitant wider range of rewards.

1. An increase in the range of statuses might stimulate the development of better criteria for determining the worth and competence of classroom teachers. Currently, seniority and college credits are the major criteria for granting the rewards of small salary increases and/or transfer to a high-status school.

2. Providing a wider range of opportunity for promotion and achievement would put teaching more on a par with the other professions, and help to attract and retain a greater number of the most competent and ambitious college graduates.

3. An expanded status system would probably decrease the use of horizontal mobility as a major avenue for gaining status, and thus facilitate a more equitable distribution of teacher talents throughout a given school system. Real opportunities for promotion might help to eliminate current demands for "combat pay" for teaching in difficult schools. As an alternative, the administration could offer promotions at a faster rate for teachers who could successfully meet the challenges of the more problematic schools.

---

[42] Max R. Goodson, "Differentiating the Profession of Teaching," *School and Society*, 86 (May 24, 1958):239–40; Edward Gross, "Sociological Aspects of Professional Salaries in Education," *Educational Record*, 41 (April 1960):130–37. Gross states that salaries should be determined by merit, which implies a system of ranking.

4. A change in the ranking system could provide the teacher with a choice of behavior in deciding how best to earn rewards for his work. Most organizations manned by professionals (hospitals, universities, clinics, research laboratories, etc.) specify several different kinds of activities that can lead to higher rank *without* completely changing one's major function (i.e., leaving the classroom, in the case of teachers).

5. A system with a range of statuses more comparable to that used in colleges and universities might help to close the status gap between teachers and professors.

6. Laymen on the school board, as well as parents of children in or out of school, have no really adequate way to judge a teacher's merits. A ranking system might provide a useful, although sometimes imperfect, criterion.

7. The development of a more formal and visible ranking system for classroom teachers could bring the decision-making process more into the open, or at least under scrutiny in the manner described by Professor Lynd in his discussion of "participative power."[43]

8. A ranking system among teachers implies that high-ranking teachers would evaluate their lower ranking professional peers in deciding on promotions, etc.[44] Although such a system does not guarantee the wisest and best judgment, it is probably superior to placing merit judgments exclusively in the hands of bureaucratically oriented administrators.

9. The suggested system of ranks might contribute to the conditions necessary for legislating increased salaries for teachers. If through an expanded ranking system the teacher could gain more prestige both inside and outside the school, the need for higher salaries might be more readily recognized by the lay public.

10. Similarly, such a system might also lead to a greater use of other symbols of rank and privilege than size of salary. Although this topic is unpopular with equalitarian-oriented teachers, it appears nevertheless to be an important one. There is considerable impressionistic evidence supporting the idea that private offices, telephones, parking spaces, and freedom of movement constitute important status symbols for the professional, without which the teacher has difficulty in claiming professional status.

A number of these possible consequences of an expanded status system in the public school can be empirically tested. The establishment of schools organized in a manner which would allow such empirical evaluation would be of utmost importance for the future of the teaching profession and, in turn, the public school.

---

[43] Lynd, "Power in American Society," p. 7.

[44] Such a system of evaluation would obviously be very difficult to implement in many large urban school systems. However, current attempts at decentralization, utilizing, for example, the "house plan" (which is being considered in the Philadelphia school system), which virtually establishes smaller schools within the large urban high school, might ultimately make collegial evaluation a feasible aspect of the status and reward system.

# part SEVEN

# Higher Education

Higher education in America has evolved from a small and highly specialized educational effort to a mammoth diversified establishment. The early colleges were perceived to have relatively few clear-cut functions—to train acceptable clergymen and provide a liberal education for gentlemen. Since the early days of Harvard, Yale, and Brown, the colleges and universities have increased to over 2,000 in number, and provide specialized training in almost all conceivable scholarly disciplines and occupational specialties. The proliferation of institutions of higher education has to a great extent been due to the many new and diverse social, economic, and political functions they have performed.

An important social function of the college or university is the key role it plays in status mobility and status retention or stability for large segments of the American population. The children of the immigrants in the great migration from Europe of 1890 to 1910 provided early signs of a trend involving higher education as a significant element in upward mobility for some of the new Americans. The large urban universities, particularly of the great metropolitan centers of New York, Boston, Philadelphia, and Chicago, along with the land-grant universities of the Middle West, became the educational vehicles for upward mobility and occupational education. A subsequent increase in college enrollments resulted from the G.I. Bill of Rights of World War II. This large-scale educational subsidy brought a new social stratum into American colleges. Boys whose families had not dreamed of seeing their sons in college were suddenly confronted with a chance for a free college education. Thus, the place of higher education as a prominent factor in the social and economic mobility of large numbers of American males has now reached full awareness in our society. Many believe that attendance in college is so important in

367

determining one's life chances that it ought to be the right of everyone to have easy access to a college or university. And states like California and New York are allocating millions to try to reach this goal.

The changes in attitude toward higher education have been further stimulated by what C. Wright Mills referred to as the decline of the "old middle classes."[1] These social strata were comprised of small- to medium-sized retailers, entrepreneurs, and the like. An important element in the family structure of the old middle classes was that the family business was passed on to the son or son-in-law. Therein the family possessed a legacy of economic and social value that could be inherited by succeeding generations. This resulted in stability and continuity in the style of life for most middle-class families.

In contrast, the "new middle classes" are comprised primarily of white-collar workers, executives, and others whose employment is within large bureaucratic structures—they are organization men. For these strata of the population the only effective legacy (if it can be defined as a legacy) a family can provide is the economic resources needed for gaining a higher education, plus, of course, the norms and values that lead to the motivations necessary for success in school. In an age of bureaucracy few can inherit either a business or enough wealth to insure the continuity and class stability of the family for succeeding generations. Each new generation must find its own place in the bureaucratized world of business and government. This apparent fact has revolutionized attitudes toward higher education among the middle strata of the United States. For all those seeking social mobility or status maintenance from one generation to the next, one or more college degrees have become critical goals. How college functions for those who fail to get degrees is the subject of one of the papers in this section.

The important changes in the social and economic functions of higher education are closely related to the great expansion in size of college student populations and those who operate the educational establishment. The aforementioned G.I. Bill of Rights brought a flood of students into college. What appeared to some as a temporary upsurge in student ranks has become accepted as normal since the 1950s. The new strata that were brought in as a result of the G.I. Bill, the apparent need for education in climbing the social ladder, and the technical demands of a bureaucratically organized industrial state, have brought not only new students but new and diverse courses, curricula, research institutes, and thoroughly transformed some of the older traditional features of the academic community.

From a certain point of view, attendance at college may function as an initiation rite for considerable numbers of American youth. Riesman and Jencks state that:

---

[1] C. Wright Mills, *White Collar* (New York: Oxford University Press, 1951).

In general, what a college does is to "nationalize" the student, taking him out of his ethnic, religious, geographic, and social parishes, and exposing him to a more cosmopolitan world in which the imagination is less restricted by preconception and ignorance.[2]

It has been pointed out that "emancipation from the older generation" takes place at colleges of all levels of excellence.[3] The lunch-counter sitins were devised and carried out by students from Negro colleges, Negroes who saw the old order as not only an anachronism but an insult to human dignity.

The colleges also serve a decided economic function in postponing the annual entry into the labor market of thousands of young people. During this postponement some are kept out of the labor force for many years: for example, girls who marry before or immediately after the baccalaureate and then start to raise families. College attendance allows the young male to mature while he is being tested and sifted into either a discipline or a vocational field where he can be trained for a place in the national economic structure. In a period of decreasing blue-collar jobs and expanding semiprofessional and professional white-collar jobs, the colleges and universities have functioned to facilitate the transition in the demands of the national labor market. The college, as the locus of initiating rites, aging and maturing, marriage market, and some time devoted to liberal learning and intellectual development, appears to be functional in providing social types who can partially, at least, meet the demands of a rapidly changing society.

The relatively substantial period of time devoted to college during the formative years of youth has led to the formation of collegiate subcultures. Although the subcultural element may vary from coast to coast, the themes are essentially the same. The greatest difference among these subcultures is probably found between the small rural residential college and the large urban university. Although relatively little is known of the college subculture, it is evident that the norms and values that arise and are perpetuated by the student subculture are an important factor in determining the nature of relationships between students ( e.g., upper and lower classmen ), faculty and students, and students and adults outside of the collegiate community. Much of what the faculty may wish to achieve in certain areas of persuasion and the dissemination of ideas can be greatly hindered or enhanced by the nature of the subculture. At large universities many administrators and faculty members know little or nothing about the student subculture, the informal networks of communication, or the characteristics

---

[2] David Riesman and Christopher Jencks, "The Viability of the American College," in Nevitt Stanford (Ed.), *The American College: A Psychological and Social Interpretation of the Higher Learning* (New York: John Wiley & Sons, 1962), p. 77.

[3] Ibid., p. 77.

of student leaders. Consequently, many attempts to facilitate communication and learning fail or are only minimally successful.

It has been obvious for some years that a substantial number of the largest universities have been beset by the problems that follow the bureaucratization of many aspects of college administration. Universities have become gigantic corporate structures with payroll, investment, and procurement functions that dwarf many large businesses. This has brought the academician face-to-face with the executive-manager types needed to manage such large enterprises, as well as their bureaucratically organized staff, clerical, and maintenance personnel. Large universities are currently in a period in which the faculties and administrations are competing for power in determining the major policies within the university structure.

During the past five to ten years the most dramatic area of growth in higher education has been in the great increase in community colleges. This development has been predominantly in the public sector of higher education. Most of these two-year colleges have been identified as county or city colleges. The major impetus behind the rapid growth was the philosophy that everyone should have access to at least two years of college, located such that the vast majority of students could live at home and commute to the campus; this is an aspect of the general attempts at equalizing access to higher education. Although the community college movement is not a direct response to the recent escalation of costs in higher education, it has served to blunt the impact for some elements in the communities in which the new colleges are located.

Although the sharply rising costs are closely related to inflation, there are a number of more important causal factors present within the structure of higher education itself. The continuous overall growth in higher education following the boom period of post war G.I. enrollments and the accompanying federal funding brought with it new expectations and desires on the part of trustees, administrators and faculty in the nation's colleges. Hundreds of four-year colleges, many of which were teacher training institutions, responded to the growing demands for liberal arts courses and curricula by adding many new faculty, study concentrations, departments and even new colleges. This expansionism led to the ultimate goal of gaining university status. Dozens of new large universities have come into being since the 1950s. The drive toward this new higher status demanded the addition of scarce resources—a situation that invariably drives up costs. Scholars with established reputations, new facilities such as libraries and laboratories, graduate schools, multi-purpose computers, research institutes, funds for graduate assistantships, plus a vast number of supporting personnel had to be acquired in meeting the criteria for university status. The established universities have driven costs up by actively competing for the best qualified faculty, administrators, students, and technical personnel.

The social consequences of the Viet Nam War not only helped to create the student protest and unrest of the late 1960s, but also forced colleges and universities to commit some of their financial resources toward bringing in more minority group members (blacks and Puerto Ricans). Since many of these new students had gained their elementary and high school education in deficient inner city schools, money had to be allocated to support facilities such as tutorial programs and special remedial courses. Active recruiting and financial aid programs have greatly increased the proportions of minority students, particularly in the large public urban universities.

Since the official ending of the American involvement in the Viet Nam War college enrollments have begun to decline. Though partly related to the bringing home of the troops, ending of the draft, the high costs, disillusionment with higher education and the declining numbers of 17–24 year olds, are primarily responsible for the change. Some of the places left vacant by the decline in "college age" students have been filled by young adult men and women and middle aged women who find college work interesting and useful in pursuing their occupational goals. New administrative units with labels like "Continuing Education for Women" (C.E.W.) have been formed to meet the academic and social needs of the older women in the student body. These, like similar units for minority students, have added a new dimension to student affairs on the large campuses.

Despite the large-scale changes and the challenge posed by higher education, as in primary and secondary education, sociologists have been slow to conduct studies of colleges and universities. The apparent importance of the collegiate period in the lives of an ever-increasing segment of the population is, however, stimulating added interest and new investigations are in the making.

# 22

# The Triumph of Academic Man*

## CHRISTOPHER JENCKS and DAVID RIESMAN

It would take a long book to describe the changes in American society that led to the establishment of national institutions and of what seems, at least in comparison to earlier times, to be a relatively homogenous upper middle class culture. The underlying factors were probably technological, but this should not be interpreted in a narrow sense. Industrial technology (e.g., the assembly line) played some part, forcing many enterprises to reorganize so as to achieve economies of scale. But this was by no means a uniform need or trend. Industrial technology in the narrow sense may have led to the creation of a Ford Motor Company, but it did not account for General Motors and still less for the Chase Manhattan Bank or General Dynamics. These were products of what Kenneth Boulding and others have called the organizational revolution, which enabled powerful individuals to exercise effective control over larger and larger numbers of people. This revolution depended on technology (the typewriter, the telephone, now the computer), but in a very different way than the industrial revolution of earlier vintage. There is no clear evidence that the large organizations created in this way were more efficient than the smaller enterprises they usually supplanted, or that they served the public better. All that can be said is that they were not conspicuously less efficient. Their spread must probably be explained in other ways. The agglomeration of power and accommodation of interests within the framework of a single institution inevitably appealed to those in a position to dominate that institution. If such organizations were not egregiously in-

---

* From: Alvin C. Eurich, (Ed.) *Campus 1980: The Shape of the Future in American Education* (New York: Dell Publishing Company, 1968), pp. 92–115. Reprinted by permission.

competent compared with smaller ones and if the ideological and legal checks on their growth were weak, they were bound to grow simply because their leaders had more power and resources available than anyone else. The ability of large businesses to retain income and thus free themselves from money-market control has facilitated their ability to grow by their own rather than Wall Street's devising.

There were, of course, many other factors involved in the establishment of overarching national institutions: the closing of the frontier and, later, the end of migration, the decline of sectarianism and religious fervor, the rise of a national market for both jobs and goods, the emergence of national magazines and, more recently, radio and television, the growth of the national government as a major force in people's lives, the unifying effect of foreign wars. These changes were accompanied and intensified by changes in the dominant political ideology of American society, in family structure and child rearing, in the character of relationships between individuals, and in individuals' self-perception. The cumulative effect of these changes appears to have been the destruction of the 19th-century Jacksonian world, in which every dissident could cut loose from his fellows and go into business for himself. The major conflicts and concords of 20th-century America were shaped within a complex of large, firmly established, loosely interrelated institutions.

Or so it seems. Actually, it might be somewhat more accurate to say that the old Jacksonian world has been overshadowed rather than destroyed. There is, after all, still an enormous amount of small business in America, both in the narrow economic sense and in the larger social sense. The evidence is not clear, but it may actually be easier to start a small business today than it was a hundred years ago, and the prospects of success, while far from bright, may be no worse than they were a century ago. On the other hand, there can be no doubt that the overall economic picture has been radically altered by the fact that the bulk of the nation's business is now done by big corporations, and that most young people considering business careers now choose to work for these corporations rather than take the risk of striking out on their own. A similar line of argument could be developed in other areas. The dissident clergyman who wants to start his own denomination has clearly not disappeared from American life; on the contrary, the number of small fundamentalist sects seems continually to grow. What *has* happened is that the big, affluent, highly organized denominations play a much larger role than they did in the Jacksonian era. Analogous changes have taken place in other areas in American life. The net result is probably not an absolute decline in opportunities for independent entrepreneurship but only a relative decline, and a parallel rise in opportunities for advancement through established institutions.

The fact that so much of the old Jacksonian world has survived right down to the present time makes it extremely difficult to date with any accuracy the changes we are describing. Historians and people generally are always torn between looking for watersheds and looking for continuities. Laurence Veysey has argued to us that the coming of the railroad was the most important break between the earlier pluralist and loosely federated America and the later, more centralized, unified, and industrialized one. In some respects the Civil War served as a catalyst for changes that had begun earlier. It both symbolized and facilitated a shift of emphasis from the second to the first word in "United States." Yet even today this shift is incomplete, its resolution depending on the nature of the issue, the local as well as the national political climate, and the kinds of deterrents local, state, and federal institutions possess.

Whatever the causes or timing of the change, few would deny that established national institutions play a much larger role today than they did a century ago and that their dominance is likely to increase. The character of American life is in good part determined within such diverse and sporadically conflicting enterprises as the Chase Manhattan Bank and the Treasury Department, the Pentagon and General Dynamics, the Federal Courts and the National Council of Churches, CBS and *The New York Times*, the State Department and the Chamber of Commerce, the Ford Motor Company and the Ford Foundation, Standard Oil and Sun Oil. It is not determined to anything like the same extent by small businessmen, independent professionals, or eccentric millionaires. This does not, of course, mean that farmers, doctors, or Texas oilmen are without influence. It does mean that they exercise influence through organizations like the Farm Bureau and the American Medical Association, and that they exercise influence mainly on other large institutions rather than directly on individuals. Institutions of this kind have in some cases crowded smaller and more marginal competitors entirely off the stage. This is the case, for example, with national news magazines and automobile manufacturers, to take two dissimilar cases. In other enterprises, such as local newspapers and home construction, small entrepreneurs can still break in. In yet others, such as intellectual quarterlies and fashion design, off-beat individuals can sometimes find a niche. Still, it seems fair to say that established national institutions set most of the ground rules for both stability and change in contemporary America.

The mere existence of well-established institutions does not, however, tell us anything about their management and control. The late C. Wright Mills used to argue that established institutions of this kind were controlled by a small group of men who had been to the same schools, shared the same values, and manipulated the rest of society to suit their own needs.[1] One of the authors of this essay earlier argued the contrary, sug-

---

[1] See especially *The Power Elite* (New York: Oxford University Press, 1956).

gesting that the activities of these institutions are subject to the veto of a wide variety of vested interests both within each institution and within the larger society.[2] Both of us still take this view. While initiative often comes from the top, this is by no means always the case—especially if the top is taken to mean boards of trustees and directors as against top administrators and professionals.

There are, of course, variations from one institution to another. In general, control over organized violence is in fewer hands than control over capital, and control over capital in fewer hands than control over ideas. The Federal Bureau of Investigation is more centralized than the State Department, but both are more centralized than the Office of Economic Opportunity or the Department of Urban Affairs. There are similar variations in the private sector. Texas oil tycoons exercise more personal control over their empires than do the Rockefellers over theirs. But almost any profit-making corporation is more completely managed from the top down than any church, university, or professional association.

Nonetheless, even the managers of the most centralized organizations, public and private, believe they have little room for maneuver. They feel hemmed in by rivals for power within their organization, by competitive organizations, by their prospective clients, by their lawyers and their boards of directors (or fellow directors), and even by their subordinates. The latter exercise their power in many ways that deserve more attention than they have gotten. Boards of directors sometimes go along with the company president because they have no ready replacement and because they fear he may take another job if he is not given his head. President Kennedy ordered resumption of nuclear testing in 1962 because, among other things, scientists threatened to leave the weapons laboratories if their hardware was not tried out. And, of course, as we shall see in more detail later, university trustees and administrators are constantly readjusting both the means and the ends of higher education so as to attract eminent scholars to their institutions.

We hope this view of America will be reflected in our rhetoric. We have chosen to speak of "established institutions," not of "the establishment."[3] We see established institutions as the framework and battleground within which most changes in the American system are now worked out, but we

---

[2] See David Riesman, with Reuel Denney and Nathan Glazer, *The Lonely Crowd* (New Haven: Yale University Press, 1950), Chapter XI. For further discussion of the difference between Mills and Riesman, see Riesman's preface to the Yale University Press paperback of *The Lonely Crowd*, 1961.

[3] It is interesting to note that the term "establishment," carried to America from England, was originally used in the way we use the term "established institutions." It applied to the Church of England and was then extended to include the Civil Service. Only in recent years has it been aimed at individuals rather than institutions, becoming a synonym for something like Mills' "power elite." See Hugh Thomas, Ed., *The Establishment* (London: Anthony Blond, 1959), especially the essay by Henry Fairlie.

do not see America as ruled by an interlocking directorate or clique. Established institutions are a mixed bag, and their ascendancy does not fully define either the character of modern American life or the expectations and aspirations of the young people who will live and work within them. Yet the hegemony of these institutions does exclude some possibilities and encourage others.

To begin with, the sources of differentiation in American life are changing. The old 19th-century divisions between Irish and Yankee, Baptist and Episcopalian, North and South, country and city seem to be losing their significance. Even the struggles between Negroes and whites and between Catholics and non-Catholics, while certainly far from settled, strike us as legacies of a vanishing past rather than as necessary features of the contemporary American system. This system is increasingly meritocratic, in Michael Young's sense of that term.[4] It tries to divide people according to competence, interests, and achievement rather than according to origin. (Background and competence are very much related, as the example of Negro failure to meet "objective" white standards indicates. But the correlation is far from perfect.) While there are still plenty of exceptions to the general meritocratic rule, and plenty of reasons for ambivalence about its increasing acceptance, it seems to us the wave of the future.

The rise of meritocracy brings with it what we will call the national upper-middle-class style: cosmopolitan, moderate, somewhat legalistic, concerned with equity and fair play, aspiring to neutrality between regions, religions, and ethnic groups. Not everyone who has money, power, or visibility in America subscribes to this set of ideals even in theory, much less in practice. There are many who take a narrower and more overtly self-interested view of the world, especially among those who have only recently climbed to within hailing distance of the top. Nor do these attitudes affect all aspects of life equally: men who think America has dealt unfairly with Negroes may, for example, see no comparable source of regret in America's treatment of the Vietnamese. Nonetheless, we would argue that the ethic we are describing, like the institutions that encourage it, is growing stronger rather than weaker.

These changes in the character of American society were inevitably accompanied by changes in higher education. The most basic of these changes was the rise of the university. This had many consequences. College instructors became less and less preoccupied with educating young people, more and more preoccupied with educating one another by doing scholarly research that advanced their discipline. Undergraduate education became less and less a terminal enterprise, more and more a preparation for graduate school. The result was that higher education ceased

---

4 See *The Rise of the Meritocracy, 1870–2033* (New York: Random House, 1959); and see discussion in Riesman, "Notes on Meritocracy," *Daedalus*, June 1967.

to be a marginal, backward-looking enterprise shunned by the bulk of the citizenry. Today it is a major growth industry, consuming about two percent of the gross national product, directly touching the lives of perhaps four percent of the population, and exercising an indirect effect on the whole of society.

The rise of the university has, of course, been gradual rather than sudden. The Civil War can again be taken as the first watershed. The first Ph.D. was awarded in 1861 by Yale. The year 1869 saw the inauguration of Charles Eliot as President of Harvard and the opening of Cornell under Andrew White. Yet it was not until the 1900s that anything like a modern university really took shape in America.[5] Perhaps the most important breakthroughs were the founding of Johns Hopkins and Clark as primarily graduate universities. Eliot's success in instituting the elective system at Harvard was also important, both in its own right and because it facilitated the assemblage of a more scholarly and specialized faculty. The 1890s saw further progress, with the founding of Chicago, the reform of Columbia, and the tentative acceptance of graduate work as an important activity in the leading state universities. This was also the period when national learned societies and journals were founded and when knowledge was broken up into its present departmental categories (physics, biology, history, philosophy, and so forth), with the department emerging as the basic unit of academic administration. Medicine and law also became serious studies of graduate study at this time, with Johns Hopkins leading the way in medicine and Harvard in law.

By World War I two to a dozen major universities had emerged and, while the number has grown slightly since then, the changes have been slow.[6] These universities have long been remarkably similar in what they encourage and value.[7] They turn out Ph.D.s who, despite conspicuous exceptions, mostly have quite similar ideas about what their discipline covers, how it should be taught, and how its frontiers should be advanced.

---

[5] For a brilliant, erudite, and comprehensive account of this development see Laurence Veysey, *The Emergence of the American University* (Chicago: University of Chicago Press, 1965).

[6] If we arbitrarily define a major university as one that turns out more than one percent of the nation's Ph.D.s each year, we find that 22 universities met this test in the period 1926–1947. By 1962 the number had risen to 30. (The absolute number of Ph.D.s needed to meet the criterion had quintupled.) Analyzing the problem another way, the dozen largest producers of Ph.D.s accounted for 55 percent of all Ph.D.s between 1926 and 1947, compared with 36 percent in 1962. See Allan M. Cartter, Ed., *American Universities and Colleges* (Washington: American Council on Education, 1964), pp. 1263–5.

[7] For evidence on this point, see Allan M. Cartter, *An Assessment of Quality in Graduate Education* (Washington: American Council on Education, 1966). The extraordinarily high degree of consensus about the relative standing of departments in all academic fields suggests that the standards used to evaluate departments must be quite uniform. Rankings over time also show remarkable stability.

(This does not mean that there are *no* differences of opinion on these matters within the academic profession. It only means that, when contrasted with trustees, administrators, parents, students, or the present authors, the outlook of Ph.D.s in a given discipline seems quite uniform. Not only were these men like-minded at the outset, but they have established machinery for remaining like-minded. National and regional meetings for each academic discipline and subdiscipline are now annual affairs, national journals publish work in every specialized subject, and an informal system of job placement and replacement has come into existence. The result is that large numbers of Ph.D.s now regard themselves almost as independent professionals like doctors or lawyers, responsible primarily to themselves and their colleagues rather than their employers, and committed to the advancement of knowledge rather than to any particular institution.

These attitudes were greatly strengthened by World War II and its aftermath. Not only in the Manhattan Project, but in other less glamorous ones, academic scientists helped contribute to the war effort, and, for this and other reasons, a dramatic increase in federal support for academic research ensued. This support soon became available not just in the physical sciences but in the biological and social sciences as well. In recent years Washington has even begun to put small sums into the humanities. Unlike previous support for universities, these federal grants and contracts are for all practical purposes given to individual scholars or groups of scholars rather than to the institution where they happen to work. More often than not, if a man moves to a new institution his federal grants are transferred, too. Not only that, but these federal grants are made largely on the basis of individual professional reputation and competence, with only minimal consideration of an institution's location, sectarian ties, racial composition, or whatever. The result has been to enhance further the status of the academician, who is now a prime fund-raiser for his institution. Since the amount of research support grew much faster than the number of competent researchers, talented men were soon in very short supply and commanded rapidly rising salaries. They were also increasingly free to set their own working conditions. The result has been a rapid decline in teaching loads for productive scholars, an increase in the ratio of graduate to undergraduate students at the institutions where scholars were concentrated, the gradual elimination of unscholarly undergraduates from these institutions, and the parallel elimination of unscholarly faculty.

The professionalization of university professors brought conflict on many fronts from the very start. Late 19th- and early 20th-century academic history is replete with battles in which the basic question was whether the president and trustees or the faculty would determine the shape of the curriculum, the content of particular courses, or the use of particular books. The professors lost most of the battles but won the war.

Today faculty control over these matters is rarely challenged, and conflict usually centers on other issues. The faculty, for example, have sought the right to choose their colleagues. While they have not usually won this right in the formal sense of actually making appointments themselves, their recommendations are sought at all reputable colleges and universities. Faculty committees are, it is true, sometimes overruled. Occasionally this is because the colleague group has rejected a notably popular teacher whose publications may not meet the standards of the guild as locally defined. Sometimes this is because a capable scholar has aroused the Philistines by, in one epoch, backing oleomargarine over butter, or today Ho Chi-minh over General Ky. Public universities are in this respect somewhat more vulnerable than private ones, holding quality constant, because of their dependence on the local legislature; but even elected state-university trustees are seldom eager to force issues of academic freedom into the open. As long as faculty members stick to problems defined by their disciplines, they are not apt to run into public controversy except in the most provincial milieus. And while administrators or trustees sometimes reject faculty recommendations, they almost never foist their own candidates on an unwilling faculty. The faculty has also sought to apply to the selection of undergraduates the same meritocratic standards that have long been used to select graduate students. Here again they have largely won the day, although marginal exceptions (geographic distribution, alumni sons, faculty sons, etc.) still stir sporadic controversy. The faculty has also sought some voice in choosing top administrators and in this, too, it has been increasingly successful. Once chosen, these administrators have broad powers to make policy (in the name and with the consent of the trustees). But even here a *unified* faculty has an informal veto at most universities and colleges.

It is important to know clearly what these victories mean. College professors have not for the most part won significant *formal* power, either individually or collectively, over the institutions that employ them. On paper the typical academic senate is still a largely advisory body whose legal jurisdiction is confined to setting the curriculum and awarding degrees. Departments, too, have little *formal* power, except sometimes over course offerings and requirements. Ultimate control mostly remains where it has always been—with the administration, the lay trustees, and in some cases the legislature (in some states the legislature's powers are being absorbed by the governor, by executive audits and the like, as well as by coordinating councils for higher education, though of course the legislature retains a veto power).

The trustees, however, are seldom what they once were. Most are more permissive than their 19th- or early 20th-century predecessors. They are also more sensitive to individuals and groups unlike themselves. They share the general upper-middle-class allergy to "trouble," of whatever sort. If there is strong internal pressure for a given course of action, they are likely to go along. They are also more likely than they once were to delegate authority to the college administration, either *de jure* or *de facto*. In part it is because the complexity of the university has increased, so that lay trustees feel less competent to deal with its affairs on a one-day-a-month basis. In part it is because college presidents are today usually Ph.D.s rather than clergymen and can therefore claim apparently relevant but esoteric expertise other board members lack. This gives the president a certain authority vis à vis his board, which was less common before the professionalization of academic work. The tremendous competition among leading and aspiring institutions means that the decisions on recruitment and promotion of faculty must be made swiftly and would be too much delayed if subjected to detailed board review. (One reason boards spend so much time on buildings and grounds is that trustees feel at home in this area, presidents regard it as useful occupational therapy for them, and decisions can sometimes if not invariably wait.) To be sure, there are enormous differences in the degree of self-confidence of trustees. Some still "meddle" regularly in the affairs of "their" colleges and universities, settling issues the faculty considers its own prerogative. Those with access to public or private money also still throw their weight around at times. But the overall trend seems to us toward moderation and an increasingly ceremonial role for trustees.

The transfer of power from boards of directors to professional administrators has not, of course, been confined to higher education. The so-called managerial revolution, while not so widespread, complete, or progressive as some of its prophets have suggested, has taken place in many nonacademic enterprises. What is perhaps unusual about the academic world is the extent to which the top management, while nominally acting in the interests of the board, actually represents the interests of "middle management" (i.e., the faculty), both to the board and to the world. Despite some notable exceptions, today's college and university presidents usually start out as members of the academic profession. When they become administrators and have to deal more often with nonacademicians, they inevitably become somewhat deprofessionalized. Nonetheless, most university presidents still see their institution primarily as an assemblage of scholars and scientists, each doing his own work in his way.[8] At bottom, they are still engaged in "making the world safe for academicians," however much the academicians themselves resent the necessary (and unnecessary) compromises. Their greatest ambition for the future is usually to "strengthen" the college, and operationally this usually turns out to mean

---

[8] Even Clark Kerr's much maligned but marvelously perceptive study, *The Uses of the University* (Cambridge: Harvard University Press, 1964), takes this view.

assembling scholars of even greater competence and reputation than are now present—though of course there are still administrators who suffer from the traditional edifice complex, and others who want innovative new programs that attract outside support even if no competent men can be found to run them.

In the course of institution building, administrators usually find it expedient to pretend that the interests of the university and of the larger society are identical. Many even come to believe it. At that point they may lose sight of some of the distinctive objectives and prejudices of their faculty. More often, however, they compromise in order to fight (or run away) again another day. This usually offends the faculty, which has the luxury of being able to go elsewhere if its insistence on its principles brings reprisal against its institution. In the course of trying to "strengthen" their faculty, administrators of upwardly mobile institutions also usually offend many of the "weak" faculty currently on the payroll. And in the course of trying to keep the peace among warring departments and contending professors within departments, administrators inevitably offend most individual professors at one time or another.

Academicians are neither a tolerant nor an easygoing species, and their apparently congenital feeling of irritation and frustration requires scapegoats. Administrators serve this purpose, and they serve it best when their actions can be attributed to nonacademic considerations. So they are usually regarded as the enemy. Nonetheless, we would argue that administrators are today more concerned with keeping their faculty happy than with placating any other single group. They are also, in our experience, far more responsive to students and more concerned with the inadequacies and tragedies of student life than the majority of the faculty. We have also found that the administrative actions that offend academic liberals and elicit bitter talk about administrative tyranny are usually disapproved by only a minority of the faculty. This minority then finds it convenient to blame the administration instead of blaming its complacent colleagues for what is done with their tacit consent. Sometimes, indeed, the dissidents blame the administration for actions the majority of their colleagues insisted on, forgetting that faculties are themselves diverse and assuming if their colleagues do not agree with them it must be because they were "pressured," "bought," or "manipulated."[9] While it would be an exaggeration to say, as noted earlier, that the faculty exercises an absolute veto over

---

[9] In a generally liberal academic setting, moreover, faculty members may overlook the significance of a small but vocal group of right-wing faculty who are not at all complacent but who tell their right-wing political and business cronies that the general run of professors (and students) is even more "subversive" and dangerous than outsiders realize. Much American anti-intellectualism depends on the pedantic documentation and conspiratorial interpretations supplied by intellectuals.

administrative action in a modern university, it is certainly fair to say, as noted earlier, that trustees and administrators only rarely override faculty opinion, and then seldom for long.

The redistribution of power in the universities has been accompanied —and to some extent caused—by a change in the relationship between the university and other established institutions. The universities, especially their graduate professional schools, have become pacesetters in the promotion of meritocratic values.[10] In Talcott Parsons' terms, they are "universalistic," ignoring "particularistic" and personal qualities in their students and professors. This means that they choose professors almost entirely on the basis of their "output" and professional reputation. Students in the graduate professional schools are selected by similar criteria: by their ability to write good examinations and do good academic work. The claims of localism, sectarianism, ethnic prejudice and preference, class background, age, sex, and even occupational plans are largely ignored.[11]

The graduate professional schools have in turn been leaders in imposing meritocratic values on the professions themselves. The leading law firms hire men who made the law review at the most competitive law schools, and the leading hospitals offer internships and residencies to doctors who did well in the most competitive medical schools. Most conspicuous of all, colleges and universities scramble for Ph.D.s who have done well in the most competitive graduate departments. The result is that many traditional prejudices affecting recruitment have broken down: local boys today enjoy little advantage over outsiders, white Anglo-Saxon Protestants monopolize fewer and fewer occupational slots, and family connections count for less than they used to. Even corporation managers with long traditions of self-interested exclusiveness have in recent years frequently yielded to a broader vision of their enterprise and of America. Big employers today recruit university graduates in an increasingly evenhanded way, paying ever less attention to "irrelevant" factors like class background, religion, and ethnicity. Partly this is because of competition for skilled specialists, partly because of the stirrings of conscience, partly be-

---

[10] Here as elsewhere we treat the graduate departments of humanities, social science, and natural sciences as professional schools no different from graduate schools of medicine, law, education, and the like. We use the phrase "graduate schools" to include all professional schools requiring a BA for admission, and the phrase "graduate professional schools" should be read in the same inclusive way.

[11] There are some exceptions. Law schools admit brilliant students who confess that they do not plan to practice law, but medical schools take a narrower view. Graduate departments in the arts and sciences will usually admit a good candidate even though they think he will "sell out" and become a scientist in industry, but they will usually reject even the most brilliant candidate if he does not plan to take a Ph.D. There is also a residual bias against girls in most graduate admissions committees, and in the past few years a bias in favor of Negroes. For historical reasons, some institutions show other idiosyncrasies, but these are of marginal importance.

cause they fear adverse publicity. Companies have grown larger, have had to rationalize recruitment policy, and can therefore no longer conceal nonmeritocratic discrimination from themselves or (consequently) from the general public. Furthermore, with the growth of democratic ideology and the decline of old-fashioned social snobbery, even college fraternities have become less exclusive, as have leading prep schools. This brings a cumulative element in the growth of meritocracy, since even if an employer wanted to discriminate he would have a hard time finding channels that made this easy for him. Legacies of earlier discrimination obviously remain both in recruitment and training—and in the feeling of appropriateness of people for specific positions. A Negro is not likely soon to become president of General Motors nor a woman president of Harvard University, but both have been Cabinet members and either might become a vice-president of AT&T.

We do not want to exaggerate the tightness of the links between the modern occupational structure and higher education. The big Wall Street and Washington law firms may hire the top graduates of the top law schools, but there is another legal world where lawyers trained in night schools pick up not-so-good livings chasing ambulances, writing wills, settling insurance claims, and generally acting as brokers between the uninitiated and various bureaucracies. Similar chasms separate the top doctors who practice in teaching hospitals from those who have no hospital privileges anywhere. There are also colleges where, as Everett Hughes has put it, the faculty not only includes no scholars but includes nobody who has ever studied under a scholar. There are still many roads into these lower levels of professional practice, and on some of them academic competence counts for less than persistence and animal cunning. There are even more roads to the top in business: sales, accounting, engineering, law, and so forth. The Robert McNamaras who come up through the top graduate schools of business administration are still nothing like a majority.

Nonetheless, the role of graduate education in job distribution seems to be growing and should be stronger than ever by 1980. At the same time, and for related reasons, the values and methods promoted in the graduate professional schools seem to be increasingly accepted in the larger society. This does not mean that the outlook of professional-school faculty and the professions themselves are ever likely to be the same. On the contrary, there will always be tension between the "theorists" in the graduate schools and the "practitioners." By the time the AMA accepts compulsory health insurance, group practice, and other reforms long advocated by large numbers of medical professors, for example, the professors will have shifted their attention to new problems and will be attacking the conservatism of the practitioners on new grounds. The same is true in other areas. The striking thing, however, is how often the opinions and practices of the professional schools foreshadow those of the profession as a whole a generation later.

The rise of the university in the late 19th century did not at first have much effect on undergraduate education. The overwhelming majority of students continued to attend special-interest colleges, and even those who attended the undergraduate colleges of universities were for the most part terminal students. While a significant proportion eventually did some kind of work beyond the BA, very few graduate professional schools offering such work had highly competitive admissions. Similarly, while administrators at special-interest colleges were often impressed by the scholarly achievements of faculty at leading universities, and some made an active effort to acquire a similar faculty at their own institution, their success was at first limited by the shortage of Ph.D.s, especially "productive" ones. As in the larger society, the groundwork for a system was being laid, and the giant enterprises that would dominate that system were being organized, but the bulk of the nation's business was still being done by independent enterprises of limited means and limited views.

The revolution accelerated somewhat after World War I, for the 1920s and 1930s were a period of unprecedented growth in enrollment. (It is always easier to redistribute resources and power in periods of growth, because the progressives can be given more without the stand-patters' appearing to get less.) By the outbreak of World War II, the majority of the nation's college students were attending institutions staffed by academic professionals—though there were still many enclaves of provincialism such as the teachers colleges, the Catholic colleges, and the Negro colleges. The professionalization of the faculty reduced the internal homogeneity of many special-purpose colleges. Upper-class colleges got literary critics with the wrong ancestors, Southern colleges hired more historians who had grown up in the wrong region or even the wrong country, women's colleges hired psychologists of the wrong sex, and Methodist colleges took on philosophers of the wrong faith or no faith at all. Such "mismatching" had, of course, sometimes taken place accidentally even in presumptively homogenous special-interest colleges, but professionalization made it far more common. It also put trustees and parents who opposed heterogeneity very much on the defensive. A New York millionaire might not have liked the idea of having his son study economics with some Jewish radical at Yale, but if the boy's teacher had been publicly defined as "one of the leading economists in the country," the millionaire's objections seemed bigoted and irrelevant. (Which did not, of course, always prevent them from carrying weight, in Montana if not at Yale.)

Until the 1950s, most undergraduates seem to have remained relatively unaffected by these changes. The proportion going on to graduate school in the arts and sciences had risen slowly, but the proportion going into law and medicine had fallen correspondingly. As a result, the overall proportion of BAs earning graduate degrees probably changed relatively little for some decades.[12]

In the late 1950s, however, the effects of the academic revolution on undergraduate life began to multiply. Both the absolute number and the proportion of young people applying to college were rising steadily. This gave many colleges a choice between expansion and greater selectivity. The faculty preferred selectivity, and this preference proved influential in colleges of all sorts and decisive in private ones.[13] As a result, the leading undergraduate colleges, both public and private, began demanding higher academic aptitude and more proof of academic motivation from their entrants. These students, in turn, found the academic profession and ancillary activities increasingly glamorous, while mostly rejecting careers in business and other fields requiring only a BA.[14] The proportion of undergraduates who wanted to go on to graduate school therefore began to rise rapidly. The same pattern was repeated to a lesser extent at less selective colleges.[15]

---

[12] Statistical measures of this trend over long periods are hard to come by. Until very recently the U.S. Office of Education's statistics lumped graduate students in law, medicine, theology, and some other professions with undergraduates. Figures on graduate enrollment and degrees included only those taking degrees in fields that offered an undergraduate major—mainly the arts and sciences and education. The proportion of undergraduates going on in professional fields like law and medicine has declined steadily since 1900, but this does not show up in USOE's figures on graduate enrollment. Enrollment in the areas which USOE traditionally defined as graduate-level have, on the other hand, risen much faster than undergraduate enrollment. The result is that USOE data greatly exaggerated the actual change in the ratio of total graduate to total undergraduate enrollment.

The *1960 Census of Population, Volume I, Part 1*, Table 173, shows that, among those completing four years of college, the proportion going on to complete a fifth did not change significantly between 1910 and 1950. Among men who were born between 1885 and 1930, about 40 percent of those completing four years of higher education went on to complete a fifth. For individuals born after 1930, 1960 Census data are not very useful, since such individuals were still returning to graduate school in significant numbers in 1960. The 1960 Census therefore tells us relatively little about trends in graduate enrollment for men earning BAs after about 1950.

[13] No doubt in individual instances there are other reasons for selectivity, e.g., the failure of a capital bond issue or the lack of building sites for expansion. In some instances, inertia favors growth; in others, stability.

[14] Among the elite students in the elite universities there has been a general rejection of business careers, even those requiring advanced degrees, but a certain proportion of men with Ph.D.s and LL.Bs will nonetheless end up in business, holding insurance against their employers by virtue of their professional training.

[15] Since the early 1950s the steady growth of graduate work in fields like education, business, engineering, and the arts and sciences has more than offset the continuing lag in first professional degrees like the LL.B and MD. A 1963 National Science Foundation survey of 1958 BAs found that 58 percent had done some graduate work. (See Laura Sharpe, "Five Years After the College Degree, Part I, Graduate and Professional Education," Washington: Bureau of Social Science Research, 1965, mimeographed.) The NSF figures include some students who had not completed a full year of graduate work and who in theory would not be entiled to report "five or more" years of higher education to the 1970 Census. It is therefore likely that the increase in the

Many if not most undergraduates came to the old special-interest colleges to kill time, get away from home, make new friends, enjoy themselves, acquire saleable skills, and so forth. Undergraduates with such aims were not, by and large, very vulnerable to faculty pressures. Most, of course, wanted a diploma, and that meant they had to meet whatever formal requirements the faculty set. But these requirements served mainly to sift and intimidate the less competent students. The abler students could get Cs without doing much work, and most capitalized on this opportunity. The spread of graduate study altered these attitudes appreciably. Today a substantial fraction of the undergraduate population wants not only a degree but an undergraduate transcript sufficiently distinguished to ensure entry into a competitive professional school of some sort. Unlike many employers, these schools are mostly reluctant to take undergraduates with poor grades. The faculty can use this fact as a weapon to make undergraduates do far more academic work than was common in the traditional terminal colleges. This external threat has been reenforced in recent years by changes in the mass media's portrait of established national institutions. These institutions are increasingly shown offering prize jobs to men who have intellectual skills. Students are therefore constantly searching themselves for signs of intellectual competence and worrying about signs of stupidity. Many cannot settle for Cs, if the graduate schools would, for they cannot accept the idea that they are only "worth" a C.[16]

The fruition of this change was the birth of what Frank Bowles has

---

proportion of BAs entering graduate school was less than the apparent contrast between NSF and earlier Census figures. But probably not much less.

More recent studies by Alexander Astin and his colleagues at the American Council on Education show that, since 1958, the proportion of entering freshmen who *plan* to do graduate work has continued to rise. In Astin's sample of 45 four-year colleges, the proportion of all freshmen planning to get some sort of graduate degree rose from 49 to 67 percent between 1961–65. This sample appears to be representative of other four-year colleges, though the percentages would be somewhat lower if junior-college entrants were included. A 1965 *followup* of the students entering 246 four-year colleges in 1961 showed that the proportion planning to do graduate work rose from 42 to 70 percent over the four years. These plans were admittedly unrealistic in many cases. (Only 60 percent of this same sample had even earned a BA at the time of the followup.) Many of the non-BAs were not even enrolled in college at the time they outlined their plans for graduate study. Nonetheless, it seems fairly clear that graduate plans and enrollment are today rising much faster than college entrance or graduation rates. Although women are generally less likely to go to graduate school than men, the recent increase has been about equal for the two sexes. This suggests that draft deferment is not the primary cause.

[16] Indeed, the enormous expansion of institutions seeking to offer graduate instruction has made places available to many who do not have distinguished undergraduate records at distinguished places. Still, the more energetic and competent undergraduate teachers generally want their students to go on to "good" graduate schools and steer them away from the more anemic ones, including the home institution at times. An undergraduate education itself tends to expose its student devotees to the names of luminaries at leading graduate schools, even though many textbooks and readers are written by men at the less visible places.

called the "university college." In our usage, this is a college whose primary purpose is to prepare students for graduate work of some kind—primarily in the arts and sciences but also in professional subjects ranging from law and medicine to business and social work.[17] It may be part of a university with big graduate schools, as is the case with Yale or Michigan, or it may be administratively independent and geographically removed from any big university, as is the case with Amherst, Oberlin, or Vassar. But even if it is nominally independent, it is a *de facto* prep school for a small number of graduate professional schools, in much the same way that Groton, Andover, and Farmington are prep schools for Ivy League and Seven Sister colleges. Such a university college usually draws most of its students from the top tenth of the national ability distribution. It seldom loses more than a fifth of them during the undergraduate years. (More than a fifth may drop out, but many return and many others graduate from other colleges.) It usually sends nearly three-quarters of its men and a third to half of its women to graduate school. If such a university college is administratively part of a larger institution, it is likely to share its faculty with the graduate school of arts and sciences. But even if it is separate, it is almost certain to draw its faculty from the same manpower pool as the graduate schools of arts and sciences, seeking the same virtues and looking askance at the same presumed vices.

The university college is the fruition of the academic revolution at the undergraduate level. Out of more than 2,000 undergraduate colleges, probably no more than a hundred today really fit the above description. Yet these are the most prestigious colleges in the country, to which the ablest and most ambitious students usually gravitate. They also attract the ablest faculty and administrators and the most generous philanthropists. And they provide a model toward which almost all the other 1,900 colleges are moving as fast as they conveniently can.[18]

Virtually all terminal colleges want to hire faculty of the kind now hired by the university colleges. Whether or not these faculty come out of the subculture to which the college has traditionally been tied is secondary. In most cases the terminal colleges also want to recruit students entirely on the basis of academic ability. They would prefer to ignore traditional considerations like geography, religion, ethnicity, and class. Specialization by sex and occupational intention is also somewhat less common among undergraduate colleges than it once was. Even administrators

---

[17] This term is used in an entirely different sense in Great Britain and parts of the Commonwealth, to indicate a budding university that has not yet achieved sufficient stability and reputation to deserve complete autonomy, and that awards degrees through another institution.

[18] For a brief description of this process of emulation see David Riesman, "The Academic Procession," in *Constraint and Variety in American Education* (Lincoln, Nebraska: University of Nebraska Press, 1956), paperback edition.

and trustees seem to be chosen more often according to the criteria of achievement, competence, and judgment that prevail in established national institutions than according to the criteria of the special-interest group which initially founded the college.

That these developments make colleges more useful to other established national institutions can hardly be doubted. They make higher education look like a fairly effective instrument for meritocratic sorting and grading of the future employees. They probably also help promote and disseminate values and skills useful in the maintenance of established institutions. The university colleges and their emulators usually try, for example, to help their students transcend whatever subculture they are born and raised in, and move them out into a slightly more cosmopolitan world. In part this is a matter of exposing students to heterogenous classmates— heterogenous, that is, by traditional demographic criteria, even though often quite homogenous in terms of academic aptitudes. In part it is a matter of exposing them to professors who know something of a larger world than the students have encountered, and who may, if they are wise or charming, lure their students into it. In part it is a matter of giving the students books to read. In part it is simply a matter of giving young people with a yen for mobility the diplomatic passport they need to cross the borders of their sexual, racial, religious, economic, or generational parish.[19]

These efforts at emancipation are, it is true, necessarily limited in scope. Some colleges manage to bring together students and faculty of diverse class backgrounds, but this diversity almost never extends to class aspirations. Wherever they come from, college students by and large plan to end up in the upper-middle classes if they can, and they meet professors who have succeeded in doing just this.[20] Similarly, while some colleges bring together students from different regional backgrounds, few mix them with more than a handful of foreigners, and even fewer create an atmosphere which appreciably curtails nationalistic biases. Then too, while many colleges attract a substantial number of students older than the undergraduate norm and all employ professors who run the full age range, few are successful in establishing really close cross-generational contacts or in counteracting the mutual chauvinism of young and old vis à vis one another. Nor can any college do much about the parochialism that comes from having lived only in the 20th century. The formal curriculum, of

---

[19] In Greek the word "diploma" meant a doubled-over piece of paper and hence a letter of recommendation. A "diplomat" was one who carried a "diploma." Today it could be said that the "diplomats" who serve as go-betweens for America's many subcultures and who hold the country together are the "diploma-holders" from these subcultures.

[20] A small but interesting minority of students, often from the upper social strata, profess aspirations for downward mobility, often identifying with Negroes as the American equivalent of the proletariat and meeting on the way down Negroes and others on the way up.

course, usually tries to overcome all these limitations, but the number of students who can significantly be affected by books has always been fairly small, especially when the message of the book is reenforced neither by human contact nor by daily experience.

These almost inescapable limitations are in most cases supplemented by self-imposed limitations, often inherited from the special-interest group that founded a particular college. Local colleges, for example, often deliberately exclude students from outside their state or even their city. While some Catholic colleges and universities seem to their traditional faculties almost to be prejudiced against Catholics in their efforts to become ecumenical, others still on occasion deliberately discourage non-Catholic applicants for teaching positions, and even occasionally screen reading lists with an eye to orthodoxy. Upper-middle-class colleges sometimes make no effort to provide scholarships for students from poorer families. White colleges often make life intolerable for black students, and Negro colleges often do likewise for white faculty. Professional schools frequently cling to a narrow view of their students' future responsibilities, and sometimes resist affiliation with a multipurpose university. Single-sex colleges, while sometimes attracted to coeducation, also sometimes cling to their exclusiveness with pride.

Just as some small businesses will probably continue to earn high returns in the interstices of a corporate economy, and local governments to take on new responsibilities despite the parallel increase in federal power, so too the old 19th-century system of special-purpose colleges will endure despite the rise of the national university system and the magnetic appeal of the university-college model. By the same token, local car dealers may survive and flourish, but the future of the automobile industry is determined in Detroit, New York, and Washington. In higher education, while the old special-interest colleges and the energies they embody may give the present much of its flavor, they do little to shape the future.

What is taking place in America is a transition characteristic of any really successful institutional invention, of which colleges are certainly an example. Special-purpose colleges were established by laymen to serve a particular purpose and were initially very much committed to that purpose. The local college was local first and a college second; the Catholic college was Catholic first and a college second; the Negro college was Negro first and a college second; and so forth. But as time goes on, these disparate institutions take on lives and purposes of their own. The college begins to change its reference group. Undergraduates stop thinking of themselves primarily as girls or Baptists or future teachers and start thinking of themselves primarily as students, having a common interest with students in all sorts of other places called colleges rather than with girls, Baptists, or teachers who are not students. Similar changes are taking place at the faculty level. Even the college president begins to think of himself less as the president of a college in San Jose, of a college catering to the rich, or of a college for Irish Catholics, and more as the president of a first-rate, second-rate, or third-rate college. More and more, his reference group ceases to be the trustees or the traditional clientele and patrons of his institution, and becomes the presidents of other colleges, many of which have historically different origins and aims.

The result is a trend toward the triumph of meritocratic academic values and the acceptance of the university college as the only viable model for the future. This model is certainly better suited to the "impossible" requirements of 1980 than any traditional terminal college would be. Nonetheless, *some* form of terminal education will still be needed then, and even for those who plan on graduate school, a mini-Ph.D. program will often be unnecessarily restrictive.

# 23

# The "Cooling-Out" Function in Higher Education[1, ]*

## BURTON R. CLARK

A major problem of democratic society is inconsistency between encouragement to achieve and the realities of limited opportunity. Democracy asks individuals to act as if social mobility were universally possible; status is to be won by individual effort, and rewards are to accrue to those who try. But democratic societies also need selective training institutions, and hierarchical work organizations permit increasingly fewer persons to succeed at ascending levels. Situations of opportunity are also situations of denial and failure. Thus democratic societies need not only to motivate achievement but also to mollify those denied it to sustain motivation in the face of disappointment and to deflect resentment. In the modern mass democracy, with its large-scale organization, elaborated ideologies of equal access and participation, and minimal commitment to social origin as a basis for status, the task becomes critical.

The problem of blocked opportunity has been approached sociologically through means-ends analysis. Merton and others have called attention to the phenomenon of dissociation between culturally instilled goals and institutionally provided means of realization; discrepancy between ends and means is seen as a basic social source of individual frustration and recalcitrance.[2] We shall here extend means-ends analysis in another

* From *The American Journal of Sociology*, 65 (May 1960):569–76.

1 Revised and extended version of paper read at the Fifty-fourth Annual Meeting of the American Sociological Association, Chicago, September 3–5, 1959. I am indebted to Erving Goffman and Martin A. Trow for criticism and to Sheldon Messinger for extended conceptual and editorial comment.

2 "Aberrant behavior may be regarded sociologically as a symptom of dissociation

direction, to the responses of organized groups to means-ends disparities, in particular focusing attention on ameliorative processes that lessen the strains of dissociation. We shall do so by analyzing the most prevalent type of dissociation between aspirations and avenues in American education, specifying the structure and processes that reduce the stress of structural disparity and individual denial. Certain components of American higher education perform what may be called the cooling-out function,[3] and it is to these that attention will be drawn.

## THE ENDS-MEANS DISJUNCTURE

In American higher education the aspirations of the multitude are encouraged by "open-door" admission to public-supported colleges. The means of moving upward in status and of maintaining high status now include some years in college, and a college education is a prerequisite of the better positions in business and the professions. The trend is toward an ever tighter connection between higher education and higher occupations, as increased specialization and professionalization insure that more persons will need more preparation. The high-school graduate, seeing college as essential to success, will seek to enter some college, regardless of his record in high school.

A second and allied source of public interest in unlimited entry into college is the ideology of equal opportunity.[4] Strictly interpreted, equality of opportunity means selection according to ability, without regard to extraneous considerations. Popularly interpreted, however, equal opportunity in obtaining a college education is widely taken to mean unlimited access to some form of college: in California, for example, state educational authorities maintain that high-school graduates who cannot qualify for the state university or state college should still have the "opportunity of attending a publicly supported institution of higher education," this being "an essential part of the state's goal of guaranteeing equal educational

---

between culturally prescribed aspirations and socially structured avenues for realizing these aspirations" (Robert K. Merton, "Social Structure and Anomie," in *Social Theory and Social Structure* [rev. ed.; Glencoe, Ill.: Free Press, 1957], p. 134). See also Herbert H. Hyman, "The Value Systems of Different Classes: A Social Psychological Contribution to the Analysis of Stratification," in Reinhard Bendix and Seymour M. Lipset (Eds.), *Class, Status and Power: A Reader in Social Stratification* (Glencoe, Ill.: Free Press, 1953), pp. 426–42; and the papers by Robert Dubin, Richard A. Cloward, Robert K. Merton, and Dorothy L. Meier, and Wendell Bell, in *American Sociological Review*, 24 (April 1959).

[3] I am indebted to Erving Goffman's original statement of the cooling-out conception. See his "Cooling the Mark Out: Some Aspects of Adaptation to Failure," *Psychiatry*, 15 (November 1952):451–63. Sheldon Messinger called the relevance of this concept to my attention.

[4] Seymour Martin Lipset and Reinhard Bendix, *Social Mobility in Industrial Society* (Berkeley: University of California Press, 1959), pp. 78–101.

opportunities to all its citizens."[5] To deny access to college is then to deny equal opportunity. Higher education should make a seat available without judgment on past performance.

Many other features of current American life encourage college-going. School officials are reluctant to establish early critical hurdles for the young, as is done in Europe. With little enforced screening in the pre-college years, vocational choice and educational selection are postponed to the college years or later. In addition, the United States, a wealthy country, is readily supporting a large complex of colleges, and its expanding economy requires more specialists. Recently, a national concern that manpower be fully utilized has encouraged the extending of college training to more and different kinds of students. Going to college is also in some segments of society the thing to do; as a last resort, it is more attractive than the army or a job. Thus ethical and practical urges together encourage the high-school graduate to believe that college is both a necessity and a right; similarly, parents and elected officials incline toward legislation and admission practices that insure entry for large numbers; and educational authorities find the need and justification for easy admission.

Even where pressures have been decisive in widening admission policy, however, the system of higher education has continued to be shaped partly by other interests. The practices of public colleges are influenced by the academic personnel, the organizational requirements of colleges, and external pressures other than those behind the open door. Standards of performance and graduation are maintained. A commitment to standards is encouraged by a set of values in which the status of a college, as defined by academicians and a large body of educated laymen, is closely linked to the perceived quality of faculty, student body, and curriculum. The raising of standards is supported by the faculty's desire to work with promising students and to enjoy membership in an enterprise of reputed quality—college authorities find low standards and poor students a handicap in competing with other colleges for such resources as able faculty as well as for academic status. The wish is widespread that college education be of the highest quality for the preparation of leaders in public affairs, business, and the professions. In brief, the institutional means of the students' progress toward college graduation and subsequent goals are shaped in large part by a commitment to quality embodied in college staffs, traditions, and images.

---

[5] A Study of the Need for Additional Centers of Public Higher Education in California (Sacramento: California State Department of Education, 1957), p. 128. For somewhat similar interpretations by educators and laymen nationally see Francis J. Brown (Ed.), Approaching Equality of Opportunity in Higher Education (Washington, D.C.: American Council on Education, 1955), and the President's Committee on Education beyond the High School, Second Report to the President (Washington, D.C.: Government Printing Office, 1957).

The conflict between open-door admission and performance of high quality often means a wide discrepancy between the hopes of entering students and the means of their realization. Students who pursue ends for which a college education is required but who have little academic ability gain admission into colleges only to encounter standards of performance they cannot meet. As a result, while some students of low promise are successful, for large numbers failure is inevitable and *structured*. The denial is delayed, taking place within the college instead of at the edge of the system. It requires that many colleges handle the student who intends to complete college and has been allowed to become involved but whose destiny is to fail.

## RESPONSES TO DISJUNCTURE

What is done with the student whose destiny will normally be early termination? One answer is unequivocal dismissal. This "hard" response is found in the state university that bows to pressure for broad admission but then protects standards by heavy drop-out. In the first year it weeds out many of the incompetent, who may number a third or more of the entering class.[6] The response of the college is hard in that failure is clearly defined as such. Failure is public; the student often returns home. This abrupt change in status and in access to the means of achievement may occur simultaneously in a large college or university for hundreds, and sometimes thousands, of students after the first semester and at the end of the freshman year. The delayed denial is often viewed on the outside as heartless, a slaughter of the innocents.[7] This excites public pressure and anxiety, and apparently the practice cannot be extended indefinitely as the demand for admission to college increases.

A second answer is to sidetrack unpromising students rather than have them fail. This is the "soft" response: never to dismiss a student but to provide him with an alternative. One form of it in some state universities is the detour to an extension division or a general college, which has the advantage of appearing not very different from the main road. Sometimes

---

[6] One national report showed that one out of eight entering students (12.5 percent) in publicly controlled colleges does not remain beyond the first term or semester; one out of three (31 percent) is out by the end of the first year; and about one out of two (46.6 percent) leaves within the first two years. In state universities alone, about one out of four withdraws in the first year and 40 percent in two years (Robert E. Iffert, *Retention and Withdrawal of College Students* [Washington, D.C.: Department of Health, Education and Welfare, 1958], pp. 15–20). Students withdraw for many reasons, but scholastic aptitude is related to their staying power: "A sizeable number of students of medium ability enter college, but . . . few if any of them remain longer than two years" (*A Restudy of the Needs of California in Higher Education* [Sacramento: California State Department of Education, 1955], p. 120).

[7] Robert L. Kelly, *The American Colleges and the Social Order* (New York: Macmillan Co., 1940), pp. 220–21.

"easy" fields of study, such as education, business administration, and social science, are used as alternatives to dismissal.[8] The major form of the soft response is not found in the four-year college or university, however, but in the college that specializes in handling students who will soon be leaving—typically, the two-year public junior college.

In most states where the two-year college is a part of higher education, the students likely to be caught in the means-ends disjuncture are assigned to it in large numbers. In California, where there are over 60 public two-year colleges in a diversified system that includes the state university and numerous four-year state colleges, the junior college is unselective in admissions and by law, custom, and self-conception accepts all who wish to enter.[9] It is tuition-free, local, and under local control. Most of its entering students want to try for the baccalaureate degree, transferring to a "senior" college after one or two years. About two-thirds of the students in the junior colleges of the state are in programs that permit transferring; but, of these, only about one-third actually transfer to a four-year college.[10] The remainder, or two out of three of the professed transfer students, are "latent terminal students": their announced intention and program of study entails four years of college, but in reality their work terminates in the junior college. Constituting about half of all the students in the California junior colleges, and somewhere between one-third and one-half of junior college students nationally,[11] these students cannot be ignored by the colleges. Understanding their careers is important to understanding modern higher education.

## THE REORIENTING PROCESS

This type of student in the junior college is handled by being moved out of a transfer major to a one- or two-year program of vocational, business, or semiprofessional training. This calls for the relinquishing of his original intention, and he is induced to accept a substitute that has lower status in both the college and society in general.

---

[8] One study has noted that on many campuses the business school serves "as a dumping ground for students who cannot make the grade in engineering or some branch of the liberal arts," this being a consequence of lower promotion standards than are found in most other branches of the university (Frank C. Pierson, *The Education of American Businessmen* [New York: McGraw-Hill Book Co., 1959], p. 63). Pierson also summarizes data on intelligence of students by field of study which indicate that education, business, and social science rank near the bottom in quality of students (ibid., pp. 65–72).

[9] Burton R. Clark, *The Open Door College: A Case Study* (New York: McGraw-Hill Book Co., 1960), pp. 44–45.

[10] Ibid., p. 116.

[11] Leland L. Medsker, *The Junior College: Progress and Prospect* (New York: McGraw-Hill Book Co., 1960), chap. iv.

In one junior college[12] the initial move in a cooling-out process is pre-entrance testing: low scores on achievement tests lead poorly qualified students into remedial classes. Assignment to remedial work casts doubt and slows the student's movement into bona fide transfer courses. The remedial courses are, in effect, a subcollege. The student's achievement scores are made part of a counseling folder that will become increasingly significant to him. An objective record of ability and performance begins to accumulate.

A second step is a counseling interview before the beginning of the first semester, and before all subsequent semesters for returning students. "At this interview the counselor assists the student to choose the proper courses in light of his objective, his test scores, the high school record and test records from his previous schools."[13] Assistance in choosing "the proper courses" is gentle at first. Of the common case of the student who wants to be an engineer but who is not a promising candidate, a counselor said: "I never openly countermand his choice, but edge him toward a terminal program by gradually laying out the facts of life." Counselors may become more severe later when grades provide a talking point and when the student knows that he is in trouble. In the earlier counseling the desire of the student has much weight; the counselor limits himself to giving advice and stating the probability of success. The advice is entered in the counseling record that shadows the student.

A third and major step in reorienting the latent terminal student is a special course entitled "Orientation to College," mandatory for entering students. All sections of it are taught by teacher-counselors who comprise the counseling staff, and one of its purposes is "to assist students in evaluating their own abilities, interests, and aptitudes; in assaying their vocational choices in light of this evaluation; and in making educational plans to implement their choices." A major section of it takes up vocational planning; vocational tests are given at a time when opportunities and requirements in various fields of work are discussed. The tests include the "Lee Thorpe Interest Inventory" ("given to all students for motivating a self-appraisal of vocational choice") and the "Strong Interest Inventory" ("for all who are undecided about choice or who show disparity between accomplishment and vocational choice"). Mechanical and clerical aptitude tests are taken by all. The aptitudes are directly related to the college's terminal programs, with special tests, such as a pre-engineering ability test, being given according to need. Then an "occupational paper is re-

---

[12] San Jose City College, San Jose, Calif. For the larger study see Clark, *Open Door College*.

[13] San Jose Junior College, Handbook for Counselors, 1957–58, p. 2. Statements in quotation marks in the next few paragraphs are cited from this handbook.

quired of all students for their chosen occupation"; in it the student writes on the required training and education and makes a "self-appraisal of fitness."

Tests and papers are then used in class discussion and counseling interviews, in which the students themselves arrange and work with a counselor's folder and a student test profile and, in so doing, are repeatedly confronted by the accumulating evidence—the test scores, course grades, recommendations of teachers and counselors. This procedure is intended to heighten self-awareness of capacity in relation to choice and hence to strike particularly at the latent terminal student. The teacher-counselors are urged constantly to "be alert to the problem of unrealistic vocational goals" and to "help students to accept their limitations and strive for success in other worthwhile objectives that are within their grasp." The orientation class was considered a good place "to talk tough," to explain in an *impersonal* way the facts of life for the overambitious student. Talking tough to a whole group is part of a soft treatment of the individual.

Following the vocational counseling, the orientation course turns to "building an educational program," to study of the requirements for graduation of the college in transfer and terminal curriculum, and to planning of a four-semester program. The students also become acquainted with the requirements of the colleges to which they hope to transfer, here contemplating additional hurdles such as the entrance examinations of other colleges. Again, the hard facts of the road ahead are brought to bear on self-appraisal.

If he wishes, the latent terminal student may ignore the counselor's advice and the test scores. While in the counseling class, he is also in other courses, and he can wait to see what happens. Adverse counseling advice and poor test scores may not shut off his hope of completing college; when this is the case, the deterrent will be encountered in the regular classes. Here the student is divested of expectations, lingering from high school, that he will automatically pass and, hopefully, automatically be transferred. Then, receiving low grades, he is thrown back into the counseling orbit, a fourth step in his reorientation and a move justified by his actual accomplishment. The following indicates the nature of the referral system:

> *Need for Improvement Notices* are issued by instructors to students who are doing unsatisfactory work. The carbon copy of the notice is given to the counselor who will be available for conference with the student. The responsibility lies with the student to see his counselor. However, experience shows that some counselees are unable to be sufficiently self-directive to seek aid. The counselor should, in such cases, send for the student, using the Request for Conference blank. If the student fails to respond to the Request for Conference slip, this may become a disciplinary matter and should be referred to the deans.

After a conference has been held, the Need for Improvement notices are filed in the student's folder. *This may be important* in case of a complaint concerning the fairness of a final grade.[14]

This directs the student to more advice and self-assessment, as soon and as often as he has classroom difficulty. The carbon-copy routine makes it certain that, if he does not seek advice, advice will seek him. The paper work and bureaucratic procedure have the purpose of recording referral and advice in black and white, where they may later be appealed to impersonally. As put in an unpublished report of the college, the overaspiring student and the one who seems to be in the wrong program require "skillful and delicate handling. An accumulation of pertinent factual information may serve to fortify the objectivity of the student-counselor relationship." While the counselor advises delicately and patiently, but persistently, the student is confronted with the record with increasing frequency.

A fifth step, one necessary for many in the throes of discouragement, is probation: "Students [whose] grade point averages fall below 2.0 [C] in any semester will, upon recommendation by the Scholarship Committee, be placed on probationary standing." A second failure places the student on second probation, and a third may mean that he will be advised to withdraw from the college altogether. The procedure is not designed to rid the college of a large number of students, for they may continue on probation for three consecutive semesters; its purpose is not to provide a status halfway out of the college but to "assist the student to seek an objective (major field) at a level on which he can succeed."[15] An important effect of probation is its slow killing-off of the lingering hopes of the most stubborn latent terminal students. A "transfer student" must have a C average to receive the Associate in Arts (a two-year degree) offered by the junior college, but no minimum average is set for terminal students. More important, four-year colleges require a C average or higher for the transfer student. Thus probationary status is the final blow to hopes of transferring and, indeed, even to graduating from the junior college under a transfer-student label. The point is reached where the student must permit himself to be reclassified or else drop out. In this college, 30 percent of the students enrolled at the end of the spring semester, 1955–56, who returned the following fall were on probation; three out of four of these were transfer students in name.[16]

This sequence of procedures is a specific process of cooling-out;[17] its

---

[14] Ibid., p. 20.

[15] Statement taken from unpublished material.

[16] San Jose Junior College, "Digest of Analysis of the Records of 468 Students Placed on Probation for the Fall Semester, 1956," September 3, 1956.

[17] Goffman's original statement of the concept of cooling-out referred to how the disappointing of expectations is handled by the disappointed person and especially by

effect, at the best, is to let down hopes gently and unexplosively. Through it students who are failing or barely passing find their occupational and academic future being redefined. Along the way, teacher-counselors urge the latent terminal student to give up his plan of transferring and stand ready to console him in accepting a terminal curriculum. The drawn-out denial when it is effective is in place of a personal, hard "No"; instead, the student is brought to realize, finally, that it is best to ease himself out of the competition to transfer.

## COOLING-OUT FEATURES

In the cooling-out process in the junior college are several features that are likely to be found in other settings where failure or denial is the effect of a structured discrepancy between ends and means, the responsible operatives or "coolers" cannot leave the scene or hide their identities, and the disappointment is threatening in some way to those responsible for it. At work and in training institutions this is common. The features are:

1. *Alternative Achievement.* Substitute avenues may be made to appear not too different from what is given up, particularly as to status. The person destined to be denied or who fails is invited to interpret the second effort as more appropriate to his particular talent and is made to see that it will be the less frustrating. Here one does not fail but rectifies a mistake. The substitute status reflects less unfavorably on personal capacity than does being dismissed and forced to leave the scene. The terminal student in the junior college may appear not very different from the transfer student—an "engineering aide," for example, instead of an "engineer"—and to be proceeding to something with a status of its own. Failure in college can be treated as if it did not happen; so, too, can poor performance in industry.[18]

2. *Gradual Disengagement.* By a gradual series of steps, movement to a goal may be stalled, self-assessment encouraged, and evidence produced of performance. This leads toward the available alternatives at little cost. It also keeps the person in a counseling milieu in which advice is furnished, whether actively sought or not. Compared with the original hopes, however, it is a deteriorating situation. If the individual does not give up peacefully, he will be in trouble.

3. *Objective Denial.* Reorientation is, finally, confrontation by the facts. A record of poor performance helps to detach the organization and

those responsible for the disappointment. Although his main illustration was the confidence game, where facts and potential achievement are deliberately misrepresented to the "mark" (the victim) by operators of the game, Goffman also applied the concept to failure in which those responsible act in good faith ("Cooling the Mark Out," *passim*). "Cooling-out" is a widely useful idea when used to refer to a function that may vary in deliberateness.

[18] Ibid., p. 457; cf. Perrin Stryker, "How To Fire an Executive," *Fortune*, 50 (October 1954):116–17 and 178–92.

its agents from the emotional aspects of the cooling-out work. In a sense, the overaspiring student in the junior college confronts himself, as he lives with the accumulating evidence, instead of the organization. The college offers opportunity; it is the record that forces denial. Record-keeping and other bureaucratic procedures appeal to universal criteria and reduce the influence of personal ties, and the personnel are thereby protected. Modern personnel record-keeping, in general, has the function of documenting denial.

4. *Agents of Consolation.* Counselors are available who are patient with the overambitious and who work to change their intentions. They believe in the value of the alternative careers, though of lower social status, and are practiced in consoling. In college and in other settings counseling is to reduce aspiration as well as to define and to help fulfill it. The teacher-counselor in the "soft" junior college is in contrast to the scholar in the "hard" college who simply gives a low grade to the failing student.

5. *Avoidance of Standards.* A cooling-out process avoids appealing to standards that are ambiguous to begin with. While a "hard" attitude toward failure generally allows a single set of criteria, a "soft" treatment assumes that many kinds of ability are valuable, each in its place. Proper classification and placement are then paramount, while standards become relative.

## IMPORTANCE OF CONCEALMENT

For an organization and its agents one dilemma of a cooling-out role is that it must be kept reasonably away from public scrutiny and not clearly perceived or understood by prospective clientele. Should it become obvious, the organization's ability to perform it would be impaired. If high-school seniors and their families were to define the junior college as a place which diverts college-bound students, a probable consequence would be a turning-away from the junior college and increased pressure for admission to the four-year colleges and universities that are otherwise protected to some degree. This would, of course, render superfluous the part now played by the junior college in the division of labor among colleges.

The cooling-out function of the junior college is kept hidden, for one thing, as other functions are highlighted. The junior college stresses "the transfer function," "the terminal function," etc., not that of transforming transfer into terminal students; indeed, it is widely identified as principally a transfer station. The other side of cooling-out is the successful performance in junior college of students who did poorly in high school or who have overcome socioeconomic handicaps, for they are drawn into higher education rather than taken out of it. Advocates of the junior college point to this salvaging of talented manpower, otherwise lost to the community and nation. It is indeed a function of the open door to let hidden talent be uncovered.

Then, too, cooling-out itself is reinterpreted so as to appeal widely. The junior college may be viewed as a place where all high-school graduates have the opportunity to explore possible careers and find the type of education appropriate to their individual ability; in short, as a place where everyone is admitted and everyone succeeds. As described by the former president of the University of California:

> A prime virtue of the junior college, I think, is that most of its students succeed in what they set out to accomplish, and cross the finish line before they grow weary of the race. After two years in a course that they have chosen, they can go out prepared for activities that satisfy them, instead of being branded as failures. Thus the broadest possible opportunity may be provided for the largest number to make an honest try at further education with some possibility of success and with no route to a desired goal completely barred to them.[19]

The students themselves help to keep this function concealed by wishful unawareness. Those who cannot enter other colleges but still hope to complete four years will be motivated at first not to admit the cooling-out process to consciousness. Once exposed to it, they again will be led not to acknowledge it, and so they are saved insult to their self-image.

In summary, the cooling-out process in higher education is one whereby systematic discrepancy between aspiration and avenue is covered over and stress for the individual and the system is minimized. The provision of readily available alternative achievements in itself is an important device for alleviating the stress consequent on failure and so preventing anomic and deviant behavior. The general result of cooling-out processes is that society can continue to encourage maximum effort without major disturbance from unfulfilled promises and expectations.

---

[19] Robert Gordon Sproul, "Many Millions More," *Educational Record*, 39 (April 1958):102.

# 24

# The Impact of College*

KENNETH A. FELDMAN and
THEODORE M. NEWCOMB

In a sense, every student who ever attends any college undergoes some
impact from the experience—even if he withdraws at the end of one "hor-
rible week." Even if, following any number of years as a student, he shows
no observable changes (say in scores on an achievement test or an attitude
scale) it is possible that the college experience has reinforced and solidified
certain characteristics that he had previously worn more lightly, and that
might formerly have been only precariously established. Between his
freshman and senior years, for example, he might have abandoned and
then readopted his initial position concerning religion as a value. Such
effects will probably not come to the attention of the researcher unless he
has chosen to make intensive studies of individuals (see, for example,
M.B. Smith et al., 1956). We have, however, had in mind a more restrictive notion of impact. We have searched the literature and compared various sets of findings with an eye to generalizations rather than to the infinite
variety of individual processes that lie behind them. We have begun with
general statements that apply to most colleges. Then we have offered a
few propositions that apply to most colleges of certain kinds, to most students affected by certain aspects of college environments, or to most students who have certain characteristics on entering college, and so on.
When possible, we offered generalizations that assumed an interplay
among whole sets of conditions. We have viewed colleges' impacts on

* From: Kenneth A. Feldman and Theodore M. Newcomb, *The Impact of College
on Students,* © 1969. Reprinted by permission of Jossey-Bass, Inc., San Francisco.

their students through the often cloudy lenses of *effects that can in some sense be offered as generalizations.*[1]

Our first finding is very general indeed. Some uniformities can be found in impacts of American colleges and universities, although the particular content of the finding reported is surely time-bound as well as space-limited.

1. *Freshman-to-senior changes in several characteristics have been occurring with considerable uniformity in most American colleges and universities in recent decades.*

Declining "authoritarianism," dogmatism, and prejudice, together with decreasingly conservative attitudes toward public issues and growing sensitivity to aesthetic experiences, are particularly prominent forms of change —as inferred from freshman-senior differences. These add up to something like increasing openness to multiple aspects of the contemporary world, paralleling wider ranges of contact and experience. Somewhat less consistently, but nevertheless evident, are increasing intellectual interests and capacities, and declining commitment to religion, especially in its more orthodox forms. Certain kinds of personal changes—particularly toward greater independence, self-confidence, and readiness to express impulses—are the rule rather than the exception.

Such is the heavy preponderance of evidence from many institutions; but each nugget of data, taken singly, represents only an average trend in a particular college or university. Though individual changes are rarely reported, we can be sure that, in each population studied, some individuals—or perhaps many—swam against the current while others—conceivably a majority—changed little or none between entrance and graduation. These facts of statistical life are not changed by the equally solid fact that nearly all studies reveal the same preponderant direction of change: it is still only a prevalent tendency.

On the other hand, neither do these considerations alter the basic findings that each of the prevalent tendencies was in one direction rather than the other. (Suppose, for example, that our data had shown a preponderant freshman-to-senior change toward greater dogmatism and declining sensitivity to aesthetic experiences.) The preponderant shift, like Mount Everest, is there, it is in this direction and not that, and it is a challenge—to our understanding if not to our powers of survival in rarefied atmosphere.

Such evidence of net change does not, however, necessarily reflect impacts of colleges. It is to be expected that at least some individuals of col-

---

[1] A few portions of this chapter are frankly impressionistic. Our own interpretations and fore-glimpses therein are not, we believe, inconsistent with the research findings considered in earlier chapters—but neither do they in every instance follow inevitably from those findings.

lege age who are not in college would, like their counterparts who are in college, show increasing openness to new experience and growing tolerance. Indeed, the available evidence on this point indicates that, as a preponderant trend, individuals who have not attended college (though eligible and acceptable) often change in the same directions as do students in college, though in lesser degree. The same culture-wide winds blow upon both populations, though college experience appears to hasten some kinds of changes, just as it may delay others.

In spite of the limitations of data on net changes, it seems altogether likely that some students in some colleges experience some changes that are *attributable* to the fact of being in college. And so our inquiry shifts to precisely such questions—*from* the demonstrations of preponderant trends *to* the analysis of particular conditions under which particular kinds of impacts can be demonstrated. This shift does not imply an abandoning of our search for generality, but rather the espousal of a different kind of general question: *under what conditions—regardless of where those conditions are found, and regardless of preponderant trends in contemporary American colleges in general—are particular kinds of impacts likely to occur?*

> 2.  *The degree and nature of different colleges' impacts vary with their student inputs—that is, entering students' characteristics, which differ among types of colleges in patterned ways.*

The public images of colleges, together with their admission policies, have the consequence that their entering students have distinguishable sets of characteristics. This does not mean that all institutions attract equally homogeneous populations of students; indeed, degree of homogeneity itself may be an important distinguishing variable among colleges. Nor does it mean, of course, that every institution's student body is clearly distinguishable from all others in the distribution of its students' characteristics. But it is clear that there are important and measurable differences among types of colleges in this respect. In most of the characteristics for which data exist there is not a great deal of overlap, for example, between most private universities and most small, public colleges.

By and large, in institutions where most entering students have high capacity most of them will have family backgrounds of favored socioeconomic status; the same students will, relative to those in other kinds of colleges, tend to be nonauthoritarian and to score high in intellectual dispositions. By the same token, student bodies that are generally low in any one of these characteristics will, in terms of probability, be low in all or most of the others. The correlation is by no means perfect, but the pattern is unmistakable.

Some of these individual characteristics—family background, in particular—will be affected little or not at all by experience in college. Others, including authoritarianism, and political and religious orientations, for example, are clearly susceptible to change during college years. Such changes, according to the few currently available studies are apt to increase rather than decrease the initial disparities among different colleges. In the absence of more complete data, we offer it only as a likely hypothesis that *those characteristics in which freshman-to-senior change is distinctive for a given college will also have been distinctive for its entering freshmen,* initial distinctiveness being in the same direction as subsequent change.

That impact is conditioned by input is hardly news, but the nature of the accentuating relationship that we hypothesize may illuminate one of the ways in which impact occurs. We suggest that two processes are at work. First, the prominence of initial characteristics—say religious attitude in a sectarian college or vocational aspirations in a technical college —indicates a readiness on the part of a considerable number of individuals to move in directions compatible with those characteristics. This readiness is then reinforced by their discovery that many others share the same interests, which are thus socially reinforced.

Such an interpretation of differential impacts among different colleges needs qualification. Accentuation is not, of course, the only process at work; this generalization, like the others, refers only to modal processes that distinguish some institutions from others. Students' initial interests may lapse, and quite new ones may be acquired—perhaps as adaptations of initial deviants to majority influence, or for any number of idiosyncratic reasons. Furthermore, in any except possibly the very small and highly homogeneous institutions, individual change tends to occur in different directions for different students, so that the process is not at all a monolithic one. But the fact remains, we suspect, that the kinds of college impacts that are massive enough to distinguish different colleges from one another are outcomes of the accentuation of initial distinctions.

3.  *Within the same college, experiences associated with the pursuit of different academic majors typically have effects over and beyond those that can be accounted for by initial selection into those major fields.*

The accentuation processes by which such impact occurs are very similar to those that result in differentiation among colleges. Individuals who elect a particular major in a given institution are not a random assortment of all its students. The preponderance of evidence now available indicates that whatever characteristics distinguish entrants into different majors tend, especially if relevant to the academic field chosen, to become still more distinctive of those groups following the pursuit of the major.

The mere fact that the same individuals, as freshmen, typically become different in significant ways, as seniors, does not "prove" that changes reflect impact of college experiences. Two considerations make such an inference questionable: many individuals who do not go to college make similar changes; and the very characteristics that determine the decision whether or not to go to college may also predetermine the likelihood of change. But the finding that initial differences among students are accentuated, following subsequent experience in college, bypasses both of these considerations. Such an analysis makes it possible to hold constant the variables of capacity and desire to attend college, and also individuals' initial status on the variable hypothetically subject to change. This is most clearly shown in Huntley's data: freshmen who initially scored highest in each value still further increased those scores if (as in most cases) they later selected a major relevant to that value—but, typically, not otherwise. Such a finding does not, of course, indicate that just going to college has a measurable impact, but it points to something more important—namely, a measured change that can reasonably be attributed to a particular combination of circumstances: a certain academic experience on the part of individuals already possessing certain characteristics. Other sources of impact also exist, presumably, but this one, at least, has been reasonably well demonstrated.

4. *The maintenance of existing values or attitudes, which, apart from certain kinds of college experience, might have been weakened or reversed, is an important kind of impact.*

Perhaps the best illustration occurs in those studies showing the persistence of pre-induction attitudes on the part of students after they join fraternities or sororities. A common aspect of this phenomenon, and perhaps an essential one, is that students are selected for membership in the Greek societies, in large part, on the basis of possessing the characteristics that subsequently persist. At least one "crucial experiment" (Siegel and Siegel, 1957) showed that students who wished to join a sorority-like group, but could not do so, subsequently developed attitudes more closely resembling those of students with whom they continued to live. Meanwhile other students who did succeed in joining the preferred group tended to maintain their previous attitudes. Since the two groups differed, initially, not in attitudes but only in that members of one group drew lucky numbers permitting them to move, the effects of residential associates are clearly demonstrated.

This process of reinforcement or consolidation is less conspicuous than that of change in individuals' attitudes and values. But it represents just as real an impact, in the sense that, in the absence of the reinforcing or consolidating experiences, outcomes would have been different. Students, like other people, tend to meet or to seek out and associate with others who have similar attitudes and values. Insofar as this occurs, processes of consolidation are ubiquitous; we suspect that they are at once the most common and the least noticed sources of colleges' impacts on their students.

5. *Though faculty members are often individually influential, particularly in respect to career decisions, college faculties do not appear to be responsible for campus-wide impact except in settings where the influence of student peers and of faculty complement and reinforce one another.*

Based on evidence collected primarily during the early and middle years of the 1960s, students typically report infrequent contact with faculty members at a personal level, nor do the majority of them indicate any strong desire for it. Many individual students do report experiences of intellectually exciting contacts with teachers, and sometimes even continuing personal friendships. For the most part, however, they expect such relationships to be professional—like those between patient and doctor, for example, only more frequent.

Their relative indifference to fraternalization with faculty members has something to do with students' consciousness of age and status differences, heightened by the symbolic significance of college as a milestone on the road from dependence on parental authority to maturity and autonomy. Students' recent and widespread expressions of concern about parietal rules *(in loco parentis)* and about their right to "a voice in decision making" represent, we suspect, not so much totally new attitudes as a new sense of freedom to voice them. The built-in differences between student and faculty culture are maintained, if in no other way, by the faculty's life-and-death power to grade students. Many students' first free association to the phrase "faculty member" might be something like "an automatic dispenser; you insert exams in the slot and it dispenses a grade."

At any rate, students perform a necessary function as socializers of one another—especially the younger by the older. Faculty can hardly expect to like the results of this kind of socialization if it occurs independently of their own endeavors, as if the two cultures were separated by a gulf.

6. *The conditions for campus-wide impacts appear to have been most frequently provided in small, residential, four-year colleges. These conditions probably include relative homogeneity of both faculty and student body together with opportunity for continuing interaction, not exclusively formal, among students and between students and faculty.*

Campus-wide impact presupposes not only a set of college influences, preponderantly favoring rather than opposing that effect, but also some degree of homogeneity on the part of its entering students. Until recently, at least, it has been a fact of life in American higher education that both of these conditions are more likely to be met in small, private colleges than in large, most commonly public ones. Many state universities attract a population almost as heterogeneous as the population of their states; their faculties are too large, and too thoroughly compartmentalized in departments, schools, colleges, and research centers, to exert uniform effects. Thus diverse influences—in quite different subenvironments within the megaversity—upon quite diverse student populations induce few *common* impacts, if any, beyond those that can be accounted for in terms of society-wide influences on young people who have somewhat superior capacities and more or less standard interests and aspirations in our society.

The "traditional" small, private colleges, on the other hand, are apt to have established images of their own—some of them nationwide, some of them mainly local. In either case, such institutions tend to attract both students and faculty who are familiar with the image, and favorably disposed to it. So it is that small colleges—inviting both informality and frequency of personal encounter, while providing relative homogeneity of student input and/or faculty influence—have had a potential for institution-wide impact that is typically lacking in large universities.

These considerations do not, of course, negate the possibility that certain subunits or odd corners of larger universities have had marked impacts upon selected students. A university consisting of congeries of small loci of diverse impacts might, indeed, be the apotheosis of effective higher education. Such "local impacts" within large universities, however, have more often been attributable to good fortune, probably, than to systematic arrangements designed to make them occur.

> 7. *In addition to the effects of campus-wide influences and the pressures of subenvironments, college impacts are conditioned by the background and personality of the student.*

Presently available information suggests that the more incongruent a student is with the overall environment of his college the more likely he is to withdraw from that college or from higher education in general. We did not find much support, however, for the often-voiced notion that, for students who remain in college, change will be greatest for those whose backgrounds are initially the most discontinuous with the college environment. Our best guess at the moment is that a college is most likely to have the largest impact on students who experience a continuing series of not-too-threatening discontinuities. Too great a divergence between student and college, especially initially, may result in the student's marshalling of resistances. Too little might mean no impetus for change. From this point of view, a college's objectives might include that of inculcating a tolerance, or even a desire, for those discrepancies that can stimulate change and growth.

Students vary in the degree to which they are open to change—in terms either of their willingness to confront new ideas, values, and experiences nondefensively or of their willingness to be influenced by others. Current evidence suggests that the higher an entering student is on either of these dimensions, the greater is the impact of college. These traits need not be unchanging aspects of a student's personality—that is, they can be affected by experiences on the campus. Therefore, the amount and nature of college impacts are not necessarily predetermined by the student's initial degree of openness to change.

8. *Attitudes held by students on leaving college tend to persist thereafter, particularly as a consequence of living in post-college environments that support those attitudes. Within-college changes, especially if accompanied by a general stance of openness to change, may be still further extended in response to new social and technological conditions.*

The general finding that attitudes change little after college years cannot be attributed simply to "inherent inertia" or to some sort of early hardening of psychological arteries. The basic fact is that one's attitudes and values do not change whimsically, but in response to new information or to new ways of viewing one's world. The older one becomes, the less the *relative* impact of any particular set of new experiences. The unique thing about late-adolescence-merging-into-early-maturity is that at this stage of development one is, in our society, maximally motivated to achieve autonomy and at the same time minimally constrained to conform to the restrictions of adult roles. The typical consequence may well be this: if one does not change during this period one is not likely to change thereafter. Or, alternatively, if one has changed during these years one may have acquired a propensity for changing oneself in response to changes in the world outside oneself.

For many of its students, in sum, college-induced changes in attitudes and values are likely to persist. Most of them are not likely again to be so susceptible to new influences, and their college-acquired stances will, to some degree, continue to symbolize independence and adulthood. For some, at least, habits of being open to new information, and being influenced thereby, will result in persisting openness to further change; such an outcome, it may be argued, is one of the goals of a college education.

No single principle has emerged in so many different guises as that of accentuation—either, under certain conditions, of individuals' initially prominent characteristics or of initial differences among groups of students. In its general form, the proposition is as follows:

9. *Whatever the characteristics of an individual that selectively propel him toward particular educational settings—going to college, selecting a particular one, choosing a certain academic major, acquiring membership in a particular group of peers—those same characteristics are apt to be reinforced and extended by the experiences incurred in those selected settings.*

The proposition is intended to be a very broad one. It is too general, of course, to apply to every characteristic of every individual. It is intended, rather, to refer to characteristics that typically distinguish, say, 18-year-olds who do from those who do not go to college, or college students majoring in physics from those majoring in French. But it is not too general to be tested in the form of specific hypotheses in particular settings (as in comparatively small groups of academic majors at Union College). Also, the proposition is intended to include reinforcement or consolidation—without measured change (see proposition 4)—as well as further heightening of initially prominent characteristics.

Furthermore, the consequences of initial selection of a college or of a major, as asserted in the proposition, imply a certain degree of correctness on the part of the applicant to a particular college or a particular major, in estimating its suitability to his particular interests. Obviously, some such judgments are wide of the mark—quite aside from the fact that decisions about colleges and majors may be made on quite irrelevant grounds. Nevertheless, the empirical fact is that many colleges and probably most majors do attract and select students in ways that result in considerable homogeneity within their student populations.

What the general proposition really asserts is that *processes of attracting and selecting students are interdependent with processes of impact.* From this point of view, colleges' impacts begin before their students arrive. By the same token, those delayed processes of selection that result in student attrition must also be considered a form of impact: the disappearance of certain kinds of dropouts not only constitutes a message to those who remain; it also removes certain kinds of influence (in the form of deviant students) upon those who stay.

Insofar as the principle of accentuation is widely applicable, it carries some educational implications, especially about the possibility of narrowing student interests and increasingly homogeneous student bodies. If colleges select only certain kinds of young people, if particular colleges select only certain types within an already limited population, if departmental majors and student peer groups apply still more restrictive criteria of selection—then is it not inevitable that every student's world becomes increasingly narrowed, including only students and a few teachers like himself?

Put thus extremely, the facts belie the charge. While some degree of homogeneity characterizes every college's body of newly arrived students, the departing seniors are not necessarily more homogeneous. Furthermore, accentuation of initial group differences is not invariably accompanied by increasing homogeneity of individual scores. (For example, at Union College where accentuation of initial major field differences was very strong, decreasing homogeneity within curricular groups with respect to the accentuated values was more common than increasing homogeneity). Findings such as these do not suggest that the output of a succession of selective processes is a standard-model senior within each college or within each department. Rather, they point to pluralistic influences acting upon individuals who, though somewhat homogeneous in some respects, are diverse in many others. The possibility of narrow intensification of interests exists, of course, as we think it should, but far from every student follows that possible path.

More serious, perhaps, is the possibility that a good many prospective college students are *de facto* preordained to flow through certain academic channels without serious consideration of alternatives. Again, the available evidence sets the fear to rest. (To take one example, according to our most complete set of data, at Union College hardly more than one-third of the students selected majors in which their initially highest values were likely to be accentuated, in the sense of being further increased. For instance, only 11 of 65 students whose initially highest value was Aesthetic majored in humanities, although ten of these eleven raised their scores for this value still higher as seniors.) What the phenomenon of accentuation of initially prominent attributes reveals, then, must be stated conditionally: *if* students initially having certain characteristics choose a certain setting (a college, a major, a peer group) in which those characteristics are prized and nurtured, accentuation of such characteristics is likely to occur. Thus its prevalence in a given institution is determined by such considerations as the actual distinctiveness of each of the settings, the accuracy by which the distinctiveness is recognized, and the single-mindedness of the individuals entering that institution. The frequency of transfers from one college to another, from one prospective major to another, and from one residential or peer group to another, suggests that a student's earliest decisions do not ordinarily result in forms of accentuation that predetermine later choices.

Impacts, from this point of view, depend on the goodness of fit between student and institution—but this formulation conceals a paradox. If we assume that a college is likely to change its students, or that it should do so, then for any one of them, as of today, the personal characteristics for which he needs to find a good fit within his institution may be different from yesterday's. If changing and searching for new good-fits are desirable experiences for a college student, then perhaps some colleges select and reward their students so narrowly that accentuation of initially prominent attributes becomes their only path to survival. Perhaps others select such heterogeneous bodies of students and provide for them settings that, educationally, are so poorly differentiated that experiences of accentuation are almost left to chance.

We suspect that, in fundamental ways, the twin experiences of self-discovery and finding a good fit involve a succession of accentuations, along with the discarding of poor fits. But colleges, too, can profit by self-discovery, and the study of its own patterns of providing accentuations is one path toward self-insight.

## A LOOK AHEAD

Tomorrow's settings for maximizing impacts on students will have to differ from yesterday's. It seems likely that the social and psychological conditions that have often been provided on small "intimate" campuses can be created within the larger (and often urban) universities increasing proportions of American students are attending.

It is customary to attribute the shortcomings of undergraduate education in large American universities, along with many of the world's other ailments, to overpopulation. The increasing "prevalence of people," together with our addiction to democratic mass education, has overstuffed our universities, which have now become gargantuan anthills. Hence their computerized bureaucracy, their impersonality, and the impossibility of impacts that are educationally relevant. So goes the myth.

If, as we are told, myths serve collective functions, then perhaps the usefulness of this one is that it absolves educators from blame—but not the social scientists, who have presumably learned to distinguish between the effects of organizational size and of organizational structuring. One cannot inquire about the optimal size of a university without also asking about its modes of internal organization—the nature of its component parts and their interrelationships. University planners have of course given thought to matters of vertical organization, dealing with hierarchical levels of power and responsibility for making decisions in discriminable areas within the life of a modern multiversity. Their organizational charts typically resemble a truncated pyramid—cut off at the bottom; they do not have enough space at the bottom of the page for any level below the department chairmanship. We do not question the reality of such a vertical organization, but we wonder about its adequacy and its desirability.

Our complaint is not merely that such vertical organizations may be overproliferated, but rather that they are too often expected to substitute for adequate forms of horizontal organization—that is, institutionalized arrangements concerning interrelationships at the same or immediately adjacent "levels." We can do no better than to quote from Katz and Kahn's *Social Psychology of Organizations* (1966), p. 222:

> The formal, hierarchical organization is an instrument of great effectiveness; it offers great economies over unorganized effort; it achieves great unity and compliance. But its deficiencies include great waste of human potential for innovation and creativity and great psychological cost to the members, many of whom spend their lives in organizations without caring much either for the system (except its extrinsic rewards and accidental interpersonal relationships) or for the goal toward which the sys-

tem effort is directed. The modification of hierarchical organization to meet these criticisms is one of the great needs of human life.

The size, in itself, of an institution devoted to higher education matters little if its internal organization is appropriate to its size. We have in mind *horizontal* organization in particular. At any given horizontal level, however, absolute size *does* matter. This assertion may be buttressed by another pair of rather general propositions:

1. Insofar as the goals of an organization prominently include psychological changes on the part of its members, as ends rather than only as means to other ends, its goals can be furthered by processes of mutual support and mutual stimulation among members of whom changes are expected. (Kurt Lewin put it this way: "It is often easier to change a whole group than a single individual.") This proposition, we suggest, applies *a fortiori*, though not exclusively, to changes in attitudes and values as contrasted, say, with the acquisition of information or dexterity.

2. The conditions that favor mutual stimulation and support must be described in interpersonal terms. They include, particularly, opportunity for continued interaction among the same individuals, allowing occasions for the discovery of mutual congeniality, preferably in varied settings—not just academic or just recreational or just residential, for example.

These propositions point quite directly to forms of horizontal organization such that, whatever the size of the institution, its human sources of stimulation and support (both students and faculty) will be distributed into as many centers as suggested by the following formula:

$$\frac{\text{Total population of the institution}}{\text{Optimal size of interpersonal environment}} = N \text{ of parallel units}$$

One may wonder, of course, whether such a form of horizontal organization might not be cumbersome. If, for example, a typical state mega-multiversity already includes a dozen or 15 separate schools and colleges, would not a further division of even one of them (say the Arts College) into another dozen or so create an organization man's, or a university president's, nightmare? We are inclined to reply that if educational considerations are really superordinate, then administrative convenience is subordinate.

If basic educational practices of American colleges and universities have changed little during the past half-century, neither have their forms of organization, and the two inertial trends are not unrelated. Our conversations with colleagues across the country suggest that there is no dearth of fresh and imaginative educational ideas, but a great deal of discouragement about the possibilities of "bucking the system." Faculty members tend to point to administrators, and vice versa, as the locus of resistance to changes. Both are right, in one sense, but both are wrong insofar as they assume that educational change must occur within existing forms of organization. Our own observation suggests that, given a single condition, new forms of horizontal organization invite, or at least facilitate, significant educational innovation. Indeed, one may go further: if new educational forms take interpersonal influence into account, then in contemporary American universities new organizational forms are a necessary means to educational ends.

The "single condition" that we have in mind, if such ends are to be achieved through such means, is a considerable degree of *local autonomy*. By way of analogy, it is a commonplace that conformity on the part of an individual is the enemy of creativeness. Just so, the exigencies of standard procedures within a single unit of a university are likely to abort creative innovations in education. Mere subdivision of a hypertrophied unit—say the Liberal Arts College of a state university—will not yield much innovation if each part is constrained to remain a miniature replica of the primeval parent. What is required is some sense of educational distinctiveness. Given a charter-built grant of autonomy, this kind of distinctiveness becomes possible.

Indexes

# Name Index

**A**

Adelson, Joseph, 74
Alatis, J. E., 293
Alger, Horatio, 34
Amerman, Helen E., 360
Anderson, C. A., 112, 200
Angrist, Shirley S., 70
Apple, Michael W., 269, 272, 274, 284, 287
Ariès, Philipe, 114, 115, 116, 119, 121
Armor, David, 41, 42, 43, 44, 51
Ausubel, D. P., 147, 161
Avineri, S., 286, 287

**B**

Bachrach, Peter, 328, 338
Bagley, William C., 15
Bailyn, B., 116, 121, 123
Banfield, Edward C., 250
Banks, Olive, 143, 155, 161
Baratz, M. S., 328, 338
Barber, Bernard, 156, 161
Bard, Bernard, 251
Barnard, Chester I., 350, 360, 362, 364
Barr, A. S., 363
Bates, R. F., 228
Bauman, Z., 142
Becker, Howard S., 262, 268, 324, 358
Bell, Robert R., 125
Bell, Wendell, 392
Bendix, Reinhard, 74, 128, 161, 162, 315, 392
Bennet, M., 157, 161
Bennet, P., 157, 161
Bensman, Joseph, 353
Berger, Bennet, 55
Berger, Peter L., 278, 283, 287
Bernstein, A. J., 163

Bernstein, Basil, 97, 98, 112, 143, 147, 148, 159
Bettleheim, B., 121, 123
Bevan, Nye, 159
Bidwell, C. E., 328, 338
Birns, P., 149, 162
Blau, Peter M., 95
Bloom, Benjamin S., 4, 161, 261, 268
Boocock, Sarane S., 74
Bowles, Frank, 386
Brademas, John, 50
Bronfenbrenner, U., 120, 123, 148, 149, 161
Brookover, Wilbur B., 83, 258, 305, 349
Brophy, Jere E., 101, 113, 306
Brown, B., 113
Brown, Francis J., 393
Brown, R., 292
Bruner, J. S., 292
Bryant, Betty H., 289
Buck, Roy C., 355
Burger, Warren, 52
Burnstein, Eugene, 362
Burt, M. K., 292
Bush, R. N., 243
Butler, Nicholas Murray, 16

**C**

Callahan, Raymond E., 15, 17
Calvin, John, 9
Campbell, Ernest Q., 74
Caplow, Theodore, 350, 351
Carlson, Richard, 7
Caro, F. G., 149, 161
Cartter, Allan M., 377
Cazden, Courtney B., 289, 292, 296
Celebrezze, Anthony, 51
Chandler, Bobby J., 360

417

Charters, W. W., Jr., 262, 268
Chayes, Abram, 38
Chinoy, Ely, 174, 184
Cicourel, Aaron U., 189
Clark, Burton, 20, 54, 55, 56, 57, 323, 391, 395, 396
Clark, Kenneth B., 34, 186
Clark, Mamie, 34
Clayton, A. Stafford, 359
Clegg, A., 143, 156, 161
Cohen, Albert, 196
Cohen, David K., 40, 44
Cohen, Elizabeth G., 238, 240, 243
Coleman, James S., 3, 32, 35, 36, 37, 38, 40, 44, 45, 46, 47, 48, 49, 50, 51, 52, 54, 55, 56, 57, 70, 80, 101, 117, 121, 123, 149
Conant, James R., 22
Connelly, K. J., 292
Corey, A., 239, 243
Corwin, Ronald G., 6, 13, 24, 349, 351, 356, 357
Coser, Lewis A., 281, 282, 283, 287, 354
Cremin, L. A., 116, 121, 123
Crockett, Harry J., Jr., 180, 181, 182, 184
Cubberley, Ellwood P., 17
Curti, Merle, 11, 21

**D**
Dahrendorf, R., 277, 281, 287
Dailey, John T., 74
Dale, R., 161
Davis, Allison, 262
Davis, Kingsley, 54
Denney, Reuel, 375
Dennis, J., 285, 287
Dennison, E. F., 116, 123
Deutsch, M., 97, 149, 161
Dewey, John, 15, 23, 34, 122, 123
Dipbrze, Wilbert, 362
Dodd, Catherine, 312
Dodson, C. J., 292
Dollard, John, 42, 262
Douglas, J. W. B., 156, 161
Douvan, Elizabeth, 74
Drabick, L. W., 355
Drachler, Norman, 49, 50, 51
Dreeben, R., 272, 287, 338
Drews, E. M., 149, 161
Drucker, P., 120, 123
Dulay, H., 292
Durkheim, Emile, 82, 83, 146, 147, 156, 327, 338
Durkin, M. C., 280, 287

**E**
Easton, D., 285, 287
Edwards, Newton, 7, 8, 9, 10

Eells, K., 97
Eisenstadt, S. N., 54, 121, 123
Eisinger, P. K., 270, 287
Elder, G. H., Jr., 115, 123
Eliot, Charles, 377
Elkin, Frederick, 74
Empey, Lamar T., 178, 184
Engels, Frederick, 156
Epperson, D. C., 55
Epstein, Jason, 38
Erickson, Erik H., 4, 118, 123
Erickson, Kai, 198
Ervin-Tripp, S., 294
Etzioni, Amatai, 243, 329, 338, 358
Eurich, Alvin C., 372

**F**
Fanon, Franz, 300
Fauset, Charles E., 351
Feldman, Kenneth A., 402
Feur, L. F., 119, 123
Fischer, G., 288
Fischer, John H., 253
Fisher, J. L., 296
Fishman, J. A., 296
Flanigan, Jean, 356
Flannery, Nick, 51
Floud, J. E., 112, 149, 162, 200, 315
Fox, William H., 361
Franklin, Benjamin, 34
Frazier, E. Franklin, 126, 128, 134
Friedenberg, Edgar Z., 269
Fuchs, Estelle, 149, 162, 339

**G**
Gardner, Burleigh, 350
Garfinkel, H., 287
Gerstl, Joel E., 164, 352
Getzels, J. W., 353
Gibson, E. F., 271, 287
Glaser, Barney G., 362
Glazer, Nathan, 375
Glick, Paul C., 166, 184
Goffman, Erving, 391, 392, 398
Golden, H., 149, 192
Good, Thomas L., 261 268, 306
Goodlad, John I., 248, 249
Goodman, Paul, 114, 123
Goodson, Max R., 365
Gordon, G. S., 349
Goslin, Willard E., 349
Goss, Mary E. W., 357
Gouldner, Alvin W., 273, 277, 278, 287
Gracey, Harry L., 82
Groff, Patrick J., 349
Gross, Edward, 358, 365
Guba, E. G., 353
Guilford, J. P., 74

## H

Hagen, Elizabeth, 361
Hagstrom, Warren O., 273, 274, 275, 276, 287
Haller, Archie O., 174, 185
Halsey, A. H., 112, 149, 162, 200, 315
Hamilton, Richard F., 170, 184
Hansen, Donald A., 164, 352
Hare, N., 280, 288
Hargreaves, David, 193, 194, 196, 197
Harriman, Averell, 33
Harrington, Michael, 138
Harrison, F. I., 150, 162
Hartley, E., 161
Haugen, E., 294
Haveman, Ernest, 168, 184
Heath, Douglas H., 119, 123
Henderson, A. M., 355
Henry, Jules, 150, 171, 269
Herriot, Robert E., 360
Herrnstein, Richard, 3, 39, 40, 43
Herskovitz, Melville J., 344
Hesa, R., 161
Hess, Robert D., 4, 78, 96, 101, 113
Himmelweit, H., 150, 162
Hodgson, Godfrey, 32
Hoehn, A. J., 262, 268
Hoggart, R., 150, 156, 162
Hollingshead, August B., 126, 130, 174, 180, 184
Homans, George C., 158, 162, 214
Houriet, R., 119, 123
Howe, Harold, 51
Huebner, D., 286, 288
Hughes, Everett C., 317, 383
Hummel, Raymond C., 244
Huxley, R., 289
Hyman, Herbert H., 150, 162, 172, 173, 174, 180, 184, 392
Hymes, D., 162, 289, 296, 297

## I

Iffert, Robert E., 394
Illich, Ivan, 114, 123
Ingram, E., 289

## J

Jackson, B., 159, 162
Jackson, Emanuel, 302
Jackson, Philip W., 262, 268, 269, 288
Jacobson, Lenore, 198, 268
Jahoda, Marie, 56
Jefferson, Thomas, 34
Jencks, Christopher, 2, 3, 32, 36, 38, 44, 45, 47, 48, 49, 50, 52, 138, 369, 372
Jensen, Arthur, 3, 39, 40
John, V. P., 97, 296
Johnson, Lyndon B., 32, 35, 52

Josephson, E., 118, 123
Just, M., 293

## K

Kagan, J., 105, 106, 107, 108, 113
Kahl, Joseph A., 4, 128, 150, 151, 169, 174, 178, 181, 182, 183, 184, 205, 219
Kandel, D. B., 117, 123
Katz, F. M., 151, 162
Katz, Fred E., 55
Katz, Irwin, 41
Katz, Michael B., 251
Kelly, Robert L., 394
Kemper, T. D., 332, 333, 338
Kennedy, John F., 375
Kennedy, W. A., 97
Kenniston, Kenneth, 117, 118, 119, 120, 123, 124
Kerman, Keith, 297
Kerr, Clark, 380
Kerr, Norman D., 354
King, R., 151, 162
Kitsuse, John I., 189, 360
Kleiner, Robert J., 126, 135, 177, 185
Kliebard, H. M., 286, 288
Kluckhohn, C., 151, 155, 159, 162
Kluckhohn, Florence R., 162, 218
Knupfer, P., 151, 162
Kohn, M. L., 152, 162
Kornhauser, Arthur, 359
Kuhler, Raymond, 362
Kuhn, T. S., 274, 288

## L

Labov, W., 299
Lahaderne, Henriette M., 262, 268
Lakatos, I., 288
Lambert, W. E., 293, 295
Lavin, David E., 70
Leighton, R., 159, 162
Lein, Laura, 297
Lenneberg, E. H., 293
LaShan, J., 152, 162
Lesser, G. S., 97, 117, 124
Levalée, Margarite, 293
Lewin, Kurt, 258
Liberty, Paul, 362
Lieberman, Myron, 349, 351, 362, 363
Lincoln, Abraham, 11
Linton, Ralph, 350
Lipset, Seymour M., 32, 38, 45, 74, 128, 161, 162, 235, 315, 392
London, Jack, 156, 162
Lortie, D. C., 239, 243
Lowenthal, L., 163, 235
Lucas, Louis, 51
Luckman, T., 278
Lueders-Salmon, Erika, 296
Luther, Martin, 9

Lynd, Robert S., 359, 366
Lysgaard, Svere, 163, 179, 181, 182, 185

**M**

McClelland, David C., 180, 184, 223, 382
McClure, H., 288
Maccoby, E., 161
McDill, Edward L., 53, 60, 70
McLuhan, Marshall, 79
McMaster, A., 280, 287
McNamara, Robert, 383
Malcolm, X, 281
Mann, Horace, 21, 34
Maratsos, M. P., 290
Marland, S. P., 120, 124
Marsden, D., 159, 162
Marshall, T. H., 317
Martin, F. M., 315
Marx, Karl, 156, 286
Maslow, A., 334, 338
Matza, David, 54, 57
Mayer, Martin, 252
Mays, J. B., 152, 162
Mead, George H., 156
Mead, Margaret, 24
Medsker, Leland L., 395
Megson, B., 143, 156, 161
Mehan, H., 296
Meir, Dorothy, 392
Melaragno, R. J., 120, 124
Mellon, Andrew, 15
Merton, Robert K., 144, 184, 322, 391, 392
Meyer, J., 240, 243
Meyer, Roberta, 101
Meyers, Edmund D., Jr., 60, 70
Miller, Herman P., 170, 185
Miller, L., 295
Miller, Van, 355
Mills, C. Wright, 142, 368, 374
Mitchell, Jonathan, 116, 124
Mizruchi, Herman P., 182, 184, 185
Moeller, Gerald H., 357, 360
Moffett, J., 290
Molnar, S., 243
Moore, David G., 350
Moore, H. A., 355
Moore, M., 235
Moss, H. A., 105, 108, 113
Mosteller, Frederick, 44, 45, 46, 48, 50
Moulton, Robert, 362
Moynihan, Daniel P., 3, 32, 33, 37, 38, 41,
    44, 45, 46, 47, 48, 49, 50, 52
Mulkay, M., 274, 284, 288
Munroe, Robert L., 302
Musgrave, P., 143, 163
Musgrove, F., 152, 163
Myrdal, Gunnar, 42

**N**

Naegele, Kaspar, 326

Nagle, John M., 244
Neill, A. S., 255
Newcomb, Theodore, 161, 402
Newman, F., 120, 124
Newmann, F., 282, 288
Nixon, Richard, 33, 45

**O**

Olexa, Carol, 186
Olim, E. G., 101, 113
Oliver, D., 282, 288
Orwell, George, 156

**P**

Parker, Seymour, 126, 135, 177, 185
Parsons, Talcott, 142, 153, 163, 216, 228,
    277, 355, 382
Passamanick, B., 349
Passow, A. H., 161
Pauling, Linus, 275
Pearl, Arthur, 187
Perrucci, Robert, 164
Perry, L. R., 143, 163
Pettigrew, Thomas, 3, 38, 40, 41, 42, 43,
    44
Philips, S. U., 298
Phillips, Margaret, 322
Piaget, Jean, 4, 283, 293
Pierson, Frank C., 395
Polanyi, M., 272, 273, 288, 291, 292
Polk, Kenneth, 186
Popkewitz, T. S., 284
Potter, David, 34
Presthus, Robert, 244
Price, E., 292

**Q-R**

Quie, Albert, 50
Redfield, Robert, 310
Redlich, Frederick C., 126, 130, 180, 184
Rehberg, Richard A., 55
Reich, Emil, 312
Reimer, E., 114, 124
Reisman, Frank, 153, 163, 259
Reiss, Albert, 351
Reissman, Leonard, 128
Remmhein, Madaline K., 356
Rettig, S., 349
Rhea, Buford, 249
Richard, J., 292
Richy, Robert W., 351
Riesman, David, 30, 369, 372, 375, 376,
    387
Rigsby, Leo B., 53, 60, 70
Riley, John, 235
Riley, M., 235
Rist, Roy, 153, 163
Roberts, K., 153, 163
Rodman, Hyman, 125, 126, 128, 130, 136

Rogoff, Natalie, 200
Roosevelt, Franklin, 52
Rose, Arnold N., 126, 128, 129, 130
Rosen, Bernard, 180, 182, 185
Rosenthal, Robert, 194, 261, 268

S

Sachar, Abram, 51
St. John, Mary Hoyt, 360
Sanford, Nevitt, 369
Schafer, Walter E., 55, 186
Schegloff, Emanuel, 298
Schneider, Louis, 179, 181, 182, 185
Schooler, T., 152, 162
Schwebel, N., 163
Seeman, Melvin, 324
Segalowitz, N., 293
Seligman, C. R., 295
Selznick, Philip, 323
Senesh, L., 279, 288
Sewell, William H., 174, 185, 205
Sexton, Patricia C., 187, 257
Shapiro, E., 299
Sharpe, Laura, 385
Shaw, George B., 256
Shils, Edward, 142, 163
Shipman, Virginia C., 4, 78, 96, 101, 113
Siegel, Sidney, 266, 268
Sigel, I. E., 105, 108, 113
Sigel, R., 270, 288
Silberman, Charles E., 38, 256
Simon, Joan, 158, 159, 163
Simpson, George E., 127, 134
Sinclair, H., 293
Singer, Milton, 310
Sizer, Theodore R., 305, 307
Smith, D., 146, 163
Smith, Marshall, 44, 45, 48
Smith, M. B., 402
Snow, C. E., 290
Spady, William G., 55, 327
Spalding, Willard B., 355
Spencer, Herbert, 52
Spitzer, S. P., 145, 163
Sproul, Robert G., 401
Squibb, P. G., 142
Stephenson, Richard M., 177, 178
Stiles, Lindley J., 360
Stinchcombe, Arthur, 74, 195, 335, 338
Stinnett, T. M., 243
Storer, Norman W., 275, 288
Stouffer, Samuel A., 218
Straus, Murray A., 174, 181, 182, 183, 185
Stryker, Perrin, 399
Stub, Holger R., 349

T

Taba, Hilda, 280
Tawney, R. R., 9

Tax, Sol, 294
Teahan, J. E., 149, 161
Terrien, Frederic W., 353
Thomas, George B., 249
Thomas, Hugh, 275
Thomas, R. K., 294
Thompson, George G., 268
Thorndike, Robert L., 361
Toby, Jackson, 322
Tressel, Robert, 156, 163
Trow, Martin, 391
Tucker, G. R., 295
Tumin, Melvin M., 325
Turner, Ralph H., 54, 155, 163

V

Van den Berg, J. H., 115, 124
Van de Riet, V., 97
Veblen, Thorstein, 11, 14, 15, 157, 163
Veysey, Laurence, 377
Vlick, Mary, 349, 357

W

Walker, J. L., 281, 288
Walker, W., 295
Walkout, Donald, 349
Waller, Willard, 19, 54, 349
Ward, C., 290, 297, 301
Ware, Marth L., 356
Warren, Earl, 51
Warren, Neil, 56
Watson, J. D., 274, 275, 284, 288
Weber, Max, 9, 329, 330, 338, 350, 355
West, Patricia, 168, 184
Westley, William A., 74
White, J. C., Jr., 97
White, W., 153, 163
Whitehead, A. N., 5
Whitehead, J. L., 295
Whyte, William F., 31, 350
Wilcox, P., 280, 288
Wilensky, Harold L., 168, 185
Willholm, S. M., 271, 288
William, Doyle, 51
Williams, F., 295
Williams, T. I., 292
Wilson, Bryan R., 309
Wilson, James Q., 305
Wilson, Logan, 357
Wilson, Woodrow, 11
Wittgenstein, L., 288
Wohl, R. Richard, 169, 185
Woodward, C. Vann, 52
Worth, Walter H., 363
Wynne, Edward, 114, 121, 124

Y

Yinger, J. Milton, 127, 134
Young, Michael, 40, 376

# Subject Index

## A

Achievement
 and legitimacy, 332–34
 motive, 180–81
 and teacher-pupil contact, 262–67
Adolescent subculture, 5
Alternative schools, 4
American colleges, shortcomings of, 120
"American Dream," 132–33
American Medical Association, 374, 383
Anti-intellectualism, 381
Autocracy in school, 258

## B

Black Panthers, 42
Black Studies, 260
Brown versus School Board of Topeka, 34–35
 retrial of case, 51–52
Bureau of Applied Social Research, 203
Bureaucracy
 definition of, 244, 246
 and educational planning, 253
 inconsistent with learning, 248–49
 and lack of incentives for change, 252
 in schools, 83–84
 and urban schools, 246–54

## C

Cambridge Institute, 33
Carnegie Commission on Higher Education, 120, 123
Carnegie Corporation Cross Cultural Education Project, 294
Caste system in the classroom, 153
Center for the Study of Instruction, 279
Cherokee Indians, 294–95
Chicago Maroon, 123
Child centered families, 19
Child centered school, 4

Childhood, and concepts of, 115
Civil Rights Act of 1964, 35
Civil Rights Commission, 40–41
Classroom interaction
 and social climate, 255
 and social processes, 255–60
 teacher as dominant in, 256
College
 administrators, 38
 and authoritarianism, 403
 change in educational practice, 413
 college degrees in the U.S., 167
 "cooling out," 391–401
 and equal opportunity, 392
 impact of, 402–14
 increase in numbers, 370
 professors, 262–65
 quality of, 168
 the small traditional, 413
 social function, 367
 special interest, 386, 389
 status system, 363–65
College planning
 by scholastic ability, 209
 by size of community, 208
Coleman Report
 effect of, 35–42, 44–47, 50, 256
 skeptics of, 50
Columbia University, 203
Communication codes
 elaborated, 97, 100–101
  definition of, 97–98
 restricted, 97, 100–101
  definition of, 97–98
 effect of early experience, 98
 and social-status differences, 101 ff
Communication and language
 and family structure, 97
 and social structure, 97
Community status, 350

423

Compensatory education, criticism of, 148, 257–58
Conflict
  in schools, 327
  in scientific communities, 272–76
  in social studies, 276–83
  in society, 327
  uses of, 327
Consensus theory of science, 273
"Cooling out" process, education and, 145–46
Credentials, importance of, 139
Culturally deprived child, 153
"Cumulative deficit" in education, 147

**D-E**

Deferred gratification pattern, 179
Deschooling, 4
Education
  affecting social change, 138
  and business, 9, 11
  and the cult of efficiency, 15–18
  differential responses to, 139
  and the family, 18–20
  "good," 139
  for gentlemen, 312
  and ethnic origins, 169
  and ideal family, 154
  and juvenile delinquency, 232
  as key to mobility, 137 ff
  and leisure, 31–32
  and occupational origins, 169
  political uses of, 157
  and price system, 11
  Puritans, 8
  and religion, 7
  revolution in, 164, 168
  and the state, 20–22
  as a secondary institution, 82
  and teacher's role, 146
Education explosion, 187
Educational Testing Service, 203, 219
Elementary and Secondary Education Act of 1965, 50
  Title III, 249
Elementary school
  reward structure, 238–39
  selection, 228–32
  socialization, 228–32
English "public" schools, 81

**F**

Family, and school class, 224–28
Farm Bureau, 374
Federal Bureau of Investigation, 375
"Feminization" of the school, 306
Ford Foundation, 51
Formal roles, 212
Formal status system, 58
  commitment to, 61, 64–66, 69–71

Formal structure of schools, 212
Fourteenth Amendment, and school desegregation, 51
Free schools, 4
Free Speech Movement, 43
Functional theory, 278

**G**

Good Opportunity Observation Device, 264–65
Graduate education and undergraduate education, 384–85
Graduation from high school, percentage in U.S., 166, 168
"Great Society," 35
Guttman scale, 181

**H**

Harvard Center for Law and Education, 51
*Harvard Educational Review*, 38
Harvard School of Graduate Education, 32
Haverford College, 119
Head Start Program, 257
Higher education
  "cooling out" function, 391–401
  and Wall Street, 383
Higher Horizons, 249
Home and School Associations, 215
House Select Subcommittee on Education, 50

**I**

Illinois Farmer's Institute, 15
Inner city schools, 307; *see also* Urban schools
Inequality
  between individuals, 48
  of income, 48
Individualized instruction, 260
Informal structure
  rules, 212, 214
  of schools, 212
  status and, 64, 66, 69, 70, 214
Institutionalization of play, 25
Ivy League, 141

**J-K**

Junior college, 395, 401
Juvenile delinquency and education, 232
Kindergarten
  and the "bad student," 92
  as "boot camp," 82 ff
  and the "good student," 92
  learning the role of student, 82 ff
  and meaningless routines, 94
  and problem children, 92
  social structure of, 93
  as training for bureaucracy, 95

Krushal-Wallis Analysis of variance, 265

**L**

Language
  as curriculum content, 289–96
  elaborated code, 148
  and family structure, 97
  learning environment, 296–302
  learning first language, 292
  learning second language, 293
  restricted code, 148
  and social structure, 97
  and teaching grammar, 290
Lee Thorpe Interest Inventory, 396
Legitimacy
  and achievement, 332–34
  breakdown of, 336–39
  and charismatic authority, 330–31
  and expert authority, 331
  nature of, 330–32
  and rational legal authority, 330–31
  of teachers, 332
  and teacher effectiveness, 334–36
  and traditional authority, 330–31
*Life,* 121, 124
Life styles, middle level, 140
Low achievement, as caused by schools, 192–99
Lower class
  aspirations of, 125 ff, 178
  boys, 148, 149
  in Britain, 146
  and educational inadequacies, 142–61
  and ethnic identification, 126
  and language (codes), 148
  and middle class values, 126
  Negro lower class, 125 ff; *see also* Black Studies
  mothers' aspirations for their children, 125 ff
  norms of, 140
  and randomness of behavior, 150
  and relation to age at marriage, 130
  training by punishment, 152
  value stretch, 126
  values, 125, 152

**M**

Manhattan Project, 378
Martin Luther King Family Center, 302
Massachusetts Act of 1647, 8, 18
Mass education, 1, 10
Maternal teaching styles, analysis of, 108, 112
Middle class
  behavior, 150
  comparison of attitudes with 15th century, 158
  conception of education, 139–40
  culture, 148–49

Middle class—*Cont.*
  families, 19
  and mastery over nature, 151
  "new middle class," 368
  "old middle class," 368
  "self directed," 153
  and status achievement, 151
  teacher expectations for, 257
  values, 147, 153, 159
More Effective Schools Program, 249

**N**

National Association for the Advancement of Colored People, 34
National Education Association, 10, 15, 21
National Opinion Research Center, 351
National Teacher Corps, 249
Navaho Indians, 159
New Careers model, 198–99
New Deal, 34
New Left Institute for Policy Studies, 33
*The New Republic,* 33
*New York Review,* 114
*The New York Times,* 43, 49, 374

**O**

Occupation and "philosophy of life," 157
Office of Economic Opportunity, 375
Office of Education, 37
Office of Graduate and Career Plans, 119
Office of Management and the Budget, 50
Open classroom, 260
"Open door" admission, 372, 394
Open schools, 4
Open-space schools, 238–43
  differentiated from open classroom, 240
  teacher interaction, 241
Organizational status, 350

**P**

Parent Teachers Association, 215
Peer group
  functions of, 224–25
  and school class, 224–28
  among teachers, 239
Personal Orientation Toward Intellectualism (POTI), 60–62, 65–66, 69–72
Philadelphia schools, 127
Platoon system, 16
*Plessy* versus *Ferguson,* 34
Project Metco, 41–43
Protestant revolt, 7
*The Public Interest,* 41, 43, 46, 47
"Pygmalion effect," 256, 295

**R**

Reward structure
  of elementary schools, 238–43
  and teacher ambition, 240–43

Role, teachers'
  affectivity of, 320–21
  and bureaucratization, 356–57
  compared to doctors and lawyers, 317
  conflicts and insecurities of, 321–26
  as diffuse and diverse, 316–20
  as distinct from literati, 310–13
  in English history, 311
  in socialization, 314–16
  in social selection, 314–16
  and technology, 312

S

Scholastic ability
  and class standing, 205
  and college plans, 206
  variation between schools, 204
Scholastic performance, 204
School achievement
  components of, 223
  nature of, 222
School attendance, 165
School class
  and family, 224–28
  informal aspects, 221
  and peer groups, 224–28
  selective functions, 216–20
  and sex differences, 222
  as social system, 216–37
  as socializing agent, 216–20
  status system of, 229
  structure of, 220–22
Schools
  and accountability, 14
  and advertising, 12
  and autocracy, 258
  comparison of Soviet and American, 120
  and "factory model," 48
  and high turnover, 215
  and informal system, 359–60
  and lay control, 354
  as marginal institutions, 49
  and public relations, 12–14
  ratio of students and supervisors, 214
  reward and punishment in, 201, 361
  roles and status in, 212
  social climate of, 258
  status and authority structure, 359–62
Science
  and competition, 274–75
  and conflict, 272–76
  controversy in, 273
Science Research Associates, 278
Secondary school, differentiation and selection, 233–36
Seminar on the Equality of Educational
  Opportunity Report, 38, 44
Sex segregation, 225
Social change and the structure of the
  school, 160

Social class
  and aspirations, 177
  and cognitive development, 150
  educational aspirations, 154
  income gap, 170
  and perceptions of teacher, 153
  and success, 182
  and value orientations, 150, 152
Social climate
  in schools, 258–59
  competition and cooperation, 258–59
Social control
  authority, 329–30
  persuasion, 329
  power, 329
Social Darwinism, 52
Social equality, 2–3
Social mobility
  and aspirations, 172 ff
  in British society, 144, 147
  and educational attainment, 207
  and intelligence, 174
  major causal agents, 138, 166
  and personality pattern, 172 ff
  process, 145
  and social origins, 170 ff
  and values, 172 ff
Social origins and effect on mobility,
  169 ff, 209
Social-self, development of, 80
Social status
  and child performance, 109–11
  in concept utilization, 105–7
  and differences in language use, 101–3
  and education, 137–41
  and reliance on school, 116
  value systems, 143, 145–46
Social values, transmitted, 125, 217
Socialization, 2, 5
  and centrality of language, 148
  of cognitive modes, 96–113
  and commitments, 217
  as development of capacities, 217
  and education, 114 ff
  and family, 77
  and learning, 77, 80, 82
  and middle class parents, 78–79
  in the school class, 216–20, 228–32
Socialization in school
  and conflict, 271, 327
  and consensus, 277
  and language, 289–96
  political, 270, 285–86
  role of teachers, 314–16
  view of society, 277 ff
Special interest colleges, 386, 389
Stanford Center for Research and Development in Teaching, 240
Status communities, middle level,
  139

Status of teachers
 bureaucratization, 356–57
 informal, 359
 in school and community, 349–59
 status dilemma, 358
 versus college professors, 362–65
 within the school, 357–59
Strong Interest Inventory, 396
Student
 as "peer oriented," 53, 58, 73
 as "school oriented," 53, 58, 73
Student image
 intellectual image, 56
 non-intellectual image, 56
Student Involvement in the Informal
  Status System (SIISS), 60–72
Student role, "good" student, 213
Student styles, 57–58, 66
 typology of, 64, 66–68
Subculture
 academic, 57
 adolescent, 51, 53, 55–56, 64–65, 73,
  117
 delinquent, 57
 fun, 57, 64, 66
 as shared with adults, 55–56
 as style, 58
Summerhill school, 255
Supreme Court, 34, 35
 Keyes (Denver school desegregation
  case), 51
 and social science data, 51
 the Swann case, 52

T

Taba Social Studies Curriculum, 280
Teachers
 effectiveness, 334–36
 legitimacy, 334–36
 personal autonomy, 304
 professional status, 251–52, 303–5
 roles, 309–26
 social origin, 306
 in a status dilemma, 349, 358
 unionization, 307
 visibility of, 353
Teachers' expectations
 in the classroom, 257
 and low achievement, 263–64
 and social class, 257
Teaching language, 291–96
 and home-school conflict, 297
Thematic Apperception Test, 180

Tracking system, 188 ff
 conformity and deviance, 196–97
 differences, 189–92
 and grading policies, 195
 implications of, 197
 performance and, 189–93
 schools (streamed), 193–95
 and self-fulfilling prophecy, 193
 and stigma, 192
 and student subculture, 197
 teacher effectiveness, 195

U–V

Ungraded schools, 4, 260
Unionization of teachers, 307
University, rise of, 377–78
University of Connecticut, 39
University professors, professionalization
 of, 378
Upper class, conception of education,
 140–41
Upper middle class
 families and maturation, 117–19
 students' need for work experience, 121
Urban schools
 and bureaucracy, 246–54
 decadence of organizational structure,
  250
 and professional educators, 251–52
 resistence to change, 249–50
U.S. Department of Agriculture, 116
Value conflict, 125
Value stretch, 126
Velikovsky case, 284

W–Y

Wabash High School, 28
Warm Springs Indian Reservation, 298
Working class
 and aspirations, 154
 culture, destruction of, 159
 and immediate gratification, 154
 and nature of man, 151
 and parental aspirations, 152
 philosophy of, 155
 and possessions, 151
 and respectability, 152
 and success, 149
 and teacher attitudes, 150
Youth
 "athletic-sports," 57
 "rebellious," 57
 "studious," 57

*This book has been set in 10 point and 9 point
Caledonia, leaded 2 points. Part numbers are
24 point Univers Bold #65. Part titles are 24
point Univers Medium #55. Reading numbers
and titles are 18 point Univers Bold #65. The
size of the type page is 27 by 45½ picas.*